A Guide through *Finnegans Wake*

THE FLORIDA JAMES JOYCE SERIES

UNIVERSITY PRESS OF FLORIDA

Florida A&M University, Tallahassee
Florida Atlantic University, Boca Raton
Florida Gulf Coast University, Ft. Myers
Florida International University, Miami
Florida State University, Tallahassee
New College of Florida, Sarasota
University of Central Florida, Orlando
University of Florida, Gainesville
University of North Florida, Jacksonville
University of South Florida, Tampa
University of West Florida, Pensacola

A Guide through
Finnegans Wake

EDMUND LLOYD EPSTEIN

Foreword by Sebastian D. G. Knowles, Series Editor

University Press of Florida

Gainesville · Tallahassee · Tampa · Boca Raton

Pensacola · Orlando · Miami · Jacksonville · Ft. Myers · Sarasota

Copyright 2009 by Edmund Lloyd Epstein
Printed in the United States of America. This book is printed on
Glatfelter Natures Book, a paper certified under the standards of
the Forestry Stewardship Council (FSC). It is a recycled stock that
contains 30 percent post-consumer waste and is acid-free.

First cloth printing, 2009
First paperback printing, 2010

15   14   13   12   11   10   6   5   4   3   2   1

Library of Congress Cataloging-in-Publication Data
Epstein, Edmund L.
A guide through Finnegans wake / Edmund Lloyd Epstein ; foreword
by Sebastian D. G. Knowles
p. cm.—(The Florida James Joyce series)
Includes bibliographical references and index.
ISBN 978-0-8130-3356-3 (cloth)
ISBN 978-0-8130-3534-5 (paper)
1. Joyce, James, 1882–1941. Finnegans wake. I. Title.
PR6019.O9F5855 2009
823.'912—dc22   2009004165

The University Press of Florida is the scholarly publishing agency
for the State University System of Florida, comprising Florida A&M
University, Florida Atlantic University, Florida Gulf Coast University,
Florida International University, Florida State University, New College
of Florida, University of Central Florida, University of Florida, University of North Florida, University of South Florida, and University
of West Florida.

University Press of Florida
15 Northwest 15th Street
Gainesville, FL 32611-2079
www.upf.com

I have discovered two things: that once you get into Joyce, you do not get out of Joyce, and that reading Joyce is a collective matter—all Joyceans are engaged in a mutual enterprise of exploring the creations of James Joyce.

I began reading Joyce many years ago, and I began by trying to go on my own. However, I soon discovered that I had to read Joyce in the company of all the other Joyceans. Reading Joyce—journeying through *Dubliners*, *A Portrait*, *Ulysses*, and (especially!) *Finnegans Wake*—requires a safari that includes all the readers of Joyce in the world.

I dedicate this book to all the Joyceans in the world, past, present, and future.

Contents

Foreword ix
Acknowledgments xi
List of Abbreviations xv

Introduction: The Recirculated *Commedia* of James Joyce 1

1

Book I (*FW* 1–216) / The Age of Gods (Vico) 25
SPACE Medium: Time and the River Flow Backward

2

Book II (*FW* 217–400) / The Age of Heroes (Vico) 102
TIME Medium: Time and the River Flow Forward: Twilight to Midnight

3

Book III (*FW* 401–590) / The Age of Democracy (Vico) 164
TIME Medium: Time and the River Flow Forward: Midnight to Dawn

4

Book IV (*FW* 591–628) / *Ricorso* (Vico) 247
TIME Medium Ending, SPACE Medium Recommencing:
The River Begins to Flow Backward: Dawn

Notes 289
Works Cited 303
Index 309

Foreword

This is a masterful study of the *Wake*, by one who has lived with the book for many ages, who communicates his understanding of the book with clarity and enthusiasm, and who leaves us with a richer sense of the possibilities of this impossible text than any critic since William York Tindall. Like Tindall, Epstein is a right witty scholar, having the rare gift of a happy turn of phrase, which makes his companionship through the *Wake* that much more welcome. The opening pages of Epstein's introduction should be mandatory reading for all who embark on *Finnegans Wake* in a graduate seminar, a reading group, or on their own. Expanding on the same expository ideas at wider and wider reaches, the guide then moves deeper and deeper into the text, like the embryonic diagram Joyce made for "Oxen of the Sun." Each ripple, each reach of the oar, takes us further into the watery center of the *Wake*. The division of Joyce's text into modes of space (almost all of Book I and Book IV) and modes of time (the more temporally explicit sections in Books II and III where the book moves chronologically from twilight to dawn) is especially helpful for those searching for a traditional narrative in the *Wake*. Epstein's synopses of particular episodes are likewise invaluable; this book is an ideal guide for any reader. *A Guide through "Finnegans Wake"* is a book that every Joycean will want to own, and it will become a mainstay of the Florida James Joyce Series.

Epstein tells an old joke from *Punch*, where a pretentious gent stands before the sea and declaims, "Roll on, thou deep and dark blue Ocean—roll!" to the delight of the girl on his arm: "Oh Harold, you marvelous man—it's doing it!" One could say the same of Epstein's book, which makes one want immediately to turn to the *Wake* and watch it work its magic.

Sebastian D. G. Knowles
Series Editor

Acknowledgments

I would like to acknowledge the help of all readers of *Finnegans Wake*, especially those with whom I discussed the *Wake*, or those whose articles and notes I read. Wakeans are an international cooperative group, and all of them are ready with suggestions on complex problems of interpretation of this most complex of texts. I owe these *Wake* readers more than I can say.

In addition to the great many Joyceans I have encountered over the decades, there are a number of Joyceans who were known to me personally and were always generous to me.

First, with early and constant help and encouragement, was William York Tindall, a great scholar of modern literature, a humane man, a deep wit, and one of the first to establish James Joyce as a fit subject for American academic study. Tindall was the director of my dissertation on Joyce at Columbia University. When I was an editor at Farrar, Straus and Giroux, I had the honor of returning the favor: I was the editor of Tindall's book *A Reader's Guide to "Finnegans Wake,"* published in 1969 and still a standard work on the *Wake*.

I also enjoyed the aid of two of the earliest scholars on *Finnegans Wake*, Fritz Senn and Clive Hart, who did fundamental work on Joyce and on the *Wake*. I met Richard Ellmann a number of times, and received invaluable help on subjects related to Joyce.

The late Alan M. Cohn was the most helpful and genial of librarians and bibliographers, and a great friend to me and to all Joyceans.

At meetings of the Joyce Society at the Gotham Book Mart, I often met such Joyceans as Padraic Colum, and the most explosively enthusiastic of Wakeans, Thornton Wilder. Wilder was on the board of advisors of the earliest Joyce journal, the *James Joyce Review*, which he helped me to establish. Wilder was always sharing notes about the *Wake* with anyone who would listen. He later passed along a huge bundle of notes to Adaline Glasheen, who carried on his work of annotation with three censuses of characters in the *Wake*.

I owe a great debt to two other friends, the late Bernard Benstock and his wife, Shari, both active forces in all subjects having to do with Joyce. Bernie's early death was a great loss to the world of Joyce criticism and scholarship. Fortunately we still have with us a friend of Bernie's and mine, Zack Bowen, the most musical and joyous Joycean on the horizon.

Among other Joyceans known to me are the most fervent members of the New York James Joyce Society—the president, Nicholas Fargnoli, and the vice president and Webmaster, Heyward Ehrlich. They have been inexhaustible sources of Wakeana, as have Sidney Feshbach and Stanley Sultan, for many years. The late Wakeans Adaline Glasheen, J. Mitchell Morse, Richard M. Kain, Hugh Kenner, Marvin Magalaner, Norman Silverstein, and Kevin Sullivan were always glad to dig out the most hidden of *Wake* facts.

The late Nat Halper was a fabulous and helpful Wakean. Two ecclesiastics, Father William T. Noon, S.J., and Father Robert Boyle, S.J., were most generous with their help on Catholic theology as well as other issues on which my ignorance was total. They were also most charming dinner companions; I miss them both very much.

I would also like to mention some Joyceans and Wakeans whom I encountered from time to time, who were likewise generous with their time and information: Chester Anderson, Anthony Burgess, Herbert Cahoon, Tom Connolly, Jack Dalton (uneasy to know but a mine of information), Bob Day (a colleague for many years), Michael Patrick Gillespie, John Gordon, Phillip Herring, Fred Higginson, Patrick A. McCarthy, Richard Peterson, Joe Prescott, John Paul Riquelme, Bob Scholes, and Michael Seidel.

I am indebted for many years of friendship to Tom Staley. I had some memorable moments with Edmund Wilson, and in 1954 I met the eminent classical scholar William B. Stanford and discussed points in his forthcoming book on Odysseus through the ages. I also met Marshall McLuhan when he was still a Wakean, and Northrop Frye, a genial man and a fountain of light on literature.

In the preparation of this book, Sebastian Knowles provided careful editorial guidance. Ann Marlowe has been the most sharp-eyed and sensitive of copy editors. I am also grateful for the assistance of Amy Gorelick and Michele Fiyak-Burkley of the University Press of Florida.

I hope that those whose names I have omitted will forgive me, since I cannot count all of those Joyceans who have helped me. They and I are both members of the worldwide band of Wakeans who, by letting their efforts sift down onto the titanic mound of commentary, are all making the *Wake* a clearer book.

What I owe to my wife, Tegwen, both of us know.

Abbreviations

M   McHugh, Roland. *Annotations to Finnegans Wake.* 3rd ed.
     Baltimore: Johns Hopkins University Press, 2006.

R&O Rose, Danis, and John O'Hanlon. *Understanding "Finnegans
     Wake": A Guide to the Narrative of James Joyce's Masterpiece.*
     New York: Garland, 1982.

T   Tindall, William York. *A Reader's Guide to "Finnegans Wake."*
     New York: Farrar, Straus and Giroux, 1969.

These sigla represent the above books throughout. Since all three books are coded closely to the text of the *Wake*, no page numbers are indicated. In this guide, I have credited all the sources I could find, including the above texts. All the other information in this book was, I believe, discovered by me, though it may have been discovered independently by others. I apologize if I have inadvertently left out credit for *Wake* discoveries made by other people.

Introduction

The Recirculated *Commedia* of James Joyce

James Joyce identifies *Finnegans Wake* as his *commedia* in the first sentence in the book: "a commodius vicus of recirculation" (3.2). A *commedia*, as Dante knew it, was not necessarily funny, but was rather a book using all varieties of language, from the most dignified to the most rowdy and vulgar. Its topic is all-inclusive: a *commedia* is about everything in the universe—and beyond.

Finnegans Wake is also about everything in the universe and beyond, but unlike Dante's *commedia*, it is extremely funny. Dante's virtues are elsewhere, while Joyce's *commedia* is an authentic comic masterpiece. Joyce declared in his Paris notebooks that the Comic is "the perfect manner in art,"[1] and there is indeed a laugh on every page of the *Wake*.

For more than four decades I have been working my way through Joyce's grand *commedia*. I began with a state of complete bewilderment, relieved only by a loud laugh now and then when I understood one of Joyce's jokes, and I have since been moving into a condition of partial enlightenment. However, from the beginning I have been fascinated, hypnotized, by the scope and ambition of Joyce's comic text. Some parts of the great book are now beginning to swim into view, but some still hide in the "semitary of Somnionia" (594.8), as I continue to tread the pathways of sleep among the shades of evening.

I feel that there are many readers of the *Wake* who are in my state, and who share my concerns. I have written this book to help them—and to help myself—share in the delight of reading this gigantic *commedia* of James Joyce the Master, that is, to provide a basic armature for readers of the *Wake*. The writing of *A Guide to "Finnegans Wake"* has spanned a number of years, using materials prepared for my undergraduate and graduate students in courses on Joyce and the *Wake*. The book is intended to be the sort of guide that I needed desperately when I myself started reading the *Wake*.

Scholarship and criticism of *Finnegans Wake* have been piling up since even before its publication in 1939. To dig into this titanic mound is like digging into the Hill of Howth itself. Seventy years of commentary on elements and sections of the *Wake*, and the philosophical, theoretical, and genetic criticism based on studies of the book, are proving indispensable to students. (For an illuminating example of genetic criticism, see Finn Fordham's 2007 book.) However, amid the enormous mound of material, there are relatively few guides completely through the work.[2] This book is, I hope, one that emphasizes the *continuity*, the long currents, within Joyce's oceanic masterpiece.

My intention is to explicate the *Wake* for the benefit of readers common and uncommon. Yet even this simple intention is sidetracked time and again by complex theoretical issues that require digging into fundamental questions of literary creation.

What is the *Wake* about? Is it about anything at all? What have Vico and Bruno to do with the *Wake*? Why is its language so odd? Is it merely a pure and simple jangle of words (as an annoyed reader shouts out on 112.4)? And does the *Wake*, as some critics assert, truly mark the bankruptcy of meaning? Is the book, as Beckett asserts, only about itself? Is the *Wake* a Cave of the Winds, a mere Blabbyrinth haunted by a wandering polyglutton?

And if you can answer those questions, try these: What happens in the *Wake*? Does anything happen? Are there characters in the book? Who are they? *What* are they?

Language as a Reflection of the World

Though the *Wake* is certainly a giant network of superheated language created by a great master, it is much more than an interlacing of linguistic signs, more than a frantic word-salad.

I believe that the *Wake* has a profoundly human meaning. It is about the center line of the life of man and woman—the creation of the family and the shift of power when the children grow up. What was always of primary interest to Joyce was the physical world and the development of people in the time and space theaters of that world—the great drama of the lives of imperfect human beings (Epstein 1971).

Théophile Gautier declared himself to be a man for whom the physical world existed. It existed, powerfully, for Joyce. For him, the real world was the material stage for the development of human beings, not simply a messy turmoil to be "transcended" for the attainment of wisdom. Paul Léon, in a letter to Jean Paulhan written four months after Joyce's death, eloquently testifies to Joyce's deep involvement with this physical world. Joyce was walking with Léon in September 1930, and a young girl complimented him on his writing.

> Joyce lifted his unfortunate eyes towards the still-sunny sky, then brought them back to the boxed trees growing along the boulevard: "You would do better," he said to the girl, "to admire the sky or even these poor trees." (Tully, 49)

In several places in *A Portrait* and *Ulysses*, Stephen Dedalus speaks for Joyce on the primacy of the physical world and its processes, notably in the Library section of *Ulysses* when Stephen rejects the foggy Platonism of the Dublin intellectuals: "Hold to the now, the here, through which all future plunges to the past" (9.89).

Joyce defends this crucial importance of "the now, the here" throughout the *Wake*. In Book IV, St. Patrick stoutly upholds the rainbow-colored world of fallen human beings against a Platonic Eastern sage who, baffled, falls on his behind with a "Thud!" as the risen sun blazes onto the daylight-flooded physical world of error and glory. Despite the *Wake*'s radical experimentation in language and form, it is a giant hymn of praise to the imperfect world of fallen human beings.

What Happens in *Finnegans Wake* and To Whom Does It Happen?

The *Wake* is, of course, circular: "A way a lone a last a loved a long the" → "riverrun" (628.15–16; 3.1). The book itself is divided into seventeen chapters, eight in the first book, four in the second, four in the third, and one in the fourth book. There is, therefore, a balance between Book I, with its eight chapters, and Books II and III, with *their* eight. Then Book IV, one of the greatest creations in modern literature, provides a lovely transition back to Book I again. However, human action, what "happens" to human beings in time, occupies only Books II and III of the work.

In a tale written by Joyce's friend James Stephens occurs the phrase "'The music of what happens,' said great Fionn, 'that is the finest music in the world'" (65). The *Wake*, like Joyce's other books, celebrates the real world and its processes in space and time. The actions of human beings in the real world are Joyce's constant subject.

So what happens in space and time in the *Wake*? To whom do these things happen? Are they "real people" or fictional characters? There are many names of real people in the book, so is the *Wake* a history or a narrative fiction?

The *Wake* as a Narrative Fiction

It seems to me that the *Wake* can be identified as a narrative fiction by a clear test. All narrative fictions are characterized linguistically by containing *nonreferential proper nouns*, that is, proper nouns whose referents depend for their existence solely on the existence of the author. If Gustave Flaubert had never existed, "Emma Bovary" would ipso facto never have existed. Histories are texts that designate people whose existence is independent of that of the author; Napoleon existed independent of the huge numbers of historians who have described his career.

Throughout the *Wake*, there are many nonreferring designations: HCE, ALP, Shem, Shaun, Issy, and a multitude of others. By this test, the *Wake* qualifies as a narrative fiction—if of an unusual type. All fictions are narratives, but the *Wake* is an unusual narrative in two ways. The first way has to do with the presentation of time. Standard narratives occur in time, but, as we shall see, only two of the books of the *Wake* (II and III) occur in time. In addition, in standard narratives, the characters are referred to by consistent names, whereas the characters of the *Wake* are referred to by many names, and in many guises or avatars.

Are Joyce's People Individual Characters or Types?

Joyce's characters are not individual Dickensian eccentrics but general types. Much of the difficulty in reading the *Wake* can be resolved by realizing that Joyce held a theory of personality in which individuals, unlike those of most modern writers, would be representatives or avatars of archetypes in a cyclical universe. Like Stephen at the end of *A Portrait*, each of the characters in *Ulysses* and the *Wake* goes like Stephen Dedalus "for the millionth time" to encounter in a myriad of masks the real world of cyclically recurring time.

The difference between the characters of Joyce and those of his fellow novelists may rest upon Joyce's status as a Catholic. Joyce, the lapsed Catholic, always kept Catholic ways of thought. The only other writers who treat their characters as types acting out general destinies rather than as unrepeatable grotesques (as in the works of Dickens, for example) are such Catholic writers as Graham Greene, Flannery O'Connor, and François Mauriac.

Church doctrine, as enunciated by Thomas Aquinas and other theologians, favors the definition of personality known as Realism that defines the essence of human beings collectively: that is, Humanity as a whole has a real existence, as opposed to the Nominalist idea that the word "Humanity" has only a linguistic existence. The Church has traditionally supported the Realist principle. The reason for this collective definition of human beings may be linked to the fate of souls at the Last Judgment. At that crucial event, each soul ends up in one of two camps. Regardless of individual differences, the most important decision ever made in the eternal career of an individual soul puts that soul into one camp or the other—the sheep and the goats, the saved and the lost. All individual considerations fail before this final collective verdict. Therefore, the Church has always held to a Realist definition of human souls rather than a Nominalist, individual definition, which would enjoin a separate, individual fate for each soul.

Joyce worked out his Aquinan theory of essential personality early in his career. In *Stephen Hero* he presented a credo defining human personality as collective, a credo to which he dedicated the work of the rest of his life. In these pages he declared that he would create a "theory of dualism which would symbolize the twin eternities of spirit and nature in the twin eternities of male and female" (210).

In all of his mature work, James Joyce would fulfill his early dreams of creation.[3] In this schema, there are only two "persons" in the *Wake*: the representatives, respectively, of Spirit and Nature, Man and Woman, HCE and ALP.[4] All of the other characters in the dream-drama are opposing or balanced avatars or hypostases of stages in human life, from childhood to old age.

SPIRIT	NATURE
HCE	ALP

YOUNG CHILDREN

Jerry and Kevin/ Glugg and Chuff	Twenty-eight Monthly Girls + Issy =
Dolph and Kev/ Cain and Abel	Twenty-nine Nightschool or Leapyear Girls

continued

continued

SPIRIT		NATURE
	ADOLESCENTS	
Shem/Shaun/Shimar Shin		Issy/Essie
Male principle is triple: testicles and penis		Female principle is duple: paired labia
	[Symbolism for sex in *FW* is three to two]	
Lipoleum Boys in the Willingdone Museyroom		Seven Rainbow Girls
	YOUNG LOVERS	
Tristan		Isolde
	THRESHOLD ADULTS	
[Fallen Man]		Isabel
Shem—below the waist		
Jaun/Haun/Yawn—above the waist		
Shem and Shaun are the principles of TIME and SPACE respectively. Together they make up a sound film, with soundtrack by Shem and still photographs by Shaun		
	MATURE ADULTS	
Humphrey Chimpden Earwicker, Pubkeeper		Anna Livia Plurabelle
Mr Porter/Finn MacCool/ Finnegan the Bricklayer		Mrs Porter
Father/Hill of Howth		Mother/River Liffey
Husband		Wife

continued

OLD PEOPLE

Four Old Men/   Kate the Hag
 Servant Sackerson

Historians/Lawmakers/Police   Muse of History

                                                       Two Washerwomen

TIME in *Finnegans Wake*

In Joyce's cyclical narrative, his use of nondesignative names may be suf-
ficient to mark the *Wake* as a "narrative fiction." However, to say that the
Wake is truly and throughout a "narrative" is accurate only on the most basic
level, since the narrative "actions" that occur seem, to some commentators,
to occur unevenly.

At the beginning of the *Wake*, time does not flow forward. Samuel Beckett, probably advised by Joyce himself, called Book I "a mass of past shadow."[5]
Any "actions" in Book I occurring in time are extremely rare and occur spo-
radically, whereas Books II and III and (partly) Book IV of the *Wake* unfold
in time, actively and consecutively.

Other commentators besides Beckett have noted the uneven distribution
of temporally organized narrative throughout the book. Of course, Joyce
was fully capable of writing an evenly paced narrative text, and even held a
theory of time that fitted neatly into a theory of narrative time. At the very
beginning of his novelistic career, in his essay "A Portrait of the Artist," Joyce
described the past as a "fluid succession of presents" leading up to the present time. It is this fluid succession of "presents," in the form of gifts, that
the Goddess of Life, Anna Livia, gives to her 111 children from her mailbag
(209.10–212.19). Since the *Wake* is Anna Livia's letter to the Lord and the
world about her husband, the *Wake* could be seen as a "fluid succession of
presents," or gifts. The temporal flow of the *Wake*—in Books II and III and
part of Book IV—gives to the reader this flow of gifts.

However, Book I has another function. It is certainly true that *A Portrait of the Artist* and *Ulysses* are each strongly bound together by temporal
links, yet the *Wake* departs radically from the temporal flow of Joyce's earlier
works. Geert Lernout has written that "the *Wake* may well be one of the first
books to lack an overall temporal framework" (119). Michael Begnal has also
observed this atemporality of Book I—"there is no 'goahead plot' to speak of

in the whole of Book I. . . . Nowhere is there plot as we conventionally know it" (1992: 119)—as has Danis Rose:

> . . . on 19 April 1926 . . . Joyce . . . had written to Harriet Weaver, "My brother says that after having done the longest day in literature I am now conjuring up the darkest night" (*Letters III* 140). . . . it is indeed clear that from the close of Anna Livia at nightfall [I.7] to the dawn-song of Kevin following the cockcrow at the end of Shaun [III.4], *Finnegans Wake* does comply with this description. An insurmountable problem arises, however, with the first part of the book which was composed before Shaun or night had even been dreamt of. To adhere to the chronological sequence, part I ought to consist of a succession of episodes corresponding to the hours before nightfall of a single day. They do not. Day and night and the following morning are inextricably mixed in them. (91)

The solution to this riddle is simple, I believe. Book I shows very little narrative flow forward, for it is not until the end of the last chapters in Book I that TIME truly "begins." The flow of TIME starts slowly at the end of I.7, picks up some speed in the Anna Livia chapter, I.8, and begins in earnest only with II.1. The *Wake* is the product of TIME and SPACE, of Shem and Shaun. As Northrop Frye says, "Shem works directly in the stream of time and supplies the energy of history; Shaun spatializes what Shem does" (16).

As Danis Rose asserts, there is no "succession of episodes" in the first book. Book I contains an overflight of a landscape in which nothing is yet happening. In this landscape we see scattered before us the elements of the narrative of the book, without narrative action taking place. This landscape is very simple: We see first a river, the mother of us all, winding through a plain. Then we see two conspicuous objects looming through the mist of a "soft" Irish morning—a large tree on the north side of the river and a large stone on the southern side. These objects symbolize TIME and SPACE, as personified by Shem and Shaun. There is a peninsula in the distance, capped with a Gibraltar-like tumulus—the grave barrow of the viceking, fallen Adam himself, the father of us all. Then Book I begins.

Almost all of Book I is a nontemporal mystery, what Beckett called "a mass of past shadow," in which the defining mode is spatial. Its function is to provide the reader with the materials of the subsequent eight-act drama and coda, in Books II, III, and IV. It is the mode of SPACE that dominates almost all of Book I. Finally, with the twilight Angelus at the end of I, viii (213.18–19), TIME and narrative sequence begin.

Books II, III, and most of IV unfold in TIME. There are two parallel temporal modes in the drama. One presents a single night, from twilight to dawn. The other moves to a much longer rhythm: the years of development of the children of a family to the point where they take over the adult functions of man and wife, father and mother, of a family. At the end of the book, the parents undergo a secular resurrection to the next generation.

The great double dream proceeds from the twilight Angelus in I.8 (213.18–19) through a midnight "Angelus" (379.27–30) to dawn and a multi-campanulate morning Angelus (601.8–29). At the end TIME stops, the blazing sun rises, the tide turns, and Anna Livia's great orgasm bears the reader back to the beginning of the book. The river is flowing backward, SPACE mode begins again, and we are introduced once more to "all the charictures in the drame" (302.31–32).

Closer Analysis of SPACE and TIME in *Finnegans Wake*

A more detailed analysis of Joyce's use of TIME and SPACE in the *Wake* reveals a crucial difference between Joyce's other works and the *Wake*. In his other works, Joyce is as clear about the passing of time as he is about the vivid appearances of his world in space. There is usually no difficulty in determining the time of the various sections in his earlier works—*Dubliners*, *A Portrait of the Artist as a Young Man*, and *Ulysses*.

Time in these works is expressed in three apparently naturalistic modes: (1) actual dates—days, months, years, holidays; (2) hours of the day and seasons of the year; (3) development of the characters over longer stretches of time. In these works we have evidence of Joyce's great ability in expressing all shades of time, from the most exact and tiny intervals to the longest and broadest rhythms of human life. At the beginning of the *Wake*, however, there is no actual expression of time, and the reader searches through chapter after chapter in vain for specific references to minutes, hours, days, seasons, or longer stretches of chronological development such as we find abundantly in the earlier books.

In fact, the reader must leaf through more than two hundred pages—*one-third of the book*—to find the first actual time described in the *Wake*. Although there is a version of the word "tonight" on 126.2 and a segue into temporality at the end of I.7, the first *explicit* time reference occurs only three pages before the end of Book I. One of the washerwomen excitedly exclaims that the dusk is growing (213.12–13), and the other remarks that the Angelus has rung, bearing the message that the Holy Spirit has entered the Virgin's womb (213.18–19), which marks the beginning of all fertility. At this point, time is finally starting, with Sechseläute, the evening Angelus at six p.m.

So what has been happening, or not happening, in the previous 212 pages? The answer seems to be that Joyce ordered the *Wake* in two modes: SPACE and TIME, in that order. As we will see, almost all of Book I takes the reader on a spatial journey to a few places—notably the Hill of Howth, the shore of Dublin Bay, the Liffey in Dublin city—and pauses to relate events that have *not yet* taken place there, or that have *already* taken place there. However, nothing takes place in real TIME at these locales, since the modes of Book I are SPACE modes.

Joyce begins his book with an enigma. The first sentence of the book seems to be describing an eastward, seaward flow of the river (3.1–3). As we later find out, the Liffey has a double flow, eastward and westward, since it is tidal. However, at the beginning of the book, which way is the tidal Liffey moving?

If a first-time reader of the *Wake* hastily reads the first sentence, the Liffey seems to be flowing seaward: that is, it has passed the Franciscan church on the banks of the Liffey known to all Dubliners as Adam and Eve's, then entered Dublin Bay and circled around the shore of the bay to arrive at Howth Castle on the southwestern shore of the Hill of Howth. However, if the reader comes to this sentence after having already finished reading the last page of the *Wake*, this seaward interpretation cannot be sustained.

There are too many oddities in this sentence for the seaward interpretation. The Adam and Eve's designation of the famous church on the Liffey is here reversed into "Eve and Adam's." The shore of the Irish Sea is described before the bend of Dublin Bay.[6] The words "past" and "back" both occur in this sentence. Most significant of all, the famous first word, "riverrun," resembles the Italian dialect word *riveran*, which means "they will arrive"— that is, the action has not yet started (M). All of these reversals and anticipations give the clue to the reverse motion of Anna Livia at the beginning of *Finnegans Wake*.

The immediate impression of this sentence on first-time readers is thus misleading. Only when these readers come to the last page do they realize that, at the end of Book IV, the Liffey has not simply *reached* Howth Castle; she has gone well into the Irish Sea. At the very end of the *Wake* Anna Livia sweeps into the ocean. She feels the deep ocean currents welcoming her— she feels a brightening up and a tightening down (626.36–627.1)—hears the seagulls offshore, and catches sight of her far-off bridesmaids, the Amazon and the Nile. In joy and terror, overwhelmed by the tides of the Irish Sea, she feels the approach of her huge, blazing, sunlit bridegroom, and asks him to take her (628.14). In the last phrase of the book, she gazes blindly into the new sun, and feels herself seized by the arms of the ocean. Then, with the turn of the oncoming rising ocean tides, she is borne backward—"A way a lone a last a love a long the" (628.15–16). She sweeps in, away from the sea, past the Hill of Howth, past Howth Castle and Environs on the inner shore of the Howth peninsula, and back through Dublin Bay into her bed within Dublin, to end up eventually at the weir at Island Bridge.

Therefore, at the very commencement of the *Wake*, the motion of the Liffey is not downstream but upstream, backward, continuing the westward movement at the very end of Book IV. The tidal Liffey, impelled back by the thrust of her mighty husband, is commencing her journey *upstream* to her eventual tidingplace.

Joyce continues the description of the reversed order of events in the first full paragraph of the book (3.4–14). Here, truly temporal events have not begun; things have not happened yet, or again. This paragraph introduces seven stages of development of a narrative, but carefully notes that none of these events has thus far taken place: Tristram has not yet rearrived; the two boys have not yet/again reconciled their conflict; the father-God has not yet/again attempted to frighten his children; the father-God has not yet/again been overthrown; the sisters have not yet/again turned into lovers of their brothers; the father/brewer has not yet/again brewed his liquor and served it; and the flood has not yet/again receded. Not one of these past or future events has yet occurred. In reading through Book I, we wait in vain for any of them to happen.

It is the word "passencore" in this passage that gives away the spatial method of Book I. Joyce relies upon an ambiguity in the French phrase *pas encore*; it means both "not yet" and "not again." Either the events described in Book I have *not yet* taken place or, since the book is cyclical, the TIME events have *already* taken place, and will take place again. Almost all the events described in Book I are thus presented prospectively or retrospectively. None takes place in the dramatic TIME mode later described in II.1 as the present pressing onward (221.17). The mode of Book I is the nontemporal SPACE mode.

To explain further: almost all of the actions in Book I feature what could be called "telling," or "psychological action." Books II, III, and most of IV feature what could be called "showing," or "dramatic action."

Nothing "really happens" in Book I. All that the reader encounters there is that some voice or voices telling in great detail events that have *already* happened, or that *will* happen. Only memory or anticipation operates in this SPACE mode, in the eight chapters in Book I.

In Books II and III, eight chapters balance the eight chapters of Book I. However, the eight chapters of Books II and III employ true dramatic action, the acting of events in "real time" (see 186.1–2). TIME here controls the "flow" of events, in several chronological modes. In these chapters, which comprise an eight-act drama probably entitled "A Royal Divorce," the events foreshadowed in Book I begin unfolding at twilight in various modes of temporal development. The night comes on, and after midnight, in Book III, the dawn slowly begins to fill the shadows of night with faint illumination of incipient daybreak. At the end of Book III, the great eight-act play finishes with rounds of applause (590.30). Then Book IV continues the process of dawning until the very end of the book, which gradually returns to the nontemporal modes of Book I.

The complete organization of the *Wake* could be represented as follows:

Book I SPACE →	Books II and III TIME →	Book IV TIME modulating into SPACE
Psychological action	Dramatic action	Dramatic action ending; psychological action beginning again
Telling	Acting out	

Time and Tide

It is this duple mode of presentation in the *Wake*—SPACE and TIME, psychological and then dramatic—that causes a good deal of difficulty in interpreting the book. If the reader attempts to read all four books of the *Wake* as a conventional and consistent temporal dramatic text, nothing but confusion will result.[7] In fact, the main function of Book I seems to be the presentation in a spatial mode all the information needed by the reader to understand the time-bound dramatic events in Books II and III, and in Book IV the final return to the beginning of the book.

Joyce assists the reader to understand the operation of SPACE and TIME by coding his text to the dual modes of the river Liffey.

Anna Livia is tidal. Twice a day, following the ebbing ocean tide, she slips downstream through Dublin city and to the mouth of Dublin Bay, where she runs into the Irish Sea. Then, with the turn of the tide, she is borne upstream by the incoming flow, through Dublin Bay and Dublin city back to the weir at Island Bridge. Then the tide turns again, and the Liffey begins to move once more toward the sea.

In *Ulysses*, Joyce used this estuary rhythm as one of the empirical indications of the rhythms of time. The reversing of the Liffey current is noted only in passing. This double rhythm governs the peregrinations of Bloom's throwaway in the course of "Wandering Rocks," as Gifford notes about the turning tides on June 16, 1904: "High tide was at 12:42 p.m.; since it is now after 3:00, the tide has turned and the current in the estuary of the Liffey is east-running" (note on 10.295).

In *Finnegans Wake*, however, the ebb and flow of Anna Livia is crucial. The backward flow of the Liffey as it is forced upstream by the oncoming ocean tide is correlated with the retrospective and prospective countertemporal SPACE mode in Book I. Then, when the tide turns at 194.31–195.6, the downstream, forward motion is correlated with the TIME mode, the temporally coded "present"-tense dramatic narrative action of Books II and III. Finally, Book IV acts out the slowing of the dying Liffey's progress downstream, until she sinks into the embrace of her son-husband-lover the ocean. The tide turns, the Irish Sea begins to enter the Liffey's bed, and time stops.

Book IV provides the great climax of the *Wake*. The TIME mode in Book IV ends with the only successful and complete act of love in the *Wake*. Earlier in the book, Anna Livia has mournfully wished that her comatose husband would wake himself up and "bore" her down (201.11–12). A "bore" is a high-crested tidal flood associated with an estuary, and it is here associated with a physical act of love. This act will eventually take place as predicted in the song at the end of I.4: the song declares that she meets her tide at Island Bridge (103.1, 3). Island Bridge is the tidingplace, where the upstream flow of the Liffey ends. The drive up the river's bed of the sea's thrust ends at the weir, and it is here at Island Bridge that the flow of the Liffey will begin to "come" downstream, moving between her two sons in true narrative TIME.

The authentic union occurs at the very end of the book, as the Liffey meets her great lover. A complete act of love takes place in the blank space between the end and the beginning of the *Wake*. Unlike the three failed attempts at sexual gratification within its pages, the blank end of the book is filled by the joyous conjoining of souls and bodies, of Spirit and Nature moved by true love.

Every day, twice a day, forever, the great act of love, the embrace and withdrawal of Anna Livia and the ocean, acts out an eternal love affair in SPACE and TIME, in enumeration and narration, the two modes of presentation in *Finnegans Wake*.

Vico and Bruno

Giordano Bruno and Giambattista Vico are invoked by Joyce in Book II as presiding over the text of the *Wake*. Here they are referred to as priests, "preteriti" (287.20), named in the Latin phrase "Jordani et Jambaptistae mentibus" (287.24). However, the roles of these two wise men in the *Wake* are not as notable as this reference and other passages seem to indicate. Joyce himself de-emphasized the roles of Vico and Bruno in the book: "I would not pay overmuch attention to these theories, beyond using them for all they are worth."[8]

The role of Bruno is less definitive than that of Vico. To be sure, the name of Bruno of Nola occurs often—as the bookstore name Browne and Nolan, among other references. Yet the most important elements of the complex systems of Giordano Bruno are not laid out in extenso in the *Wake*. Bruno's astronomical theories—the extension of Copernicus's universe into infinite space, and the relationship between the infinite starry universe and infinite God in a pantheistic embrace—play little part in the *Wake*. In III.3, the starry universe appears as the body of Yawn, but there is no indication that Yawn is God.[9]

The main contribution of Bruno to the *Wake* is his theory of the identity of opposites. Here he indeed makes a major and fundamental contribution. Dual opposition and amalgamation plays a major part on every level of the *Wake*, from the opposition and amalgamation of Spirit and Nature, of Man and Woman, to the opposition and amalgamation of Shem and Shaun, and of Issy and Essie. All the other oppositions, both large and small, owe their existence to Bruno. However, there is not much more that the Nolan contributes except perhaps his motto *In tristitia hilaris, in hilaritate tristis*.

The role of Vico is much more prominent than that of Bruno. Yet even Vico's role is limited.[10] Padraic Colum (123) recalled Joyce saying: "Of course, I don't take Vico's speculations literally; I use his cycles as a trellis." The main contributions of Vico to Joyce include the overall organization of the *Wake* into four books, corresponding in number to the three stages of history and the final *ricorso* in Vico's system, and the recurrent thunderclaps that begin the cyclical system of Vico, as they frighten the primordial giants into their caves and into theories of religion.

However, the finer aspects of Vico's system—for example, his three stages of development: divine, heroic, and democratic—do not really appear as the distinguishing principles of Books I, II, and III. There are gods, heroes, and common men in all three of the books, although, to be sure, common men and women become more evident in III.3 and III.4. Joyce's indication to his followers of the crucial role of Vico in these respects may be similar to the somewhat misleading information he provided about the structure of *Ulysses*.

Oddly enough, the closest parallel to the quadripartite structure of Vico is to be found not in the *Wake* as a whole but *within* Book II.

- II.1, which should feature the power of religion over the human giants frightened by thunder, ends with a multithunderous display (257.27–258.24) followed by an elaborate set of prayers (258.25–259.10).
- II.2 centers on the heroic conflict of Shem and Shaun, followed by a list of heroes (306.15L–308.1L).
- II.3 takes place in HCE's pub, which is filled with common men, and ends with the destruction of the common man HCE by the mob of his adolescent children.
- II.4 is a calmly lovely, if comic, *ricorso*, ending with the flow of the river downstream toward the sea, an anticipation of the beautiful *ricorso* of Book IV.

In the rest of the *Wake*, Vico and Bruno are much less evident. As in all of his books, Joyce has followed his own way in the *Wake*, with only the peripheral assistance of "Jordani et Jambaptistae."

After all, James Joyce always reinvented everything.

The Language of *Finnegans Wake*

James Joyce is one of the greatest masters of language that ever existed. However, many readers find that the language of the *Wake* provides the chief obstacle to their understanding of the book. Yet the *Wake*, as we shall see, is basically in English.

The syntax of the book can be recognized as English, with the exception of some comic cadenzas in various languages, such as the hilarious Casa Concordia passage (54.7–19). The syntax of the *Wake*, like that of all English discourses, is based on an armature made up of a limited number of common words. In fact, *Ulysses* and the *Wake* have much the same basic structures. As Clive Hart (1963, introduction) observes,

> It is remarkable that, despite the highly unusual character of the vocabulary of *Finnegans Wake*, the proportion of the 141 [most] common words, taken together, should be identical with that in *Ulysses*, to within one per cent.

And sure enough, readers of the *Wake* find that articles, prepositions, conjunctions, pronouns of all sorts, copulas, auxiliaries, and many other forms obediently perform their usual functions. Marshaled by these elements, subject and predicate accompany each other dutifully, on almost every page.

The *Wake*'s orthography is likewise basically English. The spelling in the book contains very few imported elements; there are no Southeast African suction clicks, no Welsh voiceless l's, no syllable tones as in Chinese or African languages. Except for one witty passage studded with such exotics as acute, grave, and circumflex accents (124.9–12), there are no non-English accents at all.

Only in the use of such free lexical items as nouns, verbs, adjectives, and adverbs does Joyce run away with the language, creating his own vocabulary based on English and perhaps forty other languages. Yet even here Joyce is only a trifle freer than most common speakers or writers of any language. Every time we hear discourses containing words that we do not know or novel information, we are on the borders of Jabberwocky jabber, or Wakespeech. Joyce merely takes this universal linguistic habit several miles farther than most speakers or writers have ever done.

Yet it is precisely this freedom of word choice that baffles most first-time (or many-time) readers of the *Wake*. What is the source of Joyce's extreme freedom of language? After all, in *Dubliners* and *A Portrait*, and even in much of *Ulysses*, Joyce does not seem to avail himself of such creative freedom. In *Ulysses*, however, Joyce first shows the activity of the Arranger: an intrusive speaker, defined in 1970 by David Hayman, who takes over a relatively objective text in *Ulysses* and runs away with carefree caprice.[11] It seems clear to me that the Arranger of parts of *Ulysses* has run away with the whole text of *Finnegans Wake*.

Here, then, is another enigma: why did Joyce introduce such an apparently capricious Arranger? Without further examination, it is tempting to conclude that Joyce, impelled by a surrealistic or postmodern creative gust, simply was amusing himself in *Ulysses* and *Finnegans Wake* when he handed the reins to his wild childish Arranger, a Puck or an Ariel, possessed by a mischievous, language-drunk spirit.

I do not find this explanation convincing. Joyce was not a surrealist, and he does not resemble the postmodernists, however much they may claim him as their father. A more responsible version of this interpretation might be that, since Joyce considered the comic manner the perfect manner in art, he is in *Ulysses* ensuring, with his Arranger, a wild comedy, which carries over to the *Wake*.

Moreover, in *Ulysses* the patterning of Arranging seems more carefully planned than would be accounted for by caprice or surrealist impulse. It seems to me that in *Ulysses* the Arranger begins Arranging only in the presence of darkness. This can be the darkness of the interior of buildings—the National Library, the newspaper office, the Ormond Hotel bar, Barney Kiernan's pub—as well as the natural darkness of evening and night. The early episodes are not Arranged at all; they take place in daylight and outdoors, where the operant principle is objective perception, the "ineluctable modality of the visible" (3.1), "what you damn well have to see" (9.86), "the shattering daylight of no thought" (9.1111–12). Then *Ulysses* begins to dive into darkness and into the creative fantasy of the interior mind that is the realm of the Arranger.

Katherine Anne Porter observed Joyce's preoccupation with darkness and the creation of language. She also noted the correlation of darkness with his declining sight: "His blindness was like the physical sign of his mind turning inward to its own darkness."[12]

The use of the Arranger in *Ulysses*, and the close correlation with darkness, provides a justification of the apparently capricious experiments with style in the *Wake*. Joyce allows the Arranger free rein in *Finnegans Wake*; the entire book is Arranged. The Arranger is omnipresent in *Finnegans Wake* because the *Wake* is a nighttime book, and therefore entirely within the dark purview of the Arranger. Clive Hart has suggested that Book I is a daylight book,[13] but I cannot find, in almost all of Book I, any actual time references—such as are provided in Books II, III, and IV, with the various Angeluses and the chiming of clocks and bells—until the first unambiguous time reference at 213.18–19. There is no "daytime" in the *Wake*, and therefore no objective "daylight of no thought."

The pervasive Arranging that Joyce does in the *Wake* is not, however, as elaborate or varied as that in *Ulysses*. It mainly takes the form of puns, some of them "portmanteau words" as invented by Lewis Carroll. There are two types of puns, referred to in traditional rhetorical analysis as *paronomasia* and *antanaclasis*. Paronomasia alters words to make new words that contain the meanings of the words contained within them. Lewis Carroll employed paronomasia when inventing the portmanteau word "chortle" as a combination of "chuckle" and "snort," and the word has passed into the lexicon of English.

Joyce uses puns constantly in the *Wake*—as for example in "the cropse of our seedfather" (55.8). In this phrase there are two varieties of paronomasia. In the first, "corpse" combines with "crops" to make a wholly new and richly evocative contradictory word, "cropse," combining the idea of death with resurrection. In the second, "seedfather" does not create a wholly new word, for both elements of "seedfather" are already existent words, with a double meaning contained in "seed"; only the combination is novel.

Antanaclasis, on the other hand, depends on the use of homophones or homographs, particularly those that have opposing meanings. Joyce manipulates paronomasia into antanaclasis as the light begins to dilute the darkness, in the last chapter of Book III and in Book IV. Among many examples in Book IV, a touching example occurs at the very end of the book. The dying Anna Livia mourns, "I done me best when I was let. Thinking always if I go all goes" (627.13–14). "Let" bears the contradictory meanings "allowed" and "hindered"; "hindered" is an old meaning, now only used as a term in tennis, a "let ball." Similarly, "if I go all goes" means "if I continue, all continues," as the river of time flows, but it also bears the pathetic meaning "if I die, the family falls apart," as indeed happened to the Joyce family after the death of their wife and mother.

Joyce achieves a masterpiece of technique in this long movement in *Finnegans Wake* from paronomasia to antanaclasis, when the darkness, the lack of light, in Books I, II, and III gives way to predawn illumination at the end of the book—a feat of literary creation unparalleled in modern literature.

Outline of *Finnegans Wake*

Space Mode

At the beginning of the book, nothing much is happening; nothing is moving except the river. As we have seen, it is moving westward, that is, backward. The backward and countertemporal flow of the Liffey prevents the narrative from beginning at the beginning of the book. It is a SPACE modality by which almost all of the eight chapters of Book I are ordered.

Chapter 1 opens on Dublin Bay under the misty Irish morning, the soft morning announced at the end of the book (619.20). There is a paragraph predicting the events of the book, after which we hear noises of frogs. All of a sudden we seem to be in the middle of a party, the funny funeral of the hero. But no, it is not an action but a mirage, only a faded photograph of a western scene of yesterday (7.15), like everything else in Book I. We now begin to see the function of Book I: little actually happens, but the reader gains much basic information with which to interpret the tale when TIME, and with it narration, actually begins in Books II and III.

Some of the major action in the book is then forecast by two fables, the Willingdone Museyroom fable, inside the Hill of Howth, and the Prankquean fable, inscribed on the sands of Dublin Bay. These fable tell, in appropriately reverse order, the destruction and the establishment of the family.

This chapter ends with the prediction of the coming of HCE.

In I.2 and I.3, the early history of our hero is described, including a garbled and doubtful story about how King William gave him his name. However, almost immediately rumors begin to circulate about HCE's disreputable past. Apparently he did something in Phoenix Park involving two young girls and three soldiers. At any rate, HCE always acts guilty about something; at one time he blurted out some denial of guilt to a Cad in the Park, which swiftly gave birth to a stream of scandalmongering.

Dubliners, always ready to spread malicious gossip, pass around a series of increasingly shocking stories about HCE. Stones are thrown at his house, accompanied by dozens of opprobrious epithets. A seedy balladmonger sings a satirical "rann" about HCE, and a foxhunt is organized to run down the guilty wretch. He eventually goes to earth under the neighborhoods of Dublin like a hunted fox, seeking shelter in a state of suspended animation.

The Liffey, in its journey upstream, has now entered the precincts of the city of Dublin, and we are introduced to the members of HCE's family and to other members of his entourage. In I.4, Four Old Men, senile and lascivious, contribute their totally inaccurate accounts of the past deeds of the hero. We then begin to hear about the family—his charming and long-suffering wife and his three children, two boys and a girl—and also the servants in his household and the customers in his pub.

In I.5 we are given an account of Anna Livia, and of her letter addressed to the Lord and disseminated to the world, in which she attempts to exculpate her comatose husband. At the end we are introduced to her sons, Shem and Shaun. With the introduction of the two sons, we are approaching Island Bridge, which is where the tidal Liffey ends up at a shallow weir. We are also approaching the turn of the tide, and the commencement of actual narration in TIME.

In I.6, for the benefit of the reader, we are given a quiz, in which we learn a great deal about the characters in the book. In addition, however, in the first sentence of the quiz (126.1–2), we encounter a time-word, "tonigh," a significant moment in the procession to actual TIME narrative.

Transition to TIME Mode

I.7 is made up of a masterly stream of violent invective directed by Shaun against his dirty brother Shem. Shem, as the lower half of the male body, contains the most shameful parts. Shaun, the top half of the body, is filled with puritanical hatred and fear of his own genitals and excretory apparatus. Joyce is here analyzing a phenomenon that he often encountered—the irrational, violent reaction of the audience to his uncompromising treatment of the entire male body.

Shaun's stream of invective eventually causes him to split in two, and as Justius he addresses himself directly, accusing his lower half, Mercius, of insanity. Mercius then appears, forgiving Shaun for his violence and bigotry. With the speech of Mercius TIME mode begins: "it is to you, . . . to me, . . . that our turfbrown mummy is acoming" (194.12, 13, 22). She is "coming": the debate between the brothers causes the Liffey to begin to flow seaward. She has been incestuously excited by her two sons, who represent the two banks between which she flows, like her own two thighs. It is here that TIME and narrative begin to flow—slowly at first, in I.8, the lovely Anna Livia chapter, and then, with the advent of twilight, in "real time." She is following the turn of the tide of her huge ocean-husband as it begins to ebb, far off on the horizon. The definitive beginning of the TIME narrative, the ringing of the evening Angelus at 213.14–21, the fertilization of the Virgin by God the Father, symbolizes the true beginning of every family.

TIME Mode

Book II

The four chapters II.1–4 present the first half of an eight-act play in TIME mode. It is a family drama. The half that occupies the four chapters of Book II takes place during one half of a night, from twilight to midnight. The second half, told in the four chapters of Book III, takes place during the second half of a night, from midnight to dawn.

This eight-act drama is represented in TIME in two modes. One mode, a naturalistic mode, places the unfolding story in one night, from twilight through midnight to dawn. The other mode represents the years taken up by the maturing of the children as they move to become the next generation and, thereby, destroy the power of their father.

In II.1 the very young children are playing a game in the early twilight. Shem is "it," and keeps guessing wrong answers. Three times he is repulsed by the little girls he is trying to impress. Each time, he rushes away and begins to learn about poetic creation and about sex. The third time, he returns with sexual black magic, with which he infects his sister Issy. Overexcited, she sings an improper song about her aging father, is spanked by her mother, and is dragged into the house. The chapter concludes with a thunderstorm and a prayer, as is appropriate for the first stage of Vico—the gods reveal themselves as all-powerful and thereby create the first stage of Vico, the religious.

However, two of the three children are now standing on the threshold of physical and psychological maturity.

In II.2 the three children, now somewhat older, are doing their homework upstairs in the inn. The innocent young Shaun has had difficulty with German and algebra—two subjects that share the letters ge, as in the Greek word for "mother." He now has difficulty with a third ge subject, geometry, the measurement of the mother. The crafty Shem coaches Shaun into drawing a diagram of his mother's genitals, which infuriates Shaun. However, despite his anger, Shaun is now capable of employing the rational parts of his mind to draw Cartesian lines onto undivided reality. All three of the children have learned about the nature of the maturing body, which is soon to be theirs.

In II.3 there are three performances. One is a radio play dramatizing the marriage of HCE and ALP and the emergence of the family. The second, a television play, dramatizes the murder of the father and the overthrow of paternal power. Issy then sings a charming song about the incipient castration of her father. Then the children, on the threshold of maturity, invade HCE's pub and destroy him. Shem and Shaun merge into the bottom and top half of one male body—Tristan. Issy becomes a virginal but impatient young maiden—Isolde. In II.4 the two young lovers, as Tristan and Isolde, go out to sea on their honeymoon voyage, but they accomplish little more than "French" kissing. The children are not yet mature adults. This development must wait for Book III.

Book III

The four chapters III.1–4, which begin at midnight and end at dawn, show the young man Shaun, now bearing his brother Shem uneasily between his thighs, attempting to become a mature man, one who can truly love a woman with both his soul and his body. When Shaun achieves this psycho-sexual amalgamation, he will rise up in the east as the new father-lover, like the Egyptian god Horus. Shaun is traveling downstream, from west to east, on his night journey to his rising-up place in the east as the new sun-son-husband-lover of Anna Livia.

Shaun, with Shem inside his trousers, is not yet fully a man. In III.2 and III.3 he goes through two stages of maturation. In III.2 he is maliciously questioned by his genitals, which are disguised as a donkey. Shaun evades all of the embarrassing questions that men are impelled by their genitals to evade. In III.3, in an attempt at masturbation, Shaun tries to make his brother rise up from "down under" by envisaging spanking his sister—an immature attempt at sexual action. He succeeds only in ejaculating on his own blouse—yet another evasion of mature sexuality.

III.3 is a very long chapter. In it Shaun, having fallen twice before, is now flat on his back. He is being examined by the Four Old Men. After Shaun, now named Yawn, evades as many of their questions as he can, he rises up from his own depths, and turns out to be HCE resurrected.

The newly arisen HCE is a great and proud creator, who has brought forth a mighty, but flawed, creation—the city. Dublin is beginning to appear in the growing light of dawn. Shaun/HCE has created the modern city as a wedding ring for his bride, the river, but in the course of his creation, he has imprisoned her within it. He is a true creator, but his way of showing his love to his bride-mother is to imprison her within the stone embankments of Dublin and overawe her with threats of violence. True complete love, then, still evades Shaun.

In III.4 dawn light is appearing in the sky, and we see a realistic stage set—the home of the Porter family. HCE and ALP are roused from their light slumber by a cry from Shem, who has had a nightmare. In fact, he has been frightened by the events of the previous TIME narrative. The parents rush upstairs to meet this emergency. Shem's mother consoles him. But HCE, in his haste, has forgotten that he is not wearing pajama bottoms, and all of the children are treated to a free show of mature male equipment. This startling view begins the road to maturity for the children—and is, incidentally, the source of all the rumors about HCE's antics in the park with the soldiers and the girls.

The parents return to their bedroom, leaving behind three enlightened children beginning their own journey to sexual maturity and, eventually, true love. The next generation is on the doorstep of maturity, and the aged parents fail in their attempt to make love.

End of TIME Mode and Transition to SPACE Mode

Joyce's masterpiece, Book IV, has only one chapter. In it Joyce, with total mastery of his art, recreates the physical world. Under the dawn wind, the details of a modern city begin to reveal themselves, complete with advertisements, and milk trucks delivering milk, and bread baking. There rises up a spectacular sunrise, which reveals and creates the physical world in all its rainbow-colored glory. Two champions debate the nature of the real world. An Eastern sage asserts the unreality of the real world, but St. Patrick successfully defends God's world. The world may be an imperfect creation, like HCE's creation of the city, but it is the appropriate place for imperfect human beings.

The rest of the book is told by the river, flowing eastward, as the ocean tide recedes, into the face of her great lover, who is now blazing in the eastern sky. The letter to the world created by Anna Livia, written down by her son Shem the Penman, and delivered to the world by her son Shaun the Post, is now revealed in its entirety. In it she defends her husband against the calumnies of the world. Of course, she ultimately realizes that he is truly guilty—but then, so is she, and so are all human beings in this Joycean flawed magnificent world.

The superb Soft Morning, City! section ends the chapter and the book. In this creation, one of the most marvelous passages in all of literature, the aging, blind, breathless Anna Livia flows past Howth Castle and Environs and out into the Irish Sea. As she leaves the city and the bay, she rebels against her husband's repression and strict control, and welcomes the blazing wildness of her son-husband-father-lover. She flows out into the face of the risen sun, and then dies down before the mystery of true love. The outward-flowing tide of time stops, as Anna Livia "dies," in every sense of the word, and is then borne backward by the mighty love of the sea—this time the only successful act of true love in the book.

1

Book I (*FW* 1–216)

The Age of Gods (Vico)

<small>SPACE</small> Medium

Time and the River Flow Backward

The end of *Finnegans Wake* feeds into the beginning. At the end of Book IV the sea tide is going out, and it is drawing the Liffey with it. It has been retreating since the turn of the tide at the end of I.7. At that point, when the Liffey waters began to follow the withdrawing tide seaward, the flow of narrative began. Now at the end of Book IV the tide is almost completely out, and the narrative is coming to a close. Anna Livia, the estuary, has felt the turn of the tides twice a day—the sea coming in, the sea going out, in a sexual rhythm forever. Now Anna Livia is flowing out to sea, coming to meet her son-husband-lover, who is beginning to blaze on the horizon as the sun, rising over Dublin bar at the mouth of Dublin Bay. He is rising in the east like an archangel (from the general direction of Archangel in northern Russia).

The aged Anna Livia, getting mixed in her mind and also with the bitter waters of the Irish Sea (626.36–627.1), feels the powerful ocean currents and senses the waters of her sister rivers, the Nile and the Amazon, welcoming her. She is now out in the sea, looking back with contempt at the puny bump that is the Hill of Howth.

Then the kiss of the ocean is given (628.15). Anna faints with love-death, the orgasmic tide of her end. And then the tide turns; the blazing son-husband-father enters the Liffey waters in the Irish Sea, and the river and the reader are borne backward. Forward <small>TIME</small>-narrative stops, and backward <small>SPACE</small>-description takes over. The change is expressed in the wave rhythms of the last phrase in the book (628.15–16). *Away, alone at last, and loved, along the river ran.* Anna has won free from the land and from her bumpkin of a husband and is alone at last, yet she is in the embrace of her true lover, the rising sun, and is therefore truly loved. Then the lover enters the beloved, and the river begins to flow backward—to the beginning of the book.

Book I, Chapter 1: A Misty Morning, and Two Fables

The famous first sentence of the *Wake* shows the Liffey flowing back, away from the sea and back into Dublin Bay (3.1–3). All is going in reverse: Adam and Eve's, the famous church, is now Eve and Adam's; we are moved "back" by the retreating Anna Livia from the Irish Sea to within the bend of Dublin Bay, to Howth Castle and Environs.

The commodius vicus of recirculation has turned the corner, and time stops. The commodiousness of Joyce's *commedia* now delivers us to the beginning of things, after the inferno and purgatory of the night, and the paradise of the morning coupling of ALP and HCE. Now we confront the soft morning that Anna welcomed in the last chapter—a misty Irish morning, with almost nothing visible. All we see of Dublin Bay is the face of the waters (3.14), a face with no features. Time has not yet started; it will not start again for almost two hundred pages. The first book is the equivalent of a table of contents or a dramatis personae. The eight chapters of Book I spatialize the story. They provide a paradigmatic presentation of the syntagmatic time-narrative of the later books. Now we are informed of all the things that have not yet (or again) taken place.

As the Liffey retreats upstream, other events appear in reverse order. The paragraph on the first page beginning with the reference to Sir Tristram (3.4), outlining what has not yet happened, shows events from last to first. In this chapter the two fables—the Willingdone Museyroom and the Prankquean fable—present family history in reverse: the Willingdone Museyroom shows the overthrow of the father and the destruction of the old family, and the Prankquean fable shows the meeting of the father and the mother and the establishment of the family. In the presentation of these fables here in Book I, chapter 1, destruction precedes creation. In II.3, in the TIME section of the book, the fabulous material appears in the natural order, with the story of the creation of the family (the story of the Norwegian captain and the tailor's daughter) followed by the destruction of the family (the story of the shooting of the Russian general).

In the TIME sections of the book, the natural order of the creation and destruction of the family starts with the innocent children squabbling and playing children's games and then, one by one, acquiring sexual knowledge.

With this power within them, they grow to the point of maturity, when they "threaten" the older powers of the family with supersession. The matured children presently do supersede the old powers. The sons merge and become the new power rising up blazing from the east, riding on a white horse in unbearably bright white garments ("my tennis champion son" says one of the old washerwomen at 214.27). The son/sun becomes the new lover, Tristan, of the daughter/bride Isolde, and they become the founders of the new family.

However, on the first page of the book, the Sir Tristram paragraph shows this process in reverse. The parts of the paragraph foretell all the important elements of the whole story:

1. Sir Tristram, the sexually potent young hero, the great lover, the future father, rearrives from over the Irish Sea, like the sun rising, to fight his phallic war, the successful war on the old powers and the conquest of Isolde.

2. The rocks (testicles) of the almost mature hero begin to grow, to exaggerate themselves—a state preliminary to the complete maturity of the hero.

3. A faraway voice from a fire calls the hero to maturity. This foresees the acquisition of magical sexual knowledge by Shem in II.1, when he visits the fires of Hell in his quest for poetic and sexual power (239.28–251.32). Shem's quest is successful; at the end of II.1 he has infected his sister with his knowledge. She sings a rowdy song about the (waning) sexual powers of her father, and gets punished for it (256.33–257.28), but now she, with Shem, is on the borders of maturity. In II.2, Shem tricks Shaun into confronting the sexual knowledge of their parents, and gets socked in the eye. Then all three children send an ominous Nightletter to their parents threatening them with death.

4. A young goat butts a blind old father; a young boy sees the intimate parts of the male deity or parent, as Moses saw those of God (Exod. 33:23) and Ham saw those of Noah (Gen. 9:22). It is at this point that Shem acquires the ambition to mature.

5. Twin sisters tease their brothers in childish games, games that eventually lead to maturity.

The whole book has here been summarized, in reverse order, as the waters of the estuary are borne upstream, in a countertemporal mode.

After this reverse table of contents, we hear the first of ten thunderwords,[1] each with 100 letters, with the last containing 101 letters, for a total of 1,001, a reference to another story told at night, the *Arabian Nights*. These thunder-words mark an uneasy night of rainy weather. The weather clears to some extent in the very early morning, and the next day, Sunday, is merely misty, a soft morning, to use the Irish expression.

Then, after the first thunderword, we are swept back by the rising tide to the fog-shrouded Hill of Howth. There we are given some history of the great hero who is buried there—Adam Kadmon, the original man, the viceking Adam. His size and his merry "funferal" are described, as are his penchant for alcohol and the circumstances of his fall (4.18–7.19). We peer more closely at the mound and are invited to enter it. The mound, which is looming up from the fog, contains, we soon learn, all the life stories of everybody who ever lived—the Akasic records of humanity—drifted down into a huge heap.[2]

Now we are at the threshold of the first of the two great fables in the *Wake*. The processes of creation and destruction of the family are symbolized by two root stories, which echo in myriad forms throughout the *Wake*. As befits the reverse mode of the first book, the fable of destruction, the Willingdone Museyroom, precedes the fable of creation, the Prankquean fable.

We are about to penetrate into the mound of human history, to discover the great secrets of destruction in the Willingdone Museyroom.

The Willingdone Museyroom Fable (8.8–10.23)

Joyce visited the battlefield of Waterloo in the summer of 1926.[3] On the site of the battle, just behind Mont St. Jean, there was then a cylindrical building containing on the inner walls a diorama depicting the battle at its height. (I visited this diorama forty years after Joyce; the building has since been demolished.) The visit to the Waterloo diorama provided Joyce with the landscape for the decisive battle between the father and the children.

Our guide into the Museyroom is an old woman, Kate, who serves later as the servant in HCE's pub. Old women in Joyce are the conservators of the past—consider the sisters in the first story in *Dubliners*, and the Morkan sisters in the last story; consider too, in *A Portrait*, the diary entry for 6 April: "Certainly she remembers the past. Lynch says all women do." In the *Wake*, the washerwomen at the ford in I.8 reveal all the secrets of the family whose dirty linen they are washing.

All the old women in the Wake are the remnants of young and fertile women who have become old and sterile. Kate here is the janitor of the building as well as the exhausted genitrix of the family whose secrets are to be revealed (8.8). As the guardian of life, she warns us to mind our hats going into the building and mind our boots coming out. We enter life head first, and we exit from life feet first. We are going to view some of the fundamental secrets of life in our tour.

The Willingdone Museyroom fable—the basic fable of loss of power in the family—gives in symbolic form an anticipation of the moment when power begins to shift from the older generation to the younger. To understand the relationship of this fable to the overall structure of the book, we must also take note here of the much later "realistic" account of the source of the power shift in the family, the episode in Book III where the power of the older generation first begins to erode. There the children are treated to a view of the father's lower half, front and back, and they begin to understand the power of their own lower halves.

The "realistic" account of this revelation—the basic tale of a primeval traumatic event—takes place much later, in III.4 (558.32–571.34). The aging parents in the Porter family are awakened by a cry from the children's quarters. Shem-Jerry has been frightened by a nightmare, possibly one in which the father menaces the children and is destroyed. The couple rush to the children, Mr. Porter in his haste omitting to put on the lower half of his pajamas. The half-awake Jerry—the "seeboy" (10.4–5, 20) as he is called in the Willingdone fable—sees his father's genitals, much as Ham saw the genitals of his father, Noah. The mother then warns the father (in Esperanto—*pas devant les enfants!*) that Jerry can see him, so Mr. Porter wheels about, only to make the situation worse: his little daughter, also awakened, can now see his mature male genitals. The shaggy, beastly sight (566.33) sets her to thinking about maturity and the nature of males, which then starts the whole process of supersession of the old by the young.

This traumatic event provides a great amount of the symbolic structure of the *Wake*. The description of the back and front view of the father occurs in the tale of the meeting in Phoenix Park of HCE and the Cad. Therein is the origin of all of the scandalous rumors about HCE exposing himself to some girls immodestly displaying themselves (or urinating) in the bushes, and about HCE's fears that three soldiers are going to sodomize him and/or shoot him in the back. The Phoenix Park episode, ultimately based upon the realistic display of HCE's back and front view in the morning household, reproduces the tactics in the battle of Waterloo in the Museyroom. In the Museyroom, the father confronts the sons and "fires" upon them with his huge phallus; then the girls, by immodest displays, tempt him to turn around his phallic equipment to fire upon them, at which point the matured sons destroy him from behind with a bomb, or by a display of their own masculinity.

The Willingdone Museyroom fable, or The Willingdone and His Big Wide Harse (8.9–10.23), tells the story of this traumatic, epoch-beginning and epoch-ending event in symbolic form. After we enter the diorama of life's battles, we begin to see military details.[4] At first we see only static exhibits, a series of isolated souvenirs of the battle—a Prussian gun, a French gun, a Prussian flag, a bullet (or bull) that damaged the Prussian flag, a French bullet that was fired at the bull, the triplewon hat of Napoleon, and finally a portrait of the Willingdone himself complete with seven articles of martial clothing. We are also afforded a view of his big wide harse. It is obviously difficult to tell where the man ends and the harse begins. He is apparently a hugely sexual centaur. Later, this is the way the father is seen by the children in the realistic dawning in Book III, chapter 4. The name Willingdone, besides referring to the Duke of Wellington, is highly suggestive: the "will" of the first syllable bears the Elizabethan significance of sexual power, and perhaps indicates the phallus itself. The Willingdone is a sexually potent creature, who, as we shall see, is paradoxically willing to be "done," killed, by his sons when they achieve their mature power.

But what of the children? There are three boys and two girls. The numbers three and two throughout the *Wake* symbolize respectively the male and the female sexual equipment. The two testicles and the penis add up to three; the female labia are a pair. This numerical correspondence is not original with Joyce; it was noted by Martianus Capella, who got it from Plutarch's observation in "The E at Delphi" that

> every number may be classified as even or odd . . . and since two makes the first of the even numbers and three the first of the odd, and five is produced by by the union of these numbers, very naturally five has come to be honoured as being the first number created out of the first numbers; and it has received the name of "marriage" because of the resemblance of the even number to the female and of the odd number to male. (217)

After preliminary maneuvers, the battle's action begins. At first we see the three little Napoleon boys crouching down in living death, or in the living ditch of the birth canal. They are identified as members of three British regiments of Celtic provenance—an Enniskillen Dragoon (whose depot is in Northern Ireland), a Scots Grey (from Scotland), and a Davy (a Welch Fusilier). All three of these regiments served gallantly at the actual battle of Waterloo, and sustained heavy losses. All of the soldiers from these regiments are verminous.

The Davy is stooping below the other two, who begin a Cain-and-Abel murderous quarrel. The quarrel weakens the sexual power of these boys, who represent the two testicles, and the third lipoleum boy, the Davy, who represents the temporarily immature and flaccid phallus, begs them to cease their fighting; he calls, "Assez! Assez!" The names of the three turn out to be Tom, Dick, and Harry; they are therefore Everyman in his earliest stage of development. They are also three of the four classical elements: fire (the cannon's touchole), earth (the dirt of a dike), and air (the hurrying air). Only water is missing, and later the girls provide the water.

The "Delian alps" join the scene. As the name suggests, they are the mother, Anna Livia, with her delta sexual symbol. She tries to protect the three boys from their father, the Willingdone. (Note that it is two women who protect the very young Stephen Dedalus from the anger of a father in the first chapter of *A Portrait*.)

Then suddenly we see the two girls, the jinnies, *les jeunes*, who attempt to save their brothers from the superpotent father by striking suggestive poses. Sure enough, the Willingdone gets the band up; *bander* in French slang means "masturbate" (8.34–36). In fact, the father's phallus is extending hugely, like the memorial telescope constructed by the Earl of Rosse in Ireland. No erectional difficulties for the Willingdone! It is the flanks of the girls that excites the Willingdone, reminding the reader of the sexual areas that most excite Leopold Bloom in the Circe chapter, and that very likely were the supremest objects of desire for James Joyce himself.

Les jeunes send the Willingdone a provocative message (9:5–6) in Germanoid text, warning him of whatever pranks his wife may be getting up to while he is fighting the battle of Waterloo—"Dear Arthur. We will win [*siegen*]! How is your wife? Respectfully yours [*Mit Hochachtung*], Nap."— ending in girlish laughter, "Shee, shee, shee."

The girls, to arouse the Willingdone, pretend to court the boys. Their message and subsequent behavior succeed only in getting the Willingdone's band up for the second time. Then the Willingdone sends back to the girls a scornful message (9.13–14) in a variety of French—"Dear young girls [*Chères jeunes*]. Fuck you [*Fichtre-vous*]! Women do nothing [*Dames faire rien*]. Yours [*votre*; also *foutre*, "fuck you"], Willingdone"[5]—and ends with a burst of male laughter, "Hee, hee, hee."

Then the Willingdone orders his cavalry to fire on the boys, to ghastly effect. To save the boys, the girls run away, showing their underwear to the susceptible Willingdone, whose memorial telescope extends even farther than before. The maneuver succeeds: the Willingdone swivels around to pursue the girls, and the boys see their opportunity. The smallest of the boys, the phallic Davy the Welshman, who has been stooping below the two other boys, now begins to rise up in rage and power. The other two boys, having forgotten their quarrel, join in. The two testicles cooperate with the ithyphallic Davy, and all three prepare a bomb to throw at the big wide harse of their father. However, the bomb's fuse lacks a light, and it is the Willingdone, now willing to be done (killed), who hands his matchbox to the cursing Davy, now fully erect and tumescent.[6] The Davy throws the lit bomb at the big wide harse of the Willingdone and blows the Napoleon hat of authority off the backside of that big wide harse. This is bull's-eye in the game! The power of the father passes to the next generation.

Symbolically, the father in the archetypal family quarrel always surrenders; if he did not, the secular process of development from one generation to the next could never take place. In *Dubliners*, it is the lack of this surrender, the stubborn retention of power by the paternal authorities, that is the source of the paralysis in all of the stories. In *A Portrait* and *Ulysses*, Stephen fights against the power of all the "fathers" in his generation, and ultimately wins through, with his cry of "Nothung!"

At the end of the Museyroom fable, we exit the Museyroom exclaiming, "Phew!" (10.24). (Napoleon said that when Europe knew he was dead, it would exclaim "Phew!" in relief.) We have exited the Hill of Howth, and now see a little bird running around the landscape (12.9). In other words, the mound has now appeared out of the early morning mist, and some more of the landscape is visible. Also visible are two creatures, named Mutt and Jute, who discuss what we have just seen take place inside the mound (15.12–18.16).

In our backward journey, we are now bending along the bay of Dublin, heading westward toward the city. On the clay bed of the river, alphabetical letters begin forming. We are within sight of the mist-beset city of Dublin which, with all its faults, is the frame for family life. We are about to encounter the fable of the creation of family life, the fable of the Prankquean.

The Prankquean Fable (21.5–23.15)

The fable of the Prankquean is a delightful children's tale about the creation of the family—a tale that, as we have seen, and as befits the reverse nature of the first book—takes place *after* the destruction of the family in the Willingdone Museyroom.

The fable is introduced as the product of a movement of alphabet letters on the shore of the Liffey closer to Dublin. It has a musical accompaniment (21.3–4). Spelling out HCE/ALP, a French horn "entreats" in a manly fashion, and a harp prattles forth a brittle melody played with a feminine touch, like a lark.

After this enunciation of the initials of the hero and heroine, the lovely story begins.

The fable of the Prankquean is basically simple. The wounded, comatose Jarl van Hoother, the Earl of Howth, is ensconced in his locked castle, with his two sons and his daughter playing on the floor. The Prankquean, a prankish queen or quean (wench), shows up, is offended that the castle is locked, asks a riddle, gets no answer (or only an obscene and insulting one), steals one of the sons, Tristopher (the sad one, Shem), and flies off with him to the wilderness. She changes Tristopher's sad character into a merry one, as Joyce himself once decided that the perfect manner in art was the comic, when he switched his focus from the melancholy Stephen Dedalus to the comic characters Leopold Bloom and Humphrey Chimpden Earwicker.

The Prankquean appears before the castle again, bringing the changed boy with her, and asks the riddle for the second time. Again receiving no relevant or courteous reply, she flies off with the other boy, Hilary (the merry one, Shaun), to the wilderness, changes his nature from hilarious to sad, and comes to the castle a third time.[7] She again asks the riddle, but this time the jarl, infuriated at the constant interruption of his sloth, rushes out of the castle and confronts his tormentor. They agree on a modus vivendi: the jarl is to support the newly established family, the Prankquean gets the daughter, and the family moves on.

The establishment of every family is a great mystery, much more mysterious than the destruction of the family, which has been exhaustively analyzed by Freudians. Why do a man and a woman agree to live together and to have children?

There are two basic levels in the analysis of this important fable. The first is historical, the visit of the Irish pirate queen Grace O'Malley, a real and formidable sixteenth-century person who visited Queen Elizabeth in London and addressed her as queen to queen. The Irish name of Grace O'Malley, Granuaile, was one of the codewords used by Irish insurgents to represent Ireland itself. There is a story that Grace O'Malley once showed up at the castle of the Earl of Howth, Amory St. Lawrence, and was denied hospitality: the gates of the castle were shut during dinnertime. Rightly offended at the denial of a traditional right of visitors, she kidnapped the earl's son and would not return him until the earl promised to eat dinner with his gates unlocked.

In Joyce's story, the Jarl van Hoother is a sluggish, semicomatose, self-abusing male figure. On the other hand, the Prankquean is the very spirit of action, of Life itself. Here Joyce is relying upon another level of narrative, one deriving from Indian religion. The great god Vishnu is often pictured as lying asleep on the serpent Ananta ("unending"), symbolizing the Ultimately Real itself as self-consistent and contented, resting on the unending basis of all reality. Vishnu, like the other two great gods, Brahma and Siva, is neutral and unacting, since it is necessary for them to avoid karma, the results of their actions. However, the great god occasionally stirs in his sleep, stimulated by his Shakti, his active principle, or his consort Lakshmi, or Prakriti, the active principle in nature. During the short disturbance in Vishnu's sleep he creates the known universe, which grows like a lotus from his navel. As Joseph Campbell states, "In Hinduism, the activating principle (Sanskrit: Shakti) is female energy; the quiescent is male" (192).

In the Prankquean fable, Joyce defines creation as consisting of a static principle of contemplation stimulated by the artistic principle of active creation, with the ultimate result the creation of the material universe, which was Joyce's chosen subject matter. The Prankquean, the prankish girl, is Life itself, one of the root meanings of the figure of Anna Livia Plurabelle. Life itself rounds out the characters of her sons; that is, she takes the melancholy Shem and the merry Shaun and makes them share each other's personalities.

Joyce actually shows this happening in II.2 at 287–92, near the very middle of the book, when the river flows over her banks and embraces her sons in an incestuous union. When they emerge from the baptism into life, the natures of the boys have changed, and the comments of the boys on the stream of text have changed sides. In psychological terms, Shaun, the top half of the body (pure, disembodied, cruel, intellectual, divisive), has reluctantly accepted Shem, the embarrassing lower half of the body (dirty, completely bodied, kind, generous), and they unite to form one mature human being, one creative principle using as material all of human life, as Joyce himself did.

The Prankquean fable, like every good fable, goes in threes. In fact, it incorporates all the techniques that have characterized children's stories through the ages. The organization is crystalline; parallelism is present from beginning to end. It begins with a traditional beginning: It was on a night, a long long time ago, in an Old Stone Age (21.5). Adam and Eve are introduced as a mountain and a river, and have their traditional occupations as attributed in the old Peasants' Revolt jingle of John Ball: "When Adam dalf [dug] and Eve span [spun cloth] / Who was thanne a gentilman?"

Next we are introduced to the Earl of Howth, with emphasis on his head (21.10–11). Later we see the jarl from his heels up (21.34–36). And finally we see him in an intermediate view, from his hips (22.22–23). The parallelism displayed in the fable is exquisite: first the head, then the heels, then the hips and stomach(s) of the bovine jarl. We also see the signs of his criminality: his head burnt from God's lightnings, his heels bruised by a great political crime, the St. Bartholomew's Day Massacre of 1572, and finally his gluttony signified by his heavy hips blowing a malodorous hurricane, premonitory of the later storm of creative dung, and his four stomachs, like a cow's, or a gelded bull's.

The tale is told in strict tripartite fashion, in the time-honored manner of the children's story. The Prankquean herself appears in three developing guises, asking her riddle in three stages—wit, witter, wittest (21.15–19; 22.2–6, 26–30). The three stages are also marked by flowers: the Prankquean picks a red rose and a white rose and then a blank, a rose of no color. A rose of no color may signify a Platonic rose of ideal beauty. The rose was used extensively by poets, and especially the young Yeats, as a symbol of the transient beauty of earthly life, of the temporary beauties of temporal life revealing symbolically the beauties of eternity. Here the Prankquean redeems the transience of life by her blazing activity: first Ireland is set ablaze; second, the great blaze sends all the nightbirds flying astonished from the hilltops; and finally, her great light reveals all the nightbound valleys of Ireland (21.16–17; 22.3–4, 27–28).

The jarl tries three times to tell his daughter to shut the shutter of his "shop," but all he gets time to say twice is "Shut!"—a suspiciously excrementitious exclamation—and when the finally aroused jarl orders or "ordures" (23.4), his thick speech comes out from some orifice or other as "Shut up shop, dummy."[8] In fact, in his irritation, the jarl has invented the first piece of alliterative or illiterate poetry ever created (23.9–10). The jarl has added earth (of a sordid sort) to the water (flood), fire (flaming), and air (flatus) of the now fully created world. In a reversal of Aristotle's definition of the place of the male principle as the provider of creative spirit and the female principle as provider of basic material for the creation of the universe, Joyce here shows the powerfully stimulating Prankquean as the Shakti stimulating her comatose Vishnu to create the imperfect world from dung.

The subject of the fable is the establishment of the family and the city, just as the destruction of the family was the meaning of the first fable, the Willingdone Museyroom. The fable ends with a national anthem, which sounds very much like "The Star-Spangled Banner." The jarl has said to the sea, as if he were the God of Job, "Thus far shalt thou flow" (23.11–12). The land is at last appearing from under Dublin Bay. Then the family relationships are described, as the elements in the family ship of state faring forward: the Prankquean is to control the daughter, the boys are to keep the peace, and the father is to earn the money to keep the family ship afloat (23.12–14). The ship, the wave, and the wind all act to send the ship forward. Not only does the jarl's responsibility "to git the wind up" introduce the windup of the family's affairs, but in Irish slang to "raise the wind" means to get the money. After the family relationships are defined and the family ship begins its voyage, the fable ends with the motto of the city of Dublin (23.14–15), which declares that the obedience of the citizen is the health of the state. Joyce thought that the burghers of Dublin were all too obedient for their own good, but it cannot be denied that the limitation of freedom inherent in being a city dweller is an essential element in the order and permanence of the city. Joyce will present his full portrait of the basic structures of city life in III.3, in the great Haveth Childers Everywhere poem.

After the end of the Prankquean fable, we again regard the paternal mound, which, under the busy advising of Four Old Men, is curiously restless. Suddenly the mound, offended and aroused by the oldsters' mention of the dance activities of its daughter, rears in outrage and prurient stimulation. However, the Four Old Men reassure the mound that the paternal role is being played by a new arrival to Ireland's shores, a Viking complete with family, whose initials are HCE, and who will be ultimately responsible for the famous uproar in the Garden of Eden (29.35–36), which will be acted out in Books II and III of the *Wake*.

Book I, Chapter 2: Rumors about HCE

In the next seven chapters of the book, the tide is still flowing in, and as we the readers are borne back from Dublin Bay into the city of Dublin, we begin to learn a great deal more about our city-dwelling hero HCE, his wife ALP, and his children. In I.6 we shall see them all in greater detail in the answers to a nighttime quiz. Then in I.7, after a violent tide of invective directed by Shaun at his brother Shem, the sea tide begins to turn, the river begins to flow outward, and we finally become ready for the TIME narrative to begin.

In I.2 we learn, in some comparatively clear pages, about the early life of HCE and how he got his name. Apparently the king, William, had halted in his hunt and noticed a loyal serf, Humphrey or Harold, who had hastened out to see him, bearing a pole with a pot on top. The king, amused to learn that the pot was for catching earwigs, made a stately royal joke to the effect that one of his subjects was an "earwigger," in Dublin slang a gossipy barfly. Hence the family name of our hero—Earwicker.

Almost immediately, rumors begin to spread about HCE, centering on some sort of scandal in Phoenix Park involving three soldiers and two girls. It is here that the first detailed signs of the primal scene in III.4, which has taken symbolic form in the Willingdone episode, begin to emerge. This "realistic" scene, where HCE inadvertently shows his unclothed front and back to his children, has here been transmuted into a long, unsavory story—given impetus by HCE's fear of aging and his guilt over incestuous feelings toward his daughter—about being ambushed by three soldiers in the park as he was spying on two girls micturating in the bushes.

This park story is communicated by two brothers, Treacle Tom and Frisky Shorty (39.14–43.21),[9] to other Dubliners, who join in and joyfully spread the news. Dubliners have always loved scandal, and the phrase "a nation wants a gaze" (43.21–22) combines the Nationalist song "A Nation Once Again" with the prurient interest of the patriotic populace wanting a look at the scandalous lives of the great, as they once did with Parnell. The gossip, printed in black and white with a rude woodcut illustration, spreads on the winds to all points of the compass (compass rose). It finally gets to the ears of a scurrilous balladmonger named Hosty.[10] Hosty is dirty but very popular, and he quickly draws a crowd to hear his "Ballad of Persse O'Reilly" (*perce-oreille* being the French for "earwig").

"The Ballad of Persse O'Reilly," one of the great set-pieces of the *Wake*, deserves close analysis. In this episode Joyce paints a vivid and detailed picture of a popular public event.

The melody of the ballad resembles the familiar tune "Carnival of Venice," but with one significant difference: it starts in A major, modulates to A minor, and ends up in A modal; that is, the melody slumps downward, mirroring the Fall of Man, and the tone of the ballad turns grim as the hero of the ballad is identified twice as the runaway Cain.

The ballad is first referred to as a "rann"—an Irish word for a verse, but here conveying also the flight of the "running" criminal HCE (44.7). Hosty addresses the ballad to boys and girls, skirts and breeches (44.8), thereby mocking HCE's fading sexual drive.

The hero's many pseudonyms are then detailed by Hosty. Some of the names of the hero of the ballad are: Viking; Finn; Lug, the Celtic sun god; Bug, combining Slavic words for God with the insectuous earwig, and with the Böögg, the huge effigy of the Winterking destroyed at Sechseläute in Zurich every June, as well as with Ibsen's Boyg, the cloud of self-doubt that hinders Peer Gynt's return home. We also encounter Dan Lop, Dan for Daniel O'Connell, an ancestor of the Joyce family, so they always believed, and a great political and sexual generator; he was the Liberator and the father of many illegitimate children. Here he is combined with *lop*, Polish for "bug," the whole making up Dunlop, the inventor of the rubber tire for bicycles and cars. We also encounter Lex, the law, of which HCE was the inventor; Lax, Finn MacCool's Salmon of Wisdom, *lax* or *lachs* being "salmon" in several Germanic languages; Gunn or Guinn, equivalents for Finn, with overtones of "guns"; Arth, King Arthur or Arthur Wellesley, Duke of Wellington; Barth, the flayed martyr, and saint of the Bartholomew's Day Massacre, the pattern for all treacherous acts of political and religious violence; Noll, Oliver Cromwell; Soll, the sun; Will, the Elizabethan word for drive, will, sexual desire, or the penis itself, and Schopenhauer's Immanent Will, the creative and destructive force of humanity and history; and finally Wall, Humpty Dumpty's wall.

The huge crowd bursts out in praise of Hosty (44.15–17). Then the crowd asks impatiently when the song will begin. Catching sight of Hosty ascending to the conductor's podium, the crowd begins to applaud (44.19). There is a crash of glass as some overenthusiastic clapping clown lets fall his glass of beer (44.19–20). Then the applause of the crowd is vividly conveyed by a hundred-letter thunderword in which the onset, the crescendo, and the finale of the applause are captured with great art by Joyce—the initial claques, then the first massing of clapping hands, then the surface of massed applauding hands, then at the climax the seamless noise of applause, then the dying down into solos of clapping, and finally the last few claps of one or two individuals (44.20–21).

The ballad itself is a violent satire on HCE, who, it declares, carries on his shoulders the guilt of many other figures, among them Oliver Cromwell, an evil creature to the Irish (to say "Cromwell" is Ireland is like saying "Hitler" in Israel); purveyors of contraceptives, a scandal for a Catholic audience; prohibitionists, a scandal for booze-loving Dubliners; religious reformers, a scandal for Protestant-hating Dubliners (HCE is later identified as an Anglican); dishonest shopkeepers, and all commerce in the modern world, especially American (HCE purveys chewing gum); Scandinavians; philosophers, a reference to the ultimate fate of Socrates; low-class rapists ("rotorious" in 47.8 is derived from French *roturier*, low country hick); the drunken Noah; and finally Adam and Cain.

The crowd applauds the burial of HCE,[11] and bursts out twice during the performance of the ballad, eventually suffocating with emotion while praising Hosty as the equal of Sophocles, Shakespeare, Dante, and Moses (47.19). The last identifies Hosty as the equal of the anonymous author of the Pentateuch.

With the double identification of HCE as Cain, the ballad grimly ends.

Book I, Chapter 3: The Hunting of HCE to His Den

The crowd bursts into cries of admiration as Hosty concludes on the name of Cain with a great high C from his chest (48.1). Hosty's chest C (*ut de poitrine*) is echoed by full-throated tenorial high C's from the crowd and from the many Irish tenors in it. The great volume of expelled air releases poison gas (48.5). Other Dubliners pick up the scurrilous song—merry but disreputable songsters and whistlers named as O'Hara, Paul Horan, Sordid Sam, Langley, Father San Browne–Padre Don Bruno, Phishlin Phil.

Our hero, frightened by the outcry, begins to flee. His flight is described as a *regifugium persecutorum* (51.31). The phrase is based upon *refugium peccatorum*, refuge of sinners (M). However, in the word *regifugium* Joyce encapsulates, along with the brothers' quarrel and the ultimate reconciliation of Shem and Shaun, the guilty king who is also a city founder (as in the Haveth Childers Everywhere city poem).

The *regifugium* is an extremely ancient ceremony from the early days of Rome. In this ceremony the Year-King, Frazer's Eniautos-Daemon, ends his year of magical and political power as the consort of the goddess of fertility. Technically, he is supposed to be sacrificed in some painful manner, usually by emasculation, to expiate the undetected crimes of his people—a Christ-type scapegoat. However, early Year-Kings seem to have decided that they would rather not lose their magical power and be sacrificed in some painful manner. Therefore, the devoted sacrifice would enter into a "royal flight" (*regifugium*), in which he gave himself a name signifying "nobody at all," and from which he emerged as the new king after the New Year's ceremony. In some traditions, the reborn king would undergo a couvade, emerging from between the legs of a woman and making sounds like a newborn baby.

The biblical Cain and Abel story may have provided an extremely early example of this religious complex, since *havel*—Abel in Hebrew—means "insignificant, a mere breath." Cain may have been an early example of a Year-King preserving his life and his power by giving himself a name that means essentially "pay no attention to the man behind the screen." Or perhaps, as befits Roman tradition, the fleeing king may have given himself the name Romulus, meaning "small Remus"—that is, the insignificant shadow of the real king. Note that in both cases, Cain and Romulus, the refuging king founded a city on the blood of his brother: Cain after the slaying of Abel founded the city of Enoch (Uruk), and Romulus founded Rome after his men slew Remus for his jealous mocking of them as they were building a wall.

Here this most ancient of ceremonies is acted out in Dublin. The town populace, their eyes opened by Hosty's ballad, play their part in Joyce's *regifugium* by joining in the chase (52.18–19). The spectacle of the fleeing king, in his characteristic seven pieces of clothing (52.23–31), reminds the narrator of ancient days in Dublin (53.1–6). In response to this evocation of olden days, a voice exclaims that the passage was "prigged" (53.6). The passage is indeed stolen, but from Joyce himself: it is based upon Stephen's revelation of the past of Dublin during his ordination ceremony as a artist in *A Portrait*:

> A veiled sunlight lit up faintly the grey sheet of water where the river was embayed. In the distance along the course of the slowflowing Liffey slender masts flecked the sky and, more distant still, the dim fabric of the city lay prone in haze. Like a scene on some vague arras, old as man's weariness, the image of the seventh city of christendom was visible to him across the timeless air, no older nor more weary nor less patient of subjection than in the days of the thingmote. (148)

It is no coincidence that in our backward tour through the scenery of the *Wake* we are within the city of Dublin, where the scurrilous crowds are joining in the hue and cry after their guilty king.

It is, however, Dublin generalized into the world-city. We hear the cries of the citizens in several different languages as they all hunt for peace and each other in their parliaments—four are mentioned: ulema, sobranje, storthing, duma—and ultimately in the parliament of the world, the futile League of Nations that Joyce names Casaconcordia (54.8–10). Joyce here implicitly answers those of his future critics who insist that *Finnegans Wake* is not written in English. He is saying, "If you really want to hear a cosmopolitan mishmash, here it is."

The passage may have been inspired by *Gargantua and Pantagruel*,[12] in which Panurge introduces himself to Pantagruel by begging for sustenance and money in German, Italian, medieval Northern or Scottish English, Basque, Dutch, Spanish, archaic Danish, Hebrew, Greek, Latin, and French, as well as two invented languages, Lanternese and Utopian. Joyce here seems to be trying to match or overmatch Rabelais.

It is not certain from whom Joyce got the phrases. He may have consulted several foreign-language speakers in Paris, which is how Rabelais may have acquired most of his thirteen linguistic examples. Joyce outdoes Rabelais by four languages—Joyce's international gallimaufry includes passages in seventeen languages or dialects, some hideously debased.[13] The general trend of most of the passages seems to relate to several young ladies and gentlemen seeking refreshments and the way to the toilets (and some extracurricular groin fun) in the League of Nations building. Apparently, the first entries in any practical guidebook should translate the phrases asking the way to the tearooms and the conveniences, as well as useful exchanges with pimps and hookers.[14] Let us examine five passages.

Despenseme Usted, senhor, en son succo, sabez. This phrase is a Romance language puzzle. The elements seem to be mostly dialectal Spanish—*Dispénseme*, "excuse me," with an unnecessary *Usted*; *en son de*, "in the guise of"; *sabes*, "you know"—with "senhor" in a Portuguese form. The whole phrase seems to be a polite but demotic and polyglot request for *succo*, which may be sugar. Apparently the tourists are in the tearoom.

Lick-Pa-flai-hai-pa-Pa-li-si-lang-lang. A real puzzle, the most enigmatic of the whole discourse. Despite the Sinaitic appearance, it is not any version of a Chinese language. My best guess, given the repetition *lang-lang*, is that it is a variety of pidgin, possibly based on Hawaiian or some other syllabic Polynesian language. I can make nothing of *Lick-Pa-*; *lick* transliterates no Sinaitic syllable. The next segment, *flai-hai-*, might be pidgin for "fly high," that is, take a plane. *Pa-li-si-*, mainly because of the capitalization of the *P*, might be pidgin for Paris; *lang-lang* could be an extended form of "long," which would make the phrase mean "far, far away." The whole phrase might mean something like "We took a long, long flight to (or from) Paris," a phrase from tea-table conversation at the Casaconcordia.

Epi alo, ecou, Batiste, tuvavnr dans Lptit boing going. A terribly debased form of demotic French, possibly from an imperfectly Francophone African or Canadian speaker, or a speaker of a southern French dialect. The phrase's meaning, however, is clear: *Et puis, alors, écoute, Baptiste, tu vas venir dans le petit bon coin.* "Well, then, listen, Baptiste, you are going to go to the toilet." (*Le petit coin* is French argot for "toilet."[15])

O.O. The symbol for a toilet, oo, used in Germanic and southeastern Europe, where Joyce lived for many years.

Os pipos mios es demasiada gruarso por O piccolo pocchino. Again a mixture of demotic Spanish, Portuguese, and Italian, combining to make a truly outrageous phrase about fellatio: "My prick is much too big for your little mouth." *Os pipos mios* is "my bird" in some Mediterranean languages, but the identification of the bird with the penis is a feature of Mediterranean culture from ancient times, probably going back at least as far as Aristophanes. *Demasiado grueso* is "much too thick" in Spanish; *por o* is Portuguese "for the"; *piccolo pocchino* is Italian for, literally, "little pocket," but a similar word, *bocchino*, also means, besides a cigarette holder, an act of fellatio. Has one of the tourists encountered a willing accomplice in one of the toilets of the League of Nations?

The great scandal expands. The uproar in the Casaconcordia spreads the news about our hero over the world. The fall of the great man continues to reverberate. The house of Atreus has fallen in the dust, Ilium has fallen, the hero has turned to stone like the legendary Russian warrior Ilya Morometz, but, in the words of the American spiritual, these bones will rise again (55.3–5). Our father, the ancestor of us all, is a corpse, but also, like crops, will rise again (55.7–8). The tale of the fall is indeed a sad one—it would draw tears from eyes of stone (55.20–22). Our hero, comatose, or paralyzed in the *Dubliners* manner, is traveling through the night borne along in a female Pullman sleeping car (55.19)—HCE is carried along by ALP on the river of time throughout the night.

The specific nature of his crimes is only vaguely perceived; after all, Man, suffering under the burden of Original Sin, is capable of all crimes (57.16–19). The three-two symbolic theme is here introduced. As we have seen since the Willingdone Museyroom, three is the number of mature male genitals, while two signifies the female genitalia. Three-and-two symbolizes the sexuality of the matured children, so HCE's judges and executioners are his children, as we shall see in II.3.

After a delightful picture of our hero as the Reverend Mr. Dodgson, Lewis Carroll, meditating upon a pedophilic vision of Alice (57.23–29), we embark again upon the sea of rumor and gossip in Dublin. The malicious Dublin mouths have torn him limb from limb (58.6–7). Three soldiers walking in Montgomery Street, the red-light district of Dublin, to the tune of an old song, "We Be Soldiers Three," declare that the first woman, Lily of the Cunning Hams, seduced him (58.28–30). Lily is Lilith, the woman devised by biblical scholars to explain the puzzling account of the creation of male and female in Genesis 1, followed by the independent creation of Eve in Genesis 2. The female these scholars created was named Lilith after a Babylonian demon (mentioned later on in the book of Isaiah) whose name meant "storms" in Akkadian. In the event, she was too assertive to be a "help meet" for Adam: she even wished to assume the superior sexual position! She was driven out into the wilderness and was succeeded by Eve, a much more pliable partner.

The next witness is an actress (59.4): "sweet Fanny Adams" is an English euphemism for "fuck-all" (nothing). She was once referred to as a vestpocket version of the great Sarah Siddons. Mrs. F . . . A . . ., "resting" between engagements, has been interviewed in a West End beauty parlor, telling her confidante—Issy in her double identity—that she hoped HCE would get a bouquet of oranges and lemons; the nursery rhyme "Oranges and Lemons" ends with the ominous verse "Here comes a candle to light you to bed, / Here comes a chopper to chop off your head!" The actress added in a genteel accent that the world had been unkind to him, but also that the world would be well rid of Cain (59.9–10).

"Prehistoric," obviously a classical scholar, remarks that the accenting of the scandalous fellow's name forms a properismenon (59.15–16). A garbageman and a busdriver both give their opinions. Then a chef is interviewed. "Eiskaffier" (compared to the great Brillat-Savarin, but a mere shadow of Escoffier: he can only make iced coffee) is of the opinion, given amid typically Gallic-Germanic complaints about his liver (*mon foie* and *mein leber*), is that you cannot make an omelet without breaking eggs—Napoleon's justification for ruthless cruelty in pursuit of great ends (59.29–32). An overage jogger gives his panting opinion that he knows how hard it is to collect information, but it is not cricket to climb walls and ring doorbells in pursuit thereof (59.33–35)—a comment on journalistic ethics that is still relevant.

There are further comments by such representative citizens as a barmaid, a Board of Trade official, two underwear models (Danish *benklæder* (M)), a cub courser (a trainer of foxhounds), a Buddhist would-be martyr, a seventeen-year-old revivalist who regards HCE as a brute, but a magnificent brute (60.25–26), a bookmaker, Captain Boycott, a "precentor" (a leader of choral singing (M), or a seer, from Latin *praecino*, "to predict"), the chocolate-box aristocrats Lord Doran ("Snuffbox") and Lady Morgan ("Flutterfan"), johns and prostitutes (60.35–36).

Sylvia Silence, the girl detective, contributes her well-considered opinion, with an unfortunate speech defect, an inability to pronounce the letter *r*, a characteristic shared by Lady Gregory and Rebecca West. Sylvia's opinion is that sheer greatness was his tragedy. Nevertheless, he should pay the full penalty of the Criminal Law Amendment act of 1885—the law under which Oscar Wilde was jailed. This allusion to the great Oscar Wilde scandal brings up another scandal, hardly less well known, the Charles Dilke case of 1885. Dilke, one of the most powerful politicians in England, was charged with adultery with a mother and her daughter and had to retire from Parliament, though he returned in 1892; he was too valuable to lose. The mocking song written by the Great MacDermott about Dilke—"Master Dilke Upset the Milk Taking It Home to Chelsea"—surfaces in the text (M). The commentators conclude with a sailor sitting with two girls, who make salacious comments about our hero, and finally "three drummers"—an end that refers back to the beginning at 58.23–32.

After some more desultory comment and observation, another scandal is uncovered—the great Daddy and Peaches Browning scandal of the twenties in New York. Daddy Browning, a retired taxi-company millionaire, took up with a pudgy sixteen-year-old whom he nicknamed Peaches. The scandal sheet the *New York Graphic* (the *PornoGraphic*, some called it) picked up the juicy morsel and ran with it. Here it is made the analogue of the King Mark–Isolde story and turned into a Hollywood musical from the "reel" world (64.22–65.33), ending with the film flapping (65.34), an anticipation of the sound film starting at the end of I.7.

HCE seeks refuge in a coffin, or, in paralytic-Dublin terms, a state of suspended animation. Yet even this expedient does not shield him from acrimony and obloquy. A German newspaper reporter, Herr Betreffender ("business register"; also, *herbetreffender*, "the aforementioned" (M)), tracks him to his coffin-house and threatens him with bodily harm if he does not confess his sins to the world (69.30–73.28). Herr Betreffender then shouts at him 111 opprobrious epithets (M) and follows up the tirade with a shower of stones.

Joyce may have found an original for this episode in an old newspaper, the *Dublin Evening Mail* of February 2, 1880), recounting an incident in Robertstown, west Kildare.

Outrage in Co. Kildare

Daniel Dominican came late at night to Farmer M'Con's house and threw at least 18 stones through the window. Mrs Mc'Con and the child had to leave the bedroom. Dominican kept shouting, "You won't go into the carriage to Mr Ireland and give £3 an acre for land. Are you killed now? The devil kill you!"

Since there are 111 insults, vicious if contradictory, hurled at HCE on 71.10–72.16, and since there are 111 children from the union of HCE and ALP, it seems clear that the Teutonic shouter is the spokesman for every one of Anna Livia's children—and that the children are administering the lapidation, an anticipation of the attack on HCE in the lynching section in II.3.

A large number of the insults directed at the comatose figure of HCE contain comments on his business unscrupulousness, his doubtful piety, and his political unreliability. "Goldy Geit" refers to the notorious South African gold and diamond millionaire Sir Alfred Beit, who was often criticized for his business methods, and who was one of the Jewish businessmen accused by anti-Semites of fomenting the South African war. The name carries a suggestion of the Scapegoat as well. There is also a suggestion that HCE adulterates butter with grease. He asks boastfully if anyone can beat his prices, which combines a cut-rate businessman's slogan with Parnell's reputed challenge to his rebellious followers—"If you sell me [to the English], get my price [Home Rule]." HCE is Godsoilman, an amalgam of God+soil+man, the process of the creation of Adam, with a slanting blow at "God's oilman," the sanctimonious John D. Rockefeller, a pious Baptist who made much display of his religion while forcing all of his fellow oilmen out of business. One of the funniest charges claims that HCE will send a left boot on approval, which is very likely a real advertisement for shoes sold through the mail—if the left boot fits, send the price of the pair and we will send you the right boot! It may also refer to the devil's hoof—if the left boot fits the hoof, the right boot will fit as well.

HCE is a bombastic Lombard Street victor, a successful stockbroker in the City of London, which is incidentally where T. S. Eliot worked as a bank clerk. Another phrase charges that HCE has stolen a railway car, a "rattler," and sold it—there is an echo here of a 1925 hit song by the French surrealist comic Georgius, "La Plus Bath des Javas," in which someone steals a subway train and is caught. HCE is the Ruin of the SmallTrader, a phrase that speaks for itself. The reference to HCE as a big businessman is followed up by one in German to HCE as a swindler, a *Kuhhandler* (M). And if HCE is indeed the worst that Woolworth's can sell, he must be cheap indeed—Woolworth, a major ruin of the small trader, invented the slogan that appears elsewhere in the *Wake*, SPQR—Small Profits, Quick Returns.

Many other opprobrious expressions question HCE's political correctness and the sincerity of his religious beliefs, as Joyce's own political and religious beliefs were often questioned. HCE is called an informer, which is a truly serious charge in Joyce's Ireland, and ours. However, the word may also have a philosophical meaning—that which informs, or determines the inner and outer form of an entity. Another epithet with a political overtone refers to HCE as a Bogside beauty—the Bogside is the Catholic area of Derry, the site of many events in the three hundred years of the Northern Ireland war. Another phrase echoes Cromwell's "Remove that bauble!" addressed to Parliament about the Mace—HCE is linked to Cromwell and to contempt for parliamentary representation as well as to Protestant religion. Several phrases are religious in nature but contradictory: HCE is declared unworthy to be a Protestant, and is threatened with drowning by a secret society, the Ribbonmen, but he is also called a Swaddler, a Protestant. He has been expelled from *Burke's Peerage* as unworthy of inclusion in that catalogue of nobility. He is called a bare barbarian, but confusingly he also is associated with the Grand Old Man, Gladstone, whom the Irish have always suspected of being a false friend.

HCE is referred to, in a Cockney accent, as a stodgy stage Irishman with a big arse, and then as the Iron Duke, Wellington, with a remembrance of Wellington's reluctance to consider himself an Irishman. Here is the worst insult of all—he is not even to be called an Irishman.

There are many other interesting insults directed at HCE, a number of them in his capacity as Adam. He is called a firstnighter—not one who attends the first night of plays but Adam during his first night of exile, enjoying the fallen pleasures of sex. He is a Yorkist pig, the limping burdened Richard III, with reference to his sign of a silver boar. He is called Old Fruit, but the apparently genial epithet refers to the fatal apple. The puzzling Wheatears refers to a bird, the wheatear, whose odd name probably derives from the Anglo-Saxon *hwiters*, white-arse, for its tail feathers—a jibe at HCE's big wide arse.

The Earl of Howth's open-door policy comes up in its turn, as do Cain and Abel. The lameness of the tyrant Timur-i-Leng connects HCE to perhaps the greatest killer among history's tyrants. However, HCE is also Tight before Teatime—a classic sign of alcoholism. And he is a disgraceful version of the great English cricketer W. G. Grace—cricket has a sexual significance in *FW*. HCE comes up as Barnum and Bailey—the charlatan circus impresarios combined with the Bailey lightship burning at the mouth of Dublin Bay. He is then called an artist, which is certainly a dreadful insult in philistine Dublin, but "artist" is also a drunk in Dublin dialect. The name Terry Cotter contains an obvious reference to earthborn Adam, terra cotta, but Terry Cotter is also the name of a real newsreel cameraman. HCE is referred to as two attackers of the Pope, Dante and Luther, and apparently is able to hatch the eggs of roosters: HCE can create basilisks, the evil creatures whose gaze turns viewers to stone. The phrase applied to HCE as a Peculiar Person contains a sting—God's own "peculiar" people were the Jews, but Peculiar People was also the name of a small Protestant sect. Further along, he is also a Muslim, a representative of the Sublime Porte in Turkey, combined with a drinker of porter.

HCE is an unreliable newspaper magnate, Beaverbrook, combined with the land of milk and honey falsely promised by contemporary newspapers. He is an Edomite, a member of a southern Semitic people whose name derived from the Hebrew *edom*, red soil, which also is sometimes held to be a reference to Adam, who is here equated with dirt. The Miching Daddy, the devil or the father of mischief, from the Elizabethan "miching," mischief, is another guise for our elusive hero. Finally he is an Asiatic philosopher, with phallic overtones. This harks back to the cries reported by Joyce in *A Portrait* at the first performance of Yeats's *Countess Cathleen*—"We want no budding buddhists!" (196)—and also to Andrew Marvell's description of himself as "easie Philosopher" in "Upon Appleton House." Finally, after the flinging of the 111 stones and epithets, the attacker departs, leaving HCE still in a comatose state, the representative of Joyce's paralyzed Dublin.

The last paragraph of I.3 conveys, with great poetic power, sleeping Dublin under a light rain, and HCE in suspended animation. The end of this paragraph is exquisite, with periods serving to break up the rhythm of the raindrops, and the motion of the sleeping car as it begins to slow down and stop (74.13–19). Words weigh no more to HCE than the raindrops on the ferns of Rathfarnam. Is his liver poor? Not a bit of it; he is still alive, though in suspended animation. His brains may be cool porridge, his pelt wet (German *nass*), his heart droning on, his bloodstream crawling, his breath only a puff through his nose (*pif*, "nose" in French slang), his extremities cold—all symptoms of suspended animation. His outer suburbs express his physical state—Finglas (he is toothless, or fangless), Pembroke (he has pawned all he had), Kilmainham (he has chilblains), Baldoyle (he is bald as an owl). However, his Pullman sleeping train (see 55.19–20) will stop one day. The river will return to the sea, and the comatose Irish will awake, as they did in 1916.

Book I, Chapter 4: Segue to ALP

The beginning of I.4 asserts that, as the lion in the zoo may remember the waterlilies of the Nile, so the comatose HCE may have been dreaming of the temptresses of his past (75.5–6). He may indeed have dreamed incestuous dreams of his daughter as a temptress, tempting both himself and her brothers (75.10–11).

There follows a dense patchwork of passages describing HCE's posthumous reputation. More legal mud is thrown at HCE during the trial of a methylated drunk, Festy King (Shem the Penman under a pseudonym), and the hilarious hoot of a witness named Pegger and the comment of a West Pointer, or a Wet Pinter, both obviously Dublin drunks and both further darkening the name of our hero (84.28–93.21). Festy King then leaves the stand. His disguised brother Shaun politely enquires in Latin, "Quomodo vales hodie, atrate generose?" (93.6–7)—How do you do today, my dark sir?—one of the addresses by one brother to another during the *Wake*. The drunken Shem responds with an enormous fart (93.7–9). Shem is the bottom half of the body, and this flatulent comment is entirely appropriate to his character. The twenty-eight lady lawyers in the court, the chorus of Shem's sisters as little girls, recoil in disgust at "Shame's" action, and shout "Shame" at him in versions of seven languages, while criticizing him loudly for telling dirty stories about his father (93.19–21).

The narrator comments on how the life of HCE is defined by Artha kama dharma moksa, the four elements of Hindu description of a life, and then asks the spirit of poetry (Sanskrit *Kavya*) for the key to the life of HCE (93.22–23). The phrase also means "Ask Kate the Slop for the key to the history of HCE"; she has guided tourists through the battlefield of the Willingdone Museyroom, and she operates as the spirit of history as handed down by the people, while the Four Old Men represent academic history.

The Four Old Men contribute their characteristically misleading bits to the tale of HCE (94.23–97.28). For them, the journeyings of HCE in his coffin constitute an attempt to evade the foxhunt that is constantly on his trail. They conclude that the evasive and foxy HCE has definitely slowed down (97.28). They continue to speculate on the scandals of his life and the possibility that he may have committed suicide (97.29–100.36).

The tale of HCE has been temporarily exhausted. Here Joyce has placed a great transition: HCE's long-suffering wife, ALP, is introduced, with the exhortation "Do tell us all about her!" (101.2).

Was ALP fast? the women wonder (101.1). ALP is the spirit of swiftness and change, and she may indeed have been "fast," both freely moving and immoral. The tempo of the chapter picks up after the mournful commentary on the static HCE. When the tide turns, time will run the correct way, and speedy change will characterize the prose from now on. The chorus's clamors for information (101.2–4) provide a pre-echo of the beginning of I.8. The chorus wants to know everything about HCE and ALP and his possible murder by Buckley, who shot him in the story of the Russian general.

ALP is described as the toiling, suffering wife of Adam, and her husband's household slave—taking him to her bosom when he was first born, supporting him in his labor, defending him, trying to forget his guilt, mothering all his murmuring babies, giving birth to his 111 children at the cost of her own health. She has paid a heavy price for her motherhood. Her teeth are false—the popular saying "A tooth for a child" (101.34) points to the calcium drain on poor women during pregnancy—and her hair has fallen out, another symptom of calcium drain. She has given him children, and picked him up after his fall, and given him his wake. She will be running with him until she ends up in the ocean—an anticipation of the very end of the book (101.31–102.7). Her jazzy path through the Irish countryside, her spectacular clothes and her forty bonnets, are described in swift-flowing prose. At the end of the description, she calls on her sleeping husband to crush the serpent's slandering head (102.8–17)—the theme of her letter to the world, finally revealed in Book IV.

The narrator begs us to plead for the great Mother of us all, Morandmor (containing the Danish for "grandmother" and also the indication that she reveals more and more to us), and to her as Notre Dame de la Ville (102.18–19). We are told not to tamper with HCE's mound; the curse of Tutankhamen is on it! ALP is described as having her heirs/hairs clinging to her and hanging down her back, in the rhythm of "Her Golden Hair Was Hanging Down Her Back," a song about the loss of innocence (102.22–24).

HCE's homelife is scandalous: ALP, we soon learn, presents him with pretty little Rainbow Girls from the street, with whom he spends his strength. Life, in the person of ALP, presents human beings with the life of the multicolored world, which is defended in Book IV by St. Patrick, as the sun rises and restores color to the earth (102.25–28).

The pathetic daily life of the Earwickers is succinctly sketched: quarreling today, kissing tonight, and agelong pain forever. Yet who would speak up for her overburdened husband but his wife, her body destroyed with bearing his children (102.28–30)?

This chapter introducing ALP ends in Joyce's version of an old music-hall song, "At Trinity Church I Met My Doom," which describes the suffering of a man who was enticed into marriage, thinking his wife had some money, but found himself up to his ears in debt and surrounded by crying children. ALP has sold HCE her 999–year lease, and seduced him with her body and her lovely hair. He has swallowed the bait. Here the turn of the tide at Island Bridge and the rush forward into real, narrative time is anticipated. Adam has been seduced by Eve: Fallen Man is up to his ears in time and the "hues and cries" (and crybabies in cribs) of the visible-audible world, the world that James Joyce chose as his lifelong task for artistic presentation (102.32–103.7).

The chapter closes with a lovely transition that anticipates the Washers at the Ford, and the invocation of stones and trees in I.8, to the rhythm of the biblical Psalm of the Exiles, Psalm 137, "By the rivers of Babylon" (103.9–12).

Book I, Chapter 5: ALP Described

The chapter opens with a delightful invocation to Anna Livia, which incorporates invocations to the Lord from two great religions—the Bismillah from Islam and the Lord's Prayer from Christianity (M), both addressed to the great river goddess and mother of us all (104.1–3).

Anna Livia's letter to the world about her guilty husband, to be expounded in full as daylight fills the sky in Book IV, is in reality the text of *Finnegans Wake* itself, the river of prose flowing between her two sons, the right and left margins of the book, the river of text which is given words and written down by Shem the Penman, and is delivered to the reader by her other son, Shaun the Post, as the copy of a book, a physical object made of paper, ink, and glue.

This letter to the world is here described as a feminine manifesto (104.4) praising her lord-husband. ALP's letter has been given many names in the past. The text provides 312 names for it. Most are transparent, and refer to the love and marriage of the great flawed hero and his long-enduring wife.

A few names should have additional comment. There is a reference at 104.8, which contains the Greek word *anastasis* and the Italian word *stessa*, to the constant resurrection of Anna. "For Ark see Zoo" (104.19–20) is a superb four-word poem of much resonance. It is not merely an encyclopedic cross-reference; it encapsulates an entire cultural history. The difference between an ark and a zoo is that, in an ark, the animals are enclosed for their ultimate salvation; in a zoo, they are imprisoned only for the amusement of others. For this phrase, the title of Yeats's poem "The Circus Animals' Desertion" provides a clue: in the Yeats poem, the circus animals represent the controlled and trained emotions of the symbolist poet, who tries to rise above his merely natural passions to a symbolic system. However, the poet in Yeats's poem can no longer rise above "That raving slut / Who keeps the till"—his natural passions—"In the foul rag-and-bone shop of the heart." In

Joyce's four-word poem the natural passions preserved in the Ark are stifled in the zoo of the modern world into the hollow tricks of the modern heart.

At 105.11–12 Joyce evokes the interior monologue of a giant, a terrifying creature, expressing HCE's love (German *Minne*) for ALP.

"He Can Explain" (105.14) is another economical poem. The theme is Eve in the Garden of Eden pointing to Adam, indicated by HCE's initials, to explain Original Sin.

Also at 105.14, Joyce creates a geographical conceit: the two great lovers ALP and HCE are portrayed as lying side by side like the two great lakes in Africa, Victoria Nyanza and Albert Nyanza.

The sorrows of human life appear at 105.16–17 with *usque ad mortem* (M). The complete phrase, from Matthew 26:38, is "Tristis est anima mea usque ad mortem; sustinete hic et vigilate mecum," Christ's words in the Garden of Gethsemane to his disciples. This sentence is introduced again in III.3 as *Tris tris a ni ma mea!* (499.30), a broken agonized cry from within Yawn, as the Four Old Men drill into a burning lava field of Irish historical anguish. However, the form of the phrase here suggests that only the husk is mortal; the soul is immortal, in Joyce's cyclical immortality.

Two music hall and operetta songs appear at 105.18–20—"My Old Dutch," by Albert Chevalier, and "The Jewel of Asia," from *The Geisha* by Sydney Jones—and a line from Pater's *The Renaissance* (M). All three of these phrases express ALP's immemorial age. "My Old Dutch" (in Cockney rhyming slang, "Dutch plate" = "mate") is a touching song by a man who has been married to his dear Sarah for forty years, "And it don't seem a day too much. / Oh there ain't a lady living in this world / As I'd swap fer me dear old dutch." While the original singer is male, here Anna Livia declares her love for her man. Pater's well-known words about Mona Lisa, "She is older than the rocks on which she sits," express Anna's feeling about her great age, combined with the rocks over which she flows, and the great rock that is her husband. "The Jewel of Asia," or Ayessha, is She-Who-Must-Be-Obeyed, the ageless goddess in Rider Haggard's *She*.

Joyce's own fury over the pirating of his work in the United States is expressed at 105.35–36; it was indeed a cowboy ride on several bucking broncos for the poor author!

At 106.13–14 appears another of Joyce's powerful minipoems: not only does the *Wake* itself feature a "suspended sentence" between the end and the beginning, but the sentence on the guilty HCE was suspended indefinitely. And a catchy advertising jingle for the washerwomen in the next chapter appears at 106.36–107.1, anticipating the Anna Livia chapter, I.8.

The last phrase in this descriptive catalogue is an impetuous summing up of her defense of her husband against his enemies (107.1–7). This rushing expression of Anna Livia's fury against the attackers of her husband appears in extended form as the letter at the end of Book IV, which tells the whole story in detail.

The rest of the chapter, 107.8–125.23, presents methods—somewhat misleading methods—of reading the *Wake*. Joyce here proceeds to predict, in astonishing detail, the modern, postmodern, and genetic criticism of the *Wake*.

The text of the letter, described as a graph, was dug out by a little hen from a trash heap, recalling Stephen Dedalus's description, in the Proteus chapter of *Ulysses*, of the sands at Sandymount: "These heavy sands are language tide and wind have silted here" (3.288–89). There are various suggestions from naive psychoanalytic critics (107.9), such as "a very sexmosaic of nymphosis" (107.13–14), whatever that string of psychobabble may mean. The analyst then declares his confusion (107.20–22).[16] However, as confused as the case is, the letter seems to be ultimately about family matters and the effect of family organization on general society. Family relationships determine how human society trundles along through good and evil from generation to generation (107.32–35).

Then we ask, who wrote the damn thing anyhow (107.36–108.1)? Rather than giving an answer, the narrator sententiously recommends patience (108.8–10). Several historical examples of patience are given. Perhaps the letter was the product of a radio broadcaster (108.22). Joyce then defends his own practice of substituting dashes in the French style for quotation marks; simply the absence of inverted commas does not mean that the author was incapable of stealing the words of others (108.29–36).

The narrator suggests another approach, one used often in modern genetic criticism of the *Wake*: Do not examine the text—examine the origins of the text and of its paralogisms (109.1–36). The hen-discoverer of the text is described, along with some idea of the text itself. Apparently the letter was a communication from Boston (Mass.) to Dear Maggy (111.10–11), conveying wedding and funeral news among the acquaintances of the writer, and ending with fondest regards to the twins and, in place of a signature, a large spot of tea. The letter is more important than it seems: as a missive from Boston (Mass.), it comes from "the Boss's town," Heaven, as represented by the Mass. It is, in fact, a communication from above. It is also the *Wake* itself, which begins with "Reverend" and ends with "the." That is, "riverrun" (3.1) is the first word of the book, and the last is "the" (628.16), which is close enough to various words signifying "tea." The fullest version of the letter, in Book IV, is in fact addressed to "Dear Reverend Majesty" (615.12–13).[17]

Then why, asks the narrator, is the surface of the letter so confused?—a cry echoed by many readers of the *Wake*. The answer is, the letter has been affected by being buried in the mound. If a negative of a horse melts while drying, the outline of the horse becomes a dreadfully messy combination of fragments of the portrait of a horse (111.28–30).

Warming up, Joyce directly addresses the confused reader. You feel lost in the woods? You say the *Wake* is a pure and simple jangle of words. You shout, "Call me a son of a bitch if I have the paltriest notion what the book means!" Ezra Pound may have said something like this to Joyce; Pound was certainly unsympathetic to Joyce's experiments in the *Wake*, and the American voice in the passage sounds like Uncle Ez in an irritated mood. However, Pound and all annoyed readers are reassured that, while scholars may possess the text that explains all things, any wandering scholar can pick out a good deal of meaning from the sack of the hen (112.6–8). There then follows a long and learned analysis of the letter, but it is all centered on the appearance of the letters, the paper, and other peripheral details. There is very little if anything on what the letter says—again, very like some postmodern and genetic criticism.

What there is of detail on the matter of the text is presented in 113.11–22: all that the letter writer wants is to tell the God's truth about him—mainly about how he had to see life fully (or foully), and how there were three men in him (probably the two sons and their consolidation, the Shimar Shin of the Willingdone Museyroom). Dancing with pretty girls was his only foible, but *honi soit qui mal y pense*, or, in her terms, these honeys wore flowered panties (113.16–17). Her tolerant attitude toward her husband's foibles is perhaps understandable: as we learn in the Anna Livia chapter, she herself introduced the girls to her husband, mainly to rouse him from his torpor.

After we are told that the text is, after all, a portrait of the artist (114.32), we are introduced to a long and brilliant Freudian analysis of incest, which is always on HCE's guilty mind: we dreadful old psychos, or psychoanalysts, have grimly performed the visions of our evil hearts on young Alices, when they were not yet able to resist (115.21–23). The concept of "father" is examined, by these overheated old pederasts, to the feverish interest of readers and other sneaks (115.24–28): our fathers provide food for us but also kill us ("settles our hash"). After all, young girls may prefer sex with a relative on the father's side as opposed to a maternal-line relative. Joyce is here presenting HCE's hopeful view that his daughter would rather have sex with him than with her brothers.

At 120.13–14 Joyce introduces the "ideal reader suffering from an ideal insomnia"—possibly his formula for a reader of the *Wake*.[18] We are then treated to a long and learned analysis of the letter, based in style and content upon Sir Edward Sullivan's edition of *The Book of Kells* (Atherton 1960, 62–67). Joyce admired the complexity of this medieval masterpiece, and claimed that the style of the *Wake* owed a great deal to it, especially its greatly decorated *Tunc* page (122.22). Joyce's description of the hen's letter draws upon Sullivan's analysis of the style of this page; Joyce's parody is filled with bibliographical and iconographical detail, complete with description of its typographic symbols, the secret numbers 432 and 1132 (119.26), and a cryptological analysis of the secret alphabets of the text (119.10–123.10).

In the course of this learned and irrelevant discussion the Four Old Men, representative of pedantry at its worst, are introduced on 122.11–19. The Four Old Men are also the four Gospel writers, who appear several times in *The Book of Kells*. Here, however, they are a rowdier bunch, embracers of the *Rubáiyát*'s emphasis on wine (122.11)—and sure enough, they are introduced in a *Rubáiyát* stanza (122.11–13). These debased gospellers are playing a card game, possibly whist in its original version. The game has a symbolic meaning: the lead, the six of hearts (probably), is covered by the red queen of hearts, which in turn is covered by the king of hearts. However, the opposition gains the trick when the heart king is trumped by a spade. The message may be that, from the oldsters' point of view, love is trumped by death (122.13–19).

However, this card game introduces the most pedantic and dense account of the text. Having evoked a textual critic's exhaustive and pompous treatment of the *Tunc* page of *The Book of Kells* as a model of the text (122.20–123.10), Joyce lets the equally pompous psychoanalysts have their say. Joyce was vastly amused by the conflict between Jungians and Freudians, and by orthodox psychoanalytic criticism in general. He obviously preferred his own psychology to other brands. At least, a Joycean psychoanalytical critic is capable of a comic attitude toward his work. Joyce has already mocked both Jung and Freud, the leading practioners of fashionable methods of examining Lewis Carroll and his works (115.21–23). The unsmiling analysis of psychoanalytic critics is now developed, as Jung and Freud are amalgamated into Tung-Toyd

(123.20), a tongue-tied scholar who has written at great length that the *Odyssey* has been revised from a Phoenician periplus, or travel account, according to the theories of Joyce's classical expert, Victor Bérard (123.15–17).

Then the actual accent marks of the manuscript are described as holes poked in the paper by the fork of a learned professor (123.30–124.34). Here commentators on Joyce (including the present writer) must feel uneasily that Joyce saw how lecturing and writing about his works would eventually be the bread and butter of critics and scholars. Earlier he described the stemma of his works as meals of the day (121.33–35). The narrator further remarks that the hungry scholars have mistaken a bell tolling for the dead for a bell announcing the appearance of the muffinman; that is, scholars have taken works of literature that cost writers their blood and their lives, and earned a living from them—a sobering thought for any academic Joycean.

In the last paragraph of the chapter, we are introduced to the source of the words of the letter. The Four Old Men suggest that the letter was written down by Ham, the erring son of Noah who saw his father's genitals when Noah was sleeping off a bout of drinking (125.1–2). The revelation of the father's weaknesses in the preceding and following chapters suggests that it may indeed be Ham who has written down the annals of his father. But no, Ham is Shaun the Post, who did not write the letter but only carried it. The writer is not Shaun the Postman, the chaste Joseph of Genesis and the episode of Potiphar's wife, or his New Testament counterpart, St. Joseph, the symbol of chastity, who refrained from sex with the Virgin Mary (125.14,[19] 17–18). Indeed, Shaun, as the top half of the male body, is perforce chaste, though far from emotionally pure.

No, the actual writer-down of Anna Livia's letter to the world about her husband is her son Shem the Penman, introduced by the phrase always associated with the address of Shaun, the fair son, to Shem, the dark son, "How do you do today, my dark sir?"—this time in Russian, "Kak vuy pozhivayetye, moy cherny gospodin?" However, the phrase also suggests Shaun's contempt for his smelly brother, who writes only to earn money to buy booze.

The growing prominence of the children begins in this chapter, I.5, and the following two chapters progress toward the tidal turn of the Liffey, impelled by the two sons, to the point when the narrative will move forward in time.

However, we do not proceed directly to I.7. The Nightly Quiz chapter, I.6, intervenes. Danis Rose asserts that I.5 was originally meant to lead directly to I.7, since I.5 ends with the elaborate introduction of Shem under his full designation, Shem the Penman, for the first and only time in the book. He declares that the Nightly Quiz chapter"does not add anything to the narrative. Nor does it sit very comfortably where it is positioned, interrupting the natural progression of I.5 (the identification of the scribe as Shem) into I.7 (a description of Shem)" (104). Rose does assert (102), first, that Joyce needed the quiz chapter to appear where it does, "to make sure that all of his characters (including Shaun) were properly represented in part I"; second, that the chapter was needed "to balance the episode in Part III where all of the protagonists are conjured up by Yawn"; and third, that Joyce wanted to "answer his critics" (Stanislaus, Pound, and Miss Weaver especially) who had complained to him about the obscurity of the book.

We proceed therefore to I.6, a nightly quiz in which all of the characters in the drama are presented in great detail, and in which Shem the Penman is introduced for a second time.

Book I, Chapter 6: The Nightly Quiz and the Transition to TIME Mode

The quiz chapter opens with a theatrical flourish as by the master of ceremonies of the quiz show: In the first full line we encounter a time-word, "tonigh[t]," a significant moment in the procession to actual narrative, since it is in this chapter that we encounter the beginning of the segue into TIME mode.

Then the two participants in the quiz, the questioner and the answerer, are identified. The twelve questions are set by Shem the Penman and answered—with one wrong answer, to the third question—by Shaun the Post. However, Shaun allows four of the answers to be given in the voice of the object of the question.

As we have seen, in the plan of the book, the basic symbolic natures of the brothers corresponds to the top half of the body (Shaun) and the bottom half (Shem). The bottom half, the portion with the unruly genitals, is always setting embarrassing questions to the pure intellectual top half. (The same distribution of questioner and answerer will appear again in III.1.)

First Question (126.10–139.13)

About the huge hero of the book, HCE, in the guise of Finn MacCool

This gigantic question—it has 397 parts[20]—is not randomly constructed. The question goes from tree to stone. The first clause refers to three of the largest trees on earth—the blue gum of Australia, the baobab of Africa, and the sequoia of America—as well as Jack's beanstalk, here interpreted as a bean*stale* ("talk" becoming a tale), while the last clause refers to bricks or stones (139.11–13). Thus the first question in the quiz takes us from Tree (the live tree, Shem as the principle of movement) to Stone (the static principle, Shaun). The two ultimately combine into TreeStone, Tristan, the lover, who is the third soldier as well, and the destroyer of the father, and also his successor, the creative principle of fertilization.

In the course of this huge question HCE is revealed as, among other things: city man; fugitive; department store owner, stingy boss; as Houdini, an escaper resurrected from the grave; financier; Goethe; Dublin; volcanoes, dormant and otherwise; city planner and city builder; mountain range; Ezra Pound; Viking invader; high king of Ireland; the statue of King William (mentioned in "The Dead"); many Hamiltons; Father Knickerbocker; wall builder (Bygmester Solness; Gilgamesh; Romulus) and unsteady wall sitter (Humpty Dumpty).

This section tells us a great deal about HCE, some of it so important that comment is warranted. I leave it to the reader to work on the meaning of all the elements of the 397-part question; here I will comment only on phrases not treated by M.

- 126.19: HCE had several, or seven, girls (probably Rainbow Girls) on his hearthrug. As we see in I.8, Anna Livia acts as a proxenete, or procurer, for her husband, enticing young girls to go to bed with him. As the goddess of life, Anna Livia presents human beings with the appearances of earthly life, illustrated with all the colors of the rainbow.
- 127.2–3: HCE is here a lobster (German *Hummer*; French *homard*). The crustacean quality of HCE may explain ALP's comment later that he was the only man who could eat the crusts of lobsters (624.35–36).
- 127.8–9: HCE discovered coal in his fields, and also moss roses. This puzzling phrase may conceal a Napoleon reference: Moss roses are a variety of rose with a mossy growth on the calyx and stem. There is a famous moss rose named Chapeau de Napoléon, introduced by Monsieur J.-P. Vibert of Chênevières-sur-Marne in 1826. The blossom's calyx is in three wings, like a cocked hat—as in the three-cornered hat of Napoleon (10.8). Vibert may have bred the rose originally for the empress Josephine at Malmaison (Christopher, 80–81).
- 127.11–12: Here we have a remarkable comment on social injustice by Joyce, who rarely comments directly on social issues: Harrods, Bark-

ers, Shoolbred, and Whiteley are all names of department stores in London. Joyce is suggesting that the proprietors of such stores, referred to previously as ruining small traders, are ruthless against the poor and against protesters and strikers—they out-Herod Herod, blustering against those "barking" against their policies, usually strikers and so-cialists. However, to the educated ("schoolbred") these great merchants act fairly, indeed obsequiously; in nineteenth- and early-twentieth-century slang, to behave "whitely" is to behave honorably—like a white man! William Whiteley was an egregious example of the unfair em-ployer. Strikes against Whiteley's were especially hard fought; White-ley himself sexually exploited female employees; he was frequently the target of death threats, and was shot by a bastard son.

- 128.6–7: A reference to Dublin, suggesting (puzzlingly) that the name resembles bugs, and (correctly) that the city has the shape of a cow-pat.
- 128.7–13: This passage anticipates the great Haveth Childers Every-where section of III.3, portraying HCE as a city builder. His cities are great creations with, however, some serious deficiencies. Specifically noted here: to our judgments (the original meaning of "doom," from Old English *deman*) he brought law, to our feudal manors he organized his workforce ("villains" in his "villa"); he built subways (called the Underground in London) and elevated railways grinding overhead; he built aqueducts to produce water for thirsty urban drinkers; the dust and filth in his cities encourage tuberculosis and whooping cough, and his air pollution from automobiles (carbon monoxide) resembles the results of farting; his women become prostitutes from poverty; the original inhabitants of the urbanized area are driven into the hills (become "the Ill people") by force (gunpowder); dwellers in HCE's cities always feel slightly sick (as Aldous Huxley said in *Antic Hay*, "people who live in modern cities are never quite well"), so HCE man-ufactures patent medicines (like Lydia Pinkham's) to make them feel better.
- 128.36–129.1: An important statement about HCE's relationship to his children. HCE with his "eatupus" complex is both the city of Dublin and the giant cannibal god Saturn, who swallowed his children. HCE as the city wants to reduce all of his children to parts of his own body, to avoid their overthrow of him—hence, he wants to "eat us up." He also finishes the drinks of his customers after his overthrow by his chil-dren in II.3.

- 129.7: Another of Joyce's elegant small poems: "blimp, blump." A "blimp" is a gasbag on high; a "blump" is the same gasbag, but fallen to the ground like Humpty Dumpty!
- 129.17–18: HCE's mountainous nature is reflected in references to the Andes and the Alleghanies. However, his dignity as a mountain is somewhat reduced by the overtone of Samuel Lover's comic hero of his 1842 novel *Handy Andy*. "Dumping your hump" refers to Bunyan's *The Pilgrim's Progress*, in which the hero, Christian, dumps his hump of Original Sin soon after he sets out on his journey to the Heavenly City.
- 130.19–20: A cynical portrait of HCE as a hero, probably Aeneas, hacking his way through his foes, who are here represented by the demonstrative pronouns of Latin. There is also a disturbing Greek epic reference here: in the *Odyssey* Telemachus, with the acquiescence of Odysseus, hanged the disloyal maids in the household from a cable tied to the rafters.[21]
- 130.27–31: More party games. In line 27, "twenty four" is the number of towns named Dublin in the United States (although actually there are only twelve American towns with that name). The near namesake in Poland is Lublin. And lines 30–31 are an old-fashioned riddle: the first syllable is "bud," the second syllable is "Nil" (the Nile in French), the whole word is "nul bid," the whole of it an anagram for Dublin.
- 130.34: Yet another riddling reference to Dublin: *u* and *i* in scrambled "bldn." Notice that we are overcharged for our rented rooms, which feature blind windows, here indicated by the absence of vowels.
- 131.33–35: A brilliant and affectionate portrait of Ezra Pound, who did have a most comical and confused head of hair on him, and who often displayed the bumptious, bouncy manner of a large-footed kangaroo. Pound at this time was translating Confucius's *Analects* and other ancient Chinese literature, hence the mentions of Confucius and of Tai Shan, the holy mountain in China on which the emperors sacrificed to the gods—a place-name combined wittily with Ireland, land of shanties.
- 132.8–9: A real puzzle! The surface meaning may be that we enter Dublin, or any city controlled by the giant, and are thereafter struck, or struggling, for life. After all, he does have "an eatupus complex" (128.36).

- 133.3–5: HCE as scapegoat with a shaggy neck, hanged, or crucified, for the sins of the people, and then as Christ in the Eucharist, shared out in wafers (isobaric—of equal mass) to the congregation.
- 133.23–24: HCE as judge. In one aspect he is a cruel judge with a big belly, threatening and raging like Punch to Judy; in another aspect, a more favorable one, he is full of merry quips and of brains, like an ancient Irish judge (*brehon*).
- 133.26–27: A reference to *The Last Feast of the Fianna*, a play by Alice Milligan put on at the Abbey Theatre. Joyce obviously disliked the play, which he here describes as basically a nursery version of the ancient Irish epic, with the hero beating on a toy drum. The word "shoebard" likely refers to Schubert's settings of poems from Ossian, which were about "Fingal," and based loosely on Scottish versions of the Finn saga.
- 133.31–32: A jolly publican's version of Liberté, Égalité, Fraternité—with an assurance of his drink's high quality.
- 134.19–20: HCE ("hard cash earned") as a wealthy businessman enjoying a dalliance at the Hotel Shelbourne, then and now the finest hotel in Dublin. The "shellborn" is, of course, Venus. Watling Street is the Roman road.
- 135.8–9: One of the best puns in the book! "Deutschland, Deutschland über alles!" HCE is certainly a Dutchlord, with his Germanic/Scandinavian ancestry.
- 135.36: HCE as verminous, crawling with insects. However, the phrase also contains a reference to one of the funniest anticlerical passages in English literature. "Sagarts" are priests, in Irish. In the Somnours Prologue in *The Canterbury Tales*, Chaucer defines the ultimate destiny of friars—under the devil's arse in Hell:

"Hold up thy tayl, thou Sathanas!" quod [the angel];
"Shewe forth thyn ers, and lat the frere se
Where is the nest of freres in this place!"
And er that half a furlong wey of space,
Right so as bees out swarmen from an hyve,
Out of the develes ers ther gonne dryve
Twenty thousand freres on a route,
And thurghout helle swarmed al aboute,

And comen agayne as faste as they may gon,
And in his ers they crepten everychon.
He clapte his tayl agayn and lay ful stille. (25–35)

> There may also be a reference to HCE's big wide arse. Here HCE is identified with Chaucer's Satan. This is soon followed by another comment, a serious one, on HCE as the devil.

- 136.2–4: A rich reference to a nodal point in Dante. HCE's position echoes with great clarity the position of Judas in the mouth of the central head of the three-headed Lucifer in *Inferno* 34.55–63. Brutus and Cassius are in the other two heads, but the greatest pain is saved for Judas:

> Within each mouth—he used it like a grinder—
> with gnashing teeth he tore to bits a sinner,
> so that he brought much pain to three at once.
> . . . .
> "That soul up there who has to suffer most,"
> my master said: "Judas Iscariot—
> his head inside, he jerks his legs without."

> The supine body of Judas lies within the central head of the three-headed Lucifer, with Lucifer's upper lip on Judas's lap and Lucifer's lower lip cushioning Judas's "crease" or behind. Lucifer is eternally chewing him and ripping his skin. Here HCE is given his most opprobrious role, as the greatest of sinners, Judas, in the worst position in Hell.

- 136.24–25: A hoary philosophical question, identified by M: If an old sword has all of its parts replaced, does this make it a new sword? Joyce has changed the sword to a cutlass ("cut lass") to stress the male potency at stake here. But there is more. The phrase traces back to an ancient Greek philosophical problem, the Ship of Theseus, which raises issues of identity. The ship that had carried Theseus and the sacrificial youths and maidens to and from Crete, where Theseus killed the Minotaur in Daedalus's labyrinth, was preserved at Athens. It lasted a long time, but only because all of its parts were replaced one by one. Question: Was it eventually the original ship? The conundrum had long intrigued Joyce. In *Ulysses*, Stephen despairingly evokes it to deny that he owes AE money: "Wait. Five months. Molecules all change. I am other I now. Other I got pound" (9.205–6). Like the elements of the ship of Theseus, all the materials of Stephen's body have been replaced. However, Stephen then seriously affirms his identity through time by memory, and ruefully acknowledges that he owes AE the money.

- 137. 12–13: HCE as Jesus Christ. Jesus' trial was heard before Pilate in camera, and he was crucified.
- 137.32–33: A cynical comment on the role of the United States as the bestower of freedom on the huddled masses of Europe: they just exchanged one yoke for another. Joyce later refers to the flag of the United States as the "starves on tripes" (265.L2).
- 138.9: Dublin, of course, with the North Circular and South Circular Roads, and the more than doubtful aroma of the Liffey, perfumed with streams of sewer effluent.

Second Question (139.15–28)

About ALP, a comic lovesong from her son Shaun

The next question (139.15) is based on the once common street-boys' taunt "Does your mother know you're out?" This insulting phrase always carried a strong imputation of immaturity and insufficiency. Shaun, as one half of the human body, is indeed insufficient; he is uneasily aware that he is only partially in contact with his lower half, which is constantly posing him questions difficult to answer.

Shaun responds to this malicious question with a love song to his mother, to the tune of "The Bells of Shandon." "The Bells of Shandon" was originally written by "Father Prout" as a parody of poems in English written in ancient Irish poetic forms. Shaun's poem about his mother is, therefore, essentially comic. For all that, it is a fluent work of art, and it does show Shaun's love for his mother.

The gist of the poem is that, when Shaun turns his eyes from the gigantic spectacle of his city-creating, bridge-making, and wall-building father (139.16–18), he sees his garrulous mother, the river, sleeping/slipping by her husband's side. Her whisper possesses powerful stimulative power, just as the voice of the consort Lakshmi can rouse the sleeping Vishnu to create the universe. With her burnt auburn hair and her coquetries, ALP can rouse her husband's "rudder" up, or generate wet dreams. If her quarrelsome twin sons, Shem and Shaun—who represent, among many other things, the two banks of the river, and also Ecclesiastes and Hammurabi, or Church and State—could see her prankish ways, they would burst their bounds and become reconciled. The two banks of the river will become reconciled in II.2 (287.18–292.32); at that point, midway through the book, the mother will embrace her banks and welcome the united pair as sexual partners. That is why Hammurabi and Clesiastes begin with two of the three initials of HCE; when the boys unite they are well on their way, once they generate the third "soldier," the Davy of the Willingdone Museyroom, to becoming the new father.

Third Question (139.29–140.7)

About the Inn/City of Dublin

This is apparently the question that Shaun misunderstands and answers wrong (126.7–8). The question provides many hotel names for the Inn, but Shaun answers the question with a pompous version of the slogan of the City of Dublin. Apparently, all of the city and the world is Shaun's home. Here we may see a biographical detail from the Joyce family, who lived in rented quarters all their lives. The world was their hotel, so to speak. Joyce provides a vivid picture of hotel signs obstructing each other's view: the Grand Hotel and the Splendid appear as Grahot and Spletel.

Fourth Question (140.8–141.7)

About Ireland, with the four provinces debating furiously about (as it turns out) money

The four-part question is: What Irish capital city spelled with six letters beginning with *D* and ending with *n* has the world's largest public park (the Phoenix Park), greatest brewing industry (Guinness), widest thoroughfare (O'Connell Street), and most horse-loving and tea-drinking (or God- or Eucharistic-wine-drinking) little old debilitated population? (The accent in "paùpulation" (140.13) reveals the Gypsy/Romany word *paùpus*, "little old man, grandfather.")

There is debate from other cities about some of the details of Dublin outlined in the question, but the four answerers of the question are all patriotic Irishmen, if a little muddled about problems of unifying ("harmonising") their country.

The four answerers are the Four Old Men, or the four provinces of Ireland, each here praising his own province in its characteristic dialect of Irish, each with its characteristic metal. Each of the feeble old fools proclaims his love

for Issy, the goddess of Ireland. They are also the Four Gospels, which no-
toriously fail to "harmonise" in their respective accounts of the life of Jesus.
These answerers likewise fail to harmonise when they try to ring a chime of
bells; their dreadful jangling failure represents the historical failure of the
four provinces to form a united country.

a) The Ulster speaker answers first, wrenching his capital Belfast into
"Delfas" (140.15). (Squeezing his seven-letter candidate into the six spaces
of Dublin, he conveniently forgets the requirement of a terminal *n*; for that
matter, so will the other three old men.) Ulster was the richest of the provinces, so its metal is gold. The harsh Ulster accent is reproduced, with its
Scottish vowels. Ulster's great shipbuilding industry provides the speaker
with material for his lovesong to Issy, filled with references to hammers,
rivets, the ribs of ships, and the greaseways (140.20) down which glide the
ships. The Ulster flax industry is mentioned, as is the Orange Order. Apparently what Ulster is offering Issy is rape, or at least violence.

b) The Munster speaker stretches the name of his main city, Cork, into the
six-letter monstrosity "Dorhqk" (140.21). The musical Cork accent, the accents of Joyce's father and the most mellifluous of the Irish dialects, governs
the sound of Munster's replies. The metal is silver, appropriate to the silvery
ringing of the "plovery soft accents" (140.23–24) and the descant, the lyrical
speech of that province. However, what Munster seems to be offering Issy
is to make her a household slave, cuffed to the sink and washing the dishes
(with the soapstone).

c) The Leinster speaker presents his main city as "Nublid" (140.27); it is
still certainly six letters, but with its ends inexplicably swapped. Its metal is
copper. Dublin features that appear in the answer include Georgian architec-
ture and the Guinness brewery in James's Gate. What Leinster offers to Issy
is more housework, churning butter, while her torpid husband is drowsing
in the garden.

d) Connaught's main city is presented as "Dalway"(140.36). The Connaught speaker is the most debilitated of the Four Old Men, yet the most
sexually boastful. He claims to have begun his sexual conquest of Issy like
hooking a trout, alluding to the province's fishing—salmon and eels, chub
and dace. His metal is iron, and he represents himself as Rodiron (141.3),
certainly exaggerating his sexual prowess by a great deal.

abcd) The harmonising of the four accounts is one of the greatest triumphs of Joyce. The Four Old Men attempt to play on a ring of bells, but
they are so uncoordinated that nothing is heard but a ferocious quarrel about

money, which in Joyce's view is the basic reason why the provinces cannot unite into a viable country.

The first line of the poem enunciated by the bells is relatively clear: it seems to mean "A bell, a bell, on Shandon steeple!" (141.4–5). However, the two "bell's" interfere with the rest of the line to form "Shalldoll," which converts "steeple" into "Steepbell." Then in the second entrance, which is possibly "And we'll go to Mass at Christmas, people," the "bell" and "Shandon" of the first entrance interfere with "we'll" and "Mass on" to produce "be'll" and "massplon." By the third entrance, the clash of undamped primary and secondary partials is so complex that analysis can go no further. However, the meaning of the last line, howled out by Johnny from Connaught, "Pay me my fee of threepence; the money is not equal!!" (141.7), clearly means that the money for ringing the bells—threepence for each ringer, or a total of a shilling—is unequally divided. Joyce's great skill in writing here makes a vital point about Irish history.

Fifth Question (141.8–27)

About the male servant in the bar, Sackerson/Old Black Joe

The question has many Danish terms, but the sense is plain: he is, in his own opinion, an overworked house servant. Called Sackerson later in the book, the servant is named for a famous bear in Shakespeare's time (see *Ulysses* 9.156), possibly because he is shaggy and powerful; in II.3 (370.26–371.1) he is the bouncer in the bar, who attempts to keep order as the mob of children rush up the pub steps to attack their father.

The name Sackerson may also evoke Dr. George Sigerson (1838–1925), a descendant of Vikings ("son of Sigurd"), a physician, a translator from the Irish, and a famous and much feared critic of the Irish literary movement (see *Ulysses* 9.309). By reputation, Dr. Sigerson was often brusque and bearlike to those of the literary movement who incurred his wrath.

This question and the next are about HCE's two servants, who, as the text hints, have one thing in common: they are both black. As servants in HCE's establishment, they are symbolically African slaves—a bitter commentary by Joyce on the status of lifelong servants. The answer to this question, "Pore ole Joe," is the British title of Stephen Foster's "Old Black Joe." Perhaps the British did not have enough black servants to make the original title relevant.

Sixth Question (141.28–142.7)

About the female servant, Kate, bad-tempered grumbler, keeper of the Willingdone Museyroom

Kate the Slop is an ill-tempered, aging household drudge, who has a bad word to say for anyone. Here she complains especially about her employer, who brings in all the dirt of the park to mess up her clean floor, all the time whistling "You Are My Honeysuckle, I Am the Bee," a once popular American song. She also objects bitterly to ALP's constant questions about the housekeeping: "And who ate the last of the gooseberries that were mouldering for years, and who left that there and who put that here, and who let the cat steal the chop, and who was it—you, was it—who propped the pot in the yard?" She also remembers an angry and rhythmic set of dactylic complaints about her cleaning of the lobby: "What in the name of Saint Luke are you rubbing the side of the floor of the lobby with?" She answers appropriately, "Shite!" and invites the questioner to have a plateful (142.6–7).

The end of the Kate question (141.28–29) recalls the minstrel song "Somebody in the House with Dinah," which is also quoted in *Ulysses* 15.420–23 (and which, somewhat altered, became part of "I've Been Working on the Railroad"). The song was so famous by the 1840s that British and Irish black cats were often named Dinah, as for instance Alice's cat in *Alice in Wonderland* and *Through the Looking Glass*.

Seventh Question (142.8–29)

About the customers in the bar/court of public opinion

The customers—twelve of them, who speak twelve words that end in "-ation"—are also Irish equivalents of the twelve apostles and the twelve months of the year, as well as twelve regions of Dublin and members of the Irish Dáil. They represent public opinion, especially as voiced in Dublin pubs. That the answer to the question is "the Morphios" suggests that they are changeable in their opinions, and sleepy most of the time.

Eighth Question (142.30–143.2)

About the twenty-eight plus one little Monthly Girls, students in St. Bride's Night School in III.2

This question from Shem appeals to the ambition in the little girls; he addresses them as "Your Majesties." However, the maggies are also little animals: "moggies" are pussycats in British slang, and that is what these little girls resemble—small, intensely cute furry creatures, with the distinct possibility of becoming dangerous predators when they grow up. Issy, who represents the grown-up moggies, contains within herself Salome, and a great deal of cruelty; Issy, or her twin Essie, contains the pussycat cuteness of the moggies, with their dangerous potentials fully realized.

Lewis Carroll often addressed his little correspondents as kittens. Note especially a letter written on September 17, 1893, to a little friend whose name actually was Maggie, Maggie Bowman. Dodgson wrote the letter late in his life, and the restraints that he had imposed upon himself were beginning to weaken. In this letter, which very likely Joyce read, there are elements of violence and sadism that contrast strangely with the rest of the charming fable. The letter begins "Oh, you naughty, naughty little culprit! If only I could fly to Fulham with a handy little stick (ten feet long and four inches thick is my favourite size) how I would rap your wicked little knuckles."[22]

Joyce's little maggies are the Monthly Girls, and the month is February, of a leap year, when the women traditionally have the right to ask the men for companionship or marriage. There are twenty-eight little girls, and Issy makes the twenty-ninth.[23]

The answer to the eighth question conceals the number of the moggies, twenty-eight, within itself. There are fourteen clauses in the first half of the sentence, each clause enchained with the next; the first clause picks up "war" from the question, and then they are off (142.31–35).

The next part of the answer contains fourteen enchained words, based upon the Lewis Carroll game of word ladders, in which each word is formed by changing one letter of the word before. Here the words go from "born" to "come" (142.35–143.1). The chain includes some disquieting elements: "rile" and "rule" and "ruse" suggest cunning in the little girls, and a will to rule. The little girls are part sugar and part spice, part love and beauty, part danger.

Issy herself, the twenty-ninth girl, the leap-year girl, appears at the very end of the answer—"yet comes leap year, coach and four"—as the active agent in love, picking a man to love and rule by ruse and wile: "Sweet Peg-of-My-Heart picks one man more." Besides the reference to the old song "Peg o' My Heart," the line contains the mingled joy and pain felt by Issy's lover. As the daughter of the old hen ALP, the chick pecks at the heart of her lover; Joyce himself must often have felt such mingled joy and pain when contemplating his daughter, Lucia, especially in her later years.

Ninth Question (143.3–28)

About the universe as seen by fallen Man, the realm of chance and also of ordering by repetition

The gigantic and intricate ninth question resembles, in its syntactic complexity and oratorical splendor, two passages from as diametrically opposed a pair of writers as could be imagined: John Henry Newman and Thomas Henry Huxley.

Newman, one of the writers Joyce most admired, produced a beautifully wrought sentence in chapter 5 of his *Apologia pro Vita Sua*:

> To consider the world in its length and breadth, its various history, the many races of man, their starts, their fortunes, their mutual alienation, their conflicts; and then their ways, habits, governments, forms of worship; their enterprises, their aimless courses, their random achievements and acquirements, the impotent conclusion of long-standing facts, the tokens so faint and broken of a superintending design, the blind evolution of what turn out to be great powers or truths, the progress of things, as if from unreasoning elements, not towards final causes, the greatness and littleness of man, his far-reaching aims, his short duration, the curtain hung over his futurity, the disappointments of life, the defeat of good, the success of evil, physical pain, mental anguish, the prevalence and intensity of sin, the pervading idolatries, the corruptions, the dreary hopeless irreligion, that condition of the whole race, so fearfully yet exactly described in the Apostle's words, "having no hope and without God in the world,"—all this is a vision to dizzy and appal; and inflicts upon the mind the sense of a profound mystery, which is absolutely beyond human solution.

This sentence describes the sorrowful aspects of man's life on earth, which Joyce's huge sentence touches on as well.[24]

The second source that provides an armature for Joyce's splendid question is an extremely complex sentence by Thomas Henry Huxley. Like Newman's sentence, Huxley's is close in theme to Joyce's enormous question: an objective person viewing nature would see the universe as a sort of kaleidoscope of forms, constantly changing:

> If a being endowed with perfect intellectual and aesthetic faculties, but devoid of the capacity for suffering pain, either physical or moral, were to devote his utmost powers to the investigation of nature, the universe would seem to him to be a sort of kaleidoscope, in which, at every

successive moment of time, a new arrangement of parts of exquisite
beauty and symmetry would present itself, and each of them would
show itself to be the logical consequence of the preceding arrangement,
under the conditions which we call the laws of nature.

Then, the passage concludes, "order is lord of all, and disorder only a name
for the part of the order which gives us pain."[25]

Joyce's enormous question begins with a reference to flowers, a symbol
of the little girls just described. It conceals the basic elements of its syntax
within many intertangling appositives and independent clauses, to make in
itself an icon of the complex universe that it describes. If a tired human
being, weary from his tasks in the modern dirty city, were given a glimpse
of the universe, Joyce/Shem asks, what would it look like? The answer is
"A collideorscape!" (143.28) The many repetitions of "seems" show that the
far-gazer (143.26) views a developing and changing world, a hugely complex
world of "becoming." Of course, Hamlet, who is invoked a number of times
in the question, would reject "seems": "Seems, madam? Nay, it is. I know not
'seems'" (I.ii.74).

As for the elements in the question: The gazer hoping for salvation (143.10)
is HCE, the Scandinavian fallen sinner who also hopes for his own salvation.
He is also the original Adam of the Kabbalah, Adam Kadmon, the gigantic
being who was originally coterminous with the universe but "fell" until he
was the size of a man. Shaun recalls this creature in III.3 as the giant Yawn,
the fallen creature who contains within himself all the secrets of the universe,
and who is ultimately revealed to be HCE himself, the fallen creator of human civilization. Old Copenhagen, who hopes for heaven, is also a far-gazer,
a creature endowed with great prophetic vision, and a telescope (literally a
far-gazer). However, he is also a forgetter (*Vergesser* in German); he may
once have had all knowledge as Adam Kadmon, but this knowledge is hidden within him until the investigators in III.3 recover it.

To the fargazer, the world and the universe are not permanent and un-
changing entities. His universe is not a Platonist's universe, lit by Shelley's
white radiance of eternity: it gleams with all the colors of the rainbow
(143.24–26). Joyce was not an extreme idealist, one who, as Emerson declares
in "Nature," shows "a certain hostility and indignation toward matter"—that
is, a thinker who rejects the reality of the physical world. Joyce despised the
fuzzy Platonism he encountered in Dublin. In *A Portrait*, Stephen Dedalus
rejects the cold peace of the altar for the messy life of everyday, and in *Ulysses*

Stephen, beset by his Platonist and Transcendentalist contemporaries in the National Library of Ireland, rejects them bitterly (9.85–89).

For his emphasis on "the now, the here," Joyce should be called a Descendentalist. Even though Eternity may be bathed in Shelley's "white radiance," in a habitat of spirits and angels, Joyce was sure that the many-colored glass of the physical world provided the appropriate habitat for fallen human beings. In Book IV, the Archdruid and St. Patrick debate this very question, as the sun is rising and creating anew the world of colors. In his belief in the value of the physical world, Joyce created all of his works. The literal physical world was the arena for Joyce, the world that constantly supplies surprises to the ineluctable modalities of the visible and the audible. In this belief, Joyce was entirely orthodox; for the Church, the attempt to regard human beings as angels fit for eternity was a heresy—Angelism.

However, Joyce's rainbow-lit physical world is not a disorganized mess. Shaun, in answering "A collideorscape!" (143.28), provides a principle of organization both for the universe and for his own works. The answer refers to the ancient description of the universe by Epicurus and his disciples as consisting of atoms and the void; the atoms "collide or escape" randomly, as they do in modern theories of matter. However, modern science provides an escape from chaos. Even if the interaction of the parts of the universe is truly random, they are finite in number, and they also have eternity in which to interact. Therefore they ultimately must repeat each random pattern, and this an unlimited number of times—Nietzsche's Eternal Return, a cousin of Vico's *ricorso*, and a defense by Joyce of the complexity of the *Wake*.

In the answer to this question, the changing patterns of universal elements evoke a kaleidoscope, which turns random heaps of colored glass fragments into symmetrical patterns of great beauty by repetition in angled mirrors. As the *Wake* itself repeats its stories and symbols dozens or hundreds of times, the basic story of the *Wake* emerges clearly as its own collideorscape.

Tenth Question (143.29–148.32)

About Issy, skittish virgin, young woman, cruel, capricious daughter of the family

There has already been a poetic passage in this chapter: in the second question, Shaun answers Shem's taunt "Does your mother know you're out?" with a pompous lovesong in the meter of "The Bells of Shandon." Here, however, it is the question that is blazing with passion (143.29–30). In Shem's line there is all of the "love's bitter mystery" of Yeats's poem that plays such a part in *Ulysses*. He speaks of the bitterness of love, the sourness of spurned desire, and the burning and smoke of love's blazing, a true love song in itself.

The question is a version of an Elizabethan song by Thomas Campion and Philip Rosseter: "What then is love but mourning, / What desire, but a self-burning? / Till she that hates doth love return / Thus will I mourn, thus will I sing, / 'Come away, come away, my darling.'"

Issy herself answers the question. We hear her characteristic pert and chirpy rhythm immediately:[26] "I know, pepette, of course, dear." (143.31) She is Issy, talking to herself in her mirror, a good little girl speaking to her bad little sister, Essie, who is in the mirror—Alice before and through the looking glass, so to speak.

Issy is not only Alice; she is, among others, Salome, with all the mock-naive coyness and cruelty of that dangerous dancer; in II.3 Issy sings an ominous song of the naughty nightingales (359. 32), a merry little ditty about the castration of the father. Issy distinctly resembles Gerty MacDowell in *Ulysses*—there is the same oversweetness, and the same flashes of irritation, in both girls.

The double nature of femininity provides major passages through the book. The number two is the number characterizing the female genitals, as the number three characterizes the male genitals. Throughout the book, the three-and-two pattern represents the intercourse of the lovers. In the Willingdone Museyroom the two sisters and the three brothers bear their characteristic numbers. Later, in book 3.4, ALP sings out that three for two will do for her, as her husband attempts sexual intercourse (584.10). Here in I.6, the 2/3 pattern is exemplified by Issy's lubricious whispering of "Sh sh!" and "Shshsh!" (148.4, 16), which climax in the perfect four-part Vichian pattern "Shshshsh!" (148.28).

Issy's taste in men is immature, an impatient virgin's vision of love. Her imagined lovers (144.4–13) are big, dark, sexy Hispanic hunks, football players with hairy chests, very like Tristan in the kissing and cuddling Tristan and Isolde chapter (II.4). Here Issy imagines fondling and kissing her Tristan's phallus, treating even imaginary fellatio with a delicious and outrageous mock innocence: "Oh, mind your poor tickly. Shall I put him in my mouth? Hmm. A funny place to have a finger!" (144.34–35).

She is a sexual predator in the making: she vividly imagines the delights of copulation, and declares that she does not care if anyone sees her, even a policeman or beggars(145.19–23). She believes in a fierce Darwinian strangling struggle for life and the survival in wifehood of the fittest (145.26–27). She also thrills in imagining herself as manipulating male genitalia, and as a delicious sexual prey to vampires: let's root out Bram Stoker and give him the thrill of our lives! (145.31–32). The word "thrall" also suggests that she sees herself as Keats's Belle Dame sans Merci, who has "in thrall" all the pale warriors.

Issy has the adolescent girl's contempt for her male contemporaries, who are always less mature. She remembers with amusement the attempt of a clerical Shaun at seduction. In a richly comic parody of eighteenth-century verse at 146.9–11), she tells of Shaun's clumsy approach.[27]

She scorns her father and his customers—they are all over the hill—and praises her twenty-eight school friends, whose names begin with the successive letters of the alphabet plus *Ph* and *Th*, ending gleefully with "Mee!" After she fantasizes about being spanked for her naughty thoughts (148.6), she sinks into a swoon of delight and imagines saying hotly to her dream Tristan: "Did you really never in all your life speak close to a girl before? No? Not even to the charming chambermaid! How marvelous!" (148.22–24). She ends with a vision of the marriage service (148.29–30) and a merry declaration that love laughs at locksmiths.

All in all, she is a typical young girl, with typical imagining of lovers. This is a necessary stage in a woman's maturing, as the clumsy stage of male adolescence is necessary for men.

Eleventh Question (148.33–168.12)

About Shaun himself, revealing his hatred of his brother, Shem

The eleventh and twelfth questions, of course, much like the first ten, provide information that will be of great assistance in following the TIME-narrative that begins in Book II. Here and in the succeeding chapter, the rage of Shaun against his lower half "heats up" the reversed narrative flow until the tide turns.

Shaun is furious that his lowly brother will not accept his "lower" status. Shem should be permanently "under" Shaun; the bottom half of the body is always "rising up," so to speak, and greatly embarrassing the top half. Eventually we learn that a mature man will accept both halves—the theme of Book III.

The eleventh question forms itself as a plaintive song composed and performed by Shem,[28] in which Shaun is asked whether he would ever assist his poor brother, in any circumstances. The pitiful state of Shem is presented in heartbreaking detail: he is alcoholic, on a binge, his eyes ache, he is in exile, he is ailing, he trembles and wails, he maunders in "misliness" (148.36)—a state of permanently being "misled"?—he is infested with lice, is losing his teeth, is a manacled prisoner, is blind, he begs a deaf and dumb God for something to eat. His rare merriment is filled with weeping and whimpering. He has cold blood, and lacks strength in his bones, he takes favor or abuse with the same sighing and whimpering, and he farts (a sin, the incensed Shaun insists). Shem is overly conciliatory (he says "Oh, howdy do?" even to his enemies) and, most important of all, he needs Shaun to save his "wee schoolmastered" animula, or small learned soul (149.8). Shem provides the coldly correct answer that he expects Shaun to provide—"We would rather not!"[29] (149.9–10).

We have here a self-portrait by Joyce of his parlous state of health as he struggles with the *Wake*—incipient alcoholism, varying degrees of blindness, toothlessness, low blood pressure, general pacifism, a feeling that he is chained to his never-ending *Wake* project, ambivalence about his overextensive education (a devil to learn), constant sexual urges (a devil to "lech"), and finally, as a lapsed Catholic, his dangerous religious state. However, many of the clauses in the question also refer to characteristic features of the bottom half of the body: it has no teeth and "speaks" equivocally through farts, and it is constantly urging sexual adventures on the top half.

The answer to the eleventh question is organized into eight sections.

1. Shaun denies that he would ever help his poor brother (149.11–14)

The figure and arguments of Professor Jones owe something to Wyndham Lewis, who harshly criticized Joyce as a time-besotted writer. In *Time and Western Man* and other of his writings, Lewis linked emphasis on the temporal with political liberalism, sexual uncertainty, and feeble, pacifist attitudes. Lewis himself took an extreme antitemporal position, advocating hardness of outline and concentration on the spatial aspects of the world. Joyce did not deny the spatial aspects of the world; he merely wanted to give time its due. Shaun and Shem represent two ways of looking at the world: Shaun a spatial, essentially digitalized, visual, photographic view of the physical world, and Shem a temporal, essentially analogue, aural, continuous perception of the physical world. The difference between Lewis and Joyce is that Lewis was entirely intolerant of continuity and "temporalizing" creators, while Joyce insisted on the absolute necessity of both methods of perception—spatial, with the world fragmented into still photographs, and temporal, with a continuous sound track.

In fact, at the end of the Shem chapter, I.7, the two brothers are going to combine to make up one lover of the real world, as represented by their mother, ALP. The combined mechanism works like a movie camera, with still photographs of the world combined with a continuous sound track. Shem (Mercius) will declare that it is to the combined brothers that their mother is coming, in both sexual and temporal senses of "coming." At the end of I.7 and during I.8, the narrative and the temporal flow will begin slowly.

2. The Lecture of Professor Jones on Time and Space (149.14–152.3)

Professor Jones lumbers into a lengthy disquisition on space and time. Since Shaun as the upper half possesses the head, the lecture is filled with immense learning, most of it inaccurate or based on apocryphal sources. In this respect it resembles the comments on Irish history of Garrett Deasy in *Ulysses*—both sets of comments on history and reality are fatally flawed. Apparently, true knowledge requires the complete man, Shem included.

Of course, Professor Jones attacks Time, the province of his brother, and is fervently in favor of Space. He attacks Einstein's treatment of space-time, and the concept of *durée* (psychologically experienced time as opposed to clock time) as defined by Bergson. Jones redefines these problems as the "dime-cash" problem; Joyce may be hinting at the fashionable and monetarily rewarding nature of the scientific and philosophical discussions on Einstein's theories of time and space.

Jones refers to Bergson and Einstein as drunken bitches (149.20, 28). Mingled with Jones's plethoric and syntactically clotted tirades is an unattractive anti-Semitism; Bergson and Einstein were both Jews, although Bergson during his life drifted toward Catholicism and Einstein was always a freethinker. Anti-Semitism is for Joyce a purblind single-eyed view of the world, as witness the Citizen in *Ulysses*, a denial of the necessary "darkness" of the soul.

Professor Jones then plunges into a turgid and turbid argument on definitions of "Talis" and "Qualis," to no clear end.[30] Finally, giving up hope of elucidating the complex issues he is addressing—there is a hint of Hegelian cloudiness here—Shaun decides to simplify the issue of the supremacy of space with a parable, or fable.

3. *The Tale of the Mookse and the Gripes* (152.4–159.23)

The fable, taken from the Javanese (152.12),[31] is based on Aesop's fable of the Fox and the Grapes. It is intended by Jones as a real knock-down argument, one that will prove to all objective listeners that Shaun is, and deserves to be, the natural leader in the battle for supremacy of the brothers. The fable itself is simple: a blustering bovine creature confronts some (presumably) sour grapes. However, the confrontation does not produce any obvious result, not even the result in the original fable. Moreover, the outcome is not what Shaun intends: he comes off as a blustering, shallow bully and, in company with the Gripes, is carried off by a mysterious woman.

There is a good reason for the failure of the fable. Although Shaun intends it to clearly express his superiority over his brother, he cannot carry this off, since the "root language"—the language of artistic creation—is only partly Shaun's voice, only partly under Shaun's control. The principal creative voice in the fable is the voice of Shem. Apparently, in Joyce's view, all literary creation has its genesis in the lower half of the body. When Shaun wishes to overwhelm Shem with contemptuous epithets, he is constrained to ask Shem's assistance (191.1–4).

Here we have a section of great importance for the understanding of Joyce's attitude toward language. Joyce found that the speech of great literature derives only partially from the top half of the body. Discourse from the head, which is the sort that Shaun produces, is invariably uncontrolled and overintellectual, but also sentimental. It is only with the assistance of the genitals that complete language can be produced.

A section in *Ulysses* (15.2291–2638) clearly illustrates this theme. In the Circe chapter, the sight of Zoe's bare bottom causes Bloom's psyche to split in two, and Bloom's grandfather, Lipoti Virag, suddenly appears. He is a wild creature, with a more wild and highly creative stream of language. In addition, he is the source of language. He is identified as "basilicogrammate" (15.2304), which may mean "lord of language" (as in *Ulysses* 9.454): in Greek *basilico-* means "royal" and *gramma-* means "written language." He also wears a "pshent," the Egyptian crown of the god Thoth, the god who creates by means of language, the god of libraries, as Stephen asserts in *Ulysses*. The two feathers behind his ears identify him as a secretary bird, a creature that with its protruding feathers seems to resemble a secretary with a pen stuck behind each ear. Lipoti Virag is the spirit of language incarnate, who appears as an aspect of Shem as the source of "root language."

In this section of *Ulysses*, in Lipoti Virag's whirling and uncontrolled discourse, there is one of the first appearances in Joyce's work of the free creation of *Wake* language. Lipoti's wild excitement expresses itself in irrelevant and surrealist words and phrases: "Bubbly jock! Bubbly jock!" (15.2434) and "Flipperty Jippert!" (15.2549). However, it is not only in lexical items that we see the source of linguistic creativity. In the same scene, Latin demonstratives burst forth to the rhythm of ejaculation—"Hik! Hek! Hak! Hok! Huk! Kok! Kuk!" (15.2603)—a mixture of the syntactic and the autonomic that carries conviction as to the real source of language.

At another point in Lipoti Virag's tirade, basic syntactic structures of language break loose and float to the surface: "That the cows with their those distended udders that they have been the the known . . ." (15.2452–53). In both speeches, the raging madness of the id in person has violently released such syntactically important items as relative pronouns, possessive pronouns, definite demonstratives, and definite articles. Here we see the freedom of released language.

The genitalia, the instinctual centers of the being that are the power of Shem, are also the source of all language. Joyce has released his language, and the *Wake* is the result. Shaun is, of course, uneasily aware that deep, creative language comes from the activity of the lower half of the body. In a later chapter, III.1, Shaun is questioned by his brother in the form of a donkey. The donkey's questions turn to language, and Shaun is forced to deal with the ultimate source of his language. He declares that he hates his brother "[f]or his root language" (424.17). Shaun then launches into an attack on his brother, and furiously calls Shem a plagiarist who has stolen from him (424.32–36). Notice the emphasis on "lowness" here, both moral lowness and the physical lowness of the body below the waist. Shaun next attempts to parody his brother's root language (424.36–425.3). He stole the tail of my shirt (the lower half), insists Shaun, and then proudly declares that he has produced "Shemese"—the whole chemise, in fact. The philistine is always sure that he could be a great artist, if he cared to engage in such worthless activity!

The question of language settled, Shaun embarks upon his fable based on the fable of the Fox and the Grapes. Here the Fox is a "Mookse," a moocow, and an ox, as well as a fox.[32] Joyce anticipates this fable in a section of the Oxen of the Sun episode in *Ulysses*—the tale of the Irish bull who is also a papal bull (14.582–650). The incapacity of the Church of Rome seems to have been a favorite theme of Joyce's father, and is found in Joyce's early work.

Joyce was of the opinion that the Church of Rome urgently needed many Irish churchmen to do all of its essential work. Both the Irish papal bull in *Ulysses* and the Mookse are radically incomplete below the waist. Indeed, the Mookse must walk leaning on a stick, and Shaun himself has such weak legs that he falls twice in Book III. Then what can the Gripes be but the genitals of the Mookse, hanging "bolt downright" from the branch of an elm? Here we see the upper-half/lower-half symbolism in graphic terms.

The rage shot with envy that fills Shaun resembles that of Melville's Captain Ahab, who lost a leg (and perhaps a good deal more of himself!) to the phallic Moby Dick. It is also the fury of the puritan when confronted with the disconcerting evidence given by his own lower body of the dark drives that he tries so hard to repress, in himself and in others. Joyce was very well acquainted with the furious hypocrisy of the puritan; the censors that tormented Joyce throughout his career were all Shauns, raging against the physical facts of life. Even Ezra Pound, the bohemian free soul, was embarrassed by Joyce's description of Bloom in the privy.

In this fable, despite himself, Shaun's tale ends inconclusively, with the little sister Nuvoletta trying vainly to pacify the brothers. This is not the ending that Shaun intended, but it is the one that he eventually has to produce, since his brother is the source of "root language."

The fable has also introduced some other basic elements of the story: the Stone and the Tree and the two brothers as the two banks of the river. Joyce probably borrowed the two banks of the river from the Rive Droite and the Rive Gauche of Paris, with all of their economic and political implications: Shaun, the reactionary Mookse, is sitting on the stone on the right bank of the river, and Shem, the anarchist and artist Gripes, is hanging from a tree on the left bank. Tree + Stone equals Treestone, or Tristan, the young lover. The flow of the river to her two sons is foreshadowed in this fable.

In a delightful passage, the little sister of the Mookse and the Gripes, Nuvoletta ("little cloud" in Italian), is observing the conflict of the brothers from on high, in her own little cloud (157.8–13). She is happy when her brother Shaun in a military pose is raising his walking stick "shoulders up,"[33] and she is sad when her other brother, Shem, with his knobbly knees, is making such a fool of himself. Note again, it is Shaun with his shoulders that is the top half, and Shem with the knees the lower half.

Issy/Nuvoletta tries to reconcile the two brothers, but it is all love's labours lost, in a moist setting (157.23). At last she begins to weep, and the tears fall to the earth and become a stream, which eventually becomes the river. The river herself, in the guise of a woman dressed in black, comes to each bank of the river and gathers up her sons: "Time, like an ever-rolling stream, / Bears all her sons away." We will see Anna Livia's incestuous embrace of her two sons in II.2, when the river of text broadens out to include the comments of her sons in the right and left margins (287.18–292.32).

4. Shaun cautions his erring brother (159.24–160.34)

Some condescending remarks.

5. The Lecture of Professor Jones, continued (160.35–161.14)

A return to the pompous lecture.

6. The Tale of Burrus and Caseous (161.15–167.3)

This tale is another attempt by Shaun the Butter (Burrus) to prove the disgraceful and debased nature of his brother, Shem the Cheese (Caseous). Shaun breaks into stately mirth at the thought of his brother's low nature: Caseous is a very smelly cheese indeed (163.8–11). Yet this tale, like the previous fable, contains a dismayed realization by Shaun that his sister, here called Margareena, is fond of her smelly brother. The successful suitor of Margareena will be Antonius, an amalgam of the two brothers, the third soldier of the Willingdone Museyroom, who is both the ithyphallic father-killer and the young lover Tristan, who "kills" the father by maturing into the new father. In other words, both Issy and, ultimately, her mother, Anna Livia, want a whole man, top and bottom, and will not respond to a half-man, no matter which half it is.

7. The climax of Shaun's rage (167.3–168.6)

After analyzing the Burrus and Caseous fable in his usual pompous style (167.3–8), Shaun ends his recitation with a furious alliterative outburst against his brother (167.8–17). The painapple of which Shem is ignorant is the fruit of the tree of knowledge of good and evil.[34] Shaun the puritan, on the other hand, is all too conscious of the sin of fallen Man, and the necessity to band together into restrictive religious covenants to combat together the darkness of the human understanding. Shaun is outraged that Shem will not join the crowd of clean sheep (Latin *grex, gregis*, "sheep") and sing hymns.

From here to the end of the chapter, there is a great display of Latin language and Roman law appropriate to the overeducated Shaun. The tale of Burrus-Caseous-Antonius has set Shaun's mind in a Roman cast. Shaun rushes into Roman history to declare his brother a traitor (167.18): a "topsman" in English slang is an executioner, and traitors to Rome were hurled from the Tarpeian rock. Shaun is the topsman as the top half of the body, and his brother Shem is to be hurled from the Tarpeian rock.

Then Shaun bursts into Latin. The first phrase is "Ubi lingua nuncupassit, ibi fas!" (167.33–34), which may be translated as "Where he has publicly declared it, so shall it be from now on by *fas*"; that is, "Let it be established by divine law." The second phrase, "Adversus hostem semper sac!" (167.34), may be translated as "As for the enemy, let him be divinely dealt with." T translates Joyce's *semper sac* as *semper sic*, "Be it always so!" However, Joyce may be invoking a much older law than the Roman *jus,* the law of *fas. Fas* covers the handling of the most outrageous of criminals, Oedipus or Cain. These great malefactors cannot be covered by human law, *jus.* Being too wicked for human justice, they can be dealt with only by the gods. The Latin word *nefas* covers such extravagant crimes (see 167.19). The Bible created the scapegoat for the disposition of such extraordinary crimes.

Shaun's Latin phrases are adapted from one of the earliest examples of written Roman law, the Law of the XII Tablets, created in 451–450 B.C. after the expulsion of the kings. These statutes, according to Cicero, may have been promulgated to protect the plebeians from the power of the patrician magistrates, who would otherwise have devised whatever law they wanted. Here Shaun invokes them against Shem. (T points out that Vico declared that these laws were the foundation of all Roman law.)

Shaun finishes his splenetic tirade by appealing to biblical law, both New Testament and Old Testament. His first phrase here is deeply ambiguous, a hypocritical urging for Issy to submit sexually to her feverish brother Shaun (167.34–35). If Issy falls under the influence of her sexually inflaming brother Shem and will not respond to Shaun's full-faced thunderbolt (Latin *fulmen*), let her be rebuked by the congregation as a shameless hoyden. However, the phrase also has relevance to Shem: it echoes Matthew 15–17, a section of the New Testament referring to the disciplining of an erring brother:

> Moreover if thy brother shall trespass against thee, go and tell him his fault between thee and him alone: if he shall hear thee, thou hast gained thy brother.
>
> But if he will not hear thee, then take with thee one or two more, that in the mouth of two or three witnesses every word may be established.
>
> And if he shall neglect to hear them, tell it unto the church: but if he

neglect to hear the church, let him be unto thee as an heathen man and a publican.[35]

The second phrase, intoned solemnly by Shaun (167.35–168.6), echoes Shakespeare's *Merchant of Venice* V.i.83–88, but appeals to Moses, the recorder of the Law in the Old Testament. Then Shaun—probably with Shem's assistance—bursts into poetry. He presents echoes from Scott and Burns: "Breathes there a man with soul so dead" (168.1) and "My heart's in the highlands" (168.2). *Highlows* are shoes, so Shem's hopes are down in his boots.

Shaun then picks up the poem he heard Shem begin with the eleventh question (168.3–6). Shaun answers his own question—Would Shem be rejected from the Ark by his brothers?—with a stout "ay!"

8. Shaun's final rejection/acceptance of Shem (168.6–12)

In the end Shaun rejects Shem resoundingly. Although Shaun is forced to admit—by Shem himself, perhaps—that he and his brother are bound together tightly, Shaun would deny his responsibility to Shem even if they were breast-brothers, as close as bread and salt, even had they been as close as the Idle Apprentice and the Industrious Apprentice of Hogarth, even had they slept in the same bed and been bitten by the same flea (168.6–10). Shaun echoes Milton in *Lycidas*: "For we were nursed upon the selfsame hill, / Fed the same flock, by fountain, shade, and rill" (23–24). Were they gentleman of the same family, cheek by jowl (168.10–11), Shaun would utterly refuse to assist his degraded brother.

Shaun finishes with a fine rhythmic flourish filled with fear and hate. Still, despite his furious rejection of Shem, Shaun has implicitly acknowledged his intimate association with his lower half. In the next question and answer, and the next chapter, the close proximity of Shaun to Shem is explicitly asserted.

Twelfth Question (168.13)

About Shem himself

The question "Sacer esto?" echoes the Latin XII Laws of the eleventh question, and seems to mean "Are you *sacer*?" *Sacer* is ambiguous. In its original Latin meaning, it signifies "so holy (good or bad) that it is given up for the special handling of the gods." It is close in meaning to the South Pacific "taboo."

However, it is here Shem's question to Shaun. Shem goads Shaun into admitting his indissoluble relationship with his brother, with his embarrassing lower half. "Sacer esto?" seems to mean "Are we both such extreme criminals, so taboo, for meditating an attack upon the father?" Their previous incarnation as Burrus and Caseous—that is, Brutus and Cassius—has its criminal aspects. Both Brutus and Cassius are in the two side mouths of Lucifer in Dante, for their murder of Julius Caesar, the founder of the Roman Empire. Both, with Judas, are the worst of criminals and sinners. It would seem as if Shem is asking Shaun to admit their common guilt.

Shaun's answer—"Semus sumus!" (168.14)—admits the relationship: "We are Shem." But expanding this admission is so complex that Joyce kept it for a separate chapter.

Book I, Chapter 7: Justius and Mercius and the Beginning of Time Mode

Chapter 7 opens with a long stream of invective directed by Shaun at his embarrassing, recalcitrant, and ironic brother, Shem (169.1–186.18). Shaun is so enraged that the text is unusually clear; the reader should have little trouble with this chapter. In the course of the tirade we learn a great deal about both brothers, and about the structural relationship between them.

The chapter ends with the turn of the tide, the episode in which the book stops flowing backward and begins to flow forward, though slowly at first. Shem and Shaun are, among other things, the left and the right bank of the river Liffey, as well as the thighs of ALP, and they unite to begin the long orgasm of the river as she flows to her lover, the sea.

Shem and Shaun

Shem and Shaun, the bottom half of the male body and the top half of the male body, are polar opposites in every way. Joyce himself, despite his courageous insistence on giving their due to all aspects of the human body, had misgivings about the lower, more embarrassing half of his own body, and his own baser thoughts. Niall Montgomery once reported that Joyce "could not abide his darker side, his baser behavior, his low and dirty thoughts. 'We're all animals,' [Montgomery] told him. But Joyce . . . would not accept that."[36]

Shaun insists that he is just the opposite of Shem. As the chapter unfolds, the oppositions become clear. Some of the polar oppositions of Shaun and Shem are:

Shaun	Shem
Top half of male body	Bottom half of male body
Vision	Hearing
Clear-sighted—the two eyes	One-eyed—the monocular penis
Light	Darkness
Michael the Archangel	Nick the Devil
Very popular	Shunned
"Sane"	"Mad"
Digital—analysis	Analogue—synthesis
"Deathbone"—the skull	"Lifewand"—the phallus
Apollonian—individual judgment	Dionysian—oceanic crowd feeling
Discrete	Continuous
Static	Dynamic
Stone	Tree
Theory—abstract	Creation—concrete
White light of sage's inner world	Rainbow colors of real world outside
Description—"epic"	Action—"lyric" and "dramatic"
Light tenor voice	Deep bass voice
Happy	Sad
Comedy	Tragedy
Sancho Panza—the gluttonous, garrulous comic servant	Don Quixote, the Knight of the Woeful Countenance
Brain	Genitals
Superficial learning and language	Deep feeling and poetic "root" language
Pedantic	Inspired
Justice	Mercy
Warlike and violent—the arms hit	Peaceful and cowardly—the legs run away
Intransigent revolutionary and assassin	Pacifist compromiser—"let's all live in peace"
Chauvinist "patriot"	Internationalist
Citizen	Inhabitant
Right bank of river	Left bank of river
Conservative—straight arrow	Radical—hippie
Uses aftershave lotion	Smells bad from all orifices
Belches	Farts
Arms and hands—sadism	Backside—masochism
Greedy and avaricious—the top half ingests	Generous—the lower half pours out, sometimes embarrassingly
Drinks grain liquors (beer, gin, whisky)—grain grows *up* from the ground	Drinks grape liquors ("urinous" white wine)—grapes hang *down* from the air
Prosperous	Poor
Bourgeois	Bohemian/Artist
Orthodox	Heretic
Sings	Dances
Thinks and answers	Reacts and questions
Prefers fresh food, and lots of it—the mouth takes in fresh food	Prefers processed food, and little of it—the belly "processes" the food
Butter	Cheese
Ant	Grasshopper
Fox	Grapes
Carries the message of ALP—produces the physical object, the book	Writes down the message of ALP—produces the text of the book

Shem is accused of everything bad: he is low (in all senses of the word), he is dirty, he prefers canned food to fresh food, fancies himself an artist, will not drink hard likker but prefers "urinous" wine, is a pacifist and wants everybody to be friends—in other words, Shem is a Dionysian, plunging the individual into the collective unconscious, which disgusts the bellicose and judgmental individualist that is Shaun the Apollonian.

In fact, the main function of the two brothers is to represent the two halves of the male body.[37] The difficulty of the upper half in tolerating the lower, more embarrassing half provides much of the tension and drama in the book.[38] Shaun is the pure, clean intellectual, the talking upper half, but he is also sadistic (he has the arms to hit with), and gluttonous and avaricious (the top half of the body takes in sights and sounds as well as food and drink). Shem, as the lower half, is masochistic—like Joyce himself—since he has the bottom to be hit. Shem also has the legs, which he uses generally to run away from battle. However, Shem eventually lends his legs to Shaun, who is woefully deficient in walking ability. Although Shaun is a postman walking through the world, he constantly complains about how much his legs and feet hurt; he is never on good terms with his pedal extremities, even though his brother, whose possession they are, gladly lends them to him. So undependable are Shaun's legs on their own that he falls twice on his journey through the night of Book III and finally ends up a Fallen Man, flat on his back, in III.3.

Shem's body is described by the revolted Shaun in unrelenting detail. Twenty-one bodily features are listed, each more degraded than the last. Shem is so dirty and smelly that girls exclaim "Poisse!" upon seeing him (177.12). *Poisse* means literally "sticky black cobbler's wax," but in French argot it refers to sticky, snotty little boys, the equivalent of the American word "yuck!"

Shaun is acutely sensitive to olfactory input emanating from his lower half—after all, the top half has the nose! Shem's stink earns comparison to a stopped-up sewer and a polecat. The polecat odor is referred to constantly, both here and later in the book (see 513.12–15). Shem is rejected by all clean-living cleaning women, and is an embarrassment to all sweet-smelling visiting Englishmen (183.6–8). In the Fable of the Mookse and the Gripes, the offensive odor of Shem's posterior orifice has been transferred upward, in an advertisement in the American style that Joyce admired, warning insecure males about halitosis (156.35–36). However, not even the strongest mouthwash will make a dent in Shem's inherent smelliness.

Here Joyce is making a serious point: the Enemy must be objectionable in all respects. In *Ulysses* the ancient libel about the Jews has it that Jews have a special odor that can be identified by dogs: "I'm told those jewies does have a sort of a queer odour coming off them for dogs" (12.452–53). This theme is later picked up in the Circe chapter: "The *fetor judaicus* is most perceptible" (15.1796).

Indeed, Shem the Enemy, the socially unmentionable, is so dirty, smelly, battered, and feeble that he asks a riddle about himself, "when is a man not a man?" and answers it: "When he is a . . . Sham" (170.5, 23–24). This answer shows Shem's characteristic modesty about his physical envelope, but it also suggests that Shem knows he is only half a man, an admission that Shaun refuses to make about himself.

Shem's body resembles Joyce's in many details. Shem also resembles Joyce in his field of operation. Like Joyce, Shem tells stories about his father, some of which overvalue the father, while others show up the father's failings. Joyce here insists on the importance of the father, and his dangerous relations with his own offspring, in his own work.

Other features that characterize Shaun and Shem as the top and bottom half of the body are also telling. Shaun prefers unprocessed food, while Shem, as the digestive half, wishes only for processed food—canned salmon and pineapples—and an appropriately urinous white wine. Shem has a deep bass voice, while Shaun has a light tenor. Shem is also, like Joyce himself, aware that he has diabolic roots. As the spirit of the Pit, Shem is constantly "rising up" from "Down Under," either Hell or Australia; the lower half of the world wants to have its time in the sun, so to speak. Parts of the lower half of the body can rear up from time to time, as we will see in III.2 at 462.15–468.22.

Shem, with his diabolic genital knowledge, also possesses truly deep and expressive language. As we have seen, Shaun is emotionally and artistically limited; when he needs language to insult Shem, he must ask Shem for the appropriate words (191.1–4). Notice that in the name occurring there, "Scheekspair," the pair of cheeks in the lower half are conflated with the greatest literary creator, Shakespeare. The creative function of the lower half ultimately is part of its generous, genitory, genital nature.

With the genital and excretory zones in Shem's lower half of the body, he is dirty and embarrassing. He is also masochistic, as were Joyce and Leopold Bloom: the bottom is there to be smitten. However, he is also generous—the lower half of the body gives out what the alimentary entrance of the top half takes in—and artistically gifted, since the emotional drives for Joyce are generated mainly in the bottom half.[39]

Joyce in his previous works does sometimes treat his genitals as separate characters. Indeed, Joyce once gave a name to his own penis—Ellwood—perhaps after the "gypsy" student who is the original of Temple in *A Portrait*.[40] In addition, the Parable of the Plums in *Ulysses* treats two old women on top of the Nelson Pillar. These two identical wrinkled bags dropping seeds from the top of an erection symbolize a Dublin almost completely debilitated in its tripartite genital area.

There is an even more relevant example in *A Portrait*: in a richly comic passage, Joyce describes the independence of the penis. In chapter 3, after the Hellfire sermon, young Stephen, paralyzed with fright, contemplates his genital area with horror:

> It feels and understand and desires. What a horrible thing! Who made it to be like that, a bestial part of the body able to understand bestially and desire bestially? Was that then he or an inhuman thing moved by a lower soul? His soul sickened at the thought of a torpid snaky life feeding itself out of the tender marrow of his life and fattening upon the slime of lust. O why was that so? O why? (139–40)

In the Library scene in *Ulysses*, Stephen produces a critical analysis of *Othello* in which he uses this personification of the two parts of the mind and body of Shakespeare: "His unremitting intellect is the hornmad Iago ceaselessly willing that the moor in him shall suffer" (9.1023–24). Shakespeare's violent, cruel, puritanical intellect, disgusted like Shaun with his lower half and his lower urges, destroys the Moor in himself as Shaun wishes to do with Shem.

Shaun as the top half of the body and Shem as the lower half provides a text for the whole of Books II and III of the *Wake*, which can be seen to outline the psychosexual maturing of the human male, proceeding from the initial dissociation of the top and bottom halves of the body to their ultimate uneasy reconciliation in the mature man.

Shaun throughout the book displays the horror of the puritan (especially the English middle-class puritan) at the more disreputable features of the body. In this section, and throughout the *Wake*, Joyce seems to comment on the disgust of many of his critics when confronted with the physical facts of life mentioned in his books. Yet upon examination it becomes clear that Joyce is far from having a "cloacal obsession" (H. G. Wells's phrase). In *A Por-*

trait there are few references to dung and urine, and only one fart. In *Ulysses*, in which it seems Joyce deliberately tried to include every human activity, he is moderate in his reference to defecation, urination, masturbation, blowing and wiping the nose, farting, and, in Molly's case, menstruation. (There are only two actual farts in *Ulysses*, though memorable ones.) Therefore Joyce could argue that he was quite restrained in his reference to the more embarrassing activities of the human body. Yet if nervousness over the facts of life touched even the great literary rebel Ezra Pound, with his disgust at Bloom in the privy, it pervaded the pure Platonic artists and intellectuals of Dublin, of whom Joyce wrote in "The Holy Office": "That they may dream their dreamy dreams, / I carry off their filthy streams" (151).

Joyce shows this modern middle-class squeamishness operating constantly in the pure Shaun. In the sections of the *Wake* that treat the brothers, Joyce muses on this peculiarity of the modern puritan. In the course of I.7, Shaun obsessively describes the embarrassing habits and habitat of his smelly brother. Shem's incredibly messy house, the Haunted Inkbottle, is a mousefarm filled with trash, filth, and IOUs (182.30–184.10). Shaun has called Shem's farting habit a sin; Shaun apparently sees cleanliness as superior to godliness, and judges Shem's personal habits as outward signs of Shem's inward disgrace.

Shaun extends his revulsion over his brother's habits to the greater sin of being a romantic artist. Shaun seems to regard Shem as the ultimate romantic artist. Shem's own life provides the material for his art, and Shem's own body and body fluids provide the physical material for his creation; Shem writes on his own skin with ink made from his own excrement and urine.[41]

Shem's bodily parchment is a metaphor: Joyce once said he was incapable of encountering anything that would not be relevant to his art. His own life, written on his skin, provided all the material for all of his works. As Stephen Dedalus says in the Library scene in *Ulysses*, "His own image to a man with that queer thing genius is the standard of all experience, material and moral" (9.432–33). Shem the artist is described by his unfriendly brother as "self-exiled" (184.6–7). Joyce derives the word from one of his favorite writers, the ultimate romantic, Byron (*Childe Harold's Pilgrimage*, canto 3, verse 16). The furniture on which Shem is writing the mystery of himself (184.9–10) is the material of the world as perceived by the senses, which is the "vegetable world" taken by Stephen Dedalus in *A Portrait* as the material for his art.

Joyce describes clearly the nature of the artwork created from the artist's self-image. It is not, as one might think—and as Shaun certainly *does* think—

a selfish, uselessly individualized portrait. The artist, writing of himself on his own body, produces a text in the present tense, thereby "reflecting . . . his own . . . person . . . , transaccidentated" (186.1–5). Joyce's coinage "transaccidentated," modeled on "transubstantatiated," shows how the process of creation changed the actual physical body of James Joyce into the words and paper of his works. The "substance" of Joyce changes its "accidents"—its appearance to the senses—but not its essence. Joyce foresees his own death and subsequent career. His "substance" once animated a flesh-and-blood body, but on January 13, 1941, the accidents of James Joyce changed from flesh and blood into the ink, paper, glue, and cloth of all the copies of his works. In this sense, the transaccidentated James Joyce is still with us, and will be as long as any copy of his works remains. Shaun delivers to us the physical objects of James Joyce's immortality—the ink, paper, glue, and cloth. Shem provides the "dividual" (divided) words themselves, as taken down by dictation from the song of his mother, ALP, about her husband, HCE.

Joyce also provides a vivid metaphor that elucidates this ultimate romantic definition of the artist, his works, and his immortality. The artist's works are the projection of his self-image, and the material of his works derived from his own life; here Joyce shows the artist deriving even his paper and ink entirely from himself. Shem is denied paper and ink by publishers, a detail stemming from Joyce's own experiences at the hands of the dozen or so publishers who rejected *Dubliners*. The artist must therefore provide parchment from the skin of his own body, and ink from his urine and excrement.[42]

However, the artist pays a severe price, physically and mentally, for this painfully slow act of self-definition: his own self became "chagreenold and doriangrayer" (186.8). Joyce's phrase "each word that would not pass away" (186.6) quotes the Bible (Matthew 24:35, Mark 13:31, Luke 21:33), but Joyce means it literally—that the word of Joyce will remain as long as the physical copies of his works last.

Joyce knew that he was paying a heavy price for this secular resurrection. The self that squirts ink on paper shrinks, and grows old, and becomes blind. The word "chagreenold" refers to Balzac's *La Peau de Chagrin*, in which the hero is presented with a vest of donkey hide which has the property of granting the wearer any wish, but which shrinks with each wish until the wearer is suffocated. Balzac (and Joyce) is here symbolizing the physical and moral price exacted by the fulfillment of desire. The paired word "doriangrayer" refers to the price paid by the criminal Dorian Gray, in which only his picture shows the dreadful results of his crimes. Joyce is here testifying to the drain on his health of his constant creation—shortwindedness and aging. Joyce also comments on his threatening blindness with green and gray and black,[43] evoking the three increasingly severe sorts of blindness as described in German—*grüner Star*, *grauer Star*, and *schwarzer Star*. Joyce indeed knows that he is paying a heavy price for his creation.

After the first broadside from Shaun on Shem's shortcomings, the forces of repression appear. At 186.19 a policeman in the *Wake*, who represents these forces, is astonished at the disreputable artist in his precinct. In a paragraph loaded with references to the paralyzed inhabitants of *Dubliners*, the policeman tries to reestablish the paralytic order that has been threatened by the artist. Shem, drunk and sentimental, claims that he was only trying to bring two gallons of porter home to his mother (or trying to produce moisture in his mother's genitals). The sacred word "mother," heard as "murder" by the cop, totally outrages the Germanic guardian of public order (187.13, 15). The policeman is an avatar of Shaun as a violent enforcer of order. This is made clear when Shaun addresses the drunken Shem in Danish: "How do you do today, my dark sir?" (186.32).[44]

The policeman symbolizes an important element in Shaun, an element that sums up the violence in him, the rage for order. At this point in the book, the dangerous anger that has been rising up in Shaun during his recitation of the crimes of his brother sweeps away the last of his restraint. Carried away by his fear and his rage at his own lower self and his own tendencies toward violence, Shaun finally loses what remains of his temper at the reminder of the sexuality of his mother—nay, the mere mention of her in the context of his lower half—and he begins to address Shem with violent directness.

Shaun, the outraged policeman, takes on the role of Justius (187.24–193.30), and as an incarnation of angry justice accuses Shem, his lower half, of madness. Reason belongs to Shaun, the top half with the head, which views the irrational lower half with horror and anger. Justius then "points the deathbone" (Australian magic object), and "the quick are still" (193.29)—that is, all of moving reality is frozen into a succession of still photographs, like a strip of movie film. Shaun's deathbone is his skull, in which the analysis of his outrageous brother has been taking place. The skull performs an act of rational analysis, which breaks up the problem of Shem into controllable images. In the movie that is about to start, Shaun creates the series of still photographs that, when projected in Time (Shem's principle, with sound added by Shem), makes up the illusion of continuous visual reality. The sound film starts with twilight lighting-up time in II.1 and ends with rounds of applause at the end of III.4 as the shades of night begin to pass away.

Joyce knew very well the workings of the eye, after his many eye operations. This knowledge, acquired by hard experience, he then used for his art. The principle of the eye is digital; that is, the functioning of the eye depends crucially upon a set of discrete individual events. Each retinal cell reacts to a photon of light by an electrochemical change. Then all of these individual electrochemical events are summed up into groups, and the whole is transmitted by the separate strands of the optic nerve to the visual centers of the brain. The visual, then, has digitized the moving world. It points the death-bone, and the swift, alive, living, moving actions of the world are "still," fixed into millions of individual unmoving actions.

In response to his brother's attack, Shem replies as Mercius[45] (193.31–195.4). Shem's sense is hearing. However, Mercius does not champion the audible over the visible; he includes both senses in a complete presentation of the world. Unlike the self-centered diatribe of Justius, Mercius's gigantic sentence, an orgasm-cadenza of released and releasing fluid, does not offer a defense of the individual Shem but rather a generous portrayal of both brothers. Hearing, unlike sight, is an analogue process; that is, it operates continuously. The vibrations of the air caused by an audible stimulus form a continuous wave, which in its turn causes a continuous alteration in the fluid in the organ of Corti, in the inner ear. The hairlike structures in the inner ear then react to the continuous waves of sound and send signals to the brain. While Shaun has defensively digitized the visual world as Justius, Shem as the generous, forgiving Mercius combines the visible and the audible to start the projection of the real/reel world.

The River of Time

In response to Shem's creation of the text, the river of time and reality begins to flow downstream. Shem's complex answer as Mercius takes up the best part of a page and a half. However, by leaving out several independent clauses, the basic structure becomes clear. After a ten-line spate of personal pronouns mingling "I" with "you," finally "we" emerges. Then the subject and the predicate of this huge sentence declare that it is to *both* sons that "mummy" is coming, "coming" in every sense of the word (194.12, 14, 17, 22). In this incestuous act, the two sons are (facing downstream) the right bank (Shaun) and the left bank (Shem), between which the river is to begin moving out to sea. The tide that turned at the end of the book to flow upstream, westward—the Liffey is tidal as far as Island Bridge—now turns eastward and starts on its journey downstream to the sea.

The actual TIME narrative is almost ready to begin. At this point, however, time flows too slowly to make up a complete sound-film of the world. The sound of the film, Shem's principle, begins to be audible before Shaun's principle, sight, causes the world to appear. "Quoiquoiquoiquoiquoiquoiquoiq!" (195.6)—the long word that the Movietone sound track is producing—resembles the sound made by an old-fashioned movie projector when it is first turned on. In early sound films, sound began before the visible part of the film appeared.

This croaking stutter is actually an attempt to pronounce "O," the first sound of the Anna Livia Plurabelle chapter, the last chapter in Book I. The Anna Livia chapter presents a shadowy twilight picture of the real world, and provides a transition to the actual narrative beginning with Book II.

The sound also marks the beginning of the flow of the river to the sea.[46] At the union of Justius and Mercius, the Liffey has begun to flow downstream, the right way for narrative. The Liffey ebbs and flows twice daily to a sexual rhythm with the sea tide, a constant secular copulation with her husband-father-sons. To mark and cause the beginning of this process, Mercius "lifts the lifewand and the dumb speak" (195.5); that is, the still photographs created by Justius, accompanied by the continuous sound track created by Mercius, begin to constitute a sound movie. Joyce as the proprietor of the Volta Cinema knew a great deal about film projection; the true narrative in the *Wake* is a film, a sound film of the sort that, beginning in 1927, was being projected onto the walls of thousands of cinemas around the world.

The world is about to be produced in a TIME-narrative, a sound film with the brothers cooperating to produce the world. Their incestuous coupling with their mother produces the orgasm that lasts for two more books and ends only with the end of the *Wake*. The combined senses of Shem and Shaun—sound and sight—produce the world. The combination foretells the unification of Shem and Shaun in the course of Book III, which will eventually produce the new father.

Book I, Chapter 8: Of Time and the River

The Liffey is about to flow to the sea, though slowly. To understand this chapter, it would be helpful to consult a contemporary account of the river.

A modern book on the Liffey describes in detail the course of the river of Dublin, and the origin of its name:

> The River Liffey rises in the Wicklow Mountains between Kippure and Tonduff . . . in a circle of peat hags about 550 m above sea level and a short walk east of the mountain road from the Sally Gap to Glencree in County Wicklow. Passing under the little Liffey Head Bridge on that road some 3.2 km from Sally Gap, the stream flows west down through the Coronation Plantation to empty out as a substantial river into the Pollaphuca reservoir near Blessington. Joined in the reservoir by its first main tributary, King's River, which rises at the Wicklow Gap, it flows west towards Ballymore Eustace and Kilcullen. It then turns north and then northeast across Magh Life in County Kildare past Athgarvan, Newbridge, Clane, Straffan and Celbridge to Leixlip, where it is joined by its second major tributary, Rye Water, which rises near Kilcock.
>
> Now flowing east, the river enters County Dublin and passes through Lucan and Chapelizod to the weir at Islandbridge, where it becomes tidal. . . . Eleven kilometres further to the east it flows into Dublin Bay at its artificial mouth, man-made in the 18th and early 19th centuries, between the Poolbeg and Bull lighthouses. While the total length of the Liffey's course to this place is 110 km, its distance as the crow flies from there to the source is only 23 km. . . .
>
> The origin of the name of the river is uncertain. *The Annals of the Four Masters* record that the king of Ireland in 268 was Cairbre Liffea-chair, and it is suggested that he was so named because he was fostered near the River Liffey. Later in the first millenium, that part of County Kildare lying within the loop of the river was named Airthear-Liffe and Naas was its principal town. . . .
>
> Some 40 variations for the name of the river have been recorded. They are divided into two groups, those beginning with the Irish word for river, such as Abhainn Liphthe (*Annals of the Four Masters*), Aven-lif, Avenesliz, Avon Liffey and Anna Liffey, and those using only the river-name, such as Liphi (*Annals*), Liffe, Lyffye and Lybinum. The accepted name for the river at present is Liffey, although the form Anna Liffey has been frequently used in official documents in recent centuries. This form will have led to Joyce's use of Anna Livia Plurabelle in *Finnegans Wake*.[47]

Many of the names in this description of the Liffey occur in I.8 and elsewhere in the book.

The scene for this chapter shows two banks of the Liffey with two washer-women, one on each bank. On the left bank there is a tree, and on the right bank there is a stone. The two washerwoman become the tree and the stone at the end of the chapter, as the dusk deepens.

The film (the TIME narrative) is beginning slowly, hence all that can be seen is a dark blur, a twilight effect. The film is not running quickly enough for "persistence of vision," the illusion of movement from the presentation of still photographs at a pace of more than thirteen frames a second. However, the sound track has already begun; we hear the conversation of the washer-women beginning with the word "O," which is also a feminine symbol.

First Section: The Washers at the Ford (196.1–200.32)

The speaker, one of the washerwomen, wants to know all about Anna Livia (196.1–3). The story of the great river includes the description of her dif-ficult life with her disreputable and eventually comatose husband, who was always trying to combine marriage with making love (196.24). He was from the beginning a haughty, swaggering, violent creature with a ready line of blather despite a stutter (197.5), and he was always being fiercely persecuted and prosecuted—The King versus Humphrey (196.21).

The garrulous Washers at the Ford (Irish traditional ghosts, who wash the linen of those about to die) go into all the dirty linen about HCE and ALP, beginning with his first invasion of Ireland (197.28–198.9). And just how were they married? Were they married in Adam and Eve's, or just spliced by a ship captain (197.11–13)? Note that here the Franciscan church by the Liffey quays is named in the right order—Adam and Eve's, not Eve and Adam's—since the river is now flowing the right way. However, one washerwoman scornfully dismisses the idea that they were married in church with all due ceremony, with the organ playing the "Wedding March" from *Lohengrin*—"Don Dom Dombdomb" (197.17–18).

Despite his rover fierceness, HCE ended up as a sluggish husband, always asleep and snoring like a grampus. Anna Livia often tried to rouse him, to help him make love to other women, to rouse him by showing him little street girls dressed in the colors of the rainbow. These procuring activities of ALP symbolize Life presenting the beauties of the multicolored world to fallen, comatose Man.

Many poets have declared that the task of poets is to wake up the cliche-dulled senses of human beings, to make the world vivid, as Coleridge quoted Novalis. Anna Livia, Life herself, tries to make the beauty of the world evident to her weary husband, to make ordinary life vivid to human beings. This was Joyce's own task, declared as early as *A Portrait*: After the interview with the director, Stephen rejects the ordered life of the church for the "disorder, the misrule and confusion of his father's house and the stagnation of vegetable life, which was to win the day in his soul" (162). Later, on the beach, Stephen becomes wildly exhilarated at the call of life to his soul (IV). The encounter with the bathing girl on the beach drives home the artistic task of his life: "To live, to err, to fall, to triumph, to recreate life out of life!" (IV). In his discussion with Lynch, Stephen delivers an expanded version of his artistic credo: "to try . . . to express, to press out again, from the gross earth or what it brings forth, from sound and shape and colour which are the prison gates of our soul, an image of the beauty we have come to understand—that is art" (V).

In this section of the *Wake*, Stephen's credo is represented symbolically by the endeavor of Anna Livia to wake up the sleeping senses of her comatose husband, that is, of time-dulled humanity. However, there is a realistic source for this symbol: Joyce may have got the idea for Anna Livia's activity from the reputed activity of Yeats's wife, Georgie: "George . . . encouraged her husband in his excursions and liaisons. . . . Sean O'Faolain . . . spoke of George as 'almost his procuress'" (Alldritt, 334).

Second Section: The Song of Anna Livia (200.33–201.20)

The washerwomen then relate the song (201.5–20) that Anna Livia used to sing to console herself while waiting for her comatose husband to wake and make love to her, to bore/bear her down (201.11–12)—the "bore," looking forward to the end of the book, being a strong incoming tidal surge in a river.

And what was the song she sang? asks one of the washerwomen, who is violently beating the dirt out of the underwear of a minor Irish poet, Denis Florence MacCarthy. In *Ulysses* Bloom dismisses MacCarthy's brand of Irish lyric poetry, five pages of which he has read, as "the dreamy creamy stuff," fit only for nuns and nymphs to quote in their attempt to destroy the manhood of heroes.[48] The washerwoman obviously shares Bloom's opinion.

However, Anna Livia's poem is not of this feeble sort. In fact, it is the first installment of the letter to the Lord that Anna Livia is constantly creating, the letter that finally comes out in its clearest form at the end of the book. This poem is the only time Anna Livia speaks in the whole of the book until the end. In fact, Anna Livia and Molly Bloom share this trait among many; neither of them directly intervenes in the action of the book she underlies, preferring to keep the last word for herself—Molly in the Penelope episode, and Anna Livia in her letter and "Soft morning, city!" soliloquy at the end of the *Wake*. The only speech that Molly produces in the course of *Ulysses* until the Penelope episode is a few irritable words to Leopold in the morning. Here we have the *Wake* equivalent of Molly's few words.

There is the possibility that we may be hearing Anna Livia as reported by one of the washerwomen. However, the dialect of the washerwomen— lower-class Cork dialect, as evidenced by Joyce's August 1929 recording of the end of the Anna Livia chapter—is very different from that of Anna Livia's delicate four-stanza poem, which is filled with the river goddess's combination of lyric glory and realism.

In the first and second stanzas of her poem, she swears by earth and heaven that her backside (or bankside) is worn away while she is sitting and waiting for her husband to wake up and make love to her (201.5, 8). In the third stanza, she sighs that there is no money in the house. In the fourth stanza, she shows her impatience with household duties, with her landlocked flow. In a last wild impulse, she looks ahead to her release at the end of the book and declares that if it were not for the sides of the constricting but cosy river banks that enclose her, she would leap out over the land to the swamps of the Tolka or the beach at Clontarf, to feel the wild sea breeze and the rush of the seawind into her mouth (201.17–20).

Third Section: How Anna Livia Wooed and Won Her Husband: The Attiring of Anna Livia (201.21–209.9)

Anna Livia's birth and early love affairs are detailed in reverse order, from the time when she first ran away from her nurse, to the time she was licked by a hound (204.9–20), to the time when two lads in scout's breeches went through her (204.6), to the time when a hermit, Michael Arklow, plunged his hands into the young river's hair and kissed her over and over again (203.17–26). (See Fordham 2007.)

Joyce often in the *Wake* gives physical descriptions of his characters. Here he gives a detailed and spectacular description of Anna Livia, the river goddess (206.29–207.14). As Matthew Hodgart noted (16), the description is based on that of Hera in the *Iliad*, book 14, as she prepares to seduce Zeus. But Joyce outdoes even Homer, since Joyce's goddess is richly attired in river attributes. Anna lets her hair fall in devious winding coils, and shampoos herself with water and health-giving river mud (206.29–32). Next she oils her bottom, her belly, and her genitals with unguents derived from river plants (206.32–207.1). She then weaves a garland for her hair, and makes bracelets and anklets and a necklace of river rubble, of Irish rhinestones and shells (207.1–7). Last, she makes up her face. She uses river mud as eyeshadow to look Russian and mysterious, like the great dancer Anna Pavlova, the name delivered with a smoky Slavic accent so that she is now Annushka Lutetia-vitch Pufflovah (207.7–9)—Lutetia, the original Roman name for Paris, de-riving from Latin *lutum*, "mud." She paints her lips and daubs her cheeks, her *pommettes* in French (207.10), with shades of red from infrared (strawberry) to ultraviolet, as befits one who has been a Rainbow Girl seducing fallen Man.

The lovely nature goddess now sends her virgin maids, both named for cherries, to her husband with a request for permission to leave for a while, and then, singing a version of an old song, "The clock strikes nine, the stars brightly shine, there's somebody waiting for me," flows off with her son Shaun's mailbag on her shoulder.

Her clothes are described on 208.6–26. She is wearing ploughboy's boots, a conical hat with streamers and a pin and a yellow band (crowned with yellow gorse, like the Hill of Howth itself), eyeglasses, a fishnet veil, pink stockings (salmon-colored and speckled), a haze-vapor blouse, stout stays (she is rather plump, as we see at 255.29–36), orange knickerbockers, a black and tan (!) jacket of many colors—a "joseph" (208.17)—with green epaulets and white trimmings, a pair of cigarettes in her garters, a belted corduroy overcoat with alphabet buttons (208.20), named here for the Alpheus river in Greece, and Coleridge's Alph the sacred river—two among the many river names in this chapter. She bears a fourpenny bit in either pocket to ballast her (four signifying the forces of history), and a clothespin on her nose. Chewing on something "quaint" and trailing a long skirt over the landscape, off she goes!

Fourth Section: Anna Livia's Gifts to Her Children (209.10–213.10)

Life, represented by Anna Livia, has attempted to present her comatose hus-band with the delights of the phenomenal world, in the persons of the Rainbow Girls, apparently all in vain. However, she has presents for her children as well.

As Anna Livia carries her son Shaun's mailbag over her shoulder (207.18), one of the gossips asks about the bag's contents (209.10). It turns out these include gifts for her 111 (or 1,001) children (209.27–29).

At this point Joyce enlarges on a profound pun, first made in his early essay "A Portrait of the Artist." There he describes the past as a "fluid succession of presents" leading up to the present time. In the *Wake*, present *tenses* and presents as *gifts* are conflated; here Anna Livia, the fluid life of all of us, gives each of us a succession of "presents." These appear as a succession of still photographs (contributed by Shaun).

Now we see what Life gives its children. Some of the "presents" are grim indeed; many of her children drowned, or died of disease, or killed themselves.[49]

- 210.7–8: Her son the Guardsman will receive a bullet, and it looks as if the soldier will end up shot in the stomach.
- 210.9–10: A poor little girl, living at the far end of a lane, is dying of tuberculosis, with the characteristic hectic flush on her cheeks.
- 210.12–13: Little Johnny Walker, obviously a drunk from his name, has acquired a red nose and heavy dangling hands from the circulatory problems induced by his alcoholism.
- 210.29: A humble wooden rosary for St. Brigid, the most famous Irish female saint (M), holds perhaps a suggestion that even the sainted Brigid must scrub the oaken floor of her husband's house.
- 211.2–3: Here is a biting satirical reference to two of Joyce's contemporaries, the two Irish Nobel Prize winners, Yeats and Bernard Shaw (M). Joyce's nicknames for Yeats and Shaw conceal a serious political issue— the demoralization of Irish writers before their English audience. Referring to Yeats as a will-of-the-wisp suggests that Yeats is exaggerating and expurgating his researches into Irish legends to amuse an English audience. Shaw's appellation suggests that his bark has become worse than his bite; that is, Shaw talks revolution but his contribution to real overthrow is much less than it seems. In fact, Joyce seems to refer to Yeats and Shaw as two of those Irish clowns who dedicated themselves to amusing the English rather than threatening them. In *Ulysses*, Stephen makes a cruel comment about such Irish writers amusing the English; he refers to such a pliant Irishman as "A jester at the court

of his master, indulged and disesteemed, winning a clement master's
praise" (2.43–45).

- 211.5–6: Life also has a present for Joyce himself: a Clongowes Wood
cross on his back for Sunny Jim. Joyce may have carried a load of guilt
on his back for his "libertine" beliefs, which conflicted with the orthodoxy enforced at Clongowes Wood. Yet he could not utterly reject the
orthodoxy he learned there, so his personality was split—Twin Jim.
Joyce adopted comedy as his "perfect manner in art" sometime during the writing of *Ulysses*: with the entrance of Leopold Bloom, Joyce
showed his mastery of comedy, and never looked back. However, comedy was a large part of Joyce's real personality, despite his grimly portrayed Stephen Dedalus. Joyce's family called him "Sunny Jim" (M).

- 211.14: One of the presents may have a reference for contemporary
readers: a blue bag for "Funny Fitz." Funny Fitz is to acquire sadness, a
reference to the changeover of the boys in II.2. A blue bag is sometimes
used to calm bee stings, but the phrase might refer to the bluing used
in laundry. However, it is just possible that Joyce was referring here
to John Francis "Honey Fitz" Fitzgerald (1863–1950), a Massachusetts
state senator (1893–94), congressman (1895–1901, 1919–21), mayor of
Boston (1906–9, 1910–13), and—most prominent for modern readers—Joseph Kennedy's father-in-law and John Fitzgerald Kennedy's
maternal grandfather. Honey Fitz, for whom Jack Kennedy named his
yacht, was a prominent Irish American, perhaps one of those who got
a swelled head and a large sense of his importance in the New World—
one of those transplanted Irishmen who take "number nine in yang-
see's hats" (213.36).

- 211.16–17: Joyce may also be paying off old scores with the phrase donating "a Rogerson Crusoe's Friday fast for Caducus Angelus Rubiconstein." As M notes, *caducus angelus* means "fallen angel," but the whole
name Caducus Angelus Rubiconstein is likely a reference to one of the
objects of Joyce's wrath, Dr. A. S. W. Rosenbach—"Rosy Brook"—who
bought a book, the manuscript of *Ulysses*, for less than Joyce thought
it was worth. "Caducus Angelus" suggests "caduceus," the symbol
of medicine, Dr. Rosenbach's profession. What Joyce is wishing Dr.
Rosenbach is a "black fast"—one featuring hunger and thirst, one with
very stringent conditions; the reference to Crusoe's Friday contributes
the blackness.

- 211.26–28: Joyce comments on an old subject here, public executions. ALP donates a guillotine shirt for one redbreasted criminal and hempen suspenders for another. Here is a ghastly detail of public executions: the shirt of a prisoner to be guillotined is snipped off in preparation for the lethal blade, which then makes the breast of the prisoner red with blood. The suspended Brennan on the Moor is the hero of a famous Irish ballad about a highwayman.

- 211.29–30: Here is another enigma for the reader to solve. ALP is donating a C3 peduncle for someone named Karmalite Kane. C3 was the indication in Britain during World War I of someone rejected for the military draft, the equivalent of 4F in the United States since World War II. A peduncle is a type of neck found in plants. Therefore, what Karmalite Kane will acquire will be a thin, unusable neck, probably the result of hanging, a topic that is in the neighborhood. But who is Karmalite Kane? A clue: the Harmsworth Press headquarters in London was and is in Carmelite House. The two Irish brothers, later Lord Northcliffe and Lord Rothermere, both born in Chapelizod, ran the sensational papers of the Harmsworth Press, beginning with the *Daily Mail*, the first million-circulation daily in the world. They would both qualify for the title of "Cain" for their debasing of public standards of information and their inflammatory effect on public opinion. Lord Northcliffe, whose eerie slogan (borrowed from one of his editors) was "Everything counts; nothing matters," eventually went mad. (By an odd coincidence, the most famous fictional newspaper owner of all time is Charles Foster Kane, the hero of Orson Welles's 1941 film. To be sure, it is unlikely that Joyce knew about *Citizen Kane*, which was released after publication of the *Wake*, but rumors of the making of the film might have reached him from Herman Mankiewicz, or some other person connected with the production.)

All in all, Joyce here gives the reader a disillusioned and ominous view of the "presents" distributed by the even-handed mother goddess to her unfortunate children. Then, after assigning various presents to the loafers who spread the tale of her guilty husband, Anna Livia gives to twenty-five little girls the gift of menstruation (212.16), the preparation for motherhood. She also gives to the boys bunches of grapes (212.16–17), which R&O identify as testicles.

"What a bagful!" exclaims the other washerwoman (212.20). And indeed it is a great bag full of Life's "presents," most of which the recipients would rather not have.

Fifth Section: Transition to Night (213.11–216.5)

The fifth section is one of the great sections of the book, second only to Anna Livia's "Soft morning, city!" dawn monologue. Joyce wrote about this section, especially the exquisite ending, "Either the end of [I.8] is something or I am an imbecile in my judgment of language" (*Letters*, 1:249). He later wrote that he was prepared to "stake everything" on the ending of the Anna Livia chapter (*Letters*, 3:163).

Joyce always shows especially great mastery in describing twilight and dawn, transitional areas in time. Here, by subtle manipulation of language, he shows twilight falling on the Liffey. After an initial paragraph of gossip by the washerwomen, the great final section begins.

This is the end of the SPACE episodes, and the true beginning of narrative TIME (213.12). Every story has an ending (213.12), and the SPACE story is ending here. The washerwomen lament the loss of Anna Livia's children; they all left her and went overseas, leaving only a few fragments of clothing (214.5). At this point Joyce is giving a comic rendering to the great lament of Nora in Synge's *Riders to the Sea*: "And isn't it a pitiful thing when there is nothing left of a man who was a great rower and fisher, but a bit of an old shirt and a plain stocking?"

Now TIME begins slowly, with twilight. The two old women hear the evening Angelus bell, which is here conflated with the Zurich ceremony of the end of winter, Sechseläute, and therefore with the end of the reign of the repressive father, the development of the children into the new father and mother, and the beginning of the TIME sequence: "Pingpong! There's the Belle for Sexaloitez! And Concepta de Send-us-Pray!" (213.18–19). The Swiss ceremony is combined with the loitering for sex of courting couples by the river, and the Conception by the Holy Ghost of the Messiah, the message of the Angelus itself. This Angelus anticipates the midnight Angelus, an invention of Joyce, to mark the later destruction of the Winter King himself by his children (379.27–30).

However, at the very ending of the SPACE narrative, the final passages of *Finnegans Wake* itself are prefigured. The blazing sun, which is to be seen dimly by Anna Livia at the end of the book, now appears three times, almost as a hallucination, to one of the washerwomen, the one who complains that she has been up since dawn washing rags for her tennis champion son (214.22–27). The dazzling white tennis flannels that bedeck the new son-husband-lover at the very end of the book here make an appearance three times; the washerwomen suddenly perceive hallucinations of a blazing figure at the mouth of the river, an anticipation of Anna Livia's view of her great lover the risen sun, who is also her husband-son (214.11–12, 30; 215.1).

There is another paragraph of gossip, in which it is asserted that we are all the children of Gammer and Gaffer. HCE had "married" the Rainbow Girls, had accepted the beauties of the physical world given by God to fallen Man, but Anna Livia was in the end the true wife (215.21–22). HCE is clearly identified as the scapegoat of the city of Dublin (215.27)—an identification that will reemerge at the climax of II.3 as the father-scapegoat is about to be destroyed by his children (373.12).

Then comes the final passage, a great display of linguistic technique by Joyce. The words become indistinct; the noise of the river rises as the flow of time becomes stronger. The washerwomen cannot hear each other's words clearly. They turn into a tree and a stone, as the light dies into night (215.28–36; 216.1–5).

2

Book II (*FW* 217–400)

The Age of Heroes (Vico)

Time Medium

Time and the River Flow Forward

TWILIGHT TO MIDNIGHT

In Book II, TIME begins with twilight—the time of "lighting up" (219.1), a real time usually listed in English and Irish newspapers of the period—and continues until midnight. However, there is a second, overlying TIME schema in these chapters. In addition to occupying a few dark hours, the four chapters of Book II occupy the years from the birth of the children to their puberty and early maturity. In four separate chapters, the children develop from early childhood (II.1), through early adolescence and puberty (II.2), to the border of adulthood and the overthrow of the father (II.3), to young sexuality as Tristan and Isolde (II.4).

In this second schema, the children mature intellectually as well as physically.

- In II.1 Shem acquires his magic power of creation; it is from Hell and his own lower regions that his linguistic power arises. His power is an analogue power as opposed to a digital one; that is, Shem's power is the power to match the continuity of the world with his continuous language, when he makes the dumb speak by means of a magic wand (195.5). With his magic creative power he introduces Issy to her own magic power, a sexual one. The two enlightened children then proceed to educate Shaun.

- In II.2 Shaun acquires the power of rational creation, a type of creation possessed only by human beings. He learns to draw bounding lines onto and into undivided reality, as envisaged by Nicholas of Cusa and systematized by Descartes. In this way, Shaun has learned to create a humanly describable universe, a four-dimensional Cartesian coordinate space. When Shaun directs his own magic tool, the living become frozen into still photographs (193.29–30)—that is, Shaun is introduced to a "digital" view of the world by the devices of Shem and Issy. Shaun's view of the world is basically "unreal"—he creates still photographs of a changing universe. However, the digital method and the analogue method together, Shaun and Shem, form Shimar Shin, the third soldier, and create a truly human picture of the universe.

- In II.3 the children attack their father and destroy his power. Their eyes and their ears have been opened. They see the world with their own senses, and do not accept their father's version.
- In II.4 the enlightened children, now one man and one woman, engage in kissing and cuddling as Tristan and Isolde, while the envious Four Old Men salivate and babble, and fly about madly in the form of seagulls around the nuptial vessel of the pair.

Book II, Chapter 1: The Mime of Mick, Nick, and the Maggies; Sexual Knowledge Comes to Shem and Then to Issy

Chapter II.1 was published in 1934 as a book titled *The Mime of Mick, Nick and the Maggies*. It forms the first act of an eight-act play that takes up all of Books II and III, a play that covers the development of the children into adults, the loss of power by the parents, and the accession of the children as the new parents. At the end of Book II there is an intermission, and at the end of Book III, where the play ends, there are rounds of applause, amid some tears from the tiers of seats (590.30). The cyclical family history of Joyce comes full circle.

In letters to Harriet Weaver on November 22, 1930, and to Frank Budgen in July 1939 (*Letters*, 1:295, 406), Joyce describes the action in this chapter. In II.1 the three children are still at a preschool stage, or at most early primary school. The young children of HCE and ALP are in the street playing a game called Angels and Devils (or Colours), in which one player is supposed to guess a color agreed upon by the other players. Here Shem is "it" and the color, as it turns out, is heliotrope, the color of Issy's drawers (224.26–27). Shem fails three times, since his is still the spirit of darkness, and "heliotrope" means literally "turning to the sun." Light and the sun are symbols in the work of Joyce of the power of the creative father. Shem's mind is like that of Stephen Dedalus in the early chapters of *Ulysses*: "in my mind's darkness a sloth of the underworld, reluctant, shy of brightness, shifting her dragon scaly folds" (2.72–74); "a darkness shining in brightness which brightness could not comprehend" (2.160). In *Ulysses*, Stephen releases his own paternal light when he dents the shade of the brothel light in the Circe episode. In II.1 of the *Wake*, Shem has not yet destroyed the father's light and released his own. With his darkness of spirit, he cannot understand the sunlight of mature paternal power; he cannot turn to the sun, or comprehend "heliotrope."

However, his triple failure to guess the color of the sun (or Issy's underwear) has its dark compensations. After the first failed attempt, he runs into exile and begins to create poetry, a weak poetry of a feeble romantic nature, but nevertheless a magical creation. He then returns for a second attempt, with his new power, but fails again to comprehend sunlight. He retreats this time to the depths of Hell, where he acquires a dark magical power intimately linked to sexual power. When he returns for a third attempt, his last guess seems to be another failure, but it succeeds in sexually inflaming his sister Issy, or at any rate introducing her to the dark secrets of coupling.

The twilight has deepened to curfew time, and the parents call the children in to do their homework—the werewolf is abroad! Issy, however, lingers in the street, creating a rowdy song about the coming debilitation of her aging father, "Old Father Farley," who could hardly waddle after a platinum blonde. Her mother erupts into the dark street, snatches up the overexcited Issy, spanks her, and drags her into the house. But the damage has been done: Shem's devilish creative magic has introduced both of the young children to the prospect of maturity, both physical and psychological, and now Shem and Issy are on the road to the destruction of the father's power.

Introduction and Playbill (219.1–222.20)

The play called *The Mime of Mick, Nick and the Maggies* (219.18–19), presented in II.1 as the first act of an eight-act play possibly called *A Royal Divorce*, is the tale of Michael the archangel (Shaun, the good but violent little boy), Nick the devil (Shem, the dirty but creative little boy), and the Maggies (twenty-eight little girls, school friends of Issy, and Issy herself).

The mime, and by implication the entire eight-act play, takes place every night, beginning at twilight and ending at dawn. It takes place within each sleeper's dreams, within the Feenichts Playhouse (219.2), a constantly produced Phoenix Theatre, free for everyone—there is no fee, for dreams cost nothing.

Joyce produces a detailed playbill, including the source of the play, the props, the accompanying music, and descriptions of each of the characters, complete with the names of the actors of all the parts. It is not necessary to describe the characters; Joyce has provided complete descriptions of each and their characteristic actions in Book I. They are all old friends of ours by now: HCE, ALP, Shem, Shaun, Issy, and the rest.

Since we already know so much about the players in the drama, and the themes of their interplay, only a few extra notes about the playbill should be made.

1. The play is wirelessed all over the world in all the major branches of the Indo-European language family: Celtic, Hellenic, Germanic, Slavic, Iranian, Romance, and Sanskrit (219.17). Much of the important action of the narrative portions of the book is laid out in a few sentences in the playbill. It is predicted in this playbill that Glugg and Chuff—Shem and Shaun in their latest avatars—will fight and then be reconciled and washed thoroughly by their mother (220.13–18). The major action of the whole book centers on the rivalry and the eventual exchange of places by Shem and Shaun in the next chapter (287–92), which leads the way to the eventual bearing away of the brothers by their mother, Time: in the fable of the Mookse and the Gripes, a woman carries off both the Mookse and the Gripes. As the hymn says, "Time like a rolling stream bears all its sons away."

2. Later on in the playbill we learn that there are two songs in the play, which are sung by a light lyric tenor and a hugely resonant bass (222.6–11). The assignment of songs and voices strongly recalls the music afternoon in the Sirens chapter of *Ulysses*, in which a light love song, "M'appari" from *Martha*, is sung by a tenor, Simon Dedalus, and a song of bloody revenge is sung by the "bass barreltone" Ben Dollard. Here the singers of Anna's city, Annapolis, are distinguished by their male potency or the lack of it. The top half of the body, the French lyric tenor, lacks male potency, and the bottom half, a gruff German basso, has all too much testosterone. The light tenor is called a male soprano and is given a female name, Joan Mock-Comic (222.7–8). The song itself, sung by the lyric tenor Shaun, is French in style, possibly influenced by Offenbach, and is skittish and coy. It is addressed to a soldier by a female or effete admirer.

On the other hand, the bass aria sung by Shem is deeply serious: "O Hoffung der Rache, verlass' mich nicht"—"O Hope of Vengeance, Abandon Me Not." The singer, Jean Souslevin, is a persecuted basso version of Joyce's favorite tenor, John Sullivan, who is "under the lightning" of an avenging god (*levin* is an archaic English word for "lightning")—or slightly drunk, *sous le vin*, a possible reference to Sullivan's problem with alcohol. The "Hoffnung" phrase comes from the fourth act of Rossini's *Guillaume Tell*, an opera that was one of Joyce's favorites. In the original French, the phrase begins a recitative and goes "Ne m'abandonne point, espoir de la vengeance." However, it is sung not by a bass but by the tenor playing Arnold, one of John Sullivan's greatest parts.

3. The end of the *Wake* itself is described at the end of the credits as a "transformation scene" (222.14–20). The magnificent transformation scene is a traditional ending to a British pantomime, one in which all conflicts are resolved and the whole stage lights up with all the characters present. Here the scene is a radiant wedding of night and morning, or need and mourning, and the dawn of peace—a prediction of the lovely ending of the *Wake*.

4. The credits include the information that the entire narrative is "prompted" onward by Bergson's *élan vital* (221.22).

The Mime (222.21–227.18)

The Mime of Mick, Nick and the Maggies then begins. The "argument" and the play open with a confrontation between Mick and Nick, or Shem and Shaun, under their local names Glugg and Chuff. "Chuff" is derived from the English expression "to be chuffed," meaning to be suffused with joy. "Glugg" may signify Shem going down for the third time. The game consists of one player chosen as "it," who must guess a word decided by the other players. In this game Shem (Glugg) is "it," and tries on three occasions to guess the word "heliotrope." These attempts of Shem may correspond to the three times that Joyce trod Irish soil—first as a native-born Irishman, and two more times on trips to Ireland from the Continent in 1909 and 1912.

In the first encounter of Mick and Nick, Chuff appears as an avenging angel, Michael the archangel, commander of the forces of Heaven. But the devil himself, Old Nick, has entered Glugg, who is suffering from the problems of earthly life.

In the first appearance of Issy and the Maggies, the little girls flutter like bats in the evening air—a reminiscence here of the Nausicaa chapter in

Ulysses. Among them is Issy, who announces the code word "heliotrope," the answer to the game of Angels and Devils that is about to begin, and also the color of the little girls' underwear. At the same time, however, Issy is desperately and somewhat indecently flashing her underwear like Gerty MacDowell—trying to signal the question's answer to Glugg (223.9–11).

Glugg accepts the invitation to the game, but despite his brave attempts he can only produce indecency; he is the lower half, after all. His reply contains a coded invitation to play sexual games, the nature of which he does not yet understand (223.14–15). The function of II.1 is to introduce the sexual functions of men and women to each other, but it is early days yet, and both Issy and Glugg are, so to speak, feeling their way toward each other.

The game begins. Chuff, brandishing a flashing sword, threatens Glugg. However, despite the upraised sword, Chuff's lack of male sexual power is conveyed by the alteration of the name of St. John's Wood to a feminine version. Nevertheless, the punitive aspect of Chuff's challenge is clear, from the mention of Kilmainham Prison, which is on St. John's Road (M).

In response to the challenge, Glugg, ever the pacifist, merely offers him a "trefoil," a shamrock, perhaps as a sign of peace (223.22). Here we have the actual beginning of the game of Angels and Devils; Glugg is "it" and is puzzling over the answer to the question that Chuff and the little Maggies have devised.

Wrestling with the question, Glugg seeks help from the four elements (plus the quintessential "either") and also the four Evangelists, but with no result, despite the obvious triple anagram for "heliotrope" at 223.28. The embarrassed Glugg feels as if he would like to go to the toilet, or at least leave the scene. Poor Glugg!

The Four Old Men repeat discreditable tales about Glugg's parents, who have obviously passed on their worst traits to their elder son: his truly deplorable mother (224.10), and his father, with the hairy face (*Antlitz* in German) and bulging, flashing eyes. Both provide little assistance to their son, and neither will be able to help him out of his dilemma. His mother would sing a river song to her spouse, but Glugg, sunk in ignorance—still in the limbopool, the womb (224.17)—can make no sense of the song that the river sang to the mountain, the great love song of the mature lovers.

The little girls giggle at Glugg, and titter up an arpeggio: la-do-mi-sol la-do-mi-sol si!((225.1–2). Then they issue a vulgar invitation to him (225.4). They hold their noses to indicate their opinion of his smell (the lower half always has an embarrassing assortment of odors), and tell him to pee in his breeches and play with the steam. Finally, they call him a werewolf and declare him taboo (225.8). Glugg is indeed taboo, *sacer*: as a sinbearer too evil for human justice, he is left to the attention of the gods, a scapegoat designed to bear the sins of the people into the wilderness—a role Joyce often felt was his.

Glugg decides to try to answer the riddle. He dances forward to the tune of two nursery rhymes, "Soldier, soldier, will you marry me?" and "Here we go round the mulberry bush." Issy dances forward to the tune of another nursery rhyme, "On the mountain stands a lady, / Who she is I do not know. / All she wants is gold and silver, / All she wants is a nice young man" (225.9–17). She is still trying to help Glugg; it's driving her crazy that he is so dumb. If he would only talk instead of gawking, and if he would not worry so!

She takes a bold step and shows him her pretty bottom: "Hee!" she giggles, an echo of Alisoun's "Tehee!" in Chaucer's Miller's Tale after the infatuated dandy Absolon has kissed her pretty bottom (line 3740). Then follows Issy's invitation "Speak, sweety bird!" the very Chaucerian phrase that the infuriated Absolon grinds through his teeth as a deceptive invitation when he is standing with the red-hot coulter waiting for Alisoun to make another appearance (225.20).

Apparently emboldened by Issy's rear display, Glugg—who shares with Joyce a fondness for feminine endings—embarks on the first of three attempts to guess the color of Issy's just revealed drawers. Glugg's three guesses are tinged with hellfire, but the answer is three times no (225.22–27). The references to brimstone, hellfire, and demons in Shem's answers demonstrate his mind's darkness, his devotion to devilish powers. Here Shem within his darkness is not within sight of the sun; heliotrope is beyond him.

Glugg's three guesses are scornfully rejected by the Maggies, and he is ordered to run away. Then the Maggies declare their intention of dancing around Chuff: the solar Chuff is in his heaven; all's right with the world! Only Issy is sorry for the exiled Glugg, to the tune of "Oh dear, what can the matter be?" Since Issy is the spirit of the rain, the little flowery Maggies droop beneath the drops of her sorrow. However, their mood begins to change when the warm thought of Shaun the sun occurs to them (225.32–226.20). Chuff is sheriff of the skies, and he will hang Glugg.

At the mention of Chuff/Shaun, the sun, the spirit of light and sight, we see the Maggies, dressed in their pretty clothes, as they begin a magic dance (226.24–29). The Maggies have been captivated by the glory of Chuff; they are tied in a noose of love on a marriage night. Then Issy's vapors, lit by Chuff's rays, produce a rainbow (226.30–33).

The Rainbow Girls in the system of the *Wake* represent the nubile but not yet married state of womanhood, the next step after Maggiehood. The lovely circle dance of the Rainbow Girls is described, as a number of children's songs ring out. To the tune of "Sur le pont d'Avignon, l'on y danse, l'on y danse" (226.34) the children are described. They have danced before the Flood, and they will dance after the day of Judgment. The girls dance forward in space, but in an eerie and astonishing display of Joyce's imagination, they also dance forward through time (226.33–227.2)!

As the Rainbow Girls dance forward in space and time, they become older; in fact, their mature form as women is revealed. If these little girls develop into womanhood without altering their virginal states, their final lives will be extremely sad. Joyce found the state of preserved virginity simply another name for sterility; see "The Sisters," "Eveline," "Clay," and "The Dead" in *Dubliners*, and the Nausicaa chapter in *Ulysses*, for sad proof of this.[1]

Here the Rainbow Girls end up variously as the mistress of a merchant, or a "lady in waiting" who has become a disappointed drunk, or a hysterical neurotic invalid, or a widow living only with cats, or a vituperative actress resembling Mrs. Patrick Campbell (who was famous for her vicious tongue, and who drove Johnston Forbes-Robertson almost to suicide by her cruelty), or a pathetic religious fanatic whose only pleasure is confessing imaginary lovers to her confessor, or, last on the list, a wealthy but childless fortune-teller. Dreadful fates, all of them, a catalogue of paralyzed lives for another set of stories for *Dubliners*. This is what will inevitably happen to all little Maggies who worship only upper purity, in the form of the clean Shaun, and reject the lower side of life, the dark, dangerous Shem.

Fortunately, these sad events have not yet taken place, and may never take place. The girls dance backward in space and time, forsaking their "teenes" ("vexations" in Middle English). They become little girls again, resuming their gay, innocent, happy ways, unmindful of their sorry fates (227.11–18).

Shem's Activity in Exile; His Early Romantic Poetry (227.19–231.27)

Turning our eyes from these flowers of perfection, we see the return of Shem, who has been exiled and scorned. In fact, in exile he has displayed all the outward signs of inward disgrace (227.22–23). Like Wagner's Alberich in *Das Rheingold*, he rages because the pretty girls at home have scorned and ignored him. They are all against him, the little beasts (227.27–28).

The exiled Shem's first act (227.29–228.2) is to attack and reject all the seven sacraments (M), like Stephen at the end of *A Portrait* refusing to make his Easter duty. Now Shem is indeed the Artist as a Young Man. His first works in exile resemble all too closely other works by minor Scottish or Irish writers: Macpherson's ersatz Ossian, LeFanu, Lever, Carlton, Kickham, Gerald Griffin, John Mitchel, Oscar Wilde (as Sebastian Melmoth), Samuel Lover, and Michael Banim (M).

Shem also displays the diffuse socialism of the young Joyce and the politicoeconomic principles of Leopold Bloom's Bloomusalem—Free furloughs for everybody! With ham and eggs till further orders!—along with the young Joyce's determination to go his own way (228.36–229.6). Nobody can stop him from writing what he wishes. He attacks the English—the traditional task of Irish writers—and don't laugh if he seems a bit drunk at times! He is General Jinglesome. (Joyce's use of interior monologue was compared by Wyndham Lewis (400) to the spasmodic discourses of Mr. Jingle in the *Pickwick Papers*.)

At this point, in fact, it is *Ulysses* that Shem is meditating: parody titles for eleven of the eighteen chapters of *Ulysses* are listed (229.13–16). Shem intends to uncover the secrets of his parents and his relatives. He will show the big wide harse of his father and, as Joyce does only sixty-four pages later on, display the genitals of his mother (229.17–24).[2] He will just write it all down in black and white, all about himself and his life, and thereby gain the applause, social acceptance, and financial support of aristocratic sponsors, and like Byron win international fame for displaying his romantic despair: "Was life worth living? Was it worth leaving the Liffey? No!" (229.26–230.25).

Shem remembers two early Joyce works (M): an abortive play written at the age of eighteen, *A Brilliant Career* (230.27), and Joyce's first poem, "My cot alas that dear old shady home / Where oft in youthful sport I played / Upon thy verdant grassy fields all day / Or lingered for a moment in the bosom shade" (231.5–8). The *Wake* version of this poem contains sexual overtones missing in the idealistic original, such as the word "amourement" for "amusement." However, the young Shem thought that his poem was astonishingly beautiful; his ecstasy after its creation was as poignant as toothache. The poem was in reality (as the text comments) nothing but a pastiche of exceedingly minor Irish poets, such as John Boyle O'Reilly, Thomas D'Arcy McGee, Kevin Izod O'Doherty, and (our old friend whose collected poems are in Leopold Bloom's library) Denis Florence McCarthy. The terms describing their works include writhing, gumboils, wretched horseplay, coffins and dark acid, and dense flopping hurdygurdy music. However, the fledgling artist believed that his poem sounded like nothing on earth (231.21–22)!

Shem's Dance (231.28–234.5)

Encouraged by this evidence of creative powers, young Shem summons enough morale to return home to resume the game and make another try for the love of the Maggies and his sister. Shem sees his return as a phallic dash to Issy's yonic dot. Like the old cock, the young son will win through to the post of sexual head of the family—like father, like son (232.27–28).

Shem enters dancing, and the sentence describing his dance (232.36–233.3) reproduces exactly the rhythm of "The Sailor's Hornpipe," very likely the one on the first page of *A Portrait*:

Tralala lala
Tralala tralaladdy
Tralala lala
Tralala lala.

Its appearance on the first page of *A Portrait* gives Stephen one of the characteristic symbols of his poetic efficacy, the dance. (The other symbol introduced in that section is his song.) The hornpipe on this page of *FW* also resembles a Cornish song about the devil, which is one of Shem's major masks: "Here's to the devil, / With his little pick and shovel, / Digging tin by the bushel, / With his tail cock'd up!"[3]

Shem begins guessing at the colors of Issy's drawers for all he is worth, but he is hampered by his linguistic experience in Europe (233.11–14); that is, Shem's exile has introduced him to too many different words in different languages for the resultant style to be clear to home-dwellers. Joyce is here ironically justifying his style in the *Wake*. He argues that his *Wake* language, "Shemese" (425.3), has been usefully contaminated by all the languages he has learned in Trieste and Zurich, two cities notorious for the many languages spoken there. Writers who stay at home are hampered in a different way: these parochial litterateurs are limited to different dialects of English, like the Londoner's "naow" for "know." After Shem has failed to answer correctly, the text returns to the linguistic accusation, declaring that Shem speaks English like *une vache espagnole*. This phrase, which in French slang indicates imperfection in speaking French, was originally *un basque espagnol* (233.35): Spanish Basques could not be expected to speak standard French.

The still immature Shem, nervous before the objects of his desire, falters that he hates to trouble them (233.15), but makes the attempt anyway (233.21–26). Shem's envy of Shaun's popularity is shown here by his answers:

there is a definite bias toward the yellow of jealousy. The French *jaune* occurs twice, and the third answer "nunsibellies" may refer to the color of a nun's belly—yellowish brown through lack of bathing, an anticlerical joke that Joyce used in a letter to Italo Svevo (M).

However, Shem has failed again, and again is scornfully dismissed by the Maggies. After he runs away in shame, looking like bloody Hell, his pure brother enters. At this point Shem and Shaun are compared to Don Quixote and Sancho Panza: Shem, as the hopeless spirit of sorrow, is the Knight of the Woeful Countenance, while Shaun, as the merry top half of the body, is the garrulous, gluttonous Sancho Panza (234.1–8). Cervantes himself, through the mouth of Don Quixote, acknowledges that the don and Sancho are polar opposites:

> "I am amazed, Sancho, at the insensibility of your temper; you seem to me to be made of marble, or brass, not susceptible of any emotion or sentiment; I wake, while you sleep; I weep, when you are singing, I am fainting with hunger, while you are lazy and unwieldy with pure cramming."[4]

Sun Worship (234.6–239.27)

The Maggies, those fragrant little flowers, now abandon Shem to his fate and open up to the clean sun, Shaun. In the solar rays they show up their bright colors, release their volatile oils, and become a bed of scents. They are blessed with the solar trinity (235.4–5). They innocently anticipate pure marriage with Chuff.

Shaun appears as a glorified Chuff. He is dressed in Irish colors—gold (orange), white, and green—as befits a fervent (and violent) patriot. He is also a churchman, from tonsure to almoner's toes. Most spectacularly, as befits a solar apparition, he is a round-faced shining heavenly body. His visage is rotund, like the Buddha (or Humpty Dumpty); the Buddha's mother, Queen Mahamaya, dreamed that she was pregnant with an elephant (234.12–14). Chuff is also "mickly dazzly"; that is, he is a "mickey dazzler" in the Irish phrase—he dazzles the girls with his "mickey," his penis, or general male potency. He has an oily smile and loose curls, "looiscurrals," evoking Lewis Carroll, who also had an entourage of little girls.

The twenty-nine little girls adore Chuff because they can adore him from a great distance. They dance around him more and more swiftly, as the earth dances around the sun. Recall that Molly Bloom, that earth goddess, loved Leopold, her sun, because "I knew I could always get round him" (18.1579–80).

The dance of the little girls speeds up around Chuff, as "rapid" loses its vowels (234.19, 21). All of the little Dulcineas (234.23) are enthralled by pure, shining Chuff, but not to the point of actual sex. These worshippers will open up to the bright sun, but they are naysayers about physical matters. They have the same limited view of marriage as the pathetically virginal Gerty MacDowell, who recoiled from the physical aspects of sex. What poor Gerty delicately referred to as "all that other" (13.665–66) is also far from the minds of the little flowers: they declare that Chuff's intercourse with them cannot defile them (237.23–24). The sun is 93,000,000 miles from the earth, much too far for the abhorrent physical contact.

Since Chuff as the sun seems to be rising in the east, their worship is heavily tinged with Eastern religion, looking forward to Book IV; here it is Islam that tinges their worship. The Eastern glory is exquisitely described, complete with mosques and Turkish turquoise skies (234.36–235.8).

The Maggies' prayer to Chuff begins with a triple "Sanctus!" (235.9) tinted with solar yellow: *xanthos* is post-Homeric Greek for "yellow." The vision of marriage in the heads of the flowers is a little girl's imagination of life with a nonsexual husband, complete with jealous onlookers: the sight of the idyllic home of the pure lovers will make the mouths of the envious water (235.24–25). The married life of the delicious couple, Prince Le Monade and Lady Marmela Shortbred,[5] is filled with sweetness and light—marmalade, marzipan, ice cream sundaes, charming charmeuse garments, glittering glycerine jewels, Lydia Lively fans, and (daring!) perfumed cigarettes (235.32–236.2). The allusion to Dowson's "Cynara" is as far as the narrator will go in the direction of seductive properties.

The vision ends with one of the most delightful passages in the *Wake*, describing a lively Yuletide celebration with the pair alone singing and dancing, pouring champagne, and ending with an exultant cry embedding "Anna Livia" in "Alleluia!" (236.9–18). There follows a passage from Edgar Quinet about the survival of flowers through all of human history—through political changes and through the alterations brought about by Time, which assimilates undigestable elements—and a description of the excitement of the little flowers as they prepare to worship the sun (236.19–237.9). Their understamens are open and presented to the sun; after all, flowers display their sexual members to the source of heat.

The members of their innocent school, though a bunch of little dumbbells (237.8, 13), begin their prayer to the sun, which is utterly charming. They are enchanted, chained and captured by "Stainusless"—a comic reference to Joyce's responsible brother Stanislaus, who will stain them less than his disreputable brother, if indeed they are stained at all. They declare, in their version of the gladiators' oath, that they, about to blossom, salute the heaven dweller (237.12).

Since Chuff is not unclean, nor an outlaw, nor an untouchable, he is just the sort of unthreatening lover the little girls desire. His bodily purity is insured by the best cosmetics—Harlene and Cuticura (237.28–29). He is the pure victim Abel, but also Abelard to their Heloise, surrounded by a sun halo (237.34–35).

There is indeed a great deal of resemblance between Abelard and Shaun. Shaun as the top half of the body resembles Abelard, the teacher of Heloise, after he was castrated by men hired by Heloise's guardian. Having no genitals in the first place, Shaun like Abelard is "pure," that is, incapable of endangering the purity of his sister and her little friends.

However, Shaun is not lacking in the intellectual power of the upper half. At any rate, Shaun does not think that he has anything to learn from his lower half! In this, too, Shaun resembles Abelard. Abelard kept his intellectual preeminence in the history of philosophy: he is regarded as one of the preeminent thinkers of the later Middle Ages, and his work on logic is especially valuable. Shaun also has a great deal of philosophical ability of a limited kind—see the fable of the Ondt and the Gracehoper, in which there is a great deal of philosophy, or at least a great flourishing of the names of philosophers. The top half of the body keeps the intellect pure, Shaun claims. Yet in the *Wake* the pure intellect ultimately requires the assistance of the lower half, especially the genital area, to produce the deepest language as well as the deepest type of love.

Shaun, possibly ignorant of his own motives, believes that he is pure, but there are disquieting elements in his love for his sister. In this also he resembles Abelard, who in an anguished letter about his castration and his remorse for his love affair, "History of My Calamities," confesses his mixed attitude toward his beautiful pupil: "My hands strayed oftener to her bosom than to the pages; love drew our eyes to look on each other more than reading kept them on our texts."

Shaun's "love" is heavily tainted with sadism, a prime example of what D. H. Lawrence in *Psychoanalysis and the Unconscious* called "sex in the head."

In a later chapter, III.2, Shaun excites himself with visions of spanking his sister, who has previously complained that although she surrendered to him, her bottom is sore from his spanking (232.19). In this respect as well, Shaun resembles Abelard: in the same letter Abelard admits, "To avert suspicion, I sometimes struck her, but these blows were prompted by love and tender feeling rather than anger and irritation, and were sweeter than any balm could be."[6]

Shaun is not the only one whose motives are mixed: the pure little girls refer a trifle too often to their undergarments to be entirely convincing in their innocence. Like seventeenth-century *précieuses*, they pretend to be shocked at the word "constant" (238.11), since to the dirty-minded the meaning of the word may be "standing in the *con*" (Fr., "cunt"); what could be more suggestive? However, asserting that to the pure all things are pure, they fly around Chuff, the blazing round sun, singing a version of *Honi soit qui mal y pense* (238.33–34)—honeybees swarm where honey-golden sunlight lies in pools. Finally they describe themselves in words associated with the Virgin Mary, with suggestive overtones (239.10, 16). These virgins are as yet physically virginal, but they are very impatient virgins indeed. Yet they still keep technical purity: they are united in heaven, where there is no marriage or giving in marriage, according to Christ (239.13). And these bright brides-elect dance around and around, in the Italian version of "Ring around a Rosy" (239.27–28).

Glugg Returns (239.28–255.11)

While these circular ceremonies of consent are taking place around heavenly Chuff, Glugg has been in Hell (239.30, 32–34). To the nursery melody of "Oats, peas, beans and barley grows," Beelzebub and Ahriman (the Zoroastrian spirit of evil and darkness) are bellowing and bedimming the atmosphere. Shem lies in the position of Lucifer in the last canto of Dante's *Inferno*, bottom upward as seen from Heaven (239.34–35). Two children's games describe Glugg's position: London Bridge has fallen down and cannot be bridged by pins and needles (or puns and riddles), and Glugg is mocked by the brides-elect of Chuff.

Yet Glugg rises up and, with the help of his mother (242.25–243.20), returns to the quest, as Dante was called from his dark wood by Beatrice and the Virgin Mary. Glugg in his exile in the underworld has learned a great deal about the nature of his family. Among other things, he realizes the imperfect nature of his parents' marriage: since the Earwickers are Protestants, an orthodox Catholic would regard their marriage as a form only. The reference to W. G. Wills's play *A Royal Divorce* at 243.35 further illustrates Glugg's knowledge of the weak spots in the relationship of his parents.[7]

The lamplighter comes by to provide the illumination for "lighting up" time. Jewish religious holidays begin at twilight, and here Sukkoth, the Feast of Tabernacles, is announced. The source of the word "tavern" is *tabernaculum*, so the religious references announce the solemn rites of the opening of HCE's tavern. The bells in the temples ring; the singsong begins in the synagogue. Curfew is also announced, as the traditional French warning to children to come indoors—"The werewolf will get you!"—sounds out. Come indoors, where the home fires are being lit (244.3–10)!

Joyce's writing is especially powerful when he is describing transition states such as twilight or dawn. Here the advent of twilight produces some of Joyce's loveliest phrases. Note the great beauty of the passage describing the onset of night (244.13–14, 25–28).[8] In this exquisite passage, the four stages of the coming night are laid out for the reader, in the terms that the Latin writer Macrobius employed in his notes on the *Somnium Scipionis*: *conticinium, concubium, intempesta nox,* and *gallicinum*—first the coming of silence, then the entry into bedrooms, then dead of night, and then cockcrow (244.31–33). All the beasts in the zoo say their evening prayers and prepare for sleep (244.33–245.4); Joyce has suggested that the pub is near a zoo. (Joyce's grave in Zurich is also near a zoo.)

The Siemens arc lights go on, in Dublin and all around the coast. All the little fishes in the bay begin to forget their theological quarrels and go to sleep (245.9–13). Girls and soldiers come out adventuring, and stroll in the park three by two (245.19–20). Three/two is always the *Wake* signal for male/female sexuality.

The pub awaits customers, with all in readiness (245.26–246.2). However, the opening of the pub keeps a religious flavor; the Jewish holidays Shevuoth and Purim appear on 245.35–36.

We hear the first call from HCE to the children to come into the house. He is the father but also Thor, the god of thunder and lightning and the head of the Aesir, the Norse gods. He violently orders his children to come home (246.6–8). ALP is also anxious for the children to come home and begin their lessons. However, Glugg has not yet finished with the game.

Glugg returns for the second time. He is described as an unchaste chestnut colt (246.36). He has matured: as he is called unchaste, he obviously has had some sexual experience in his travels. The coulter (knife; also the share of a plow, as in Chaucer's Miller's Tale) here has a sexual significance as well.

Glugg is greeted by someone, with a message that suggests both that he has come back and that he is finished, in some sense, perhaps that he is through with his apprenticeship. He replies that he is both true and through (247.12–13), thereby acknowledging that he is indeed present, but also that he has remained true to his spirit, in the sense that Stephen Dedalus remained true to himself through all of his tribulations. Shem is greeted, possibly by Shaun. The cross-talk team of Shem and Shaun greet each other throughout the book as "How do you do today, my dark sir?" (Shaun to Shem), and "How do you do today, my blond sir?" (Shem to Shaun). Here it is Shaun who greets Shem in classical Greek. Shem replies in sorrow, "Why? Why?" in classical Greek, and stammers that God knows why he is suffering, and that everything is ruined and meaningless (247.12–16).

Glugg is mournful, and he weeps, partly because while he was away he acquired a sense of vision, and he uses it to imagine his inaccessible sweetheart in the nude, black from her dark hair streaming to her knees, although white from the garters up—an intensely erotic vision (247.19, 32–34). This acquisition of sight by Shem is symbolically equivalent to the rising up of the Davy in the Willingdone Museyroom, which is the preliminary to the destruction of the father by the third, phallic son.

Glugg uses his newly acquired vision to gaze at his sister up in the stars (asters), who is doing her best to signal him the "heliotrope" answer to the game (248.6–7). She tries several times, first sounding it out (248.8–10), then presenting it as sets of riddles (248.11–14, 33–35), then sounding it out again (249.14–16), and finally spelling it in Hebrew letters (249.16–17). Her mouth is described in detail as a "house of breathings," complete with lips and cheeks, teeth, hard palate, soft palate, and uvula. Issy seems prepared to embrace the combined brothers, once the pure Shaun has acquired the dark knowledge of sexuality that she desires (249.17–19). The saucy little girls then dance in a ring around Glugg and laugh at him. He declares mournfully that they pretended to help while all the time they shouted naughty words at him, and that it is not cricket—twenty-nine girls against one man (249.34–36)! Still, he decides to try once again.

The third try of Glugg introduces one of the most mysterious sections of the book. The meaning of his third set of guesses has not been successfully annotated, but the effect is magical, in the literal sense. From now on, for several pages, the text is soaked in references to black magic, a sexual magic which is extremely powerful and under the influence of which Issy is transformed into a little sorceress. The purpose of this chapter is to show how Shem infects his sister with his guilty knowledge, with which they both will infect their pure brother, Shaun, in the next chapter. In this chapter, two of the children have moved out of their ignorance over the edge into a maturing sexuality.

The three enigmatic answers of Glugg, and his equally enigmatic pantomimes accompanying them, require close analysis. He asks first if they have pink ribbons, and pretends to be tied in ribbons around his rump. He next asks if they have dirty hands, and pretends to be cleaning their chimneys. He then asks if they can leave their homes, and pretends to be cutting them up and spitting them out (250.3–9).

The first question, as M shows, is derived from a German children's song and game, "Morgen ist die Hochzeit da!" (Tomorrow is the wedding). The lines from the song are "Willst du dieses Mädchen haben, / musst du rosa Bändchen tragen"; that is, "If you want this girl, you must wear pink ribbons." It obviously refers to marriage, and shows the trend of Glugg's sexually infused thought.

However, there are further possibilities of interpretation for this passage. Glugg pantomimes being tied with ribbons around his rump and his head. The word "rumpffkorpff" introduces a significant metaphor. The nineteenth-century scientist H. D. Ruhmkorff in Paris perfected the induction coil. This device is made up of a core of iron strips bound about with a "primary wire." When this wire is connected to an electricity source, it magnetizes the core, and if a secondary wire is wrapped around the primary wire, an electric current is "induced" into it. If the secondary wire has exposed termini, the induced current causes a spark to flash across the "spark gap" from one terminus to the other. In the *Wake*, this tripartite device is a metaphor describing the relationship of the three children. The "ribbings" that Shem winds about his "rumpffkorpff" represent the primary wire of the induction coil; Issy as the core is magnetized by her brother Shem's sexual desire for her; and the two of them will eventually in II.2 induce a current in Shaun, the secondary wire, to produce an enormous spark. In fact, the spark gap itself is mentioned on 232.33.

The second question, as M again shows, is derived, like the first, from a children's song and game with sexual overtones, "Hänschen seet in'n Schosteen" (Jacky sits in the chimney corner). I have discovered a related version of this German dialect song, "Jänsken satt in'n Schosteen," in which Jacky is sitting in the chimney corner and shining his shoes. A pretty young girl comes up and asks him to shine her shoes. Jacky sets about his task with a will, and she really gets her shoes shined! It sounds as if this euphemistic song has a strong sexual reference, much like the first.

The sexual content of this song is reinforced by the words in the pantomime following the second question: "He makes semblant to be swiping their chimbleys." "Swiping their chimbleys" is a recurrent phrase in a salacious British folk song, a version of which is sung in Dylan Thomas's *Under Milk Wood*:

In Pembroke City when I was young
I lived by the Castle Keep
Sixpence a week was my wages
For working for the chimbley sweep.
. . . .
Poor little chimbley sweep she said
Black as the ace of spades
O nobody's swept my chimbley
Since my husband went his ways.
Come and sweep my chimbley
Come and sweep my chimbley
She sighed to me with a blush
Come and sweep my chimbley
Come and sweep my chimbley
Bring along your chimbley brush!

The third question and its pantomime are puzzling, but they too seem to have strong sexual overtones. M notes that the phrase derives from a source in one of Joyce's Buffalo notebooks (VI.B.33.33), "Adieu, adieu, frau Scheisdens," which is described as possibly from a children's game. The third pantomime shows Glugg violently destroying the maidenheads of the maidens. What they are saying adieu to is their virginal innocence, their *Scheiden* or vaginas, at least in Glugg's fervent visions!

The narrative voice later declares, puzzled, that Glugg has evidently failed for the third time (253.19–20). However, Glugg has *not* failed. In this extremely important passage, something fundamental and magical has obviously occurred. Just after the three sexually charged questions and pantomimes, black magic and threats to fathers fill the darkening air. The six subsequent paragraphs also need close analysis:

I. The first paragraph that follows the questions has a number of functions. The little girls are ordered to be quiet in three languages, Irish, German, and Italian (250.11–12). Then come references to adultery and the presence of an enigmatic figure who seems to combine fathers, aunts, and uncles. There are allusive threats to fathers, resting on a pair of passages from *Hamlet* about fathers. One is addressed by the prince to the young Ophelia:

> HAMLET: I say we will have no more marriages. Those that are married already—all but one—shall live. The rest shall keep as they are. To a nunnery, go. (III.i.149–51)

This implied threat by Hamlet to his stepfather King Claudius provides the appropriate menace to paternal power in this section of the *Wake*, which prepares the plot against HCE that comes to fruition in II.3. The other allusion is to Hamlet's savage mockery at IV.iii.52–56 where he addresses Claudius:

> HAMLET: . . . Farewell, dear mother.
> CLAUDIUS: Thy loving father, Hamlet.
> HAMLET: My mother. Father and mother is man and wife, man and wife is one flesh, and so, my mother.

Joyce's aunt/uncle takes Hamlet's conceit one step further: Claudius is both aunt and uncle, but the threat in *Hamlet* reinforces the threat to the father in the *Wake*.

II. The Shakespearean atmosphere thickens with the next paragraph (250.16–18), which not only associates the guilty HCE with the guilty Macbeth but also declares that the father's sexual potency is gone. The obvious reference is to Birnam Wood having come to Dunsinane, and to Macbeth's fear-filled hallucinations at *Macbeth* II.ii.39–40, 46–48 (M).

HCE, who has himself overcome his own father to become a father, is represented by the guilty Macbeth, who has murdered his symbolic father Duncan, and who fears that the same fate will overtake him. However, Joyce gives the overthrow a particularly sexual significance. A burning "would" puts the auxiliary "will" into the past tense. "Will" as an Elizabethan noun frequently has a sexual significance, and sometimes even signifies the penis.[9] Here it is Shem's phallus that has come to dance in the "inane," the emptiness of the "inane" referring to "woman's invisible weapon," the empty vagina. Shem and Shaun, when combined into one glamorous, irresistible lover, will symbolically murder the father, and the cold, aging father, lacking breath, will sexually leap no more.

III. There follows a paragraph (250.19–22) that, to judge from its style, is mocking a children's book, the gist of which is to introduce the girls to the handsome young lover.

IV–V. The next paragraphs are thick with black magic, merriment, and fear. The hazel fork, the vervain, the blasting rod in 250.23–26 are all instruments of the black magician from a manual of black magic, the *Grand Grimoire* (M). Four demons from the *Grimoire* are evoked at 250.27.[10] Black magic is here the magic of sexual desire and performance, the creative power discovered by Glugg in his sojourn in the underworld among the demons.

The Prankquean, who can force change in the family power structure, here mingles with Shem's power of black magic her own power, that of changing the relationship of the elders with the children. The children are irreversibly becoming sexually mature and are all soon to be obsessed with sex (250.29–30). This theme is associated with fauns in the phrase that ends the paragraph (250.32–33). The sentence evokes Mallarmé's "L'Après-Midi d'un Faune," in which a young male's introduction to sexual desire is vividly conveyed. In the first performance of the ballet made from the poem by Debussy, Nijinsky caused a great scandal as the Faun by finishing his dance with an obviously orgasmic shudder.

VI. The last paragraph of this passage (250.34–251.3) is written in a merry horse-race rhythm, showing the eagerness of the children to get to their destructive and constructive goals. Also evoked is Attila, a figure of fear, who here stands for the apprehension felt by the father at the growing power of the children, and his anticipation of his own imminent downfall.

The outcome of all this black magic, Prankquean power, and youthful impatient rhythm is to transform Issy into a young witch. The demonic poetic power of sex evoked by Glugg has entered the little girl, transforming her into an accomplice of Glugg and a magnetized core for Joyce's induction coil. As M notes, 251.10–14 describes the recipe recorded in the *Malleus Maleficarum* for the making of a witch: "the Devil, a Witch, and the Permission of Almighty God." Joyce's version of this recipe refers to a hungry devil, a young witch, and the permission of Almighty God. The magical transformation of Issy into a young witch is accomplished at night. Shem is so overcome by the transformation he has brought about that he ejaculates (251.12–14, 16–17).

Issy remains impatient with Glugg; she could shake him, and when he is gauche she goes dead with embarrassment. However, we see that she has been definitely turned on by Glugg's magic: she begins to have visions of him as a tutor and a lover—Abelard and Heloise revisited. She declares hopefully that a sexual relationship between an impressive teacher and his lovely pupil has been common in all times and societies since Adam and Eve, and her eyes begin to swim in anticipation of the affair. She also says, in a provocative reference to the grammar of love that she is engaged in learning, that she will owe him a great deal (IOU) if he becomes her lover (251.27–32).

She knows that the dreams of love that are sweeping over her are produced by black magic and witchcraft: her word "exaspirated" is really "*x* aspirated," that is, "hex." However, the main model in her mind for her relationship with Glugg is Paolo and Francesca da Rimini (251.23–25).

Chuff becomes alarmed at the change in Issy, and challenges Glugg anew (252.7–13). Both boys are wishing the other dead. St. Mowy founded Glasnevin monastery; "prospect" refers to Mount Prospect, the name of Glasnevin cemetery. *Glasnevin* means "pleasant little green" in Irish, and the Pleasant Grin is Eliot's "chuckle spread from ear to ear," the jolly grin of the skull. Mount Jerome is the Protestant cemetery of Dublin (M). In addition, Glugg is wishing that Chuff would become a "family tree," that is, become his own coffin, and Glugg's use of "abedder" contains the Welsh word *bedd*, which means "grave."

Issy, despite the fumes of love swirling in her head, is still annoyed with Glugg. She wishes that he would offer marriage to her, and start thinking of babies. However, all that Glugg will do is sing romantic love songs to her: "Come into the garden, Maud" and "Thine eyes are stars of morning" (253.11–18).

Twilight (255.12–259.10)

Darkness deepens. All of this doubtful, noisy, and precocious activity seems to have caught the attention of the head of the household. He suspects—correctly!—that his children are up to no good. At any rate, he wants the children to come in and do their homework. He begins to bestir himself (255.4). He produces his wife from his side (255.27–30), like Eve from Adam, and sends ALP out to gather in the children.

ALP is indeed a plump little tailor's daughter and the agent for furnishing ship material ("the Ship's Husband," as she is called in II.3). She is generally delectable: she stands five feet five inches tall, weighs 150 pounds, and has breasts, waist, hips, thighs, knees, and feet in proportion. However, she is not in a good mood. She seizes the boys by their ears and hauls them off into the house to do their schoolwork (256.1–10). She shouts at them to stop their play; the names of ten Irish writers are produced as reproaches by the angry matron—Burke, Kendal Bushe, Sheridan, Goldsmith, Yeats, Synge, Wilde, Shaw, Swift, Sterne. After all, creation is the original sin![11]

Their schoolwork is waiting for them (256.17–32)—Bible study, French, grammar, history, physics, Latin, Eugene Field's poem "Wynken, Blynken, and Nod," the story of Sinbad the Sailor, Uncle Remus stories, politics, chemistry, and—most important of all, as we will see in the next chapter—geometry.

Rebellious Issy remains sulkily outside, while the air is filled with rumors of war and ominous odors (garlic put up by the superstitious innkeeper to keep away vampires, perhaps) (256.33–34). Garlic and the Gaelic League are here invoked, along with the rumors of war, and the clock chimes for eight p.m. (257.8–10).

Issy, now a young witch, her eyes newly opened by Glugg's spells, begins to sing a dirty song about her father. The song reveals a mockery of the father's fading sexual powers and of his futile attempts to pick up young women, as it sings of Father Barley who tried to pick up a platinum blonde, Old Daddy Deacon who could once place his piece of bacon but who now cannot hold a candle to the young boys of the family, bold old Farmer Burleigh who woke up in a sexual fume, a hurlyburly, but could hardly waddle after the objects of his affections, old Daddy Achin playing Punch to young girls' Judys, and Old Forester Farley, who with his advanced age and vanished powers had given up hope of being the Holy Spirit to young girls' Virgin Mary (257.24–26).[12]

ALP, furious at Issy for disregarding her orders to come into the house, is also angry at the disrespectful tendency of Issy's song. When authority is threatened, it responds with violence, and here ALP seizes her daughter, takes down her pants, and gives her a spanking (257.13–14, 16–17, 19–21, 23–24).[13]

Note that one reason for ALP's anger and fear is that Issy is creating a song; Issy is called "Shakespeare" by her angry mother, and accused of creating a "panto[mime]." Since creation is a sure sign of rebellion in the children of the archetypal family, Issy richly deserves her spanking, as her mother, and God thundering overhead, insists. As we have seen, creation is the original sin in the *Wake*. It was first committed by God, when he created the universe—"The attribution of Original Sin to God is one of the basic axioms of *Finnegans Wake*"[14]—and when human beings create, God flies into a jealous rage and thunders furiously at his turbulent and imitative offspring.

Then we hear a thunderword, which is basically the sound of ALP spanking Issy combined with HCE shouting "Shut the door!" in several languages. In the Prankquean fable, which foreshadows this event, the jarl keeps trying to get the daughter of the family to shut the door, and always fails to have it done in time. To shut the door means to prevent change occurring in the family, but the jarl fails in his attempts in the fable, and here HCE fails in his attempts as well. The family power is beginning to shift to the children, despite all that the parents can do.

The thunderword is followed by applause from the audience, mingling with the sound of the spanking. The audience has been carefully attending to the mime, the first act of eight in the narrative drama, and they highly approve of the drama so far. However, the applause sounds as three loud claps of thunder overhead (257.30, 33; 258.19).[15] The Lord is joining the parents of Issy in condemning her ominous creations. Then the curtain drops "by deep request"; Issy really wants her dress down where it belongs!

The damage has been done. The words "Ragnarok" and "Götterdämmerung" creep into in the text to foreshadow the end of the old order (258.1–2). Still, the violent ending to Issy's song has accomplished a temporary peace. The thunder has cleared the air, and all the worried and unhappy inhabitants of the earth have trembled and crouched in fear—for the moment (258. 20–24).

There follows a lovely evening prayer, addressed to the "Loud"—after all, loudness is the most salient characteristic of the God who has just thundered his children into silence. The prayer combines elements of the Litany of the Saints ("Christ, hear us, Christ, graciously hear us"), Jeremiah 21:13 ("Who shall enter into our habitations?"), and the Anglican Book of Common Prayer ("Give peace in our time, O Lord") (M). The sayer of the prayer hopefully begs of the Lord that the children will enter the house, will be obedient, and will do their homework (258.31–32). Note that the prayer defines evil as nonmatter, in the Augustinian manner as the privation of good.

The process of time will change trees into stones, thereby producing Tree-Stone, or the young lover Tristan (259.1–2). The prayer continues with a special appeal for the repose of the children, amending the words of the Book of Common Prayer to "Grant sleep in hour's time" (259.3–4). It also prays that the children will not catch cold, or soil their beds, or commit crimes related to adultery or adulthood.

The prayer, however, contains a substantial threat to the children in the persons of the twin guardians of the home (possibly the two pillars of the front door) (258.34–36). These two guardians seem cheerful enough—their description evokes the twin Cheeryble brothers of *Nicholas Nickleby*, the cheery benevolent brothers who make everything come out right at the end. Note, however, that they have bombs in their fists.[16] When these cheerful armed men order the children to say their prayers and go to bed, they are speaking for the parents, who want only that the children remain obedient. It is too late for this outcome, however; Shem's black magic has transformed Issy into a little witch, and both now intend to do the same to Shaun.

The prayer ends with another borrowing from the Book of Common Prayer, appropriate enough for the Protestant household of the Earwickers: "Lord, have mercy upon us, and incline our hearts to keep this law" (M). However, Joyce alters the prayer to create a statement that could describe all of Joyce's work: "Loud, heap miseries upon us yet entwine our arts with laughters low!" (259.7–8). Joyce's work certainly contains life's miseries aplenty, yet the low laughters of the book, and the low joking of Joyce, the master of modern comedy, sound below all of the sorrow, and produce what Joyce in the Paris notebooks regarded as "the perfect manner in art"—the Comic.

The chapter ends with a yawn down the vowel scale—"Ha he hi ho hu"—and a sleepy mumbled "Amen" (259.9, 10).

Book II, Chapter 2: Dividing the Undivided—A Geometry Lesson

Chapter II.2 is written as a text with two sets of marginal notes, plus footnotes. The two boys write the marginal notes—originally Shem on the left and Shaun on the right, but then they change places. Issy writes the cheeky footnotes. In the "real-time" schema of the *Wake*, twilight is over and night has begun. In the other temporal schema, the children have matured from the preschool or elementary stage of II.1 into secondary education.

The rebellion of the children proceeds apace, and with their rebellion, Shem and Shaun develop into one complete male human being. In II.1 Shem already acquired knowledge of the physical world, and with it a dark, sexual, poetic magic with which he infected Issy. In the educational sequence of Book II, it is Shaun's turn to acquire adult knowledge. However, the knowledge that is unwittingly and unwillingly acquired by Shaun is not Shem's *éducation sentimentale*, an acquisition of emotional experience, as in II.1. In

II.2 Shaun, that part of the body that contains the brain, acquires principles of rational analysis. It is only then that the adult male is constructed, as the two halves of the body are amalgamated into one young man by the incestuous embrace of their mother (287.18–292.32).

What completes the development of Shaun is schoolbook learning, especially the tenets of rational Cartesian analysis as applied to geometry. Reality is continuous, but Descartes introduced digital "artifice" into the measuring of the continuous universe. The maturing Shaun learns, against his will, to draw the line somewhere—that is, to segment undivided reality, and thereby to be able to grasp the structure of the universe (292.31–32).

The digitization of continuous space historically began with Zeno's paradoxes: "Since what [Zeno's] Dichotomy tries to do is break a continuous physical process down into an infinite series of discrete steps, it can be seen as history's first-ever attempt to represent continuity mathematically" (Wallace, 71). But it was in 1637, with the publication of Descartes' treatise on geometry, that the modern treatment of the digitization of space began. Descartes is the hero of this chapter. His name and his tenets occur in several places: "Cartesian spring" (301.25); "reborn of the cards" (*re-né des cartes*) (304.27–28); *cogito ergo sum* (304.31).

Descartes, by creating three-dimensional coordinal space, created a method for describing motion in space. The Cartesian coordinal space "digitizes" continuous space for the purposes of description; it is therefore an "artificial" method, in that it falsifies the continuous nature of space for human purposes. It is here that Shaun learns to "point the deathbone," by which he creates still photographs of moving reality, in order to provide half of the motion picture of the real world that is *Finnegans Wake*.

From the very beginning of his artistic career, Joyce had a geometric metaphor in mind. In the original essay "A Portrait of the Artist," Joyce characterized the process of describing a human being as "tracing the curve of an emotion." ("Tracing a curve" is a term from geometry: locating separate points on the graph that satisfy the equation to be represented, and connecting the discrete points.) Joyce located his young hero in space geometrically in *A Portrait*, where the young Stephen Dedalus, in his first contact with education, works out his geographical position in the created world. Stephen begins with his name and spirals to The World and then The Universe.

However, unlike Stephen, Shaun is located first in the universe, and then spirals down to the upstairs room in HCE's pub, where he is vainly trying to understand geometry. The text of II.2 begins with four views of the origin of the universe, beginning with the highest view—the universe seen by Cartesian methods. The undivided universe of space is here divided by human rational Cartesian means for the purposes of measurement and description.

The first phrase in the chapter, "As we there are where are we are we there" (260.1), establishes the three Cartesian coordinates, and locates us, by the artificial devices of segmenting undivided space, in the universe. This phrase is glossed by Shaun's pretentious phrase in the right margin, which means "whence and where" (260R).

Two more methods for describing the origin of the universe are then unfolded. There is an enigmatic phrase "from tomtittot to teetootomtotalitarian" (260.2). "Tom Tit Tot" is a demon from an English version of the story of Rumpelstiltskin (M); he has power so long as you do not know his name. Here he corresponds to a God with an unknown name—YHWH in the Judeo-Christian schema—with great creative power. This is the god of the early religions. "Teetootomtotalitarian," on the othe hand, represents the modern scientific universe, one set spinning like a top and described by scientists in a unified scheme controlled by invariant laws.

Joyce here presents the ultimate deity, the Kabbalistic Ain Soph,[17] who is introduced by Shem's cheeky comment in the left margin about a great spirit with a hairy face (260L). This refers to the highest element in the Kabbalistic structure of Ain Soph, the Makroprosopos, the Great Face, which is a face seen in profile with a long white beard. Within the beard is another, smaller visage, seen full-face, with a black beard, known as the Mikroprosopos, the Small Face. The hairy face reminds us, too, of the face of Stephen's father at the beginning of *A Portrait*, where he is telling Stephen the story of the moocow. Hairiness, the sign of the mature male, is also associated there with paternal creativity, both literary and universal.

The intention to describe the universe from beginning to end is present in the phrase "tea tea too oo." "Tea" is the first syllable in "teetootomtotalitarian" and "too" is a "preecho" of the last word in the chapter, "too," at 308.25.

260.8–15

The viewers spiral down from the beard of Makroprosopos through the nine Kabbalistic Sephiroth to the earth, and travel through all of the Liberal Arts. The Prankquean's riddle, the symbol of action pressing onward relentlessly and letting the chips fall where they may, is evoked at 260.5–7, complete with a nervous prediction from the father that he will end up shot if the education of the children continues.

Issy, her eyes now completely open, participates with sinister enthusiasm in the process of development. She adds a comment of her own on the beard of Makroprosopos, in her first footnote (260n1): if her father, HCE, that old Herod the child-killer, were to attack her or rape her, she would counterattack and pull his beard, and be sentenced to "nine months" in jail for assault, or rather would bear his child. As usual, Issy is ambivalent about her father.

Then the text spirals down from "whence" and "where," from Unde and Ubi, down to "while" and "whither" (260.8, 9, 14); appropriately, the three dimensions of Descartes are supplemented by Einstein's fourth dimension, time. The spiral downward, pompously described by Shaun as an itinerary through the universal (260R), reverses Dante's constant spirals *upward* through Purgatory, and proceeds through seven levels of education. Joyce's version of the masters of the seven liberal arts and sciences in Limbo contains some studies more respectable than others, in the Joyce style. History is represented by Livy, language by Mezzofanti, physiognomy (an appropriately doubtful "science") by Lavater, astronomy by Tycho Brahe (a reference to the Milky Way is made by Issy), philosophy by Bishop Berkeley, art by Gainsborough, and music by Guido d'Arezzo (with Shem's cheeky representation in 260L of Guido's "gamut," do, re, mi, fa, sol, la, si, do—or ut (M).

260.14–262.2

HCE and ALP are represented as 1 and 0, and the barrow in which HCE is buried is merged with HCE's inn. The father and mother are shown in various guises: as a muscular blackguard making love to a hoyden, as the maker of the universe mating with a rainbow maid (that is, fertilizing the fallen world that he has made, an act of superfetation), as a comatose line—a length without breadth or breath—a corpse buried in a mound—HCE—and finally as more a crowd of human beings than an individual (261.18, 21–22), thereby reinforcing the collective nature of Joyce's characters.

HCE's hugest manifestation is as Ain Soph, the Kabbalistic "Unlimited," but Issy, who respects nothing, refers to this universal God as simply a name for grapejuice (261n3). During Prohibition in the United States, Prohibitionists actually denied that Jesus ever drank wine; therefore, they insisted, the use of wine in the Mass was not canonical, and grapejuice could be substituted!

HCE is also represented by the erect masculine numeral 1, side by side with ALP, the feminine 0, making up the perfect number 10 (261.23–24). Both parents are invoked by their initials as we approach the inn (262.1–2).[18]

262.3–19

The viewers end up in Limbo, where the great sages carry on their university.[19]

The approach to the inn is performed in stately rhythms (262.3–6). Issy's comment on "Knock" locates the landscape as the underworld: she instructs the reader to knock, and the merman below the tidemark will answer, "Go to Hell!" (262n1).

We are actually approaching the land of the dead, to end up in Limbo among the great pagan poets and philosophers, who will educate Shaun in dangerous secular learning. Dante includes in his infernal university Homer, Horace, Ovid, Lucan, the heroes celebrated in Homer and Virgil and Roman history, and also, oddly placed among them, Saladin. The philosophers, led by Aristotle—the master of those who know, the most honored of all by Dante and by Joyce—are Socrates, Plato, Democritus, Diogenes, Empedocles, Thales, Anaxagoras, Heraclitus, and Zeno. A truly distinguished university faculty!

The rhythmic approach to Limbo continues with a password (262.7–10). Here Issy's previous mention of Hell is reinforced by "I'll be damned!" at 262.9. Hell is further evoked by the next quatrain (262.11–14); that is, God, infuriated by HCE's capture and naming of ALP, thus initiating a rival creation to His own, threw the man to earth, where, like Dante's Lucifer, he hollowed out a huge conical excavation.

This evocation of eternal death for our fallen parents is followed by a fragment of the requiem (262.15–17). The perpetual light of the hymn is spluttering on its wick; the light of human knowledge is always uncertain.

The poetic entrance hymn ends with a reference to Nicholas of Cusa's *Of Learned Ignorance* (M), an appropriate title for a chapter on education in the lower secular sciences, and a resigned "So be it" (262.18–19), containing a reference to sows, which, besides representing acceptance, also contains a sting. It will be recalled that Stephen Dedalus referred to Ireland as the old sow who eats her farrow. Here the sow represents human history, which the speaker accepts, with all its imperfections, as the price to be paid for human life and for the development of human families.

262.20–281.13

The text shouts to us to go into the inn (262.26–27).

And sure enough, we are finally at HCE's inn, which is complete with staple ring to tether your horse and stepping-stone to mount it, and with the heads and wings of various beasts and fowls on the walls (262.20–25). It is a busy scene—the children are doing their homework, the drinkers in the pub are drinking, and HCE, the publican, is merrily making mints of money (262.27–29). The children at their tasks upstairs are as diligent as the drinkers in the bar (263.21). We are, as Shaun declares sagely, in the realm of physical determinism (262R). All is on track for the inevitable development of the children into adults. The cycle has revolved millions of time; at 263.13–15 we see HCE cycle through HCE-CEH-ECH. It has always been that way, secure and unchanged though heretical and unfortunate, from the Garden of Eden onward (263.18–21).

The whole family is there—the father, the mother, the two boys (becoming three young men) and the little girl (becoming two young girls), the mountain and the river, the tree and the stone. The location of the inn is Chapelizod, a town three miles to the west of Dublin and the traditional home of Isolde, the bright-haired daughter of Aengus (M) (265.19–20). Many of the features of Chapelizod are described (264.15–268.6), and our camera's-eye vision takes us to the inn and up the stairs to where the children are studying.[20] The nature of their studies—appropriately secular studies for fallen humanity, the creation of artificial means to segment the originally continuous creation—is made clear by the evocation of the rainbow at 267.12–16.

The children's studies are outlined in the next fourteen pages. Arithmetic is first (268.7–16), then grammar (268.16–270.28).[21] Secular and religious history follow in some detail (270.29–276.10), to the last syllable of recorded time—Out, out, brief candle! Finally, Issy begins to practice letter writing, to prepare herself for her life's task as a mature woman writing her letter to the world about her guilty husband (278.7–281.15).

Although Issy is uncomfortable in her chair (278n2), she toils away, licking her pen and her lips, occasionally blotting her paper, and rubbing her eyes. She launches into an excited footnote filled with visions of married love and the joys of housewifery, a delightful and delight-filled cadenza similar to that of her mother later on (279n1).

The penmanship exercises end up with her reproducing the text from Edgar Quinet about the flowers surviving all the battles of history (281.4–13).

Of course, her brothers will have their say about her accomplishments. Shem satirically denies the power of the Quinet passage, mocking the feebly Nietzschean ambition of the writer, who can only thrust to zero effect (281L), but Shaun approves of her efforts, since literature is, to this militant fellow, simply an adjunct to warfare (281R).[22]

Now the readers approach the central portion of the chapter—the creation of the diagram of ALP's genitals that Shaun is tricked into drawing by his jealous brother Shem. In the introductory paragraph (281.15–27) there are strong echoes of *Othello* and the fatal handkerchief, the *fazzoletto*. Issy predicts that the boys will change sides as a result of Shem's trick. She declares that Shaun finds it difficult or impossible to "spend" (281n4), and one of the meanings of "spend" is to ejaculate. In this she is correct; the top half of the body is in fact incapable of sexual expression, and will be until the boys change over with each other.

282.1–304.3: Central Theme

AMDG

The central segment of the chapter—like the compositions that Stephen Dedalus, and Joyce himself, wrote for his Jesuit instructors at Clongowes and Belvedere—is headed at 282.6 by the Jesuit motto AMDG, Ad Maiorem Dei Gloriam, and ends twenty-two pages later at 304.3 with the conventional ending of all such compositions, LDS, Laus Deo Semper. (Issy knows how the game will end; at 282n2 she giggles the initials). However, unlike those pious compositions, the composition here is a creation that, like all creation, is presented as an aggression against God the Father and his monopoly of creation.

At this point, we are close to the center of *Finnegans Wake*. In the course of this composition, ALP will broaden out to both margins of the text, to cover both banks of the river on which her sons sit, and take them both to her incestuous bosom: "Time like an ever-rolling stream, / Bears all her sons away." The two sons have excited their mother to orgasm, and it is to both of them that their mummy is coming (194.22). The incestuous embrace causes the amalgamation of her two sons into one uneasily integrated male human being. Freud wrote that any couple in bed engaged in sex must come to terms with incest. The unified male, having come to terms with incest, will destroy his father in the next chapter, II.3, and then travel on, with Shaun carrying the letters through the night and Shem curled up like a cod in a pot inside

Shaun's trousers, emerging only on occasion with embarrassing questions for his host. Finally, the combined creature will rise in the east as the new father.

282.7–286.24

Shaun's difficulty with geometry, the study that measures Mother Earth, is here explored in detail. The introductory paragraph of this dangerous composition establishes the mastery of Shem over Shaun in this educational task (282.1–4). Shaun is the boor here, working under the control of Shem, the lord.

The adult Shaun's rational mind will ultimately be the source of the divisive sciences by which he divides the undivided universe. As a child, however, Shaun has great difficulty with the advanced mathematical keys to the division of space. We are first introduced to his methods in dealing with elementary arithmetic (282.7–283.20). He does well enough (282.8–9), even though he is forced to count on his fingers, and manages to have a good time with arithmetic. His ways of counting seem rather rowdy, resembling the progress of Hogarth's Rake, from aces and heavy drinking to vaginas, doubtful literature, and dicing (283.4, 8–9). Issy comments in a footnote (283n2) that Shaun is getting to be more like his father every day, on the road to ruin.

However, the higher branches of mathematics confuse Shaun greatly (283.20–29). Geometry and algebra puzzle him; he could reckon with numbers, but it seems unfair to switch to letters of the alphabet for unknowns. These two subjects are worse than his problems with German, in reading Goethe's *Hermann und Dorothea*. Those who struggled through Goethe's long classical poem in school, where it used to be a favorite set book, will sympathize with Joyce's description of the poem as "German diarrhea"!

The key to Shaun's puzzlement with these three school subjects is what algebra, geometry, and German have in common: the letters *ge*, the Greek root for Mother Earth. Shaun lacks knowledge of the facts of his mother's intimate anatomy, and Shem is all too eager to introduce him to them.

This passage leads straight to Shem's trap for Shaun, and the introduction of Shaun to the facts of life, which in its turn leads to the uniting of the children into a force that, in the next chapter, will lead to the destruction of the father. Issy senses that a crucial point has been reached in the narrative, and also senses that the father will kill them all if he knows of the plot. Her footnote "Slash-the-Pill lifts the pellet. Run, Phoenix, run!" (283n3)—inserted into the text just as Shem is setting out on his subversive voyage—warns the boys that the father is aware of their rebellion. Her comment contains an allusion to a poem by Robert Graves, "The Halls of Bedlam," which is about a mad father who kills his children: "Father in his shirtsleeves / Flourishing a hatchet. / Run, children, run!"

Oblivious to this warning, Shaun leafs through his geometry textbook with great incomprehension (283.32–286.2), concluding that the whole thing is equivalent to chaos doubly confounded. He then comes upon the problem set for homework, which is the first problem in *The Elements of Euclid*: "Construct an equilateral triangle" (286.19–20, 21–22). He contemplates the problem with his thumb in his mouth (286.20–21). The equilateral triangle is, of course, the symbol of his mother, "Ann"—the three-letter symbol is ALP—but innocent Shaun does not realize the dangerous territory he is entering. Perhaps he thinks that he can cross over the beach, the "littoral," like the Hebrews entering the Holy Land by crossing the Jordan dryshod, in the Book of Joshua.

286.25–287.17

Shem kindly offers to help him construct the triangle.

The first thing Shaun must do, the cunning Shem says, is pick up a fistful of mud. Any little mud that comes out of "Mam" will do (286.31; 287.7–8). Why? Shaun asks. Shem quotes Euclid's "There's no royal road to geometry" (M) (287.4–5), while Issy gleefully comments, "Will you walk into my parlor, said the spider to the fly?" (287n1). The spiteful Shem persists in his seduction of the shy Shaun, and Shaun amiably goes along.

Shem instructs Shaun to unbox his compasses and place the sharp end of the compass at a place on the Irish coast to be called *a* or "olfa"—the alpha and omega of the dangerous process. Shem identifies the place as "the isle of Mun, ah!" (the Isle of Man was in Roman times called Mona, which is also Italian for "cunt"). "O!" responds the still clueless Shaun, thereby closing the alpha-omega series and joining in the crime.

When Shem tells Shaun to unbox his compasses, the question "I cain but are you able?" is met with an amicable nod, and Shem says, "Good! So let us 'seth' off" (287.12–13).[23] Seth, the third son of Adam and Eve, the successor to Cain and Abel, and also the Egyptian god Set that killed his brother Osiris, completes the triad of potent sons. As we saw in the Willingdone Museyroom, the two brothers represent the two testicles, and the third brother, the phallic Davy, once he rises above his two brothers, destroys the Willingdone. Here the same process begins. Now everything for the plot is in applepie order (287.16–17)!

287.18–292.32

Shem's plot to force Shaun to see his mother's genitals gets under way, and the river herself intervenes.

The stream of text, which until this point has been narrowly flowing between the marginal comments of her two sons, now broadens out to both margins. Anna is, in effect, incestuously embracing her sons and, like the Prankquean, causing them to share each other's qualities. Time is, literally, bearing all her sons away. The two sons become one combined young man, a young man of mixed motives and deeply conflicting drives, much like all modern men. Until the end of the book, the two share each other's qualities, and are now one and the same growing male adult—rational, uneasy Shaun, bearing his uncontrollable brother Shem curled up between his thighs.

Anna Livia's augmented flow begins with an account in Latin, which seems to describe the writing of the *Wake* itself, by Joyce sitting in Paris. The Latin inscription ends with an invocation of "the wisdom" of Bruno and Vico, declaring in general terms that the boys have been taken into the bosom of the stream, and have embraced their mother (287.23–28).

The broadened river is described over the next five pages, with eight phrases separated by semicolons, and one colon. The eight phrases describe the career of Shem, and his acquisition of forbidden knowledge, especially knowledge of his mother's anatomy. Of these, the seventh and eighth are the most significant for the future trend of the book. The seventh phrase (292.12–21) declares that if you could look inside the mind of Shem, you would find a great confusion and an equally great amount of information.

The eighth phrase (292.21–32) contains the most important bit of information in the mind of Shem—that for the completion of the children's task of overthrowing the parents, Shaun must learn to divide the continuous universe artificially into digitized segments (292.31–32). That is, the cream of the meaning of what Spengler called our Faustian age, the modern age of analysis in which we live, is that, whether you are happy (like Shaun) or sad (like Shem), common sense is going to whisper to you, in a terribly upper-class English accent, that you must really draw the line somewhere. Joyce's critics had all been declaring that Joyce had crossed the line of decency in his books; here Joyce is acknowledging that to balance the grasp of the undivided universe existing in time and space, it is necessary for rational human beings to draw Cartesian lines, and to divide undivided reality, for the whole work to be complete.

293.1–304.3

At this point Shaun, seduced by the subversive Shem, promptly begins to draws the Cartesian lines that will end up as a diagram of the genitals of his mother.

At first Shaun does not realize what he has done. He exclaims in admiration, "Another grand discovery!" (294.12–13). The awed Shaun thinks that Shem is so clever that he is bound to end up in the madhouse (294.15–16), another reference to the "madness" of his unruly brother.

Shem keeps guiding Shaun's hand, and keeps commenting gleefully about the forbidden areas he is limning. Shaun begins to feel a certain uneasiness as the diagram grows complete: "This makes us an identical pair of accomplices!" (295.26–27). The accomplices are indeed hard at work to topple their parents. Here Shem is connected to Stephen Dedalus at the point of his own triumphant destruction of the paternal light in Ulysses.[24] Shem makes water flow for Dublin, but also carries Siegfried's sword of manhood up his sleeve (295.17–18). Shem here asserts that he has attained sexual maturity with the acquisition of his phallic sword, Nothung. However, it is both of the brothers who are engaged in the task of causing the river to flow, to "come" forward between her thighs, with her two sons as river banks.

Shem and Shaun have now changed positions. Shem, formerly a deep bass, is now on the top, singing tenor, and Shaun is precariously holding on to the bottom, singing bass. The two join in a well-known song by Percy French (296.13–19). Shaun is about to fall from his position as Michael the archangel and is holding on precariously to the angelic rank that was formerly his by right.[25]

Shem, hissing like the serpent in the garden of Eden (297.4), tells Shaun that he will make him see the home, or whole, or hole, of their eternal Gaeamater (296.30–297.1). As he gleefully describes Anna Livia's anatomy, Shem anticipates the final sexual act of the book, when the incoming tide begins to enter Anna's estuary again, when the tidal bore rushes up from the Atlantic (297.31–32).

The meaning of his drawing begins to dawn on the once naive Shaun. Mother of us all—quite a coincidence (299.3, 8)! Shaun is looking in the wrong place, says Shem. Even so, Shaun is getting a haunted expression on his face, as if he had seen the devil, the spirit that forever denies, according to Goethe. Shaun must look down, not up, says Shem. Shaun does look down, and he immediately sees what Issy has been writing. He then begins to understand what sort of message he will be carrying to the world. He also accepts his role as the drawer of Cartesian lines delimiting the undivided spaces of the universe. In a version of Alexander Pope's injunction, Shem counsels Shaun to drink deep or avoid the "Cartesian" spring (301.24–25), the spring that is also the source of his mother's waters.

Shaun's eyes have finally been opened, and he sees all the characters in the book of the family, as presented in a dream-drama (302.31–32). In other words, Shaun now can read *Finnegans Wake*! Shaun also sees all the great creators in Irish literary history—Steele, Burke, Sterne, Swift, Wilde, Shaw, and W. B. Yeats (303.5–8).[26] The force of human creation has been let loose and, since creation is the original sin in the *Wake*, the Father is in great danger.

Shaun then becomes enraged with Shem, as Cain was enraged at Abel. Shaun is now the guilty Cain; the changeover of personality has altered his virtue into Shem's vice: as the Bible says, "And Cain was wroth with his brother" (303.15). Again, as in the Bible, Cain's "countenance fell" (Genesis 4:5), but in addition, Cain's fist rises up (304.1–2), and he punches Shem in the eye.

Shaun's outrage may be more than the usual Oedipal complex of emotions about his mother; it may have a specifically Irish Catholic origin. Brendan Gill commented that Irish Catholic boys

> brought up by nuns and priests, wished that every woman, even every mother, could remain a virgin; the fact that women made love, and especially that one's own mother made love, or had once made love, was intolerable. (Wolff, 254n)

The indignant Shaun has blackened Shem's eye, which now bears an ebony circle around it (304R). There may be here a reference to the Egyptian myth of Horus and Set. In *The Book of the Dead*, one of Joyce's primary sources, Set, the god of unlimited areas, who will not draw the line somewhere, fights with Horus, the "god of limits," who *will* draw limiting lines. Set destroys one of Horus's eyes. Horus retaliates by destroying Set's testicles.[27]

We can apply the Egyptian myth to this section of the *Wake*, if we recall that the boys have changed sides. Shaun (the good Horus) and Shem (the bad Set) have now embraced their opposites and become one uneasy human being. Thus we see that Shaun (who is now Set) has blackened the eye of Shem (who is now Horus), but Shem-Horus has ensured that Shaun-Set will lack testicles and therefore must still rely upon Shem as the lower half to perform the fertilizing function for him. Shaun-Set has ensured that Shem will be blindly locked up within Shaun's trousers until Shaun "releases" him for sexual purposes. From this point, the unified Shaun carries the word through the night, and Shem curls up in Shaun's trousers like a cod in a pot (593.21–23).

Then the river retreats to its former banks, but the children have changed sides: Shaun is now on the left bank and Shem on the right. As a matter of fact, Shem has almost completely silenced himself: whereas in the first half of the chapter he was very garrulous, making 91 comments, after he changes sides he makes only 10 comments. Shaun, on the other hand, made only 28 comments in the first half of the chapter; he makes an equal amount, 29, in the second half, plus all the names of the 56 subjects of the essays that he and Shem will write, and the countdown to the Nightletter. It seems that here Shem has become the (almost) silent partner of the two, content with his place inside Shaun's trousers.

The school composition, which has begun with AMDG, now ends with LDS, here appearing as a Wagnerian lovedeath—love is death, how simple! (304.3)—a preparation for the first lovemaking of the children in II.4, the Tristan and Isolde chapter. With the completion of the composition, Joyce has opened the door to the children's creativity, transforming a tiresome classroom task, a writing assignment, into the symbol of a creativity that is highly dangerous to the older members of the family. From now on, the maturing children begin to force their parents from their positions of power.

LDS

The gleeful Shem thanks Shaun for the blow (304.5): now Shaun has lost his purity and is a fit accomplice. In calling Shaun "Pointcarried," Shem refers not only to the greatest French mathematician, Henri Poincaré, but to *poing carré*, the "square (big) fist" that has just struck him. Shem is seeing rainbows (304.8–9), first, from the physical effects of the punch in the eye but, second, as a symbol of Fallen Man. Man has, like Henri Poincaré, boldly created what never existed before—the means to describe the universe—thereby evoking the rage and fear of the God of the Creation.

Meanwhile, Issy is watching in fascination. She is more than ready for her part in the attack on the parents (304.19–26).

304.26–306.7

Shem then sings a song of triumph, one that emphasizes the man-made Cartesian system now in the power of Shaun. Shem is made "a reborn of the cards" (*re-né des cartes*), so "cog it out, here goes a sum" (*Cogito ergo sum*) (304.27–28, 31). Shem continues (repeating the forger Pigott's spelling error), "And that celebrated sock in the jaw of yours has dispelled all my hesitency." Now there will be no more hesitancy, however spelled; the children are going for the kill. And just to emphasize the sexual nature of the coming triumph, Shem inserts in the left margin "cunctitititilatio," defined as the stimulation of a "tricky" female with much tickling of thighs, but the spelling, probably an English or Italian schoolboy joke, draws it out in excitatory and masturbatory rhythms, with the sexual numbers two and three prominent, ending with a long hissing ejaculation (305L).

306.8–308.29

The three children, now united in an aggressive force, begin to "create" in a great stream of school compositions.

Fifty-two heroes from ancient and modern history—befitting a chapter devoted to the heroic age of Vico—are the topics of their compositions, or one a week (306.15–308.1). At the end of the list they declare triumphantly that their "connection" has come through, as if a Paris telephone number has been reached: *Gobelins dix-sept, six et neuf!*

The children then begin a count of ten, as if they were referees counting out a fallen prizefighter. And finally comes the deeply ominous Nightletter (308.20–29).

At first, the Nightletter seems to be no more than a Christmas and New Year's telegram to their parents and all the old folks at home. However, the wording could not be more threatening. Pop and Mommy fade entirely into Pep and Memmy, and the old folks become the old fuckers below and beyond. All the old folks are dead, or soon will be.

What the babes mean to do will shortly become very clear indeed. The word resembling "preposterousness" in the message means literally the replacement of what was before by what comes after. That is, the children will take over from the older generation, and they will hang all the oldsters. If there were any doubt about the murderous intentions of the children, the skull and crossbones drawn by Issy in her last footnote should remove any ambiguity. Issy's final comment reinforces the Cartesian theme of the chapter: we wish you eggs and jokes for skull and crossbones at school, and we hope that Pop will enjoy himself over our drawing the line. That is, the children, enlightened by their new ability to draw Cartesian lines to describe the universe, will start drawing lines of another sort. It is perfectly clear that the line that the children will draw will be around their father's neck.

Book II, Chapter 3: The Death of the Father

M notes that the first sentence of the chapter (309.1) conceals an acrostic, spelling out I'M NOMAN. This chapter contains the attack by the enlightened children on their father, foreshadowed by a radio play, a television play, and a song. Effectively, the attack reduces Everyman—our hero HCE—to Noman, a father who has lost his power and efficacy. The maturing of his children frightens the stammering father,[28] and from the end of this chapter he hides among the dead (309.2–3), until he reemerges in Book III, chapter 3.

The introductory section (309.11–311.4) then presents an elaborate description of a radio that is playing in HCE's pub. Also described is an ear (310.8–21), Shem's organ and the human organ that will receive and interpret the first story, the tale told over the radio. The ear is treated in considerable detail: tympanum, meatus, Eustachian tube, the organ of Corti, and the three bones of the inner ear—hammer, anvil, and stirrup—all making up the internal labyrinth of the ear, which is described in otological terms (310.21).

I. Radio Play: How Kersse the Tailor Made a Suit of Clothes for the Norwegian Captain (311.5–332.35)

The scene is HCE's pub approaching midnight, at the height of its activity The customers in the pub, all drinking lustily, are listening to a radio play told by Shem. It is about a humpbacked Norwegian captain and how he tried to purchase a suit of clothes from a Dublin tailor. After three voyages, and successive failures by the tailor to fit the captain, the captain marries the tailor's daughter and sets up a family.

This tale comprises one of the most difficult sections in the *Wake*, mainly because it is so full of foreign words, many of them Scandinavian and Germanic. However, its general trend is clear. It tells of the initial meetings of HCE and ALP—he being the Norwegian captain, she the tailor's daughter. As the account of the founding of the family, this tale corresponds to the Prankquean fable of I.1.

The story, originating with Joyce's godfather, Philip McCann, was often told by Joyce's father, and it was mentioned in *Ulysses* (4.215). Ellmann writes (1982, 23) of

> McCann's story, told to John Joyce, of a hunchbacked Norwegian captain who ordered a suit from a Dublin tailor, J. H. Kerse of 34 Upper Sackville Street. The finished suit did not fit him, and the captain berated the tailor for being unable to sew, whereupon the irate tailor denounced him for being impossible to fit. The subject . . . became, by the time John Joyce had retold it, wonderful farce.

As Joyce's father embroidered the story, the tailor then urged the irate captain to scrunch up into various postures, to make the clothes fit. In another version, bystanders praise the tailor's ability to fit such a misshapen creature.

The listeners in the pub are drinking freely, and HCE, the red-faced pub owner, a Scandinavian with merry winking eyes, is pulling the levers rapidly, setting up drink for all customers, while his bouncer, elsewhere named Sackerson, is scanning the crowd for troublemakers (310.22–311.1). Apparently the radio story has already begun; there is some discussion among the customers, punctuated by drinking, about where in the story they are now. Finally the dialogue of the tale is heard: the captain asks the Ship's Husband, the supply agent for the ship, where he can order a suit of clothes. The Ship's Husband knows just the place: Kersse the tailor, successor to Ashe and Whitehead, Clothes Shop (311.24).

The plot begins, with many references to the Prankquean fable. The captain enters the tailor's shop, orders the suit of clothes, and departs on a voyage (311.25–314.6). As the tailor begins to create the suit of clothes, another thunderword resounds, as God the Creator becomes alarmed yet again at the signs of creation among his children (314.8–9).

"That's all mighty purty, but what about his daughter?" urge some of the more romance-minded customers (314.30). The tailor and his wife are aware that they are getting older, and they do not seem averse to a marriage between their pretty daughter and some likely lad. The life story of the tailor and his wife is summarized. Once they were newlyweds, singing "The young May moon is beaming, love" (318.13–14). Their present loving state is evoked by Robert Burns's touching poem about an aging couple, "John Anderson, my jo," with echoes (318.14, 27–28) of the closing words "Now we maun totter down, John, / And hand in hand we'll go / And sleep the gither at the foot, / John Anderson, my jo" (M).

The tailor, like the captain, is an aging man chewing his food morosely, a man bent under a hump of guilt much like Richard III's, all of which is evoked by phrases from Shakespeare (with an assist from Colley Cibber): "Now is the winter of our discontent—Off with his head! So much for Buckingham!" (318.20–21).

There is some drunken conversation among the customers, in which HCE is again identified as the humpbacked villain Richard III (319.20), and then the story continues. The captain returns and tries on the suit. It does not fit. The enraged captain curses the tailor (320.12–17), then rushes off to sea for a second time. He sails around many oceans and enters many ports (320.18–321.33). When he returns, the tailor comes forward with another version of the suit of clothes. It fits even less well than the first time, says the captain—his own father would not know him—and again the captain curses the tailor (322.8–13).

The tailor loses his temper and accuses the captain of being impossible to fit (322.35–323.24). The gluttonous captain's belly is too big, his hump makes accurate fitting impossible, and his hips are so fat that he seems to have his pockets filled with potatoes. In fact, the captain is spherical, much like Falstaff, "plump Jack"—"Banish plump Jack and banish all the world!" As Carlyle found out in *Sartor Resartus*, it is impossible to tailor garments for the huge irregularities of the physical universe, or for the oddities of human personality.

The listeners burst into laughter at this outburst from the tailor, and then there is an intermission, in which we hear announcements, a weather forecast, news bulletins, and some advertisements.

The announcement apparently concerns someone's coat and trousers, which are to be returned to the postmaster at Clontarf. The telephone number of the postmaster—"Clontarf, one love, one fear" (324.20–21)—refers to 1014, the date of the battle of Clontarf, the last battle won by the native Irish against invaders, so the articles of clothing may belong to Brian Boru, the victor, and chief victim, in the battle. Joyce may here be referring to the independence of the Irish won after the Anglo-Irish war. There is also an alternate address to call about the coat and trousers (324.21–22), which, besides the reference to Finnegan, may contain a reference to Joyce's early vocal career: the judge at the singing competition at which Joyce won a bronze medal was Luigi Denza, who wrote "Funiculi, Funicula."

The weather forecast tells listeners the evening is rainy, caused by a sudden ridge of low pressure (324.31–32), with mist in some parts and local drizzles. We already know that the night is rainy because of the constant claps of thunder in the book. However, the outlook for tomorrow is brighter, visibility good—in fact, the "soft morning," a misty morning that is heralded in Book IV (619.20) by ALP. The news bulletins announce the crash of the Hero and his fall in "Aden," the approaching nuptials of his children, and the burial of the hatchet, signifying the advent of peace (324.36–325.1). There are also advertisements for Guinness, Lynch's tea, and the Buchmanite Oxford Movement (M), as well as a horse race and a harp quartet concert. Then the story recommences.

The Ship's Husband suggests that, to resolve the conflict, the captain marry the tailor's daughter (325.13–326.20), and after some difficulty in convincing the tailor (326.26–329.12), the marriage is arranged, and the captain is caught and caged (329.13): the captain's ravens (Hugin and Munin, which are the two ravens of Odin) unite with the tailor's daughter's doves in a reference to the raven and dove of Noah's ark, and to the establishment of a new world.

The wedding of the captain and the tailor's daughter (329.13–332.35) is elaborate. Beginning with the illumination of Dublin and the ringing of all the bells, it is truly a jubilee—you could hear the cheering as far as the Welsh mountains across the Irish Sea (329.14, 20–21, 30–31, 32–33). The Norwegian national anthem and the new Irish national anthem, "The Soldier's Song," ring out to signify the union of the Norwegian captain and the Irish maiden (330.7–8). He got a berth, and she got a household, declare the listeners (330.28).

The tale ends with the words that Joyce insisted was the only way to end a fairy tale: "And they put on the kettle and they all had tea" (330.25–27). The Norwegian words to end a fairy tale occur two pages later (332.1)—"Now the story is ended."

However, before the actual end of the story, the transition to the next story is established. The next generation, the twin boys, begins to knock at the door (330.30–32). They are without an apple because they are still innocent, in that they have not yet overthrown their father.

Entr'acte: Kate (332.36–334.31)

To show that history is moving onward to the next stage of the attack on the father, there is an intermission, in which Kate enters. She is the spirit of history; she was the guide in the Willingdone Museyroom, and she is here to introduce another version of the tale. She stays long enough to establish the transition to the second story and then leaves, shutting the door.

II. Television Drama: How Buckley Shot the Russian General (334.32–355.9)

The next tale is a television drama, showing the clearing sight of the children as they fix a bead on their father, much like the Davy in the Willingdone Museyroom. Joyce never actually saw a television set in action (Hart 1962, 158–59), but he kept up with all scientific matters of his time. After all, one of the main inventors of television, Vladimir Zworykin, was working on the television iconoscope in Zurich during Joyce's stay there.

This bloody television drama, told by Shaun, begins with a New Zealand war song and dance, a Maori *haka* (335.4, 16–17, 19–20, 23).[29] The martial air is identified as Maori by various references to New Zealand and its capital, Wellington (335.13, 17, 18). The name Wellington also ties this story to the Willingdone Museyroom tale, which is likewise about the destruction of the father by the children. The evocation of New Zealand, a land "down under," identifies the presence of Shem, the spirit below the waist, who will provide the phallic weapon for the superseding of the father by the new generation. Whenever "down under" is required, as later in III.2, the phallic apparatus rises up to do its duty.

The story is about an Irish sharpshooter, Buckley, who after initial hesitation shoots a Russian general during the Crimean War. This tale, Ellmann relates (1982, 398), was also drawn from the repertoire of Joyce's father.

> Buckley, he explained, was an Irish soldier in the Crimean War who drew a bead on a Russian general, but when he observed his splendid epaulettes and decorations, he could not bring himself to shoot. After a moment, alive to his duty, he raised his rifle again, but just then the general let down his pants to defecate. The sight of the enemy in so helpless and human a plight was too much for Buckley, who again lowered his gun. But when the general prepared to finish the operation with a piece of grassy turf, Buckley lost all respect for him and fired.

Joyce once told the story to Samuel Beckett, and said he was having trouble finding a place for it in the *Wake*. When Joyce got to the point where Buckley finds it in his heart to shoot the general, Beckett commented that the general's act of wiping his behind with a clump of sod was "another insult to Ireland" (Ellmann 1982, 398n). Joyce found in this remark the proper link to the *Wake* (353.15–19). R&O (197) suggest that there is also a link to the insulting way the Willingdone, in his fable, hangs up the hat of the lipoleum boys on the tail of his big wide arse.

The gist of the story is announced on the same page: "The strength of the Russian general is known throughout the world; let us see what a little fellow can do!" (335.20–22). The pub customers call for the story to begin. They announce the names of the two men who will relate the shooting, "Butt" and "Taff"—Shaun and Shem (337.32–33, 35–36). The customers seem to regard the two assassins as flowers, budding relentlessly against Old King Winter and overthrowing him by virtue of their developing into maturity.

The television story begins with a spate of Russian, for the Crimean War. We now see the two participants, who are elaborately described in the stage directions for this television show; the second sense—sight—has been added to sound, to make up the whole broadscale drama of the attack on the father.

Butt will be the actual killer of the Russian general; Taff is simply a subtle instigator. Butt as Shaun represents the murderous intellect.[30] Butt starts off by describing the seven articles of clothing of the Russian general, all of them associated with the Crimean War. These also associate the general with HCE in all of his aspects (339.10–13). There follow some hostile comments on the general. These are mingled with references to operas, all of a suitably bloody, imperial, and martial cast: *Il Trovatore*, about the murder of one brother by another; an aria from Meyerbeer's *Les Huguenots*, about a soldier firing cannons at a nunnery; a reference to Glinka's *A Life for the Czar*, in which a peasant saves the czar from assassination; and later Lortzing's opera *Zar und Zimmermann* (Czar and Carpenter) (341.9, 16, 17; 349.4).

There then follows an interlude, in which the television switches away to a horse race, the world-renowned Caerholme Event (341.18–342.32). Evidently this horse race, while originating in Ireland, is universal in application. Joyce reinforces his theme of uncertainty by reminding us through the name of the race that the odds against any event occurring are a thousand to one, or a guinea to a gooseberry (342.15–16). He also reminds us through the name of the prize for the race, The Liverpool Silver Cup, that there is many a slip 'twixt the cup and the lip. In fact, given the random nature of events in the universe, the odds against any particular event occurring are very great. However, given eternity, all events can reoccur without limit.

Here the events that occur foreshadow the coming destruction of the father. Sure enough, the order of the horses in the race (342.19–26) reproduces the war map of the Willingdone Museyroom, indicating the destructive nature of the "race." The Willingdone Museyroom is also evoked by exclamations of *Pamjab!* and *Bumchub!* that recall the "bombshoob" sought madly by Shimar Shin (10.9).

The father-horse, ECH, Emancipator (owner HCE), later called Immensipater, is rushing after the flanks of his two daughters, both owned by their mother. Immensipater is hotly pursued by his three sons: Shem, a man made of ink; Shaun blazing with wrath, like the Bailey lightship; and Shimar Shin, the phallic Davy, whose name here suggests ratatouille but also echoes a volley of machine-gun fire, appropriate to the executive assassin of the group. These three are at this point bay geldings, since the sexual power is still monopolized by their father.

Homo Made Ink		Furstin II
Bailey Beacon →	Immensipater →	
Ratatuohy		The Other Girl

The resemblance of the order of the racehorses to the order at the end of battle in the Willingdome Museyroom episode is not coincidental. Such a thing to happen here! exclaims the announcer, adding that the Lord Mayor is profoundly annoyed, or amused (342.26, 28). The Lord Mayor may well be subject to conflicting emotions: he is about to be deposed. However, as we will see, the loss of the paternal power is, in a real sense, a great relief to the guilty holder of that power, who has been haunted by the guilt of destroying his own father.

The discussion between Butt and Taff recommences. Butt describes how the general began to defecate, with a fierce smell. Butt draws a bead on the general, but hasn't the heart to fire (345.2–3). What fun! exclaims Taff. You hadn't the heart! (345.8–9).

There is then another intermission, in which reference is made to the holy marriage of the Winter Father with his mother-sister at Christmas (346.4–7). The wild Arabian Nights riders, driving furiously like King Jehu in the Bible, derive from the Zurich holiday of Sechseläute. This annual festival takes place in June, at Johannisfeuer, "jehumisphere," which M identifies as St. John's Eve, or Midsummer Eve. The end of the festival features the wild racing of the Zurich guilds, dressed in their medieval costumes, around the Böögg, the representation of Old King Winter, a huge conical pile of faggots topped with a bearded paper face. At the ringing of the evening Angelus at six p.m., the winner of the guild race will toss a torch on the pile of faggots. When the flames reach the head, which is filled with fireworks, Old King Winter's glowering countenance will explode, signaling the end of the old regime and the advent of the new order of springtime. Here Old King Winter, HCE, is close to the end of his reign.

The discussion continues until the quality of the television picture suddenly improves. The electronic operation of the television set is described in detail (349.6–16). The screen lights up to show the figure of the Russian general, here dressed as Poppy O'Donohue, the general of the Jesuits (349.19–20)—the Russian general and the head of the Jesuit order, the authority figure of both Church and State. This figure exhibits several medals. He appears clearly to the brothers, who then can "see" their father with great clarity. They both become the "seeboy" of the Museyroom fable who, having risen up from between his brothers, becomes enraged by the sight of the father and madly seeks the means to destroy him. The same thing happens here: when Poppy O'Donohue sacrilegiously attempts to pluck the fruit of the Tree of Immortality in the Garden of Eden (350.1–2), he has taken one step too far. The father's attempt to avoid his fate, his death and succession by his sons, brings about his downfall.

Butt alters his appearance to seem like Oscar Wilde (350.10–12), who also attempted to destroy a father, the Marquess of Queensberry, the father of his lover. Then Butt, after a moment's hesitation, hovering like Mahomet's coffin between heaven and earth (353.6), prepares to do his duty. In a spate of references to World War I, Butt declares that before the apparition could draw his Lewis machine gun, "I shot him like a white slaver! Humpty Dumpty is dumped, the unbeliever!" (352.14–15).

He dared me to do it, insists Butt, and I did do it (353.10–11). Remember that the father in the Willingdone Museyroom assisted in his own downfall by tendering his matchbox to Shimar Shin. Butt, amid references to the battle of Clontarf, the last battle won by the native Irish for seven hundred years, describes how he carried out the murder "when I saw him, while twelve o'clock was rolling all over our Lord's land Ireland, and heaving up that sod of turf to clean his, to wipe himself, and sticking out his bottom . . . at that insult to Ireland!" (353.15–19). The account of the killing contains a number of historical references. The word "rolland" (353.15), which obviously points to the *Song of Roland*, also signifies the great bell Rollant in Ghent, which rang as a signal for the Spanish soldiers to murder all the inhabitants of the resisting Protestant city. Another phrase, "an exitous erseroyal *Deo* Jupto" (353.18), besides referring to HCE's big wide harse, echoes Psalm 113, "In exitu Israel de Aegypto," which not only celebrates a great liberation from tyranny but is also the psalm used by Dante in his Can Grande letter to illustrate the quadripartite exegetical method of medieval literature. In the same line "instullt," referring to the insult to Ireland, may contain the German word *Stuhl*, which means both "chair" and "excrement"; the boys intend to pull down the tyrant from his seat of power, which is also the seat of relieving the bowels.

Butt calls, "Ready, aim, fire!" in Italian, and shoots (353.19–21). The shooting of the general with a crozier suggests the crossbow of the Ancient Mariner. The "cockshock" suggests the death of Cock Robin, as well as the destruction of the father's phallus. Of course, "rockrogn" announces Ragnarök, the cyclical Norse end of the world. For Joyce, the passing of the creative power from the father to the sons is indeed the end of one world and the beginning of a new world.

The killing of the Russian general sets off an even-more-than-horrible titanic explosion, which occurs at exactly twelve o'clock midnight (353.22–32). The atom is annihilated, an astonishing anticipation by Joyce of the atomic bomb.[31] However, it is also true that the world is created *ab nihil*, from nothing, by the word, the "etym"—a double meaning befitting Joyce's theme of creation and destruction. The destructive aspect of the deed, the destruction of the Winter King or the Russian general, is balanced by its creative aspect. The deprived sons acquire power. They become aristocrats by this creative destructive act, and in a male version of "Cinderella," plump country bumpkins "fairygodmother" themselves into landaus as the London elegants in the London elegance of Piccadilly. The transformation is worldwide; it occurs in Hawaii and Africa, in Rome and Athens, in space and time.[32] This vivid image of destruction echoes Stephen Dedalus's description of the end of history in *Ulysses*: "I hear the ruin of all space, shattered glass and toppling masonry, and time one livid final flame" (2.9–10). Both *Ulysses* and *Finnegans Wake* center on the loss of power by the older generation in favor of the children.

Butt and Taff, now one and the same person, are ideally reconstituted (354.8; 355.1). The destruction of the dominant father causes a shift of power within the family, and allows the sons to become one person, a young man on the road to maturity. From this point on in the *Wake*, Shem and Shaun are one person, an unevenly developing young male adult bearing his genitals uneasily in his trousers.

Commentary on Story by Customers and HCE (355.10–359.20)

The customers and HCE discuss the story. HCE is uneasily aware that both stories are relevant to him and to his family predicaments, and so he tries to universalize the stories, to attract attention away from himself. He gives an example of arousal by literature: he was reading a piece of literature while on the toilet and found himself unintentionally aroused—well, all men have lecherous impulses, and you are not guilty for what happens involuntarily! His customers are skeptical.

Song of the Nightingale (359.21–361.35)

This section, amid constantly increasing signals of danger to HCE, contains the contribution of Issy, a delightful aria all about castration of the Father.

The radio voice returns and declares that we have been listening to an excerpt from John Whiston's production of *The Coach with the Six Insides*. Who the six inside passengers are is not explained: the Earwicker family contains only five members. However, there is a geometrical figure called a tesseract, which has in fact "six insides." It consists of a cube centered inside a larger cube, with each vertex of the smaller cube attached to the corresponding vertex of the larger cube, making six slant-sided inside polyhedrons in three dimensions, or folded into four dimensions, if time is considered the fourth dimension. The relevance of this figure to *Finnegans Wake* is not clear.[33]

HCE is now very uneasy indeed. He is haunted by his guilt: the stories are called ghost stories, to be continued in a fear-filled night (359.26–28). In fact, the whole atmosphere is becoming distinctly ominous.

The song of the swallow and the nightingale follows. In this section, Joyce has the swallows sing out (359.28). It will be recalled just what the swallows and the nightingales were singing about in *The Waste Land* and in "Sweeney Among the Nightingales": Procne and Philomela were singing of the ghastly rape of Philomela and of their intention to avenge themselves on the guilty king Tereus by feeding him the stewed-up flesh of his own son. Here the song is just as ominous, if a bit more jolly. Joyce's nightingale sings to commemorate a violent act, in this case castration rather than murder. However, the castration of HCE ends up with the loss of the father's power, so the castration is a kind of murder after all.

The song is introduced by a radio voice setting the scene for the nightingale song.[34] The setting is lovely: dewy bushes shelter nightingales amid rose scenery at dusk. The names of thirteen composers sound out in this introduction: Rossini, Haydn, Pergolesi, Meyerbeer, Bellini, Mercadante, Beethoven, Wagner, Bach, Gluck, Glinka, John Field, and Mozart. The Swedish Nightingale Jenny Lind appears twice, once in "Jinnyland" (359.35) and once combined with Florence Nightingale (360.2).

An imitation of the nightingale song segues into the "Tit-Willow" song from *The Mikado* (360.2–3). This phrase reminds us that Issy is really two twin girls, a good little girl and also (as here) a very bad little girl, a real Salome. The two girls are going to sing a Willow Song. Koko's song in *The Mikado*, "Tit-Willow," is comic indeed, but it too has ominous aspects. Koko is singing it to keep from being boiled alive by the emperor for killing the crown prince, and Koko's only chance to avoid a dreadful death is to woo the ugly and violent Katisha. This he does with the song about the unrequited love of a dickybird, which leads to the bird's suicide. Not really a lighthearted song at all, especially when one recalls the original "Willow Song," Desdemona's song in *Otello*, also sung against an extremely ominous background. Willow Songs from Shakespeare's time on have traditionally been sung before death. Here Issy/Essie's Willow Song announces the moral death of HCE.

Let every son of a bitch keep still in reverence! orders the announcer (360.3–4). The three lurking soldiers, the two testicles and the phallus, now described in musical terms, get ready to do their duty (360.4–5). The song begins ripplingly (360.22); the beginning of a real nightingale solo consists of a series of light chirps leading into long, heartfelt, sustained notes. The triple "rip" may also provide a murderous hint here of the three soldiers combined with Jack the Ripper. Then the nightingale announces herself (although in reality only the male nightingale sings) as a bulbul, the Iranian word for "nightingale," expanded by an Italian affix indicating large size.

The nightingale's song is a hypnotic, mesmerizing chant, weakening its intended victim, HCE. The chant is directed at his phallus, by many indications. The "will . . . willy . . . wouldn't" sequence recalls the use of the modal auxiliary "will" and its past tense version "would" earlier, in "a burning would is come to dance inane" (250.16), where the Elizabethan meaning of "will" includes not only volition but specifically male sexual desire, and in fact the penis itself.

The intense concentration on the "willy" immediately spreads out to include the testicles as well (360.25–27). The druids would cut the holy mistletoe with a golden sickle on the sixth day of the moon (M), and *gui* is French for "mistletoe." In Bellini's *Norma*, the moon priestess takes the place of the druids in their mistletoe ceremony. However, the whole mistletoe ceremony is a symbolic representation of a castration, with the *grappes*, or clusters, of mistletoe on the oak representing the genitals of the oak.

The naughty girl then gazes even more closely at the father's phallus, and comments feverishly and mockingly on its size and on the comparative smallness of her own genitals (360.31–34). At the thought of the enormous male instrument of pleasure, the singer begins to experience *dessous troublants*, to quote *Ulysses*—ants in her pants, we would say—and happily envisages letting her harlequin boyfriend look up at her underwear (360.36–361.1). She ends the song with more praise for the size of the imagined phallus, and further imagines with delight the entry of the phallus into her diminutive receptacle, here envisaged, to the tune of "Ding, dong, bell, Pussy's in the well," as a cat, with obvious punning possibilities (361.13–15). Swift's epigram about twelve men in armor easily defeating one man in his shirt is adapted to Joyce's use as "man in his armor," which means a male wearing a condom.

The song ends with self-praise—What a nice old buzzard! But what neat young girls!—and another ominous phrase declaring the singer's intention to kill "Kelly," meaning HCE (361.15–17). Here all the leaves begin to laugh at the thought of the dark games to follow. The little girls are aware only of their joy at the overthrow of their father, and do not realize that the death of the older generation inevitably involves their own. The episode ends with the evocation of the ending of many *Arabian Nights* tales—"And they all lived happily ever after until the inevitable end came and Death took them all" (361.18–31).

Commentary by HCE (361.36–367.7)

HCE has been listening nervously to all of this, and he begins to sweat with fear (361.35). However, he rallies bravely, and begins to defend himself. What you say may be true, but we are all guilty! HCE depends on the shaky legal maxim that what all are guilty of, none are guilty of. He launches into a complex defense claiming that he was misunderstood, and that anyway no one has the right to stop human freedom in any way. Revising Parnell's proud claim that "No man has the right to fix a boundary to the march of a nation,"

HCE declares (365.26–27) that no mother has the punishing ability to cut off a man's phallus, to make of no effect the lurch of emotion that leads to the sexual act. He insists that all boys and girls owe him a debt of gratitude for introducing sex to the world, and he comes to a Falstaffian period—full stop (366.30). The text comments that HCE then sat down, Punct! (367.7).

Midnight Attack on the Father by the Children (367.8–382.30)

The midnight attack on the father by a mob of his almost mature children, the climax of II.3, is choreographed with great care by Joyce. The ferocious marching song of the children, who have landed on the coast on their raid, is interspersed with panicky comments by HCE and the Four Old Men and fragments of earlier songs, along with bombastic but ultimately vain commands by the forces of Authority.

What happens first in this central section is that HCE, unnerved by the Song of the Nightingale, summons up the forces of Authority: the Four Old Men, and Sackerson, the bouncer of the bar. The Four Old Men enter (367.8–36) and attempt to establish order with "Guns"—that is, firearms and also the Buddhist precepts of the Gunas—but are buffeted by waves of fear (368.1–23). There is also an Omar Khayyam parody (368.24–26), a "Casey Jones" parody (368.27–29), physical description of the Four Old Men (368.30–369.15), and a commentary by the Four Old Men (369.16–370.29).

The Four Old Men wear masks, which they immediately doff (367.8–9). They begin chattering, and are identified as our old uncles possessed by impotent sexual desire (367.14). They are also identified as the four Evangelists (367.15–17), complete with the figures traditionally associated with them: the angel for Luke, the lion for Mark, the ox or calf for Matthew, and the eagle for John (367.32–33).

However, these evangelists do not bring messages of peace and love; they are frightened, senile forces of repression. Joyce, a brilliant analyst of politics, was very well acquainted with the habits of authority when threatened: in a crisis, all geniality and compromise suddenly vanish, and blind violence takes their place. For example, in *A Portrait*, the pandying of Stephen is directly connected to the fear and guilt of the ecclesiastical authorities in Clongowes directly after the death of Parnell, which had set off volcanic political passions, as evidenced in the Christmas Day dinner scene (see Epstein 1971, 35–51).

At this point in the *Wake*, the fear growing in HCE produces a climate of violent repression. The Four Old Men begin to produce incoherent but vehe-ment moral precepts, all adding up to categorical imperatives not to frighten old people. The Buddhist moral precepts, the Gunas, are here merged with actual guns, perhaps those of the First World War.

After the parodies of the Rubáiyát and of the American song about Casey Jones, the railroad engineer who wrecked a train, we suddenly begin to see with the eyes of the matured children what the Four Old Men look like: one has a square large face with an atlas jacket; the second has bright brown eyes and blue sacks for shoes; the third has a peaked bookish nose over a lousy shirt; and the fourth has red hair and a straw-colored belt (368.30–33). We now see clearly the weak faces of old authority, as if they were four Garrett Deasys.

In a few pages, the raging children will see their father in a blazingly clear light. The main feature of this section of the *Wake* is the clearing of the eyes of the children, so that they can see what pathetic, powerless creatures the older generation turn out to be. However, Joyce always despised physical violence. The children "overthrow" the father in a purely Joycean way: they lose all respect for him, as does the young man in Hawthorne's "My Kinsman Major Molineux." The loss of respect for authority figures is the main lever for revolutions of all kinds, and here also the clarity of the youthful vision overturns the old order.

Joyce was a great analyst of the psychological forces surrounding revolu-tion. In the third section of *A Portrait*, the Jesuit fathers at Clongowes Wood school suddenly allow Father Dolan to punish the students illegally, since the forces of order fear that the students will react to the death of Parnell and start a rebellion. It is only the determination of Stephen Dedalus that halts the reactionary counterrevolution (see Epstein 1971, 36–51).

Here in this section of the *Wake* (370.30–371.5), the violent forces of order suddenly erupt. To reinforce the orders of the old men, Sackerson, the vio-lent policeman, enters with a "Boumce!" Note that the conventional Eliza-bethan and Jacobean representation of a cannon noise—"Bounce!"—is here spelled with an *m*; after all, it is the good cannon of Michael the archangel that is going off, not the cannons of Old Nick the devil—hence the letter *m*!

It is *Polizeistunde,* official closing time. The "boumcer" Sackerson has come in to pump the fear of the Lord into those sons of bitches! Only four minutes more! (370.30–371.1).

HCE attempts to strangle the vipers in his bosom (371.2–5), but it is too late for paternal violence. A mob of HCE's children has landed on the sea-coast (indicated by the crowd's cry invoking Ostia, the port of Rome). His maturing children are coming to destroy him.

The destruction of HCE, the wildest section of the night episodes, is accomplished in a triumph of Joyce's art, an intermingling of songs and comment that deserves careful analysis.

The War March

The mob of HCE's grown-up children march toward the pub, striding to a powerful tune with a savage lyric. Their marching song is not Hosty's "Ballad of Persse O'Reilly," although that hostile rann plays a part in this violent scene. At first, the words sung by the distant mob are indistinct, but then they become all too clear (371.6–8, 18–20, 30–32; 372.25–27; 373.9–11).

The language of this poem is interesting. Although the meter is a pounding iambic tetrameter, the war march owes much of its savage power to the many accented closed syllables, that is, syllables that begin and end with consonants. For example, in the fourth and fifth stanzas, all but four or five of the sixteen accented syllables are closed. The poem also draws power from the high number of double consonants and diphthongs, which give the mouth a great deal of vehement exercise.

The words of the war march have a rich background. The basic source is the old nursery rhyme about Tom, the Piper's Son. However, as Glasheen and M make clear, a more proximate source is a Dublin parody of the nursery rhyme devoted to an enormously popular eighteenth-century castrato, Giusto Ferdinando Tenducci, known as Senesino (1736–1800?). His great fame began in 1762, with his solo aria "Water Parted" in Thomas Arne's *Artaxerxes*. Joyce quoted the name of this solo to evoke the hydrological cycle of ALP, and the inevitability of history.

Water parted from the sea
May increase the river's tide.
To the bubbling fount may flee,
Or through fertile valleys glide.

Though in search of lost repose,
Through the land 'tis free to roam,
Still it murmurs as it flows,
Panting for its native home.

A. War March—First Stanza (371.6–8)

The words of the first stanza of the war march, sung just as the mob of children land on the seacoast, are blurred by distance and the wind. HCE is identified as dour and Germanic, and there is some confused comment about him in youth and old age.

B. Ballad—First Reference (371.11–17)

In response to the first stanza of the war march, HCE remembers the funeral and wake of the Giant. Now, however, the funeral is for "Himhim" (371.10)—himself.

There follows a bloated version of some lines from Hosty's "Ballad of Persse O'Reilly," with HCE's characteristic stutter enormously amplified.

A. War March—Second Stanza (371.18–20)

The words of the second stanza are much clearer than those of the first; the mob is closer. By all the rules of sexual sport, it is correct that young people should be allowed to charm away the night with dalliance, while the aged are dumped down to take care of daily affairs. It will be recalled that in the Willingdone Museyroom the Willingdone eventually surrenders a light to set fire to the fuse of a bomb of his raging son Shimar Shin, and thereby acquiesces in his own downfall.

In the embracing of night, we have here an echo of Wagner's *Tristan und Isolde*. In the love scene in the second act, both Tristan and Isolde dismiss the day as garish, and embrace darkness and night as the proper setting for love. Night is equated with the peace of death, light with the suffering in life. Here, in my translation, are two typical passages from the opera:

> TRISTAN: The day! the day! The jealous day! To the day, the greatest enemy, hatred and mourning! As you put out the torch, I wish that I could put out the light of impertinent day, to avenge all of love's sufferings! Is there no pain, no sorrow that does not awaken with its light?

> TRISTAN and ISOLDE: (*together*) Oh eternal night, sweet night! Highly exalted night of love! Those you hold, those you smile upon, how could they without suffering awaken? Now banish suffering, lovely death, desired with yearning, love-death! In your arms, devoted to you, primeval sacred warmth, freed from the suffering of awakening!

There are deep implications in this evocation of darkness and night. Darkness and warmth are the signs and conditions of youth in *A Portrait* and *Ulysses*; light and day are the signs of the powerful father in both books. However, it is only when Stephen acquires his own paternal light that he is ready to become a mature artist. In the *Wake* the attempts by Shaun-Tristan at sexual activity—the kissing and cuddling in II.4 and the sadistic visions leading to masturbation in III.2—and the old people's attempt at sex in III.4 are all failures. It is only at the end of the book, when the sun-son-husband rises up in the east, that a true act of bodily and spiritual love is accomplished.[35]

B. Ballad—Second Reference (371.22–27)

After an allusion to "The Campbells Are Coming" (371.21), there is a second reprise of "The Ballad of Persse O'Reilly" in HCE's guilty mind. The pubkeeper tells his customers to leave the pub.

A. War March—Third Stanza (371.30–32)

The first line of the third stanza evokes the tree and the stone, soon to be combined into Tree-Stone = Tristan. The children will steal HCE's crown, and use it to brew their drinks.

C. The Old Men Panic (371.33–372.24)

We now hear many echoes of the Prankquean fable, as signs of the establishment of a new family.

The Four Old Men and the customers try to escape from the pub. The Four Old Men are identified at 372.12 in a phrase evoking Cicero's treatise *De Senectute*, "On Old Age," here combined with a clear "scenic" vision of the oldsters by the children. The seeboy of the Willingdone Museyroom, who sees his father and then destroys him, is here expanded into the clear-sighted children of guilty fathers.

A. War March—Fourth Stanza (372.25–27)

HCE's cane and hat, two signs of paternal power, and symbols in *Ulysses* of Stephen Dedalus's artistic efficacy, are here destroyed or stolen by the rebellious children.

D. The Gathering of the Children (372.28–373.8)

The children have gathered for a picnic combined with a lynching party (372.30), and the Four Old Men are at their wits' end trying to escape. There is a savage game of Hide and Seek, with the Old Men trying to hide and the mob seeking them. The shouts of Hide! Seek! Hide! Seek! seem to echo *Sieg Heil!* a reference by Joyce to the use by the Nazis of savage youth—young yahoos—to overthrow the old order in Germany and the world. Joyce may also be recalling the use of youths by unscrupulous demagogues in Ibsen's *League of Youth*, evoked at 310.17.

The four fear-tossed waves of Hide and Seek rise to a huge crescendo at 373.7 as waves of panic rising from alpha to omega.[36]

A. War March—Fifth Stanza (373.9–11)

The mob of "yahooth" race up the straining stairs, and announce the exit of the old bugger and ogre, the Winter King.

Destruction of HCE by the Children (373.12–380.5)

Now, at the beginning of the violent climax of this violent chapter, HCE as scapegoat and guilty Richard III is suddenly revealed in a blaze of light. He is described as the scapegoat (373.12) with a phrase that derives from "Hircus Civis Eblanensis" in the Anna Livia chapter (215.27), in which HCE is identified in Latin as "the [scape]goat of the city of Dublin." However, the phrase is here changed in significant ways; the goat is combined with Orcus, the Roman god of the dead, and the apple of the Garden of Eden is combined with "nuncio." That is, the apple of the Garden of Eden has caused the fall to death of HCE, the "chiefest" of sinners, and the annunciation to Mary of the birth of the new generation, the young Messiah.

All of this is now clear to the sharp eyes of the new generation, as the "seeboys" confront the crouching, hairy scapegoat bowed beneath the hump of his guilt. The children shout that he should be ashamed of himself, hiding that shape in his coat, and for resembling so barefacedly the greedy prince, Richard III. The identification of HCE as Richard is followed by the first thudding blows directed at the guilty father (373.16).

Shouting that their father thought they would never grow up, or wake up (375.18–9), the children proceed to destroy their father, or at any rate to reduce him to a nullity. They pull down his pants and kick him like a football

(373.31–32; 374.19–20; 375.3–4, 21–22). They brand him and set him on fire (374.32–33; 378.17; 379.13). They hang him (377.8–9, 17–18) and crucify him (377.36–378.1).

After these attacks, they think that he is dead as a doorknob (378.1–2). Nevertheless, despite all their effort, he remains obstinately alive (378.17; 379.13). Despite the battered father's stubborn powers of survival, the Sechseläute ceremony has taken place. The power of the Winter King has been destroyed, and the midnight Angelus rings out (379.27–30). There is, in reality, no midnight Angelus, but Joyce supplies one. The blows landing on the humped scapegoat at 379.7–8, 27, 28, 29, 30 are combined with the phrases associated with the Angelus—the bell for Sechseläute and the Conception by the Holy Spirit of the Messiah and the new age.

The sexual authority of the old father has been destroyed; the Winter King has abdicated; Falstaff's staff has fallen, as when he, with buck's horns on, is attacked in Windsor Great Park by the disguised merry wives of Windsor (379.18–19). The new sexual order, the new order, the new powers, the sexual order of the children—three to two—is now in place, and alpha has ended up as omega.

Coda

The mob of HCE's children rush out of the pub. The bar is empty, leaving behind only HCE, the pubkeeper, now poor old King Roderick O'Conor, dancing merrily about and singing, and finishing up remnants of liquor left by customers (380.6–382.26). Roderick O'Conor was the last High King of Ireland, and he was left a shadow king when the Normans were invited in on a domestic quarrel and remained as conquerors.[37] However, HCE is anything but upset at his loss. Battered and ruined as he is, he wanders around the empty pub, pouring the leftover drinks into one glass and draining it, and singing a merry song (381.23–24). Eventually he slumps onto a chair or commode.

HCE's many almost-mature children now amalgamate into two lovers, Tristan and Isolde, on their honeymoon voyage. With some of Joyce's characteristic grace in describing twilight effects, the reader sees the ship of the young lovers sailing away into the starry night.[38] As we will see in the next chapter, Old King Mark is comatose in the hold, and the Four Old Men as seagulls are singing their farewell to the old order. The ship is sailing from the Liffey away to lands of night (382.27–30).

Book II, Chapter 4: Tristan and Isolde

The tale of Tristan and Isolde opens with the sound of four seagulls shrilly screaming a contemptuous song about old King Mark, who has been superseded by the two lovers. The seagulls' song can be heard any day around any port in the world. This song is a triumph of Joyce's demotic poetry, poetry produced by other sources than professional poets, as is the ending of the *Wake* itself.

The seagulls' song begins with a line that has become famous in modern subatomic physics: *Three quarks for Muster Mark!* (383.1). The physicist Murray Gell-Mann, seeking a name for a newly postulated constituent of atomic particles, pondered that (as it then seemed) there were three of these fundamental objects for each subatomic particle. Three quarks in one particle brought the Joyce line to mind, and the rest is history.

The song of the seagulls reveals Mark's total loss of power. He has even lost his title: King Mark has become Mister Mark, without much of a bark, and all he can do to find his shirt and his semen-speckled trousers in the dark. The four seagulls laugh a foursquare laugh at him (383.8–14). They anticipate that Tristan is the young spark that would "tread" her (the term for the sexual attack of the cock on the hen).

In this section, Joyce brilliantly conveys the sound of the seabirds overhead screaming shrilly amd gleefully (383.15–18). "The death of Cock Robin" provides the form for this last sentence; the mention of death recalls the desire for night and death in Wagner's opera. The German form *kuss* recalls Wagner, but the alteration of the names of the two lovers—"Trustan" and "Usolde"—spells out Tristan-Adam's trueheartedness and the ultimate betrayal by Isolde-Eve. In the original French legend, Tristan marries a second Isolde; these two Isoldes are the basis for the mirror doubles of Issy-Essie, the good little girl and the bad little girl. In the original legend, the bad Isolde of the White Hands informs Tristan mendaciously that King Mark has not forgiven him, which plunges Tristan into despair. Later, in III.3, one of the anguished voices crying out of the gulf of Irish history inside the great mound is Tristan's, crying that he was true to his bride of the brine (see 499.30–32; 500.21–22, 25, 27, 30; 501.3).

The nuptial ship and the winds blowing it are described (383.19–384.5). Then the Four Old Men, narrators of the chapter, are introduced in a passage that reproduces the motion of four waves, each one breaking on the one before (384.6–17). They burst out in a version of an old American college song:

"Glorious, glorious! / One keg of beer for the four of us. / Glory be to God
that there are no more of us, / 'Cause one of us could drink it all alone!"

History of the World Turned Upside Down (386.12–395.25)

The four senile historians then launch into an account of world history—all
wrong, and with the sexes confused, as are their own.

Johnny (386.12–388.9)

The four Evangelists—"Mamalujo" in Joyce's manuscripts and in the text—
are here presented in scrambled order, which echoes their total confusion,
augmented by impotent sexual excitement. Johnny babbles on and on about
the facts of Irish history, which he gets as wrong as did Garrett Deasy in
Ulysses, obsessing about a "half a tall hat" over and over, confusing genders, calling his colleagues and himself "heladies" (386.14–5) and turning the
male heroes of Ireland into women: Daniel O'Connell becomes Mrs. Dana
O'Connell, and his statue, looming over the Liffey at the foot of O'Connell
Street, is relocated as "prostituent" behind Trinity College (386.22–23); Sir
Roger Casement becomes Lady Jules Casemate, and his 1916 landing in Ire-
land becomes "her" landing in the year of the flood 1132 s.o.s. (387.22–23).

After a great deal of nonsense, Johnny finally gets to the story of Tristan,
and presents it in reversed, farcical, and vulgar form (388.1–6). Mark, the
king guy, is kicked into the yard, and his nephew Tristan, a tactful lover,
enters farcically from a fire escape in his nightshirt. Isolde tumbles for him
and into bed, and her knees loosen, to the tune of the orgasmic love-death
that ends Wagner's opera.

Marcus (388.10–390.33)

Marcus takes up the tale, summing up the Irish provinces in Joyce's brilliant
formulation of Irish history as "Ulcer, Moonster, Leanstare, and Cannought"
(389.5). "Ulcer" for Ulster is particularly succinct and accurate. "Moonster"
for Munster suggests the mooncalf stare of the provincial peasant. "Leanstare" for Leinster displays the unemployed leaning against the walls and
staring vacantly. "Cannought" for Connaught shows the ignorance and incapacity of the inhabitants of that backward province.

Marcus proceeds to describe the violence of Irish history accurately as
"Killorcure and Killthemall and Killeachother and Killkelly-on-the-Flure"
(389.6–7). When he eventually gets around to the Tristan story, he evokes a

Byronic Tristan gazing into Isolde's eyes, and the passage ends with an echo of lines from *Childe Harold*: "Roll on, thou deep and dark blue ocean, roll!" (389.22–28). This Byronic echo is overlaid, and undercut, by a cartoon from *Punch* that Joyce certainly knew, as he knew all the classic jokes from that publication:

> (*Young cockney with his girl, paused on the seafront at Margate facing the sea, elegantly quoting Byron with a gesture*): Roll on, thou deep and dark blue ocean, roll!
> (*Starry-eyed young girl, gazing up in wonder at him*): Oh Harold, you marvelous man! It's doing it!

Lucas (390.34–392.13)

It is difficult to say just what Lucas is talking about, except that he is reproducing the same background noise as the two preceding Evangelists. It is possible that the lack of relevancy in his monologue, and in Matt's that follows, is due to their excitement at the approach of the great kiss and cuddle of the two postadolescents on their narrow loveseat.

Matt (392.14–395.25)

Matt Emeritus takes up the tale. He, like the others, wanders in senile confusion among genders and historical errors. However, he ends with an introduction to the big kiss of Tristan and Isolde, with allusions to *The Book of the Dead* and the Egyptian return of the soul to the body after death—"the opening of the mouth." Matt refers, trembling with impotent desire, to the three-two sexual symbol, and the kiss ("pogue") that opens the door to freedom and heaven (395.22–25).

The Kiss (395.26–398.6)

Apparently Isolde, in the tradition of Celtic maidens taking the active role in sex, initiates the kiss. Overcome with desire, with a queer little cry of "joysis crisis" she unites her lips with Tristan's (395.29–33). The phrase "joysis crisis" is one of Joyce's poetic triumphs: Isolde's ecstatic cry of "Jesus Christ!" combines with a "joyous crisis," a perfect description of sexual swooning allied to orgasm.

The big kiss given by Tristan to Isolde—truly a "French kiss" in twentieth-century American slang—is described in great comic detail, in terms of a football match (395.35–396.3). The massive missile of virile victory, Tristan's tongue, penetrates through the lines of Isolde's ivory teeth, eliciting a triumphal cry of "Alris!" which combines many of the letters of the lovers' names. This amalgamated cry is reminiscent of the mental cry of "Siopold!" in the Sirens episode of *Ulysses*, after the tenor solo given by Simon Dedalus and overheard by Leopold Bloom (11.752), in which the singer and the audience are united in one great artistic cry of joy.   It is significant that both this kiss and the attempted sexual encounter of the aged HCE with ALP in III.4 are described in terms of sport—the kiss with football, and the sexual encounter with cricket. It has been suggested that here Joyce is satirizing the widely held theory of British schoolmasters that sport would reduce the sexual stirrings of their young male charges.[39]

Well, the four old fools are beside themselves with vicarious delight. Their version of the great medieval princess makes her look very much like a horse and not very intelligent (396.8–10). A modern feminist critic would note that for these senile droolers the Irish princess is only a body, the dream object of adolescent males such as Tristan, and of declining old wankers such as themselves.

They find every justification for Isolde's disloyalty in the disability of old King Mark. "How can you blame her!" they exclaim, and mock the drowsy feeble old king, with his straggly beaver beard, his feeble, dutiful kiss goodbye, his plodding walk, his cheap clothes, and his toupee (396.13–18). They exclaim that it would be too much to offer such a pathetic old wreck so much as a pinch of hen shit (396.19–20), thereby passing judgment on themselves as equally pathetic creatures.

This sexual encounter between the young lovers is the first of four in the *Wake*. The others are in III.2 when Shaun's self-excitation leads to a feeble ejaculation, in III.4 when the attempt of the aging HCE only demonstrates his impotence, and, between the end of Book IV and the beginning of Book I, the final embrace of ALP and her son-husband-lover the sea. Only the last is a true love encounter. The French kiss in II.4 is merely the contact of two immature bodies. As in the other works of Joyce, the only successful sex acts here are those in which the mature bodies and the mature souls of the man and the woman join in a total embrace.

When the Kissing Had to Stop (396.21–398.33)

At any rate, whoever was guilty, the two swooning adolescents were kissing most passionately while the four oldsters made pathetic attempts to masturbate to the rhythm of the kissing (396.21–28). Finally, as all things must, the kissing has to stop. The old men, viewing the kissing as a mere mechanical rubbing of bodies, describe the action in mechanical terms, as the action of a motor car (396.29–33).[40] Eventually Tristan's pulpy tongue falls out of Isolde's mouth, plop! after he has popped the question. Ah now, it was totally terrific! exclaim Matthew, Mark, Luke, and John. And then they begin their babble once again, leading up to their closing serenade to their beloved Issy.

The Senile Serenade (398.29–399.28)

The four old men sing to their love in their characteristic dialects, including their characteristic metals (gold, silver, copper, and iron) and the name of one Irish province, Ulster, and a town in each of the other three (Dingle, Balbriggan, Cong).

Matt, the representative of Ulster, sings his song first, and a grim, violent song it is, as befits the violent history of the province that Joyce called "Ulcer." In Joyce's time, Ulster was the wealthiest of the provinces, and here Matt entices Issy with the gold in the bowels of the Bank of Ulster. The Scottish overtones of the Ulster accent are conveyed with the reference to "bawbees" (shillings). The aggressive Orange ignorance of the Catholicism hated by the North comes out in Matt's theologically grotesque reference to the mother of the Holy Ghost (399.1–2). The song of the North ends, appropriately enough, with the word "murder!" (399.2). Of love for Issy, there is not a shred, just a powerful urge to possess her violently.

Mark, speaking for Munster, produces a stream of lovely language in the most musical dialect of Irish English, the dialect of Cork, the native dialect of Joyce's father. Mark's poem consists of a come-all-ye addressed to the nymphs of Dingle beach in Kerry to greet Brinabride, an Aphrodite riding the surf in a curragh of shells and wearing a blue mantle that recalls the blue mantle of the Virgin. Brinabride, the bride of the briny waters, is the deepest name for the beloved of the Irish bards, as we see later on in III.3 when, from the depths of the mound of Yawn, the molten streams of Irish history burst out (499.35–501.5).

Then Luke, the representative of Leinster, in a debased, weary, and jolting passage, asks to be her nurse until he dies. He proffers nothing more for her than a warm sleep in his overcoat, and he dismisses young Irish heroes as "highsteppers" who certainly died bravely enough for her, but who will not support her. The tired old man can only offer to beg money for her.

John, the most senile and boastful of them all, claims that he spent all of Friday and Saturday making love to her—one of the more improbable claims in the book. He also identifies her as Maud Gonne, Yeats's beloved (399.22). Maud Gonne refused to marry Yeats, once asking scornfully, "Who would marry Willie?" Would the spectacular Maud even consider making the pathetic Johnny her lover? Joyce here dismisses the claims of all of Ireland, made by the Nationalist poets, to be the lovers of Kathleen na Houlihan.

The definitive answer to the various claims made by the ridiculous old men is given by their donkey, who produces loud heehaws of scorn after they have finished, saving his loudest heehaws for Johnny (399.29–30).

Joyce then provides one of his loveliest transitions (399.31–34), as the adolescent lovers at midnight prepare to enter into their adult phase in Book III. The light on the nuptial ship moves down the river as the tide flows down to the sea. The Four Old Men drink their beer, while the ship takes its predestined course. The lot of all of Ireland is cast; the development to adult status is going to take place.

The name "johnajeams," combining John and James, Shaun and Shem, is borrowed from Hamlet's soliloquy in act II, scene ii. There Hamlet, reproaching himself for delaying his revenge, compares himself to a village idiot, "John-a-dreams." The rest of this section is also borrowed, from Hamlet's speech to Horatio in act V, scene ii, when Hamlet, having revealed his misgivings about the duel with Laertes, stops Horatio from calling off the event: "Not a whit; we defy augury; there is special providence in the fall of a sparrow. If it be now, 'tis not to come; if it be not to come, it will be now; if it be not now, yet it will come; the readiness is all. Since no man has aught of what he leaves, what is 't to leave betimes? Let be." Here, in the middle of the night, Joyce allows his inevitable process to go forward—"led it be"—that is, let it go forward as it is "led" by the flow of the river. Here, as in *Hamlet*, we see the "spirit of reconciliation" (*Ulysses* 9.396). Shaun has joined with Shem to make "johnajeams," the combined adult man who bears his genitals uneasily in his trousers, and whose process of maturation is described in the next book. There the uneasily reconciled brothers step forward as a complete man, a man of mixed motives and drives, like all men.

3

Book III (*FW* 401–590)

The Age of Democracy (Vico)

TIME Medium

Time and the River Flow Forward

MIDNIGHT TO DAWN

Book III is devoted entirely to the development of Shaun to the stage of guilty fatherhood, to the assumption of the power, the guilt, and the suffering of the superseded HCE. Each chapter in Book III shows a step in the slow maturing of Fallen Man. In III.1 he is named as Shaun, and he falls for the first time. In III.2 he is Jaun—*jaune* for the yellow sunlight he is eventually to produce. He is also a mixture of Don Juan and a sadistic pedophile. Finally, he is Haun (he is vanishing like a ghost)—and he falls for the second time. In III.3 he is Yawn (semicomatose) and, as Rose suggests (44n1), he is Dawn itself since, at the end of this chapter, already the more somber opacities of the gloom have vanished (472.19–20), yet in III.3 Shaun has not only fallen, he is flat on his back. In III.4, as daylight grows, he is the old man asleep on the bed next to his old wife, a completely fallen man, getting ready to give away power and sexual potency to his son, the rising sun of Book IV.

Shaun has become Dawn. At the end of this book, daylight has almost dawned, and the ambivalently precious crown of maturity, with its burden of guilt, has passed to the new father, Shaun, who thenceforward walks through life bearing Shem, his genitals, curled up in his pajama trousers like a cod in a pot (593.22–23).

Book III, Chapter 1: Shaun Evades the Questioning of His Lower Half

Joyce first sketched out Book III, which he called "the four watches of Shaun," in 1924–25, and worked on it for years. Originally conceiving III.1 and III.2

as a single chapter, he separated them for publication in *transition* (Hayman 1990, 37), then kept the separation for the published book to preserve the symmetry of the four-chapter model.

Joyce explained III.1–2 to Harriet Weaver as "a description of a postman travelling backwards in the night through the events already narrated. It is written in the form of a *via crucis* of 14 stations but in reality it is only a barrel rolling down the river Liffey" (*Letters*, 1:214). The "barrel" is the combined Butt and Taff of II.3, in their reversed forms as "tub" and "vat," now one and the same person. Shaun is the modern conflicted male, bearing his genitals uneasily within his trousers. The genitals occasionally rouse themselves to produce difficult questions for Shaun to answer or (for the most part) to evade.

The west-to-east journey of Shaun (plus hidden Shem) also prepares the way for the great dawn scene in Book IV. One of Shaun's personae is that of Horus, the sun risen as the reborn son of Egyptian religion. Everyone knows that the sun "travels" from east to west during the day, but what happens afterward? Somehow the sun has traveled during the night back to its eastern springing-off place the next morning. The Egyptians unraveled this enigma by claiming that the sun travels under the earth in a boat from west to east, in time to rise up the next day. This is the "travelling backwards" of Shaun. In his vessel, a barrel, he voyages all night with the flow of the eastward-flowing Liffey, until in the morning he is ready to arise as Anna's tennis champion son clad in his blazing white flannels, at the mouth of Dublin Bay.

The Bedroom at Midnight (403.1–17)

Our attention is first called to the chiming of bells, a definitive chiming from alpha to omega. The narrative voice declares that it must be twelve o'clock; however, if we count, we hear only eleven chimes. Here we have a tribute to the relativity of Irish chronometry. Something similar is seen in part 5 of *A Portrait*, where Stephen is about to leave for his university classes: at this point the clock in his house shows a quarter to twelve, though the right time is twenty past ten, and as Stephen walks to the university, a clock in a dairy that he passes shows five minutes to five, but a clock nearby chimes eleven o'clock (see Epstein 1971, 104–5). The chimes near the Earwicker household in the *Wake* are no more accurate than those that Stephen hears or sees in *A Portrait*.

We now read one of Joyce's most beautiful sentences, describing the low beating of the hearts of the couple (403.5). We are in the Earwickers' bedroom, viewing the slumbering HCE, and dimly by his side ALP, his Anasta-sia (403.10–11). Anastasia means "resurrection" in Greek: ALP is the spirit of continuity.

The window reveals a foggy night, which will lead to a "soft" (misty) morning later on. There is a white fogbow (403.6), a rainbow effect caused by mist illuminated by gaslight. The rainbow itself, always a symbol of Fallen Man, is unfurled in words that stud the paragraph: "ruddled" expresses red, gorse is yellow or orange, broom is yellow and green, *blau* is blue, "hindigan" suggests indigo, and *Veilchen* is a violet (M).

The first thing we see is the nose of HCE, wrinkled, tinted by drinking. Next we see his blond hair. Then the narrator descries the face of HCE, which is wobbling indistinctly in the misty dark. However, with the word "remem-brandts," Joyce paints a clear picture of HCE's battered face for the reader—he compares it to the self-portraits that Rembrandt painted in his old age, faces battered by life and experience (403.10).

HCE is sleeping uneasily. He is having a nightmare: a black demon is looking hungrily at ALP (403.12–14). The staring demon, resembling a blue-toothed man, has a beaked nose like a wild Indian, and a horny hide. The name that HCE calls him, Gugurtha, resembles the name of the famous Numidian king Jugurtha, the enemy of the Romans—which in turn sug-gests that the demon is black. (There is a black nightmare figure in *Ulysses*, Haines's black panther.[1]) However, the form of the name Jugurtha in the text, "Gugurtha," suggests Gogarty. Did Joyce suspect that his onetime friend Gogarty had wished to make a play for Nora? Is this part of the background of *Exiles*?

The demon muses hungrily that ALP is the most beautiful woman in the world, and that he would like to eat her up. She would stick to the roof of his palate, he murmurs (403.14–17). Then HCE furiously banishes the demon from his dreams (403.17): "Hence! Away! Do not come near! Go to black! I switch off my mental light!" (Latin *apage* = "begone!"; *monite* = "beware!")

The demon may be banished from HCE's dreams temporarily, but the source of HCE's fear is permanent: he fears that his son will supersede him and take away his wife, as indeed he will. HCE is hagridden by this fear throughout the whole book; the father fears the maturing of the son, and sees it as his destruction. The demon is the maturing Shaun, who now, preceded by churchbells, puts in a memorable appearance.

The Entrance and Appearance of Shaun (403.18–407.9)

The unnamed narrator, who turns out to be the donkey of the Four Old Men, declares that he was just about to fall asleep when he heard a chime of bells ringing for midnight—the "chimes at midnight" that Falstaff admits he often heard as a rowdy young man.[2] The narrator notes that all is dark except for the highlights on the river and some garments, probably left over by the washerwomen of I.8 (403.22–404.3).

In another of Joyce's lovely nighttime phrases, a broad tone is heard, and all the creatures of the wood call out for Shaun (404.4–9). The four elements are here: the "breath" is air, the "woodfires" are fire, the "hummers in their ground" add earth, and the fourth element, water, is already provided by the dark gleaming river. This passage is a parody of an important passage in part 4 of *A Portrait*, when Stephen hears that he is going to enter the university and realizes what his mission in life is to be, and just before Life greets him in the form of a lovely girl. At that important moment he hears "fitful music . . . out of a midnight wood" (165), just as the narrator of this *FW* passage hears the melodies from his own midnight wood.

Shaun gradually appears. In a beautifully modulated passage, Joyce conveys the measured emergence of a figure from the dark wood, complete with expanding vowel clusters and a stagy vocabulary emphasizing the words "lo" and "'twas" (404.9–15).

Shaun's appearance too is stagy (404.16). He is dressed in seven articles of clothing—overcoat, brogues, jacket (with huge red buttons much too large for the buttonholes), waistcoat, necktie, frilled overshirt with his motto embroidered on it in the Irish colors of green and white and orange, and perfectly creased trousers. The Willingdone, the Jarl van Hoother, and later High King Leary are likewise dressed in seven articles of clothing, so Shaun is staking his claim as the father-authority figure.[3]

The donkey-observer is overcome with admiration at the sight of Shaun (405.11–17). The repeated reference to sight (Shaun's sense) and his "beamish brow," as if Shaun were the spirit of the beaming sun, confirms that Shaun is the spirit of external appearance, while Shem is constantly hidden away from sight.

The donkey explains Shaun's buoyant health and his rosy schoolgirl complexion (407.7) by Shaun's eating habits, which are indeed impressive. Shaun, the top half, the half that eats, eats incessantly (405.22–23). His input in his twenty-four-hour mealtime (German *Mahlzeit*) is more than copious. He consumes well over forty types of food and drink during the day, including a blood orange, bacon and eggs, rice pudding, cold steak, then round steak (very rare), rice and peas, Yorkshire pudding, chops, goulash, pumpernickel, an onion, a saddlebag steak,[4] a swig of porter, sweet and Irish potatoes, broth, then some more eggs and bacon, beans, another type of steak, a duckling, cold veal, cabbage and green peas, a finger of gin, bread and dulse (a type of seaweed) and jam, a swig of wine, another swig of wine (the Greek wine Mavrodaphne), custard, tea, butter, ham and Jaffa oranges, a bottle of Guinness, and a tart to end all. John McCormack was a notable glutton, eating and drinking everything in sight and becoming quite obese early in life, but he was a piker compared to Shaun. Shaun may have started out in life as a thin young man, but his weight increased outrageously as he grew up (407.5–6).

Shaun's Performance Begins (407.10–409.7)

"Overture and beginners!" (407.10) is the callboy's traditional cry at the commencement of the performance of a play—the overture is beginning, and those actors who are to be on stage as the curtain goes up should take their places. Shaun yawns melodiously down a scale (407.27–28). He begins to speak, mainly to complain about how much his feet hurt. He has walked a great deal, of course, but then, he is always complaining about the lower half of his body. He notes professionally that the curtain is up, and that the house is full of people who came in on free tickets, "deadheads" (407.35, 36).

Shaun now speaks about his brother. He states unconvincingly that he is fond of "that other," but insists that his brother is unoriginal (408.24–25). In fact, the gist of his responses to all the questions of the donkey is that he, Shaun, could write very much better than his disreputable twin, although Shaun's attempts at "Shemese" are less than competent; the top half needs the lower parts to create literature as well as physical offspring.

The Fourteen Questions (409.8–426.4)

The fourteen questions (although not all are questions) in III.1 expose the uneven maturing of Fallen Man, the male human being, a process that always contains many backslidings and self-questionings. The purpose of this chapter is to show Shaun uneasily becoming aware of his physical being, and of the physical universe. St. Francis referred to his own body as a donkey, and here in III.1 the donkey represents the male body, especially the unruly lower half, which is always making double-edged remarks and posing disconcerting questions to the uneasy rational and virtuous mind housed in the upper half.

The donkey-inquisitor slyly and obsequiously nudges Shaun into admitting that he has a tangible body, that he is not, in fact, made of smoke and mist (413.31), and that the invisible universe has an irreducible "meaty" base (419.3–4). The universe is material and real. Shaun's own body is real, not a tinted cloud similar to the body of Christ as seen by the heretic Valentine, "spurning Christ's terrene body" (*Ulysses* 1.658–59). In the last chapter of the *Wake*, the dawn chapter, we will see St. Patrick, over the objections of the idealistic Eastern sage, advocating the material universe, colored with all the tints of the rainbow, as the appropriate environment for Fallen Man.

As we noted before, Emerson wrote in "Nature" that idealists and Gnostics showed "a certain hostility and indignation toward matter." This emphasis on the physical is a most important Joycean theme, both in the *Wake* and elsewhere in Joyce's works. Joyce was a man for whom the visible, physical world existed—for whom, as Wallace Stevens wrote, "The greatest poverty is not to live / In a physical world" ("Esthétique du Mal," XV.1–2). However, Shaun hates the physical world and constantly tries to deny the material body and the material universe. His antimaterial attitude echoes that of the shallow Platonists in the Scylla and Charybdis chapter of *Ulysses*. In that chapter, Stephen rejects AE's assertion of the importance of "formless spiritual essences" (9.49) and insists firmly to himself, "Hold to the now, the here, through which all future plunges to the past" (9. 89), which is, as we have seen, a materialistic credo for Joyce himself in all of his own creations.

The bottom half, the ass, now begins his insidious questioning. The lower half of the body is always luring the upper half into admissions that the upper half would rather not make. The number of these remarks may represent the fourteen Stations of the Cross, which depicted fourteen stages of Christ's crucifixion; self-pitying Shaun sees himself as martyr and saviour. However, Shaun as saviour has weak spots, specifically those beneath the waist.

I. Question and Answer (409.8–30)

Shaun shows a characteristic evasiveness throughout this chapter; in fact, he once answers one of the donkey's questions with the answer to another. Here his first word in response to the first question is "Goodbye," and his last word is "Adieu!" (409.11, 30). (Later, we will see that the eleventh question of the donkey requests an Aesop fable, which Shaun has already recited in answer to the eighth remark.)

The donkey begins with a gently malicious question as to whether Shaun was given a permit to carry letters—that is, whether Shaun is an independent agent, or is under orders from someone else, or from some other part of the body! Shaun, of course, evades the question and continues to complain about his feet. He also shows that he has recognized the donkey as a Shem representative by saying in Italian, "How do you do today, my dark sir?" (409.14–15), the characteristic manner of Shaun greeting Shem throughout the book.

In this section occurs the phrase "in echo rightdainty" (409.12), which refers to the first tenor aria in Rossini's *Barber of Seville*, "Ecco ridente in cielo" (Behold [the dawn] smiling in the sky). Here Shaun looks forward to the dawning of the next day, which will also feature himself as the new father shining in the eastern sky, and the appearance of a new center of physical paternal creativity, which Shaun hopes will be him alone. This aria occurs also in the next chapter (468.20), as Shaun attempts to ejaculate; there as here, the Rossini aria indicates Shaun's desire to claim physical maturity as the risen sun.

II. Question and Answer (409.31–410.19)

The donkey continues the previous line of questioning, remarking that Shaun's activities might not be under his own control but under the orders of others (409.32), again suggesting a certain lack of originality and independent action by Shaun. Shaun responds that he never wanted to do a stroke of work, but was condemned to walk the highways, and then complains again about his feet.

III. Remark and Response (410.20–27)

The donkey, proceeding to soft-soap the suspicious Shaun, predicts that Shaun will ultimately bear the letter of ALP to the world about her erring husband, and Shaun complacently agrees that that is certainly a possibility. In fact, he does end up creating the physical representation of Anna's letter, the millions of separate copies of *Finnegans Wake* in print. Shaun is here announcing that he will be a publisher!

IV. Question and Answer (410.28–411.21)

"Where are you able to work?" asks the donkey, surrounding the question with fulsome and elaborate compliments. Shaun describes his area of employment, and ends with praise of his home, and an affirmation of its sanctity—he believes in working at home, unlike his wandering brother. However, Shaun's belief in Ireland as his realm of operation is at least partly based on desire for money—and he enunciates a greedy credo (411.21).

V. Remark and Response (411.22–412.6)

The donkey then observes that the home-dwelling Shaun seems to have painted the town with patriotic gore (411.23–24) while the donkey Shem (Joyce himself) was away in Europe. Joyce is here referring to the Easter Week uprising, followed by the Anglo-Irish War and the civil war that followed, all of which took place while Joyce was in Zurich and Paris.

Shaun replies with an oily smile that he is proud of his bloody actions; he speaks in the rhythms of "The Wearing of the Green," asking how the donkey heard of the murderous uprising (411.25–26). The reference to *Il Trovatore* (411.29) and the quotations from the aria "Stride la vampa" (411.31–32) draw a parallel to the murder of one brother by another in Verdi's opera. Fratricide was certainly taking place in Ireland from 1916 to 1923. The weapon by which Shaun's revolutionary murders were committed was wielded by the ithyphallic Davy of the Willingdone Museyroom, the third soldier who rises erect from between his testicular brothers and slays the father, and later murders the Russian general (412.5). Here Shaun admits that the executive weapon for the overthrow of the old order must rise up from down under—an admission, whether Shaun realizes it or not, that Shaun ultimately requires Shem for a definitive change in the power structure of the family.

VI. Question and Answer (412.7–413.26)

The donkey again praises Shaun's voice and follows up with a puzzle, a question that is very difficult to understand, both from the point of view of syntax and of content (412.9–12). The original version as recorded in Hayman's *First Draft Version* (221) is "—Do you mean, I insinuated, that verdure or varnish will?" This is not much help, and the usual commentators do not provide much light.

It is just possible that this section contains a reference to a brilliantly satirical passage in chapter 2 of Dickens's *Our Mutual Friend*, in which Dickens describes the nouveau-riche Veneerings:

Mr and Mrs Veneering were bran-new people in a bran-new house in a bran-new quarter of London. Everything about the Veneerings was spick and span new. All their furniture was new. . . . For, in the

> Veneering establishment, from the hall-chairs with the new coat of arms, to the grand pianoforte with the new action, and upstairs again in the new fire-escape, all things were in a state of high varnish and polish. And what was observed in the furniture, was observable in the Veneerings—the surface smelt a little too much of the workshop and was a trifle sticky.

If so, the donkey is insinuating that Shaun is a Johnny-come-lately, a pretentious newcomer. However this may be, Shaun obviously knows what the obscure question means, because he responds with volcanic rage. As T remarks, "The sixth question . . . is so obscure that his sudden and heated response is surprising."

Shaun's testy reply contains a good deal of detail about Irish postal practices, and ends with a number of references to Swift's correspondence with Stella, neither of which is much help in understanding this passage.

VII. Question and Answer (413.27–414.13)

The seventh question picks up the Swift references in Shaun's previous answer, and goes on to refer to Shaun's opinion of himself as a body made of tinted smoke (413.27, 29, 31). That is, Shaun may regard himself as merely a spirit without any material taint, which was perhaps Swift's own opinion of himself; Swift rejected with horror Stella's advances, and all references to the human body. Therefore we have here a return to the theme of Shaun's hatred of the material and the physical, and to the donkey's attempts to make him face the fact of his own materiality, to make Shaun realize that he is indeed Fallen Man, Man fallen into the material world.

Shaun responds, "Oremus" (413.32)—Let us pray (T)—and at length points out that he is inside a barrel (414.10–13). He then ends his reply as piously as he began it, with "Qui tecum vivit et regnat" (414.13), the ending to the Offertory of the Mass (M) but also an invitation to all to share the contents of the barrel.

VIII. Request and Response (414.14–419.10)

The donkey, accepting the invitation to drink from the barrel, offers the second half of the Eucharist, the eating of the wafer, in a Russian context: "So vi et!" Then, feigning admiration, the donkey begs Shaun for a song. Shaun, however, would rather tell a fable, the fable of the Ondt and the Gracehoper. This fable, like the Mookse and the Gripes, represents an attempt by Shaun to justify his hatred of his brother but, like the previous fable, merely shows Shaun to be a pompous, self-deceiving philistine. However, the fable also represents a powerful attempt by Shem to remind the flesh-mistrusting, Gnostic Shaun of the physical reality that inescapably underlies the spiritual universe.

At first the Gracehoper is constantly happy, always dancing and singing, while the Ondt starts out as a very serious, solemn, even sullen, Germanic person (416.4–5). Here the Ondt resembles Stanislaus Joyce, to whom his brother James once remarked, "There's a queer, grim, Dutch touch about your phiz. I pity the poor woman who wakes up to find it on the pillow beside her" (S. Joyce 1958, 139). However, in the course of the fable, the brothers change emotional tone: the Gracehoper ends up weeping, and the Ondt almost bursts with joy. Here the crossover of the brothers symbolized in II.2 is reprised.

The fable itself is charming and its prose is generally transparent. The Gracehoper, as befits Shem with the legs and appurtenances thereunto appertaining, was always dancing, and making sexual advances to four types of insect—flea, louse, bee, wasp—behind a watering pot, and all of this to kill time. He was happy on account of his "joyicity" (414.23). He and the little girl insects were dancing like Valentin le Désossé and Jane Avril, in two of the famous Toulouse-Lautrec posters (415.11). If science, the Gracehoper thought, can tell us nothing about God, at least the arts can tell us something about the little details of God's universe (415.15–19).

The Ondt, on the other hand, is not at all happy; in fact, he is boiling with rage and jealousy. "What a sight for the gods!" he bellows, while making faces at himself in his looking glass (415.26–28). The Ondt is a well-built fellow, about as tall as a shilling in pennies (416.3–4). He prays to the Egyptian gods of the underworld, and asserts his own virtue (415.33–416.2).

In the meantime, the Gracehoper is getting into trouble, as his summertime antics give way to wintertime suffering. His debts and his whoring after pretty little girl insects have finally overwhelmed him. He begins to starve to death, and actually begins an act of contrition (416.19–20). The Gracehoper, the embodiment of the temporal dimensions, has eaten up all of his time; that is, he has consumed months and centuries, and even eaten his clock (416.21–25). In the depths of the winter, at "Chrysalmas" time (416.26), he wanders through the freezing streets, sinking into delirium through hunger and cold. The snow and the hailstones are falling about him, and the ferocious wind of Trieste, the *bora*, is raging through the streets, blowing the cobblestones up to the roofs, and tearing slates off the coffeehouses. The Gracehoper mistakes the ugly whistling tornado for a lovely sizzling tournedos, a steak, and he feels that Ragnarök, the Norse Last Day, has come for him, as the huge wind calls his name—"Graussssssss! Opr! Graussssssss! Opr!" (417.1–2). He is filled with remorse for his own heedlessness, and determines that when he meets with the Ondt, his brother will see a great change in him.

The Ondt, on the other hand, is now filled with a joy as deep as his brother's despair. The Ondt is sprawling on a divan in his sunroom, in his slippers, smoking a special brand of Havana cigars, with his underwear sliding off his distended abdomen. He has plenty to eat and drink—mainly monkeynuts and an infusion of mint—and he is as happy as a beachboy on the Lido. The former playmates of the Gracehoper—the flea, the louse, the bee, and the wasp—are now the Ondt's playmates. They are biting his legs and his thighs, and kissing him fondly. The little wasp, Vespatilla, is blowing "cosy fond tutties" up his undershorts (417.19–20)!

The Ondt is totally delighted. His happiness combines features of the Muslim paradise of houris and the Christian Heaven of faith, hope, and charity (417.24–31). Crowning his joy is the image of the suffering Gracehoper dying in the street of cold and hunger. After all, one of the joys of the Redeemed in Paradise, we are told, is the contemplation of the suffering of the Lost in Hell. The Ondt bursts out laughing. Let him be the lonely artist in Paris, bitten by lice and fleas, exploited by Parisian parasites; I'll be a laughing rich professional, with my high fees (418.1–2)! Note the presence of the brother brewers of Guinness, Lords Ardilaun and Iveagh. In addition, the mention of high fees suggests another crack at Joyce's old enemy Gogarty, the rich doctor.

The Ondt sings a satire on "Yankee Doodle," still mocking his poor brother's artistic pretensions, and follows up with a prayer to money—pounds, shillings, pence, and glorious wealth (418.2–4). The Ondt laughs and laughs, and the episode ends with a Kiplingesque poem, in which the weeping Gracehoper forgives his laughing brother, and entrusts his four insect playmates to his care. However, the Gracehoper's forgiveness is tempered with a sting: Why can't you beat time? The Gracehoper seems to be warning the space-worshipping Ondt that time will pass, and the positions will be reversed.

Here we have the polar oppositions characteristic of the brothers: when one is happy, the other is sad. In the course of the fable the brothers will change over, as they do in the book itself. The Ondt will become happy, and the Gracehoper will weep, and then time will pass and the reverse will take place. The most important aspect of this fable, however, is that the Grace-hoper's knowledge of physical reality will infect the Gnostic Ondt, and so here the brothers again will share each other's knowledge. The relevant lines in the poem ending the fable describe the nature of the universe (419.3–4). That is, the immaterial "invisible" universe of the Gnostics, the idealist's universe in which physical reality is entirely illusory, as Blake insisted, has a meaty reality that is just as real as the spiritual elements in it.

This meaty reality will underlie the daylight ending of the *Wake*. Physical reality will come back with the rising of the sun and the re-creation of the rainbow colors, the return of the real world to Fallen Man. The Eastern sage, with his knowledge of the white radiance of eternity, will give way to the colors of the real world, defended by St. Patrick, and the Gracehoper will finally achieve the grace of Fallen and Risen Man.

IX. Question and Answer (419.11–421.14)

The donkey expresses an extreme, and patently insincere, admiration for Shaun's linguistic gifts. But then the donkey asks if Shaun could read as well as his brother. Shaun explosively asserts that he can read any language— Greek, Latin, Persian, Ottoman, Coptic (like James Clarence Mangan (M)). Mainly what Shaun can read is his mother's letter to the world.

There follows Shaun's attempt to read the letter. However, all that he can read is the outside of the envelope. That is, Shaun as the head cannot, without the assistance of the lower half, understand the message that Anna Livia is sending to the world about her husband. The letter itself is given the clearest description yet in the book, as the letter carried by the postman Shaun, son of HCE, and written down by Shem, brother of Shaun, who gives written form to the utterances of ALP, mother of Shem, in which she argues the case for her guilty husband (420.17–19). Of course, we do not yet know the contents of the letter; this must wait until the end of the book, when many things become clear.

The inscriptions on the envelope reflect the pilgrimages of the Earwicker family (and the Joyces) around Dublin. It also bears the many stamps of the postal authorities which record failed attempts to deliver the letter. Some of the stamps in postmasterly English would read:

Gone. Try Opposite House. Not Known at This Address. Left No Address. No Such Person. No Such Number. Expelled from This Address. Opened by Mistake. Shot at Sight (!). No Such Street. Removed to

Phibsborough. At Sea. Dead. Please Send On. Wrongly Spelled. Seized
by the Crown. Blown Up. Search Unclaimed Mail. Condemned by the
City Authorities. Back in a Few Minutes. Closed for Repairs. Deserted.
Back to the Post Office. Razed. Lowered. Vacant. Mined.

Finally the postal authorities locate the elusive HCE: Here's the bailiffs! Step
to Hell out of that, Earwicker!

X. Remark and Response (421.15–422.18)

The donkey suggests that Shaun has as great a gift for language as his celebrated brother Shem. Celebrated! exclaims Shaun. Notorious is the way he
would describe him. He then looses violent invective against Shem, which
shows Shaun's constant uneasiness about what his own bottom half is up to.
He thinks that his mother is far too kind to the disreputable Shem, and he
totally rejects the suggestion that Shem is any relative of his.

XI. Request and Response (422.19–424.13)

The donkey asks for a fable of Aesop, possibly trying to trap Shaun into
creating a shallow triviality and thereby proving his linguistic and literary
unfitness. Here we have one of the donkey's comments that is out of order,
or perhaps Shaun's answer is out of order; the fable has already been told in
answer to the eighth question.

Shaun responds, not with a fable, but with another violent attack on his
brother. He accuses Shem of immature Byronism: Shem's early work shows a
"pillgrimace of Childe Horrid" (423.8), a grimace of the immature poet finding the world not as he would have it, as a bitter pill. And even then Shaun
insists, hiccuping nervously, that *he* gave Shem his language! Again we see
Shaun's unconvincing assertion of his own linguistic originality.

XII. Question and Answer (424.14–424.22)

But why, meekly asks the donkey, do you so hate your brother? What is the
real reason for the animosity? For his root language, retorts Shaun (424.17).
Over and over again, the root cause for his hatred of his brother is the feeling
that Shem is the source of true language. As in the Lipoti Virag episode in
Ulysses, the root of language is to be found in the id, or in physical terms, the
genitals, the lower half of the body.

Shaun's anger causes him to utter the forbidden word "invrention"
(424.20), thereby invoking Creation by the Word, forbidden to mortals by

the jealous God of Creation. This brings about the last thunderword, which bears elements significant of Ragnarök, the Scandinavian Last Day. With 101 letters, the last thunderword makes up, with the other nine thunderwords, a total of 1,001, as in the 1,001 Arabian Nights, also a collection of tales told at night, just like the *Wake*.[5] Since the thunder has ceased, the rest of the night will be clearing, leading to a misty, "soft" morning, in Book IV.

XIII. Question and Answer (424.23–425.3)

The donkey maliciously suggests that Shaun could produce such magic language on his own, a cue that Shaun picks up with alacrity. Shem's creations are all stolen from him, from Shaun (424.32–35)! He then launches into a ponderous parody of what he takes to be Shem's frivolous and meaningless language (424.36–425.3). The "yesses" of *Ulysses* merge with the writing down of Anna Livia's letter with a goose quill, to form a satiric portrait of Shem's tale of a shirt, written on a chemise. In *Ulysses* Joyce presents the Irish expression "as fast friends as an arse and a shirt" (14.638–39). Here the arse of Shem and the chemise become close associates, a scene Shaun finds disgusting and infuriating.

XIV. Question and Answer (425.4–426.4)

The last question arrives, and with it the end of the Stations of the Cross. Again, the donkey needles Shaun with the insincere compliment that Shaun could certainly use such doubtful words himself if only he would take the trouble (425.6–8). Shaun falls into the trap and asserts that of course he could stoop so low, but he never would. In fact, he would burn alive any salacious diarist or Zoroastrian spirit of fiery evil who would inflame his mother by uttering such inflammatory language in her hearing (426.2–4). As we have seen, Shaun is just as guilty as Shem of inflammatory language. Anna Livia is stimulated by the language of both boys, which is why she "comes" to their bidding in II.7. The next chapter will show Shaun to be a master of sexually inflammatory language, as he inflames the little Nightschool Girls with his sadistic pedophilia.

The First Fall of Shaun (426.5–428.27)

After unconvincingly evading the donkey's questions, Shaun overbalances, falls into the river, and vanishes—the first Fall of Man—leaving only a whiff of smoke, to the melody of "E lucevan le stelle" from *Tosca*. The passage is one of Joyce's masterpieces of twilight transition: the stars shining, the earth strewing aromatic breezes, the donkey creeping in the darkness, the dark air wafting odors that turn out to be tobacco (427.10–13).

Next, to the tune of "The Cat Came Back," a folksong about resurrection, Joyce ushers Shaun off the scene. Joyce ingeniously shows the dimming and vanishing of Shaun's belt lamp by suppressing the vowels of the repeated phrase: "the lmp wnt out" (427.14–15). Then the donkey-inquisitor bids him farewell, and predicts the eventual sunrise.

The chapter ends with a blessing from the donkey (428.10–14, 26–27). In the blessing, the word "trampthickets" may contain a hidden reference to maturing into sexual powers: in part 2 of *A Portrait*, the first awakening of Stephen Dedalus to the possibility of sex occurs near a tram, its floor strewn with used tram tickets, as Stephen is about to go home from the children's party at Harold's Cross (see Epstein 1971, 190). Here also Shaun, like young Stephen, is poised on the first step of sexual maturity.

Book III, Chapter 2: The Sermon of Jaun

Chapter III.2 contains the second stage of sexual maturity of Fallen Man. Shaun is here called Jaun: Don Juan for his obvious sex appeal, plus the French *jaune*, "yellow," for the yellow sun that he is to become at the end of Book IV.

The chapter consists entirely of a sexually inflammatory sermon preached to the little girls of St. Berched's nightschool by their favorite chaplain, who intends to excite himself with fantasies about spanking his sister for his own "sadisfaction." Jaun's vehement and graphic preachings on the danger of physical sexuality, actually, are designed to arouse his own passions. He is, in reality, masturbating during his sermon. He himself acknowledged his activity, saying that he cannot "belabour this point too ardently" (436.19–20)! His feverish sermon and his threats to Issy constitute a series of attempts to get his phallic lower half, Shem, here called Dave the Dancekerl, to rise up from "down under." Shaun succeeds in erecting his phallic brother Shem, but Shaun's manipulation of the phallus produces only a feeble ejaculation, a second immature act of sexuality after the French kissing in II.4.

Sadomasochism in the Works of Joyce

This chapter shows a type of immature sexuality, a self-gratifying stage, which the combined "sons" will pass through on their journey to full maturity. In the course of Jaun's sermon on sexual temptation, a sermon much more calculated to inflame sexual desire than to quell it, Jaun shows himself to be a violent and hypocritical philistine, and a sadistic pedophile. In fact, Jaun is the sort of man who should not be trusted within a hundred miles of young people, of either sex.

There is a deep streak of sadomasochism in the works of Joyce, but its nature and focus change as Joyce's work develops. In *Dubliners*, there is the extreme sadism of the "old josser" in "An Encounter." In *A Portrait*, Stephen feels a frisson of excitement at the thought of the flogging of a fellow student. In *Ulysses*, there are the fantasies of Bloom, most elaborately acted out in the Circe episode. There are also the notorious letters of 1909 from Joyce to Nora, in which Joyce's extreme masochism is displayed.[6]

However, there is one difference between these acts of sadomasochism and the sadomasochism in *Finnegans Wake*: the earlier episodes are all directed at boys and men, whereas the sadism in the *Wake* is directed mainly at young girls. (Jonathan Swift exhibits similar propensities at several places in *Journal to Stella*.) The two chapters of the *Wake* in which these sadistic acts occur are II.1, where ALP spanks Issy, and this chapter, III.2, in which Shaun excites himself into an erection by visions of spanking the little nightschool girls and his sister.

In III.2, with Shaun vehemently urging sexual abstinence upon the nightschool girls while exciting himself with visions of spanking them, Joyce is making a serious comment about authority. Beneath the extreme hypocrisy of Shaun we see the sexual basis of rigid authority, in which ferocious assertions of morality are enforced by extreme violence.

In fact, it almost seems as if the insistence on obeying to the letter all categorical maxims of conduct has as its real purpose the infliction of sadistic acts on helpless sinners. In *Ulysses* Joyce himself provides a powerful comic example of the connection between sadism and sexual excitement: after the croppy boy , in one of the hallucinations in Circe, is hanged and his " violent erection . . . sends gouts of sperm spouting through his deathclothes on to the cobblestones," the hangman declares, "I'm near it myself" (15.4548–49, 4554).   Here Joyce has been anticipated by Shakespeare. The mad Lear, seeing clearly for the first time the injustice of human institutions, reproaches the servants of justice for hypocrisy. Lear recalls that he once saw a beadle whipping a prostitute, and that the servant of justice had an erection. Lear comments bitterly, "Thou hotly lusts to use her in that kind / For which thou whipp'st her" (IV.vi.160–63).

However, the only result of Shaun's visions of spanking his sister is an ejaculation on his shirt, much like Leopold Bloom's in the Nausicaa episode of *Ulysses*. This chapter provides a graphic portrait of an immature male performing an ultimately sterile act of masturbation. Here we see the second unsuccessful act of immature male sexual assertion. There will be a third attempt at sexual assertion in III.4, the unsuccessful sexual drama between the old man HCE and his sardonic wife ALP, in which she scornfully says that HCE never wet the tea, never succeeded in ejaculating (585.31).

As we will see, it is only at the very end of the *Wake* that a complete sexual act is accomplished, as Anna Livia flows out to sea toward her blazing consort on the horizon as the book ends and begins.

Introduction (429.1–432.3)

Jaunty Jaun—Shaun as Don Juan and the yellow sun—is now on the next leg of his journey back to his rising-up place, and he is still complaining about his feet. He is resting against a log, which is also Sigurdsen, the policeman, fast asleep.

Twenty-nine little girls from St. Berched's nightschool regard the log with distaste, but when Jaun appears, they all come buzzing around him and begin to tousle his hair and take liberties with his genitals (430.19–23, 30–31). Jaun, for his part, greets them kindly and asks how they all are. In fact, he inquires with suspiciously close care about their dress, keeping a keen eye on their little legs and bottoms (431.4–7). He also keeps a more than loving eye on his sister Issy, to the tune of an old Irish love song, "I Know My Love by Her Way of Walking" (431.14–17). All in all, Jaun displays a warm sense of sensuality on seeing his little friends.

Shaun the Postman begins addressing his sister with appropriately postal enunciation of express mail and general delivery of diction (431.21–22). Issy's letters, which we saw her beginning to write in II.2, are referred to (431.29–432.3); the mature woman is always writing a letter to the world about her guilty husband, and Issy is hard at work preparing for the role.

Maxims (432.4–434.34)

After mentioning some clerical acquaintances, Shaun begins his sermon to the little girls with a series of moral maxims. He gives himself away almost from the outset. Under the guise of a rainbow-colored search for the proper part of his breviary to consult, Shaun shows that he is not sure whether he is there to instruct his young flock or to cover them with livid bruises in acts of loutish violence (432.30–33).

The maxims all add up to exhortations against sexual activity, unless it is performed with wealthy marriage in mind (433.32–33). In the pursuit of marriage, all stratagems are allowable.

Shaun reveals a disturbing view of sexual activity with one of his first maxims: Never give up your heart until you "win his diamond back" (433.14–15). Under the surface of a crass instruction to make sure of marriage before giving way sexually—an exhortation resembling Mephistopheles' cynical serenade in Gounod's *Faust*—Shaun betrays his fear and hatred of his brother, and of all physical expressions of love. A "diamondback" is a rattlesnake. To refer to a venomous reptile in the context of marriage shows Shaun's mental imagery: if the penis is a rattlesnake, the physical act of sex is deadly dangerous.

Shaun also begins quite soon debauching his young charges, and exciting himself with fantasies of punishing the little girls for engaging in salacious activities, ones they never would have imagined if he had not mentioned them. Never let seducer's hands make free of your body, he warns, and never lie over the end of a sofa wiggling your little bottom (433.27–28, 15–16). Note the continuing reference to female bottoms.

There follow more maxims focusing on hips and bottoms. Wear girdles, and never take them off at parties and leave them in the men's lavatory (433.23–25)—it was a scandal of the 1920s that young girls at parties would shed their corsetry to dance wildly. Jaun then gets even more intimate: he warns them to be sure to dress where no one is looking and to be careful of peepers before they urinate in bushes (433.33–34).

He warns them against wearing lace (434.21–23), and to avoid amorous emotions, which might lead them to be attracted to young men (433.22–23). At the thought that his young charges might look with loving eyes at boys, Shaun simmers with sadistic anger and imagines the impact of whalebone switches punishing such fair vanity (434.25–26).

Shaun next imagines young girls riding in trams who do not keep their eyes chastely on the advertisements or on the tram driver, but allow young men to look at their legs (434.26–34). This passage is full of literary references—to Dickens's *Our Mutual Friend*, *David Copperfield*, and *The Old Curiosity Shop*, and to Oliver Wendell Holmes's *The Autocrat of the Breakfast Table*—but the main reference, a hidden one, is to D. H. Lawrence's short story "Tickets Please!" In this story a darkly handsome tram dispatcher, who has had his way with many of the female conductors of the trams, is finally mobbed by them and humiliated, a fate that Shaun may find queerly attractive. Shaun warns the girls that if the young man looks at their skirts they may become sexually aroused, and then who knows what could happen?

Attack on Artists and Philosophers (434.34–435.16)

The literary atmosphere brings on the next stage of the diatribe, an unbridled attack on culture and on books. Shaun is a hypocritical, sex-mad philistine, a "wowser," to use an American term of the 1920s. Shaun is practicing as a "vice crusader" of the sort with which Joyce was only too familiar. It is at this point that Shaun launches into a furious attack on culture, and specifically on the work of artists and philosophers. Shaun is convinced that all artists and intellectuals are actually prurient creatures burning with his own brand of sexual desire—an extreme example of projection, and also an extreme example, in D. H. Lawrence's phrase, of sex in the head. Shaun asserts that "autists" care only for themselves, and are oily bearded pimps, smut salesmen wishing to kidnap young girls for the white slave traffic in Buenos Aires (a notorious center of the trade), and lascivious young men who take girls to see plays of doubtful morality (434.34–435.3).

These "intellectuals" also try to seduce girls into posing in their undies, or totally "undraped" (an oily euphemism), for salivating and masturbating painters and a baker's dozen of dirty cameramen filming pornography. These "hogs" comprise Hogarth with his "line of beauty," Botticelli, whose female bottoms are indeed frivolous and silly, Tintoretto tittering, Veronese exhibiting hypocritical *vergogna* (Italian for "shame"), Correggio with powerful *coraggio* ("sexual power" in Italian slang), and Masaccio masturbating with his "extrahand" or *mazzaccio* (slang for "big, nasty penis") (435.7–9).

These dangerous sensualists, oddly enough, include poets and philosophers, in this case Byron and Berkeley (435.10, 11). This pair represent the polar opposition of Shem and Shaun, romantic poetry and icy idealistic philosophy. All intellectuals and artists are suspect, it seems. Joyce here develops a powerful metaphor describing the uneasy relationship of Shem and Shaun as the earth itself, with its ice-cold poles being Shaun and its hot equatorial regions being Shem, who is always hunting like Nimrod for a sexual thrust (435.12–14). Shaun ends this part of his diatribe with scornful dismissal of other oily euphemisms for images of naked women (sweet little girls—*süsse*

Mädels in Viennese dialect) and a reference to a contemporary scandal, Hedy Lamarr's nude swim in the 1933 Czech film *Ecstasy*.

More Maxims (435.16–439.14)

Shaun resumes his maxims, which include such gems as "If you look on a boa, you will never wear strawberry leaves" (435.20–21). Again the penis is referred to in revulsion as a snake. The whole seems to mean that the little victim of seduction will never more be a virgin—or perhaps will never marry an English duke, whose diadem traditionally features strawberry leaves.

Among several too intimate injunctions to mind their digestions and not get constipated, there is a delightful observation on public morals: "Secret satieties and onanymous letters make the great unwatched as bad as their betters" (435.31–32). Masturbation is the poor man's enjoyment here; the great unwashed cannot afford expensive works of pornography, but fantasies can suffice, and they cost nothing! Joyce was well aware that he himself had benefited from the publishers' stratagem of sparing private-press literature from the restrictions of ordinary trade publishing.

Shaun builds up another head of steam as he produces more strictures on sex. Keep out of doorways with young men, and sailors (436.13–14). He prefers love of the usual sort, like sister and brother, with overtones of cisterns (436.14). Like Gerty MacDowell, who "would be just good friends like a big brother and sister without all that other" (*Ulysses* 13.665–66), Shaun still feels a timid inclination to avoid sex, since that would involve his hated brother. However, he does wish for some physical contact: he wishes to be his sister's lover, even if the action smells of cisterns and is not more moral than visiting a brothel. After all, he will be no more than a husband-in-law (436.16), since anything more would involve the active participation of Shem. Shaun is, of course, attempting to make Shem rise up with all his power—the usual hypocrisy of the head in dealing with love! Eventually, under the pressure of sexual stimulation, the timid Shaun will take his leave, and his erected brother Shem will take over.

Exciting himself with visions of prostitutes, Shaun flies into a second flight of sadistic rage: Just put your head coyly on your lover's shoulder, but recoil if he begins to react. If you do not, I'll be apt to spank your bottoms until they are burning (436.33–437.1)! He finishes the lecture with intimate instructions about menstruation, surely too intimate for his young audience.

After another sadistic outburst (439.3–6), he proceeds to the related area of book burning.

Book Burning (439.15–441.23)

Book burning was a sensitive subject to Joyce: the first edition of *Dubliners* was burnt. Shaun is moved by the spirit of sadism into this area: if it were not for his powers of restraint, he would burst out against those who would seduce youth by literature (439.22–25). He is obviously on a crusade to fulfill the Reverend Bowdler's desire to keep any evil author from bringing a blush to "the cheek of innocence" (alluded to previously at 185.11–13).

Shaun says that he would burn the books that grieve youth and mislead it, in a fire greater than Savonarola's Bonfire of the Vanities or the burnings of the Alexandrian library (439.34–35). Joyce is here referring to contemporary events: there were famous book burnings in May and June of 1933 in Germany, led by Nazi groups and Nazi students. Shaun then recommends respectably anodyne reading, including the novels of Father Finn, S.J.

Threats (441.24–445.25)

The thought of extending his personal crusade for the purity of his family to society in general excites Shaun's "sadisfaction" further (444.10–24, 25–29; 445.4–9, 14–22). His sadistic threats grow to a crescendo, combined with assertions of his sexual prowess. He refers to his "bishop" (445.8), employing Herman Melville's transparent euphemism for the penis. Shaun reminds the girls that any illegitimate baby that results from sex games will be their responsibility to raise (444.10–14).

In fact, Shaun is totally driven by sexual forces: in his diatribe, the word "myself" is combined with the word "sex" to form the powerful "myselx" (444.18). His ferocious attack combines D. H. Lawrence's lovemaking in the head, a cruel emotion when divorced from physical sexual drive, with physical violence (445.23–26).

More Threats, Laughter and Anger Mingled (445.26–455.29)

There are more threats, but Shaun is beginning to feel his phallic lower half, his "magic fluke" (451.8), responding to his exhortations. His increasing excitement makes him feel warm—"I'm not half Norwegian for nothing!"—

an anticipation of his future role as the rising sun (452.35–36). His increasing heat means that he will be off on his journey sunward. However, even though he is about to leave the schoolgirls, he asks them not to mourn for him; he will be rising up soon enough to marry them, so *sursum corda* (453.22–26)—hearts up!

Shaun laughs heartily at the thought of the heaven of love that awaits him and his worshipful disciples. Then, becoming fierce once again, he bids farewell to them, with a final description of the joys of heaven, both spiritual and, by now, physical, awaiting all of them—and all that they have to do to attain this glory is to die. After death, there will be delight forever in the presence of God the Father (454.27–455.29).

Gluttony (455.30–457.24)

All of this exercise has made Shaun ravenously hungry, and he describes the enormous meals he expects to recruit his strength: strong tea, bully beef, potatoes and peas, colcannon, haggis, soup, legumes, nuts, bacon, spices—all go down and become the body of Shaun. The food is musically masticated and then changes into its chemical form; the words for the food become scrambled and then simplified into bare vowels and consonants—"xooxox xxoxoxxoxxx" are boiled protestants (potatoes)—until he is full up like Falstaff (456.20–24).

Shaun declares that his anger is assuaged and his hunger is relieved, and that he is going away. His incipient departure signifies that the upper half, the intellectual part, is giving way to the lower half, whose representation, Shem, is about to rise up from down under. That is, Shaun's violent and greedy masturbatory fantasies have succeeded in arousing him to an erection.

Issy (457.25–461.32)

Issy is saddened at the thought that Shaun will be leaving them, but whispers to her bad little self in the mirror that sexual joys await her. Issy is a virgin, since in the archetypal family only the mature mother has experienced physical love in its complete form. However, Issy is a most impatient virgin. Unlike the pathetic Gerty MacDowell, who wants to avoid "all that other," Issy yearns for physical love. She is fully capable of attracting male sexual attention, and she knows it. In fact, she imagines opening Shaun's trouser buttons and viewing his "petit bonhomme," his fascinating concealed naughty bits;

she feels for his manhood (459.24–29). She fully intends to seduce Shaun, when he has finished his journey from west to east and finally rises up as the sun in the morning. Issy looks forward to a complete act of union, the only one in the book, the act of love that takes place after the cock crows for the dawn, a complete physical and moral union occurring between the end of the book and its new beginning. She knows that all of Shaun's sadistic bluster is the sign of an incomplete man, and she imagines her own delightful charms and his reaction to them (461.21–28).

However, to Shaun's continuing chagrin, she desires *both* brothers—that is, a complete man. She asks both of her brothers to teach her the facts of love, to warn her which to— She is about to sneeze. She has earlier felt a tickle in her throat (458.10–11). Her "ah ah ah ah . . ." (461.32) is the preliminary to ah-choose!—that is, she is asking the two brothers which of them she is to take on first—but the pious Shaun misinterprets her incomplete word and finishes it for her: "ah-MEN!" His word choice and hers agree, however, in that both signify that she will choose and know men, *all* men, and presumably all of the aspects of men.

The Accession of Shem (461.33–468.22)

Shaun gives a farewell toast to Issy and the other girls—a farewell because he feels that his concentration is shifting from his own upper intellectual and rhetorical half to his lower half, which he has been belaboring vigorously all the while.

He declares that he is leaving behind as proxy his brother Shem, for their "consolering" (462.17).[7] Shaun acknowledges that Shem provides his interior voice (462.16). The name that Shaun gives Shem here, "Dave the Dancekerl" (462.17), is rich in significance. Dave is, among other things, the Davy of the Willingdone Museyroom, the third soldier, the finally erect phallus that signifies the end of the father's potency and that destroys the Willingdone. He is also, as the designation tells us, a dancer: one of the signs of Stephen Dedalus's artistic potency, from the first page of *A Portrait* to the Circe episode in *Ulysses*, is dancing.[8] Dave is also a "dansker," as the son of the Scandinavian HCE.

Finally, Dave is King David, the ultimate symbol of the royal power of art.[9] (David danced as well as sang; see II Samuel 6:14, 16.) Here Dave the Dancekerl is the finally erect penis of Shaun, dilated by his belaborings and sadistic visions. Shaun declares to Issy that she should embrace Shem, to the tune of Ottavio's lyric tenor aria from *Don Giovanni*, "Il mio tesoro" (462.22). However, Shaun adds insincerely that she should keep a table between herself and the ithyphallic Shem.

Dave himself appears, entering to the words and music of the Count di Luna in "Io tremo" from *Il Trovatore*—"Lumtum lumtum! Now! The froubadour! I fremble!" (462.25–26)—announcing the arrival of the count's hated rival Manrico, who is really his brother, though he does not know it until the end of the opera, after he has killed him. Shaun loves and hates his brother, who has the red nose of a drunkard, which is also the inflamed glans of Shaun's penis (463.19–20). As befits the male genitals, Dave looks like the jack of clubs, with the characteristic shamrock triple formation "like the knave of trifles" or trefoils (463.35).

Dave has been an exiled convict in Australia, literally "down under"; his head is shaved in the convict's cut (464.8–9), and he bears a prison pallor (463.34–35). Shaun points out his "penals" (465.5). Then Shaun thrusts Issy into Dave's arms and feverishly encourages them to embrace each other (465.1–13). He encourages them to entwine their legs (*enjamber*), and to bite each other. The increasing heat of the sexual ceremony is causing clouds of holy incense to rise up: *Weihrauch*, *thuris*, " frankincense," and *idos* are respectively German, Latin, English, and Greek terms for incense (M). In this heated and aromatic passage Shaun refers to Byron's incestuous relationship with his half sister, Augusta Leigh (465.17).

Shaun continues to egg the pair on, evoking Yeats's pairing of the Queen and the Beggarman as analogue to the sexual entwining of the two—the Lady of the Lake and the Convict of the Woods (465.36). Why, they might be Daddy and Mummy (466.1)! However, Shaun seems to detect a certain hesitation in the sexual entanglements of the two, a growth of scruples (466.8). He advises Shem to be more cruel in his lovemaking, invoking Jack the Ripper's sexual sadism (466.13–14).

Then Shaun encourages Shem to sing, to rekindle the fading passion, and Shaun will join in (466.24–26). As before (see 222.6–11), Shaun sings in a merry but epicene lyric tenor, and Shem produces a booming melancholy prayer for assistance (466.31–32)—"From the danger of the bull, from the pestilence that flies by night, have mercy on me in my sorrows!" The pretentious but ignorant Shaun as usual misunderstands Shem's Latin, but he admires Shem's deep voice, a full octave below his own (466.35–36; 467.8). The "stones" probably refer to Shem's manly testicles.

But all is in vain. Shem is too shy, Shaun's motives are mixed, and the act of masturbation ends only with shamed, sterile ejaculation: the Irish national emblem, here sterile, is creeping down Shem's shirt (467.10–12). The prevalence of masturbation is Ireland's lack of blooming—the Irish national unblooming (467.11)—its shamrock of shame. The sadistic visions of Shaun have ejaculation as their aim, but Shaun's phallic Dave the Dancekerl achieves only an ejaculation without fertilization, a pure act of autoeroticism.

This theme of Irish masturbation, taken up most definitively by Patrick Kavanagh in his long poem *The Great Hunger*, is treated early in the work of Joyce. In *Stephen Hero*, Joyce sardonically declared that the famous purity of the Irish peasant was the product of masturbation:

—. . . I fully recognise that my countrymen have not yet advanced as far as the machinery of Parisian harlotry because . . .
—Because . . . ?
—Well, because they can do it by hand, that's why!
—Good God, you don't mean to say you think . . .
—My good youth, I know what I am saying is true and so do you know it. Ask Father Pat and ask Dr Thisbody and ask Dr Thatbody. I was at school and you were at school—and that's enough about it. (55)

Joyce's brother Stanislaus wrote in his Dublin diary a parody of the song "Mr. Dooley" that includes the lines "For 'It's masturbation / That kills a nation,' / Said Dr. Dooley-ooley-ooley-oo" (58).

After a final attempt to get more than a feeble ejaculation from Shem (468.12–19), Shaun, falling toward guilt and human glory, seems to content himself with the hope that the sexual union at sunrise will be more satisfactory than the failure in this chapter (468.20–22). Shaun has passed another stage in his reverse journey toward the east, where he will become the rising sun. He foresees the great embrace at the end/beginning of the *Wake*. That is, at sunrise—which is evoked by Rossini's tenor aria "Ecco ridente in cielo spunta la bella aurora"—a union of the brothers Mick and Nick must come to pass and, also, amid thunder and lightning, a true act of physical and moral love.

The Second Fall of Shaun (468.23–471.34)

The girls mourn Shaun, because they are sorry that their favorite is leaving them. According to Joyce's letter to Harriet Weaver of August 8, 1928, the girls use a liturgy borrowed from the Maronite Christians of Lebanon, with twenty-nine words in the mourning ritual, one for each of the girls. The rite itself, exalting Shaun as a series of lovely trees, is from the apocryphal book of Ecclesiasticus 24:17–19 (M).

As Shaun begins to leave, the girls cry out twenty-nine different words for peace, in several mangled languages (470.36–471.5). Joyce noted that such a series of cries of peace sounded around the world on November 11, 1918, at the armistice in World War One.

Then Shaun attempts to leave, but only falls into the river. This is his second fall—he is now a doubly Fallen Man.

Receding of Shaun, Advancing of Light (471.35–473.25)

Shaun, now named Haun—he is fading from view—is bid a fond farewell by the sardonic narrator, with many good wishes. The long night is beginning to fade into day. The narrator predicts the rising of Shaun as the phoenix, the Bennu bird, the symbol of the rising sun, and notes that the night is ending (473.16–20). The alteration of the word "vanished" into "sphanished" (473.20)may mean that the narrator has noted that the sun has already risen in Spain, five hundred miles to the east of Dublin. The full rising of the sun and the crowing of the cock of dawn are boldly predicted at the end of the chapter (473.20–25).

Book III, Chapter 3: The Psychoarchaeological Inquest on Shaun

The giant chapter III.3 consists of two parts: the Starchamber Quiry, a huge mask-play in which HCE evades his questioners brilliantly until he can evade them no longer, and his towering Haveth Childers Everywhere soliloquy, in which HCE the great Master Builder is celebrated.

The Starchamber Quiry (474.1–532.5)

The chapter opens with Yawn moaning melodiously, like an angel whose lovely little bottom has been stuck with a pin (474.13–15). The Four Old Men, now a coroner's jury, come upon Yawn and are struck with awe and fear. In fact, anyone would be awestruck: Yawn is titanic, gigantic. As Adam Kadmon, he is the original Adam who, in the Kabbala, is coterminous with the universe. His Fall consists of dwindling down to human size, but at this point he is the whole universe. Our fear and awe—expressed in seven words for "fear" followed by increasing numbers of exclamation points, in seven differ-ent languages (475.1–2)—represent the reaction to sublimity. The number of the words and of the exclamation points, seven, is also the number of colors in the rainbow, the number of Fallen Man.

Evoking awe in contemplating the vast universe (475. 12–17), Joyce shows himself to be a great painter with words. He produces a masterly and viv-idly colored portrait of the starry universe, culminating in the Milky Way. Yawn/Adam Kadmon here also contains the Akasic records of theosophy. As these are the repository of all history, human and nonhuman, Adam Kad-mon contains within himself complete knowledge of everything that has ever happened. By the ancient Greek theory of the Microcosm, all of that knowledge is available to him by introspection, even when he has dwindled down to human size. In this chapter, we the readers are given a tour through the whole of history, from the Creation of the universe to the creation of the city.

Eventually, coming down to the earthly plane of our narrative, Yawn is also the Hill of Howth, which is becoming dimly visible through the di-minishing night shades. From this point in the book, the physical universe becomes increasingly visible, until true daylight appears.

Beginning of Investigation (474.16–477.30)

The Four Old Men, interspersing four of the fear-words with a series of disrespectful comments on the wailing from the mound (475.12–17), com-mence their "starchamber inquiry" (475.18–19). The psychic fishermen climb onto the huge Yawn and begin to spread their drifting, colored, gleaming nets (477.11–12, 19–20). The phrase describing their nets, one of Joyce's love-liest sentences, evokes phrases in the well-known poem by Eugene Field, "Wynken, Blynken, and Nod." This poem is about a child going to sleep, which reminds us that the action in Books II and III represents a dream: "'Where are you going, and what do you wish?' / The old moon asked the three. / 'We have come to fish for the herring fish / That live in this beautiful sea. / Nets of silver and gold have we!' / Said Wynken, Blynken, and Nod."

Yawn's Early Evasions (477.31–478.2)

Yawn is very evasive in his answers to the four inquisitors, but we are the beneficiaries of his evasiveness: he rambles all around the physical and psy-chological universe in his attempts to avoid a clear answer to the question "Who are you?" As the ancestral mound of all human beings, he contains the knowledge of all human beings. As the Akasic records, he contains all of universal history. Therefore, we are given a huge tour around the universe of things and men, from the creation of the universe itself by God Almighty to the creation of the city by our hero, HCE.

In the telling, however, Joyce gives an Irish turn to his tour: it is Irish voices that we hear, from beginning to end, and it is Irish history, the sorrowful history of defeat and betrayal and suffering, that gives the tone to Yawn's comments. It will be recalled that Stephen Dedalus in *Ulysses* regards history as "a nightmare from which I am trying to awake" (2.377). The sorrowful tone of Irish history also accounts for the melodious moans that emerge from the mound. Phantoms from Irish history and stages in the history of the Irish begin to speak.

- SWIFT (478.3, 5, 26–27, 29–30): Swift's is the first voice we hear, mourning for the lost opportunity to love his two girls, Stella and Vanessa.
- TRISTAN (478.19–22): Tristan's is the second voice we hear, speaking in French.
- PATRICK (478.26–27, 29–30, 34; 479.13–14): Patrick speaks up, mourning for his lost congregation in the woods of Fochlut. The woods evoke wolves: Parnell is quoted, as begging his followers not to throw him to the wolves (479.14).

The mound finally identifies himself, but enigmatically, as three persons in one (478.26) combining Tristan, Jonathan Swift, and Patrick, with a soupçon of Parnell and Joyce himself. There is also a strong suggestion that Shaun is "part Nick"; that is, Yawn is acknowledging that his lower half exists, however much he may deplore the embarrassment of below-the-waist activities and structures. The word "dieudonnay," however, is a puzzle. It appears later as "Gottgab" (490.8), which likewise means "gift of God," but the significance is obscure, perhaps deliberately so. There may be a reference here to the eldest of the inquisitors, Matthew, whose name derives from the Hebrew *mattityahu*, which does indeed mean "gift of God." But why only one of the Four Old Men?

There may be a pattern in the choice of these three main persons from Irish history: they may represent the two halves of the body, the two soldiers, and their reconciliation in the third soldier and in the risen sun in Book IV. Swift denied the necessity for physical love, and recoiled violently when Stella and Vanessa declared their love for him. Swift's disgust for the body is notorious, and forms a large part of Shaun's equally extreme hatred of the physical. Tristan, on the other hand, had no trouble with the physical side of love; it was the moral aspect of his love for Isolde of Ireland that wrecked him—his betrayal of King Mark—as well as his sorrow at his own betrayal by the second Isolde, his wife Isolde of the Lovely Hands. We see here the conflict between the upper and lower halves of the body inside Shaun, acted out by two of the three parts of Yawn. Patrick (and Parnell) may represent the third soldier, the erect phallus, which is the executive part of the loving male body, and which, in the person of Patrick, triumphs over the cerebral sage in the debate over the physical world in Book IV, as the risen sun recreates the world of human beings.

Vikings and Ancient Irish History (479.17–482.5)

The specifically historical section of the chapter begins with an evocation of early history: Viking invasions of Ireland, the incursion of the ancestors of HCE, and the activities of wolves and foxes in the primitive Ireland of the autochtonous Irish and the Scandinavian invaders. Patrick makes his appearance at 482.5 with his characteristic exclamation in impatient moments, "Mudebroth!" (M).

The Four Old Men break into one of their interminable quarrels (482.7–485.12). Then one of the four asks the question that the reader has been trying to ask throughout the book: Are we speaking the English language or "sprakin sea Djoytsch" (485.12–13)? Are we on sea or land? Are we speaking English, or floundering along in a special Joycean language? Then one of the Four Old Men pulls himself together and begins another round of questioning, which however elicits only a spurt of pidgin English (485.29–34).

The questioner impatiently asks the mound whether he is Patrick. The mound answers in a three-line poem (486.3–5), which indeed identifies him as Patrick—or "Quadrigue" in a Q-Celtic form (McCarthy 1984, 617). The rhyme encodes the number 432, the traditional date of the second arrival of Patrick in Ireland, in answer to the prayers of the pagan Irish in the woods of Fochlut. Then one of the Four Old Men tries a bit of ancient magic: he presses a piece of burial jade to the temple, the lips, and the breast of Yawn, and asks what Yawn sees, feels, and hears. The result is three riddling answers:

1. When the burial jade is pressed to Yawn's temple and he is asked what he sees, the answer (486.17–19) seems to refer to someone obsessed with love, with overtones of French. The reference is probably to Tristan; the Tristan legend achieved its most elaborate development in French.

2. When the jade is moved to Yawn's lips and he is asked what he feels, the obscure answer (486.23–25)suggests the dead Lady of Shalott, and the white arms perhaps Tristan's betraying wife, Isolde of the White Hands. However, the comment by the questioner alludes to Swift's two lady friends Stella and Vanessa, so the whole interchange may evoke the yearning Swift.

3. Pressing the jade to Yawn's breast elicits the most enigmatic answer (486.30–31), which involves a hopping creatures slapping his feet in a puddle of bran. Since the three figures being evoked include Patrick, it is logical to assume that he is here, but his presence is difficult to see.

Then the three-part vision fades, without having provided much in the way of useful information to the three questioners.

Exploration of Shaun's Soul (486.30–532.6)

There follows a long section of fifty pages, one of the most difficult and complex passages in the book. The depths of Yawn's soul are being plumbed by the inquisitors, and in the course of their investigations, the deepest regions in the universe open their depths.

At first there is evocation of Patrick, Bruno of Nola, and Shem (described bitterly by Shaun). Finally one of the questioners, fed up with obscurity, asks the reclining figure to sing Hosty's "Ballad of Persse O'Reilly" from the end of I.2, but in answer gets only a piece of the mocking ballad about the aged King Mark sung by the seagulls in II.4. From its satirical tone, one of the questioners identifies the voice as the savage satirical voice of Swift, and Yawn's answer seems to indicate that the questioner is right (491.21–22).

The next eight pages are laid out as a gigantic crescendo, which culminates in the heartrending release of the historical anguish of Ireland at 499.30–500.34. Then the next thirty pages lead to the discovery of HCE within the depths of Yawn—the father resurrected in his son (532.6).

The whole passage begins with the evocation of the Viking queen Ota, wife of the Viking invader Thorgils, sitting upon the altar of Clonmacnois cathedral, uttering prophecies (M). One of the Four Old Men salaciously refers to this provocative act by envisaging the plump bottom of the nude Viking queen on the altar (493.19–25; 552.29–30). To which Yawn, duly roused, replies that the male sexual organs and feminine nudity vote for continuation of life (493.26).

Then the sexual excitement of Yawn lights up the whole universe, and introduces an astronomical cadenza on the glories of the physical world and the loving depths of heaven and the human heart. The rainbow of Fallen Man appears, to certify God's gift of love and consoling peace to human beings. The onset of human love brings the search of the Four Old Men to a much deeper level, and leads directly to the mysteries of death and resurrection, and the horrors of human history, the nightmare from which Stephen Dedalus wishes to awake.

The glories of the cosmos (494.6–495.33) reveal the secrets of the family, as Yawn associates the astronomical universe of the stars with the activities in the archetypal family—the giant father surrounded by his tiny children dancing sarabands around him (494.27–28). Yawn then exposes the intimate details of the family imbroglios, of which he may have read in the letter from Anna to the world that he is carrying. However, he declares that there is nothing in the letter to be ashamed of: honi soit qui mal y pense, with a nod to the panties of the great queen (495.27–28).

Yawn and the old men air the family's dirty laundry yet again (495.34–499.3), and end with the evocation of HCE dead and resurrected. Yawn, in one gigantic sentence, describes the funeral of HCE, with all the visitors and the general excitement (497.4–499.3), and with HCE lying bottom upward like Dante's Lucifer (498.35).

One of the Four Old Men gives the particulars of the death scene and the songs of mourning (*nenia*) and sacred dances (M). There are also words for "death" in twenty-nine different languages, as the chorus of little girls mourn HCE, their "bappy"" the word combines "pappy" with "bap," a type of bread (499.4–11). The speaker ends with a requiem. The requiem is not as definitive as it seems: there is a pepperpot in the neighborhood that makes the corpse sneeze (French *éternuer*) (499.11–12). Then Yawn asserts that HCE's fire is not yet out, and hints at the presence of HCE within him, and also at the resurrection of the father at the end of the book. There's lots of flame in the clownish father's wick! The keening of mourning has passed. Long live the new king (499.13–14)! The key of life has passed from Anna's lips to the lips of the resurrected father-bridegroom, as the heroine passed it to her imprisoned foster brother in Boucicault's *Arrah-na-Pogue*. In a similar way, the dying Anna passes it to HCE in the penultimate line of the book, where the keys to heaven have been passed, and life begins again (628.15).

The mention of death and resurrection sinks us abruptly to a much deeper level in the mound. Here Joyce is repeating some insights that he first developed in *Ulysses*, in the Glasnevin episode. In that episode Bloom, making nervous jokes in the cemetery, has two uncanny metempsychotic breakthroughs. Under the oppression of his thoughts about death, Bloom twice unconsciously evokes his great original, Odysseus. At one point he finishes his joking about resurrection with an apparently irrelevant reference to dust in a skull with the phrase "Troy measure" (6.682). Dust is not measured in troy ounces, but a window to the past, to the Trojan War, has suddenly opened in Bloom's mind, haunted and oppressed by thoughts of death and resurrection. The second metempsychotic moment occurs as Paddy Dignam's coffin sinks into the earth—certainly a solemn moment. As the coffin disappears, Bloom suddenly thinks, "If we were all suddenly somebody else" (6.836). In the *Wake* also, the solemn references to death and resurrection push the investigation suddenly to depths far too low for the old investigators to control. This section (499.15–501.10) deserves close analysis, especially since I suspect a typesetting error in the beginning of it.

First, one of the old men greets the recumbent figure (499.15), with the mound hailed as the master of resurrection. Then another of the old men greets the adipose figure in similar terms (499.16). However, the next sentence (499.16–18) is, I believe, wrongly assigned to this second old man. The text of this chapter is, after all, "the most seriously texually corrupt of all" (R&O 243). It would be much more appropriate to begin a new paragraph and assign this sentence to HCE; the speaker declares that he had four drinks in the morning and two at lunch and three more later on, but "Your souls to the devil! Do you think I'm dead, or drunk?" The four-two-three configuration may also have been intended to be four-three-two, the Patrick number 432, but the sentence ends with a version of what the revived corpse says in the original song "Finnegan's Wake": "Thanam o'n dhoul, do ye think I'm dead?"

Then two of the old men debate the best way to continue the investigation. One asks the other if he means to sit there coddling his penis (499.20). The other responds irritably that if he cannot use one version of magic power, he can use another (499.26–27). He intends to use priestly-poetic magic—an "ollav" is an ancient Irish priest-poet (*ollamh*)—to elicit a more satisfactory reply from the mound.

The result of the spell is immediate and startling: a deep, eerie sound from the depth of the mound. "Oliver!" shows the presence of the *ollamh* as well as the fearful memory of Oliver Cromwell, whose ruthless cruelty forms a large part of the dark Irish memory. The reference to an earthpresence is not clear; it may be a poltergeist, or a dangerous gnome or kobold. Some sort of frightening spirit is being summoned by the spell. The sounds emanating

from deep in the mound may resemble groans or the warlike skirl of bag-
pipes (499.28–29), or the sound of snare drums (500.1). Watch out!

The Horrors of Irish History (499.30–501.10)

Now begins the most powerful passage in *Finnegans Wake*. What had been a
delicate musical moan at the beginning of the chapter here suddenly emerges
as a roar of pain. The stream of utterances, borne upon a white-hot river
of anguish, is heartbreaking and deeply frightening. The cries make up a
portrait of a millennium and a half of tormented Irish history. The voices
are of those anguished dead who have not fulfilled their greatest desires on
earth. Yeats once exhorted all people to "go down empty to the grave." These
spirits have not gone down empty; they are still tortured by their unfulfilled
desires.

The first utterances emerging from the mound refer to the sorrow of
Tristan, his sad soul, his bleeding heart, his bowed head, his open generous hand, his familiar footstep (499.30–32). Besides the reference to Tristan,
the utterance forms a (slightly distorted) lament for a lost, generous leader:
Where is the Prisoner of his Love for us? Where is the Bleeding Heart? Where
is the Good Herd Laid Low? Where is the Open Hand? We no longer hear
his Wonted Foot on our doorstep!

The Latin phrases come from Matthew 26:38 and Mark 14:34: "Tristis est
anima mea usque ad mortem"—"My soul is sad even unto death"—the words
of Jesus at His lowest depth of sorrow, in the Garden of Gethsemane when
he asked his disciples to watch with him. (See also Jonah 4:9.) The following
word, *lignum*, possibly refers to Christ's anticipation of His crucifixion on
"wood." HCE in the depths of the mound is expressing his great sorrow and
suffering.[10]

What is emerging from the mound is the authentic voice of Irish history—not the history of dates and kings and treaties, but the bloody, sorrowful voice of human beings suffering through the nightmare of history from
which Stephen Dedalus wishes to awaken. The stream of anguished voices
blazes like lava, completely overwhelming the Four Old Men, who are, like
Garrett Deasy, the representatives of academic history. They try vainly to
stem the flow, but it blazes on. The old men recognize with dread the dead
giant of Ireland coming alive, as indeed he did in 1916 (500.1–2, 2–3). Then
the voices of the dead burst out of the mound:

• (500.4) The dark foreigner and the light foreigner (Shem and Shaun; the
Danes and the Norse) invading Ireland again.

• (500.5) Funeral sounds, now with a grating, ominous overtone.

• (500.6) The warcries of the Fitzgeralds, Norman by origin but now the fiercest of Irish families, versus Parliamentary troops of Cromwell hot to avenge Protestant English settlers killed by the native Catholic Irish. The brutal English acts of revenge in the seventeenth century made Cromwell a name of enduring horror to the Irish.

• (500.7–8) The ferocious warcries of the invaders, now accompanied by a snare drum.

• (500.10–11) The screams of the Irish women when they see English yeomen, famous for their cruelty,[11] rushing at them. Competing cries of "Redshanks!" evoke the original Celtic inhabitants of Ireland (M), and "Up Lancs!" is a cry of encouragement of English troops from Lancashire engaged in suppressing dissent in Ireland by the usual dreadful methods.

• (500.12–13) Catholic voices, as identified by the Four Old Men: "The Cry of the Deer" is a hymn by St. Patrick (M), and the white hind represents the Catholic Church in Dryden's "Hind and the Panther" (M). The terrified old men hear the ferocious hunt, and they clamor for peace, or perhaps for information as to who has the legal title to the land.

• (500.14–16) In the rhythm of one of the surviving prayers of St. Patrick (M), the names of Irish newspapers: the *Irish Times*, the *Irish Independent*, the *Freeman's Journal*, the *Daily Express*. Here are prayers for the intentions of the Irish equivalent of the pope with his infallible messages; in Ireland, the function of papal bulls is performed by newspaper editorials. (Joyce himself wrote for the "dully expressed.")

• (500.17–18) Strike, kill, and slaughter! The Sluagh na hEireann—the Army of Ireland—was a nationalistic society. The cry "Choke the Pope" is a traditional Protestant cry of hatred.

• (500.19) The beginning of the Lord's Prayer—"Our Father" (M)—swallowed up in general uncertainty as to just what the people are praying for, and to whom.

• (500.21–2) The anguished cry of Tristan that he has been betrayed by the bride of the brine, Isolde—or rather by both Isoldes, by both of the girls Issy and Essie, the first (German *erste*) and the last one (Danish *sidste*) (M). It is also the voice of Swift mourning his coldness to the two girls named Esther.

• (500.23) The anguished voice of Swift picking up the theme. His desire to be merged with the girls ("Us! Us!"—cf. 628.13–14) modulates into his basic egoism ("Me! Me!") which rejected Stella and Vanessa while he was alive.

• (500.24) An English sergeant major hoarsely urging forward his occupying troops, with a slight suggestion of Wagnerian Germanic violence in Bayreuth.

• (500.25–31) Fading funeral sounds, mingled with the voice of Tristan exclaiming over his betrayal by the girls, and the voice of Parnell producing his clearest exhortation to his followers—to get his price if they must betray him to the English—and finally the voice of Swift helplessly and vainly uttering his eternal love for Stella.

• (500.33) Last in this series of voices of the helpless and frustrated dead, and most frightening: the voice of James Joyce himself begging for forgiveness from his mother, Mary Joyce, for having made her last moments in life sorrowful.

The voices begin to fade, and the Four Old Men finally succeed in stanching the dreadful flow of sorrow, betrayal, and pain (500.34–501.9). After a final sputter of funeral sounds and a last truncated call from Tristan for the bride of the brine, the old men regain control and ask for the title, whatever that may be. Then they restore the theatrical lighting that has been extinguished by the cries of anguish. They have reestablished the telephone connection, and give their respective telephone numbers: *Ségur cinquante huit* (Ségur 50 08), and *Gobelins quarante quinze* (Gobelins 40 15).[12]

As the lights come up, the revelation of the blazing and terrible depths of human history introduces the reader to some of the most fundamental aspects of human life. Then the mound, in its attempts to avoid the answers to the old men's questions, takes the reader on a tour of the history of the world, from its very beginnings—the Creation, the Tree of Life, and a description of the first family of the world.

History Tour: Creation of the World (501.10–503.3)

The history tour begins with the state of the world at the Creation. The first aspect of the new world that Yawn describes, under the prompting of the old men, is the bonfires, creating light (501.24). They are vividly described as having their blue beards streaming to the heavens (501.29). Joyce derives this description of bonfires from Aeschylus's *Agamemnon* 305–6: the beacon fires announcing the fall of Troy "send up with unstinted force a mighty beard of flame" (*phlogòs mégan pógona*).

During the original night, the great Creator, the titanic original male mountain power, was engaged in a huge, merry act of love with the great original female valley power. The Creator was bouncing around like an india-rubber ball (501.31–33). There was weather of all sorts on the original day—hot, cold, rain, snow, wind from all directions, fog and frost, hail—in fact, chaos doubly confounded (501.34–502.10). All four classical principles and all four classical elements were there: hot, cold, moist, and dry; earth, air, fire, and water (502.17–24). The sea was visible from the beginning, with whitecaps as far as the eye could see, and every effect of stage weather was present except for thunder, which in the Viconian scenario comes later (502.25–503.3). Note that the natural effects are here described as stage properties, anticipating the stagy presentation of everyday reality in the next chapter, III.4.

History Tour: The Garden of Eden, with Stone and Tree (503.4–506.23)

The next scene in the tour of the original world is the Garden of Eden, which includes the Stone and the Tree of the original Wake landscape. The Stone is symbolic of arrested time, the Tree of living development. The Tree is Yggdrasill, the Norse tree of the universe, and the Tree of Life in the original Garden of Eden, and Darwin's Tree of Life. There is also a snake in the garden, both the original snake of the Bible and the snake of Norse mythology that gnaws at the root of Yggdrasill.

Both the Tree and the Stone are introduced in Yawn's answers to the questioners' inquisition concerning the Garden of Eden, and its "common or garden" contents (503.4) symbolic of the Tree. Yawn complains of the nasty dirt and ashes around the everlasting ash tree (503.7). The dirt is the principle of the Stone, which is reinforced by the ashes and the ash tree.

The questioners and Yawn then settle down to explore the garden and its contents. The garden is portrayed as a kitchen midden where Adam and Eve first met (503.8–9). One of the questioners asks if the place is at Woful Dane Bottom (503.21), a real place in Gloucestershire (M) but also descriptive of HCE's big wide arse, later displayed in extenso at III.4 (564.1–565.5).

The Stone then appears in a few sentences from Yawn and the questioners. Yawn begins, and describes the sun, or flag, of old Ireland and its green-gray-and-black coloring (503.22–27). Green, black, and gray are the three sorts of blindness as described in German; Joyce with his severe medical problems with his eyes was well acquainted with these terms.

Here the old flag is the flag of blindness and death, a flagstone, in fact, a tombstone of every Tom, Dick, and Harry, marking the peace of the grave. A sign on the stone warns that trespassers will be prosecuted, or rather that tricky pissers will be set apart in pairs (503.29)—that is, that young girls who piss in the bushes (that old scandal again!) will be paired up with young men and placed in seclusion with them.

The Stone's partner, the Tree, is described in brilliant detail, in one of the most vivid and elaborate set pieces of the book (503.30–506.18). The tree is made up of three great trees of tradition:

1. *Yggdrasill, the ash tree of Norse tradition.* Yggdrasill is the Worldtree. Its roots go down to the underworld, and its trunk and roots connect to the nine kingdoms of the underworld, to Middle Earth, and to the kingdom of the gods. The goddess of the frozen underworld, Hel, controls the kingdom of Niflheim. The Eagle of Intelligence roosts in the branches at the top, in which the stars shine; between the brows of the eagle is a hawk. Below the surface lies a dragon or serpent, Niðhoggr, gnawing at the roots of the ash tree. There are other animals on or near the tree—many snakes, and four deer biting the foliage and causing pain to the tree. A squirrel, Ratatosk, runs up and down the tree carrying messages, usually malicious, between the kingdoms and the rest of the tree. There are three springs at the foot of the tree.

2. *The Tree of Life, in the Garden of Eden.* Adam and Eve were expelled from the garden so that they would not eat of the fruit of this tree, which confers immortality. However, humanity will ultimately get the chance to eat of this tree, as foretold in the Book of Revelation.

3. *Darwin's Tree of Life.* Darwin conceives of earthly life in a famous metaphor:

The affinities of all the beings of the same class have sometimes been represented by a great tree. I believe this simile largely speaks the truth. The green and budding twigs may represent existing species; and those produced during former years may represent the long succession of extinct species. . . . From the first growth of the tree, many a limb and branch has decayed and dropped off. . . . As buds give rise by growth to fresh buds, and these, if vigorous, branch out and overtop on all sides many a feebler branch, so by generation I believe it has been with the great Tree of Life, which fills with its dead and broken branches the crust of the earth, and covers the surface with its ever branching and beautiful ramifications.[13]

Joyce's Tree of Life shares characteristics with all three of these great trees. Joyce's Tree is like Yggdrasill in that it contains all the different types of human and animal activity. Joyce's Tree includes all human genders and all levels of human society. Like Darwin's Tree of Life, Joyce's Tree embodies the processes of human and animal evolution. Finally, like the biblical Tree of Life, Joyce's Tree represents a type of immortality—not, to be sure, a personal immortality, but a secular immortality made up of the life, death, and resurrection of the archetypal family. In fact, later in this chapter, III.3, we see the hero HCE, who was overwhelmed in II.3 by the lynch mob made up of his children, resurrected from the depths of Yawn.

The great Tree is introduced by a question from one of the Four Old Men, who asks whether there used to be a tree in the garden. Yawn replies that there had been, a giant ash tree (503.30504.1). We are fed and clothed from the Tree of Life, but we are also brought to death (burked) by it, and we can read the story of life from it; our reading is in its leaves. The great tree was standing in both southern (Sumerian) sun and northern (Cimmerian) shade—the beginning of the theme of antithetical inclusions characteristic of Joyce's Tree of Life (504.6, 7).

One of the old men commands Yawn to describe the Tree, to give a poet's bird's-eye view (504.16). Yawn complies. In one magnificent sentence, he describes a titanic structure teeming with life of all sorts, species, genders, and social levels: Tudor queens and whorish Idaho shopgirls, babies growing as buds on its branches,[14] birds swinging like mad King Sweeney of Irish legend on its topmost branches, and apples—the traditional apples attributed in English-speaking countries to the tree of the Garden of Eden—moving from alpha to omega, bouncing up to the heavens and down to earth (504.24). Yawn describes criminals in the Tree waiting to be hanged at Tyburn, with their bones strewing the Tree's roots, and young impatient reform-school inmates (Borstal boys) seeking the secrets of sex—the origin of spices—from the feminine aspects of the Tree (504.26–28).

He describes dissenting heretics and schismatics (for example, Darwin and Gibbon), fighting like the Guelfs and the Ghibellines, praying to the east and projecting curses to the west (504.30–31). He describes Kilmainham pensioners—imprisoned Irish revolutionaries—throwing up stones at the branches to bring down her fruit, and bold young girls trying to reap husbands from the Tree, and cock robins hatching mistletoe from the Tree.[15] The speaker describes the yellow sun and the white moon in the ash tree's branches, as they are in Yggdrasill, appearing as honeysuckle and white heather. There are birds and animals approaching, flying around its branches and rubbing themselves on its bark, and hermits of the desert, like St. Jerome, studying Hebrew with its triliteral forms (505.4). Finally, as a grand climax, there are the acorns and pinecones bursting out of the Tree (505.4–5), manifesting its uncontrollable plenitude (505.5–6). Plenitude is a characteristic of God, the characteristic of His huge fullness of creative power, of which the Tree has a generous helping.

On the Tree is also a serpent slithering in its satin gleaming garment down the trunk, a snake of the sort that inhabited the Garden of Eden, and also like the serpent/dragon that gnaws the roots of Yggdrasill (505.7–9). Yawn finishes with a mention of the leaves whispering since the Creation and the branches twisting around and shaking hands with each other forever. The huge description is punctuated with a word evoking the eternal cycling and circling around the great tree, "Evovae" (505.13), an abbreviation for *[et in secula] seculorum amen*, meaning "forever."[16]

Yawn and the old men engage in an excited coda, saying the Tree is exalted; nobody ever saw anything to equal it (expressed in bird terms); indeed, it is a tree of liberty (505.14–17, 21)! Yawn then gives the name of the tree (505.29)—*Apfelbaum*, German for "apple tree," an appropriate name for the tree from the Garden of Eden, with overtones of rising up and falling down, like Man himself, falling for his disobedience and then rising through the Fortunate Fall.

History Tour: The Fall (505.32–506–33)

The allusion to the Fall of Man provides a bridge to the description of the archetypal family (505.32): the foolish Adam, his frau, and the penis![17] Or, as one old man exclaims, the world, the flesh and the devil—how this Luciferian affair smells of trouble for us!

The same old man asks, "Was Adam, the combination of man and angel, knocked on his sore bottom as a result of his adventures around the tree?" Yawn answers by relating how Adam gave names to all creatures, and thereby committed the sin of creation, which God resents as encroaching on His prerogative. The climbing snake it was (506.2) who flattered Eve into getting Adam to commit the first sin. This caused God, the Master of the House, to punish the serpent by forcing him to crawl on his belly forever. Joyce describes the first Tempter, in a sentence ending with violent hissing (505.36–506.8).

The presence of the serpent immediately recalls the Fortunate Fall of Adam and Eve (506.9–10). "O felix culpa!" exclaims the old man. Yawn and the old man agree that Adam's sin was needful, alluding to "O certe necessarium Adae peccatum" from the Exultet (M). The mention of Adam's sin brings up necessarily the redemption by the sacrifice of the Second Adam, Jesus, who was crucified on the Second Tree. The old man begins to sing a verse from the great old American spiritual "Were You There When They Crucified My Lord?": "Were you there when they laid him in the tomb?" Then Yawn sings another verse from the same song: "Sometimes it comes on me to tremble, tremble, tremble" (506.11–14).

And that was how Adam, and HCE, first fell.

Description of Adam/HCE, His House and Family (506.34–513.28)

The next twenty-five pages (506.34–531.26) are very confused. They seem to be about the Earwicker family—where they live, what they do. However, what with Yawn's desperate evasiveness, the multiplicity of his masks, and the quarrelsome nature of the questioners, the surface is turbid.

The reader should take heart: this is the last truly difficult section of *Finnegans Wake*. When HCE emerges from the depths of the universal night of Yawn, there is a clear run to the end of the book. Daylight is beginning to filter into the sky, and many things are becoming clearer.

The next few pages of this difficult section (506.34–508.11) are certainly about HCE and his big wide arse, which he has displayed previously as the Jarl van Hoother and the Russian general, and which will feature prominently in III.4, when we the readers are given a tour of HCE's bottom displayed like Phoenix Park, and when the children get a much too clear view of HCE's belongings.

In this section, the questioner poses a series of queries about "a man of around fifty" (506.34). (Joyce was in his fifties in the 1930s, when he was deeply engaged in these chapters of the *Wake*.) All the Earwicker dirty linen is washed all over again. HCE's trousers come down again and his bottom is yet again on display. Yawn reports the display, and the questioner exclaims, "What a curious sight of HCE's bottom!" (508.11). Another questioner follows up with a hybrid Greco-Latin phrase apparently meaning "Today his underpants fell down?" (508.12) (M). Yawn's confirmatory "Ay, another good button gone wrong" reminds the reader of the valiant back button on Bloom's trousers that flies off and breaks Circe's spell in *Ulysses* (15.3439–41). Here HCE's posterior is again in sight, and viewed from the feminine angle (508.21, 22).

There is more than a hint that HCE was not displeased to be viewed by his little daughter in her twin forms Issy and Essie, here symbolized by P/Q

(508.23–28). In fact, one of the questioners suggests that HCE deliberately uncovered himself in the presence of his daughter (509.21–23). Yawn replies with a rowdy poem based on an American original:[18] "A man can laugh through the whole of a farce, / A man can laugh through the whole of a play, / But a man can't laugh through the hole of his arse / Because he isn't built that way" (509.30–33). Yawn then follows with an account of HCE's lowering his trousers and creating by defecating, like the Jarl van Hoother, thereby producing a great earthly and poetic creation (509.33–36).

The next tale taken up is the marriage and settling down to child-raising of HCE and ALP (510.6–512.33). The wedding of HCE and ALP is the main concern of the speakers here. There is considerable emphasis on HCE's drinking habits; the *trou normand* referred to (510.20) is the ritual drink with which the Norman French break every major meal. However, at the wedding of HCE and ALP, at least the priest and the bride were sober, or so the narrator thinks (510.34–36). The best man at the wedding was Magraw (511.2), who will turn out to play a major part in the married life of the couple as the Other Man in the Earwicker menage.

ALP herself is now described (511.12–512.26). As usual, she is a splendid sight. Yawn says she wore silver and bronze jewelry, and a bunch of keys (or shamrocks) on her shoulder most prominently (511.29–31). Yawn and his questioner discuss admiringly the love and conquest of the pair—tiptop really (512.20). The questioner's praise of the pair ends with a prediction of the final, successful act of love at the end of the book at Dublin bar, where ALP will meet her resurrected lover in the morning (512.23–26).

The following sections deal with the name of their house, which invites visitors to Toot and Come-Inn (512.34), and with the children. Shaun is described in a few sentences (513.7–8). Being the top half, he is here called crazyheaded, which as an incomplete "head" person he surely is. Shaun is, however, partly representative of his father; from the claw of the lion, one can imagine the beast himself, as suggested by the Latin phrase *ex ungue leonis* (M).

Shem gets a much more elaborate treatment (513.9–24), one that deserves to be analyzed in detail. This brilliant passage is filled with testimonials to Shem's dancing ability—after all, he is the lower half that bears the legs! "Jambs" refers to Shem's legs, and there is a reference to *Top Hat*, the 1935 film starring Fred Astaire and Ginger Rogers. Other dancing references in this passage are to Russian knee-bend dances as performed by Nijinsky; the Easter sun, which according to Catholic unofficial tradition dances for joy on Easter Sunday; "Ta-Ra-Ra-Boom-De-Ay!"; and the first lines of the song "You Should See Me Dance the Polka!" Shem is a rumba dancer who fell and crashed; he is an imperial dancer (czar) who dances the czardas, and he whirls like a dervish. He has dancing in his blood like a disease. Finally there is a reference to Maria Taglioni, the first dancer to go up on point. Yawn comments that Shem got his dancing ability from his father, who went dancing the tripudium (513.22) in his fifties. The tripudium is a Latin sacred dance, one that Stephen Dedalus dances wildly in the Circe episode of *Ulysses* (15.4013). Joyce himself would on occasion launch into a wild "boneless" dance of the sort that Stephen Dedalus dances in *Ulysses*.

Shem is also gifted, like Joyce, in singing. There is a reference (513.14) to the amateur singing competitions in a town near Naples, Piedigrotta, where the local tenors, baritones, and basses shout and cry out (*schreien* in German), that is, show their abilities every year; Caruso himself first appeared at Piedigrotta, as a baritone.

So Shem has both singing and dancing abilities. In the works of Joyce, from the first page of *A Portrait*, where young Stephen both sings and dances, through *Ulysses*, song and dance are the twin marks of the artist. The figure of King David, a royal singer and dancer, is alluded to in *Ulysses*—as Stephen Dedalus walks away from bondage in the house of Bloom, he hears "a jew's harp in the resonant lane" (17.1244)—and it appears prominently through all the Daves and Davys in the *Wake*, including Dave the Dancekerl.[19]

However, there is the usual drawback to Shem's lower-half dancing ability; he comes from Tophet, Hell, the lowest part of the universe, and he is a devilish dancing dervish. The bad smell of the lower half is also referred to—you can sniff him, and he stinks like a polecat (513.13).

There is then a short reference to Issy (513.25–28). That is, she is made up of thoughts of Tristan, and sorrows (threnes), and thoughts of trinities—her two selves and Tristan, perhaps—and trains of wedding gowns.

Further Examination and Quarreling (513.29–525.9)

The Four Old Men are described, engaging in their usual scandalmongering (513.29–514.4). One of the scandals they air is about the rowdy goings-on in HCE's house, which is next described. Yawn calls it "Eccles's hostel," an obvious reference to Bloom's address in *Ulysses*, but then Yawn corrects himself and gives an encrypted version of "Finn's Hotel," the house's name: ." i .. '. . o .. l" (514.18). Then other names are suggested (514.22–28).

Finn's Hotel is a most appropriate name for the house of the archetypal family. It is also the name of the hotel where Nora worked as a chambermaid when Joyce met her. Danis Rose suggests that *Finnegans Wake* itself was originally supposed to be entitled *Finn's Hotel*, which is quite a plausible suggestion, since the name would combine the figure of Finn with a tribute to Nora.

Other family scandals are aired and ventilated, including HCE's dubious business practices (514.29–31). The old men urge Yawn to go into more detail about HCE, which he does in a long paragraph (516.3–30). HCE's bellicosity and the many "pious and pure wars" (Vico's phrase) that HCE waged are described in a long discussion, which merges into an account of the episode of the Cad in the Park, and what the Cad did afterward, pegging stones at HCE's house and calling him names—all the old scandals, in fact (517.2–521.9).

The inquest is interrupted by a ferocious quarrel among the inquisitors, apparently started by Matt of Ulster, who is impatient with the disorganized questioning methods of the aged Johnny from Connaught (521.10–522.3). When they finally get back to business, Yawn keeps saying, "Hah!" (522.13, 19, 23). Apparently he is pleased that the Four Old Men are such incompetent inquisitors. However, under pressure, Yawn says that he is not responsible for his utterances of "Hah!" and that he had something inside him talking to himself (522.26). One of the old men suggests that Yawn get psychoanalyzed (as Mrs. McCormack suggested to Joyce), a suggestion that Yawn indignantly rejects, as did Joyce (522.27–36).

Further pressure on Yawn produces a long disquisition delivered in the voice of the low-class gossips that spread the stories about HCE in the first place, which led to the making of Hosty's ballad (523.21–525.5). At the end of this prolix performance, Yawn begins to warm up sexually, but hypocritically suggests that cold water can calm his sexual urges (525.3–5). At this, one of the inquisitors—probably the impatient Matt, to judge from the Scotch-Irish overtones—furiously reacts to this further example of Yawn's evasiveness (525.6–9). That is, Yawn has a big tongue, but only a small head.

The Salmon of Wisdom Emerges (525.10–526.19)

Another of the old men interrupts Matt, and takes the question further; in fact, this old man begins to see a huge fish in the dim depths of Yawn. The fish is the phallic Salmon of Wisdom, or the even more phallic human conger eel, which bears HCE's initials (525.26). All of these ichthyal and ithyphallic creatures bring an intensely sensual atmosphere to the text, and evoke Yawn's memory of the seven Rainbow Girls.

This sexy reference to the rutting of maids in the fishery (525.13) causes a deepening of the search. Sex sinks the net of the four fishing inquisitors to a depth not yet achieved (525.10–13). In response, Yawn mentions the names of five girls. However, the sentence has seven words alliterating in "l" (525.14). The old questioner takes this to be a reference to HCE's carryings-on with the seven Rainbow Girls (525.12–15). Joyce declared that HCE had seven wives, according to Ellmann (1982, 636n). The Joyces always claimed that Daniel O'Connell was a collateral ancestor of theirs; HCE shares O'Connell's sexual propensities. It used to be said in Ireland that you could not throw a stone over the wall of any orphanage in the land and not hit one of Dan O'Connell's bastards.

Matt urges Yawn to go further in his reference and to sing a stanza from Hosty's ballad. Yawn complies: it turns out to be all about fishing. In response to Yawn's rash reference, the four suddenly see, emerging from the depths, the Salmon of Wisdom, for which they have been fishing in vain. The four desperately try to land the huge fish, but must settle for a promise that someone will eventually land him. Yawn pleasantly agrees that one day the Salmon of Wisdom will be caught. The reference here may be to the Judaic tradition that on the Day of Judgment the great sea creature Leviathan will be caught and will be served up at a banquet of the Righteous.

However, the mere sight of the Salmon of Wisdom has enlightened the questioners. Who will catch the fish? they ask. Yawn replies with a riddle, one that refers to the mystery of the third soldier, which as we have seen refers to the erect penis of the son moving to destroy the old father. They are three in one: they comprise Shem and Shaun, and the shame that separates them (526.13–15). The shame that separates them is not the hypostasis of the Father and the Son and their mutual love, which is the Holy Spirit, but the mutual shame of fathers and sons. This phrase can be elucidated by a statement in *Ulysses* about the unavoidable conflict between fathers and sons, who "are sundered by a bodily shame so steadfast that the criminal annals of the world, stained with all other incests and bestialities, hardly record its breach" (9.850–52). That is, fathers and sons are separated by so fundamental a "breach" that there is no record of a father raping a son. The word *em* is Hebrew for "mother," so the shame that sunders fathers and sons is based on a profound animosity, the deep-down understanding that they are both fighting for the mother—an Oedipal conflict so deep that the combatants cannot even approach each other. Here in the *Wake*, the shame that sunders them also sunders *em*, the mother—the winner splits the mother sexually.

Issy (526.20–528.24)

One of the inquisitors admires the reference to the three boys, but wants to know about the girl(s) in the family (526.17). Yawn responds with a reference to the urinating maidens in the bushes, and evokes the girls bathing themselves, cleansing their faces with Pond's cold cream, and looking at themselves in the streams of their mother (526.28–33). The inquisitor enthusiastically welcomes the vision of nubile nakedness narcissistically admiring its own inverted reflection, like Alice, in mirrors and streams (526.34–36).

All of this overheated sexual discussion evokes Issy, who eventually speaks up for herself, or perhaps this is merely another mask of Yawn's ventriloquizing. Issy is her usual coy, cruel, self-absorbed, virginal self, constantly talking to herself in the mirror (527.3), and impatiently awaiting a perfect man, one with mustached lips. Her little *dessous troublants* (527.31) get excited at the thought of him. She has a vision of her marriage with her Prince Charming, with wedding marches by Father Mendelssohn, who is always mindful of their sins (528.8), amid elated cries of "Kyrie eleison," "Christe eleison," and "Sanctus!" (528.8–9). Then she gradually fades out.

The four old men respond ecstatically to this vision of their hard-up hearts' desire. They imagine her in Herrick's silks ("That brave vibration each way free"), and envision the Sechseläute bells of the Angelus ringing out. The Virgin is to be impregnated by the Holy Ghost, or by them (in their dreams!). Or is she having a lesbian love affair with herself instead of experiencing the Conception by the Saint Esprit (528.17–18, 23–24)?

Here ends the enquiry of the Four Old Men.

Introduction of Brain Trust (528.25–532.5)

The sensuality of the atmosphere—the Rainbow Girls, the phallic fish, Issy's inflammatory remarks—has a radical effect on the Four Old Men. Abruptly the tempo and intensity change and the inquisitors are rejuvenated, metamorphosing from four quarreling, inefficient old fools into four highly efficient young inquisitors—the brilliant young braintrusters (529.5).

The term Brains Trust, later shortened to Brain Trust, was invented in July 1932 by James Kieran of the *New York Times* to describe the young academic advisors of Franklin Delano Roosevelt at the beginning of the New Deal. Here in the *Wake*, the energy of youth is evoked in the eventually successful effort to find the depths of HCE's soul. It will be recalled that in *Ulysses*, Leopold Bloom twice feels his youth renewed upon sexual stimulus, first after reading in *Sweets of Sin* "Young! Young!" (10.624) and then after ejaculation resulting from Gerty's display on the beach: "Goodbye dear. Thanks. Made me feel so young" (13.1272–73).

The bright young inquisitors renew their questioning of Yawn, this time with great force. At their urging, HCE tries two more masks, responding with the voices of Sackerson and Kate (530.23–24; 530.36–531.26), but in vain; the questioners are having none of that! In an invocation of great power (531.27–532.5), filled with alchemical spells calling up the spirits of air and fire and earth and water, and culminating with "Fee Fie Fo Fum!" they force the evasive HCE to come from behind his shop shutters (French *persiennes*, slatted shutters), and doff his masks, and appear on his own. After HCE exhausts his final four masks, the inquisitors force him to doff all masks (531.34; 532.5) and to rise up, in different forms at first, then as himself, as the great Master Builder of the City.

HCE's Last Masks

The final masks are those of Adam, of a BBC announcer, and of a Communicator who channels the voice of Oscar Wilde. That is, the three masks are arranged in an A-B-C pattern: A(dam)–B(BC announcer)–C(ommunicator). With Oscar Wilde, they amount to four masks, so they might be the final forms of the first four voices in the chapter—Tristan, Swift, Patrick, and Parnell.

A. Adam (532.6–534.2): The first words of the resurrected HCE, the city creator, are "Amtsadam, sir, to you!" These words introduce HCE as a city builder (Amsterdam), but also as Adam; on continental railroad schedules, Amsterdam is regularly abbreviated as "A'dam."[20] HCE is also a government officeholder (German *Amts-*, "official"). Further, these first words of HCE form a code message that identifies HCE as the eternal city-builder: the first letters of the phrase spell out *asty*, the classical Greek word for "city."

However much HCE tries one more act of concealment, he is given away by his characteristic stutter (532.7–533.3). HCE feels a good deal of guilt over his incestuous desires for this daughter, and as usual he frantically denies everything before he is actually accused of anything. He tries desperately to deny his urges, but only makes matters worse (532.18–533.3). He would have his daughters arrested for even thinking of such a thing (532.27–29)!

To cover his all too obvious guilt, he launches into fulsome praise of his wife: she is my dear true wife, with the smallest shoe size outside Chinatown (533.4–6). My private chaplain can testify as to my sexual relations with her in our four-poster bed (533.8, 12–13), with the Four Old Men looking on (533.14–21)—as they do in the next chapter. In fact, our home was altogether like *Et dukkehjem* (533.18)—Ibsen's *A Doll's House.*

HCE, having (as he thought) disposed of the charges against him, ends as if completing a radio broadcast, with the stock prices and the state of the agricultural market and "That will be all for today. Goodnight everybody. And a Merry Christmas!" (533.33–534.1).

The inquisitors are not impressed, and comment cynically (534.3–6).

B. BBC Announcer (534.7–535.25): The second mask that HCE tries on is that of a calm BBC announcer (534.7). The radio commentary at the end of the first mask perhaps suggests the voice of the second mask: HCE may think that it is safer to speak through an independent medium than to confess in propria persona.

The English spoken by BBC announcers was for a long time considered to set the standard. However, our mellifluous announcer has an odd taste in literature: an indecent limerick about a street paver, or paviour, in Belgravia. M reports a version of this limerick, which brings in disbelief in "the Saviour." I would argue that Joyce was alluding to another version. I have taken the liberty of rewriting the limerick—or rather, as I think, I have reconstructed the original:

There once was a man from Belgravia,
Who tried to find work as a paviour.
   He walked down the Strand
   With his tool in his hand
And was fined for indecent behaviour.

It should be noted that Joyce has the word "paviour" in his text, which suggests that my version is close to the one that Joyce knew.

The whole speech of the BBC Announcer is given up to a defense of himself. There is literally not a teaspoonful of evidence against me! I swear by the Thirty-Nine Articles (another reminder that HCE is an Anglican). This is followed by a violent attack on the Cad, who started the rumors about HCE and his misdeeds. How dare this low disgusting creature attack me! When I was the Lord Mayor of Dublin, Bartholomew van Homrigh, I shook hands with the king (535.1–12)!

The BBC Announcer ends with a deluge of insults directed at the Cad, and at the two girls in the park. The whole story of his misdeeds is obscenest or Ibsenist nonsense (535.19). The Cad is submerged under a rain of insults of the sort that were originally directed at Ibsen when he was first introduced into England.[21]

The four inquisitors seem to have ignored the fulminations of the announcer. They call on the next mask-wearer, Old Whitehead, and ask him to broadcast his comments (535.22–25).

C. OW (535.26–35): The next voice we hear is that of Old Whitehowth (535.26), who combines in himself Oscar Wilde, as the initials suggest, and a Commentator, and the top of the Hill of Howth. Joyce derived much of the Oscar Wilde passage from a spiritualist source.[22] Wilde, through a medium, was supposed to have written, among other things, "Pity Oscar Wilde—one who in the world was a king of life . . . dear lady . . . Oscar is speaking again . . . I am infinitely amused by the remarks you all make. . . . Shame on Joyce, shame on his work, shame on his lying soul."

The voice then begs for pity; he has been through a thousand hells and is calling *de profundis*, from the depths. Open your ears! He has a number of Wilde's characteristics at his death: white hairs, failing memory, bodily weakness. However, Wilde was not thirty-nine years old, as the text suggests. The age of thirty-nine is not significant in the life of Wilde: Wilde at the beginning of his legal ordeals was forty years old, and died at the age of forty-five. In addition, Old Whitehead is deaf as an adder. The deafness that is mentioned was never a characteristic of Wilde, though he did develop an ear condition, diagnosed in his last illness as ototis media, which originated in an attack of syphilis when he was twenty, or perhaps from a fall in prison, or both. The ear condition led to meningitis, which heavily contributed to his death (Ellmann 1988, 580, 581).

Wilde/HCE asks to be judged not by his disreputable life but by his fruits, which in the case of Wilde are his books—and they are indeed impressive. He ends by introducing the title of the great poem that follows, asking pity for poor Haveth Childers Everywhere (535.34–35).

We are then informed that we have been hearing the voice of Old Whitehead through a Communicator. (When Yeats's bride began channeling spirit voices in the autumn of 1917, one of the designations for the spirits was Communicators.) This Communicator is a spirit from Rio de Janeiro who is named Sebastian, as in Sebastian Melmoth, Wilde's pseudonym during his exile and at his death. There are a number of other Wildean references, addressed to the Communicator: Felix Culpa combines with an open *culo* or bottom (536.8–9), a comment on Wilde's sexual preferences, and a pitying reference to Old Whitehead's career—yesterday he consorted with the nobility, and with Nobel Prize winners, but he died in a madhouse (536.12–13). However, his voice is still young and his mouth is red, even though his blond hair is mostly white (536.21–24). The commentator suspects that Old Whitehead is a sacrificial lamb for him, bearing his burdens.

Now, however, all the masks finally drop off, and HCE speaks in his own voice.

Haveth Childers Everywhere

The Great Male Soliloquy (536.28–554.10)

The eighteen-page Haveth Childers Everywhere section is the purest and most powerful expression of male creativity, as Joyce saw it, with all its flaws and grandeurs.[23] This male soliloquy is second in power only to the other great prose lyric, the Soft Morning, City section at the end of the book, which is the great female soliloquy.

Both of these great prose lyrics provide examples of a genre invented by Joyce, one that could be called the "demotic prose lyric," of which Molly's soliloquy is the finest example before those in *Finnegans Wake*. Other examples of the demotic lyric in *Ulysses* are the section on water in Ithaca (17.163–228) and the shorter section on fire in the same chapter (17.255–74). In these "poems" Joyce creates a great picture of the world, using only the lyrical equipment available to ordinary people.

The Haveth Childers Everywhere soliloquy is an immense, and immensely merry, poem about the creation of cities, especially Dublin, which HCE made as a wedding ring for his bride, ALP. The city of Dublin is appearing through the mist and the vanishing shades of night as HCE begins his great city poem. It is, like Molly Bloom's soliloquy, in eight huge prose paragraphs—occasionally interrupted by a quartet of one-line comments from the inquisitors.

Joyce, the Master Builder of literature, rejoiced in cities, the creation of Man the Master Builder in concrete terms. As Tindall says,

> The gaiety of the Master Builder's boast, transfiguring all the dread of cities with their dopes, rioters, and muggers, is that of Joyce, builder of another kind. The London of T. S. Eliot, like the Paris of Baudelaire, is a kind of hell. Shelley's hell is "a city much like London." Not so Dublin, which, whatever its paralysis and dirt, was dear to Joyce, a city man entirely. Building and rebuilding—even their often discreditable

results—are gaiety's occasion. Being the Master Builder of Dublin or of the *Wake* is fun. (272)

It is at this point—when the city is beginning to appear through the mists of night, and when we begin to see the river flowing through the stone embankments of Dublin—that we must consider the true relationship between HCE and ALP. So far we have heard only the apparently insincere praise by HCE of his little wife, while all the time he is yearning feverishly for the embraces of the Rainbow Girls and of his own daughter, Issy. However, this strategic attitude of public affection for his life partner, a strategy adopted to conceal his incestuous urges, actually conceals a true affection, if one that is deeply possessive in nature. The City, the creation of HCE, acts as a bind and a trap for ALP. As we will see, the city that HCE made as a ring for his bride effectively constricts her maidenly freedom. At the very end of the book, she tries to spring free of it (627.32). Yet immediately afterward she sees his arms, those terrible prongs, rising up to embrace and trap her again (628.4–5).

I. HCE's Profession of Innocence (536.28–538.17)

HCE begins by asserting that he has revealed everything in his past and is confident that he has nothing really bad on his conscience. If he is given even a short jail sentence, he will think that extremely unfair. He says a prayer (536.34–36), and ends with a slam at his critics, that they are also guilty, and that people who live in glass houses should not throw stones (536.36–537.1). He predicts the sunrise, which will take place in the last chapter, and connects it to Western conquest of the East (537.11). He then begins to talk about his beloved, for whom, as it will appear, he made the great city. He denies, with an oath to Fricka, the Norse goddess of marriage, that he, like King Cophetua, attempted to seduce a beggar maid to be his queen (537.31–32). Though he certainly desires to seduce young maids, he keeps insisting that for no money would he do such a thing.

II. HCE Raids the Coast and Defeats the Irish (538.18–540.12)

Yet the theme of sexual desire keeps returning, and leads directly to the description of the city. Although HCE denies seeking for such young girls, he declares indirectly that he has triumphed over the three soldiers and has taken away their women. He refers to the tripartite structure—which, as we have seen, stands for the male genitals—as three Deucollions (538.29, 30, 33). "Collion" means "testicle," as in Middle English *cullion* and French *couillon*, so "Deucollion" means "two-testicled." The three Deucollions are the nicely hung young bachelors of the Museyroom fable (10.3–4). Yet despite the tripartite sexual potency of the soldiers, HCE has stolen their girl.

Joyce here evokes a story by Henry James, "The Lesson of the Master," to drive home his point. He refers to the story twice, at 539.8–9 and at 540.28.[24] In the James story, an old master, a great writer named Henry St. George, tricks a young writer into giving up his beloved to him by claiming that she would hamper the young writer, while he, the old writer, is past his prime and cannot be harmed anymore! The lesson of the master is how to trick his worshipful young disciples. Here HCE, the Old Master, claims that he has taken away the intended of the three soldiers.

HCE then describes how he, the Viking rover, landed on the coast and began to build a home, which is combined with his pub, for his abducted bride (539.17–22). He is now well launched upon his description of the city that he built. He has built his city of magnificent distances (539.25), which nevertheless has muddy bogs within it.[25] It is walled and fortified (539.25–26). Joyce ends this paragraph with a description of medieval Dublin (540.3–8) from Holinshed's *Chronicles*, quoting from Stanihurst (M).

The Four Old Men join in with praise of the small Irish town of Drumcollogher, which they seem to think is the town being described. "There is only one house in Drumcollogher," as Percy French wrote (M). They urge visitors to see the town, no matter what else they see. In fact, the last old man says that you should see Drumcollogher and die, a phrase originally devised for Naples (M).

III. Dublin Begins to Appear in the Morning Light (540.13–545.23)

Now the description of the town begins in earnest, with the beginning of dawn light. The town has changed a great deal with time, and yet remained the same, a place of mingled good and bad, true and false. It also combines details from a great many large cities of the world.

The first detail is a London detail: where the triple tree of Tyburn, the tripartite gallows, once stood there is now Marble Arch, the traditional place for the disaffected to voice their grievances (M); where once malefactors were hanged, now murmuring masses of protesters hold meetings and march (540.15). There is a special significance in the choice of this place for the first city detail: it combines the murderous authority of the city officials with the safety valve of democratic protest, thereby summarizing the whole range of political relations.

The next comment provides a brilliantly comic Shakespearean note on the commercial activities of the city: "where the bus stops there shop I" (540.15–16). Authority is first established, and then the commerce of the city comes in. The next few clauses strengthen the note of authority, with the mention of sheriffs and bailiffs, but HCE reminds us that although the authorities of the town include the police and the murderous Black and Tans (540.21), these policemen are only human, after all (540.21–22); that is, Unter den Linden, the policemen, or horneys (M), can meet their sweethearts.

Joyce then gives credit to Ibsen, who defined for the modern world the rural and urban types of humanity. There are eight plays of Ibsen mentioned with close approximations of their Norwegian names (540.22–25). At this point Joyce's cynicism about public law and finance, probably inherited from his father, takes over. The obedience of the citizenry—that is, their passivity—is the foundation of the health of the town; Joyce provides a version of the motto of Dublin (540.25–26). However, the town has a certain tranquility even though it is ruled by thieves and murderers: our finances and lives are in the hands of the highwayman Jack Sheppard, and our assurance of life—our life insurance, in all senses—is controlled by the crime-master Jonathan Wild (540.26–28).

Law has been established, even though the instruments of order are frequently unlawful themselves. The town has achieved a certain peace; old abuses and dangers have abated. The bullying duellists Hair-Trigger Dick and the other "blueblaze devils" described by Maria Edgeworth have passed away; thugs are rare, lepers are hidden away, and teachers and doctors have mitigated the plagues of disease and ignorance (540.29–33). HCE says complacently that all is truly good, *valde bonum*, the words used in the Vulgate in Genesis 1:31 to describe God's approval of his creation (T).

Most early cities were built on hills for defense, like Troy or Jerusalem. HCE's city is built on seven hills, like Rome or Edinburgh (541.1) (M). In the city itself, there are several huge erections—the churches of St. Nicholas and St. Michan, the Eiffel Tower, the Woolworth Building, and other skyscrapers (541.4–7).

Taxes and other money matters are then taken up: by finance and imposts (taxes) the city builder grew, and by weighing out precious metals by ounce and scruple, he grew outrageously (541.7–9). He collected medieval taxes of murage and lestage, and he made money, literally—he established a mint and struck coinage, as the early Norse king of Dublin Sitric Silkyshag did for Dublin (541.9–12). However, like everything else in the city, the money was a mixed blessing; it provided the source of financial power, but it also was dissipated in gambling dens, pawnshops, and IOUs (542.12–14)—*mont-de-piété* is French for "pawnshop."

The inevitable next step in history involves the commercial prosperity of the cities, which invariably roused the envy of those not benefiting. Hordes of invaders rose up to attack the centers of wealth. The cities organized themselves for defense (541.14–24). Brian Boru, whose names in Irish means Brian of the Tributes, a financial title, repulsed the Norse invaders at the battle of Clontarf. Wellington kept Napoleon from taking Brussels at the battle of Waterloo—"Waterloo, morne plaine!" in Victor Hugo's words.

Martial law kept unruly elements passive, as in the bloody suppression of rebellion in Warsaw (541.23) in 1863 by the Russian general "Hangman" Muraveyev. To be sure, Muraveyev was hardly the only bloody suppressor in history. Joyce might as easily have pointed to other military leaders and soldiers in the age of revolt, such as General Galliffet in Paris in 1871, General Radetsky in Vienna in 1848, the yeoman cavalry at Peterloo, the Germans in Belgium in WWI, or the British Tans and Auxiliaries in Ireland. The city creator gives life to his children, and takes it away bloodily when they show signs of independence.

Our double-dealing civic hero then created the gulf between the rich and the poor (541.24–25). He made prayer feasts in the corpulent and religiose upper city, the acropolis, and created hunger in the lower city (Niederdorf, meaning "lower town," is part of Zurich). The division between the upper city, the region of wealth and power, and the lower city, the realm of hunger, is known in dozens of older cities of the world. The fragment "praha-" evokes Prague; Kafka's novel *The Castle* takes as its central theme the contrast between the servants in the lower city and the inaccessible mysterious authorities on the hill.[26]

HCE claims that he drained the sloblands of Dublin and created the suburbs of Fairview, Rathgar, and Rathmines. Beggars were sheltered in the Dublin Mendicity Institution, whose complacent and corrupt officials prospered on the beggary of others, an old abuse noted by, among others, Dickens. At similar institutions, the Poor Law Guardians of Dublin were the most prosperous and reactionary citizens of the town (541.26–27).

HCE also had a double standard in patriotic matters. How many English soldiers did he drill mercilessly on Salisbury Plain? And how many English soldiers did he drown in a dreadful wreck (541.28–29)? In that awful event of 1807, commemorated in song and described in a history of the time as "perhaps the greatest tragedy that ever took place in or near Dublin," two army transport ships, the *Princess of Wales* and the *Rochdale*, were wrecked off Seapoint near Dublin, with the loss of more than five hundred soldiers and officers. The history records: "The long shore presented a sight too horrible for description." Joyce is here reporting for yet another time "the unconscious cruelty" of the English,[27] which he commented on in his essay on Daniel Defoe, and in *Ulysses*.

By changing the hundred pipers mourned in the song to three hundred pipers and two and two (541.29), Joyce is returning to the 3/2 sex motif, with the three soldiers and the two girls in the park. In sexual matters, our civic hero likewise had a double standard. For sleek sleeping beauties, he spun veils of night; to the sleeping female beasts among the poor in the city, he turned a deaf ear (M). It is not only the sexual aspect of social distinction that is being treated; the "two nations"of Disraeli are here also. Beautiful melodies sounded in the wealthy West End, while in the slums of the East End the poor were roaring like beasts (541.30–34). There was disease in the poor districts, tuberculosis and beriberi (541.36–542.2), which was a vitamin-deficiency disease possibly induced by a diet of potatoes (M).

However, HCE did not entirely neglect the health of the city. He created the Dublin water system, which at first conveyed water through tubes made of the trunks of elm trees (542.4–7).[28] He then created the Dublin transit system (542.7–9). He put up drinking fountains in the streets, with chained cups (542.9–10)—actually the creation of Sir Philip Crampton (M). Other cheap beverages, such as tea or coffee, were provided at various shops (542.10–14).

HCE then created the political system of Dublin: in Foster Place, near the old Parliament of Ireland building, he allowed political rallies to be held; suffragettes and conscientious protesters chained themselves to railings, but older women and the mothers of Dublin approved of the political arrangements imposed by HCE (542.17–22). He needed soldiers, so, like Napoleon, he encouraged childbirth. When children were born, he would command "bringem young" (542.26–27). Evoking the name of Brigham Young suggests that HCE would have encouraged polygamy, for the increase in children that it produces; and, like the Jesuits, he knew that if children were brought to him when they were young, he had them for life.

To encourage childbirth, HCE set up maternity hospitals, and he also imprisoned prostitutes, so that the sexual energies of Irish men should turn exclusively to their childbearing wives (542.27–29). Dressed as Lord Mayor, in gold chain, neckcloth, and sashes, he jaunted about his town, and at the same time, as a legless beggar, he trundled about the streets like jelly in a bowl (542.34–35).

He had a curious double policy about prostitutes. Despite his discouragement of them, he knew that they helped keep money circulating, so he sent them out on the streets to refresh the jaded men of Dublin; however, to keep the semen for legitimate childbearing purposes, he made sure that the Dublin men could not ejaculate—he psychologically castrated them or otherwise damaged the function of their genitals (542.35–543.3).

HCE was a very active ruler, both for good and for bad. He sent out myriads of Irishmen around the world, some as convicts to Botany Bay in Australia, and some as colonists to America, where they set up twenty-four Dublins (543.3–6).[29] He was widely praised as a ruler, but schoolboys were less enthusiastic about him—they called him a son of a bitch, and he punished them (543.6–10).

The light stealing into this predawn stage of the night begins to show the scene clearly, and now comes the description of the actual city of Dublin. HCE was a great builder. The more secretly he built, the more was his landscape filled with houses; he constructed his Vanderbilt house at midnight, and in the morning he was surrounded by many roofs—the houses sprang up like mushrooms in a field (543.11–13).

He compares himself, not for the first time, to Solomon the Magnificent (543.13–15). Solomon disclosed his glory to the Queen of Sheba, who, as the Bible indicates, was most impressed: "the half was not told me," she marvels (I Kings 10:7). However, the biblical Solomon did not quite "disclothe" himself to her; at least the holy text does not report so! And just like everything else in this section, the identification of the glory of HCE as that of Solomon has its dark side. The quote from the Sermon on the Mount, about the lilies of the field, puts Solomon in his place: it asserts that the flowers were more gorgeously arrayed than "Solomon in all his glory" (Matthew 6:28–29). In the book of Ecclesiastes, which was traditionally attributed to Solomon, and which Joyce certainly had in mind when he wrote this passage, the magnificent king takes no pleasure in all of his accomplishments, which rivaled those of HCE: "Then I looked on all the works that my hands had wrought, and on the labour that I had laboured to do; and, behold, all was vanity and vexation of spirit, and there was no profit under the sun" (Ecclesiastes 2:11).

With the physical town beginning to appear in the dim light, Joyce shows just what sort of a town it is (543.15–545.23). HCE's creation is flawed but magnificent. It contains all sorts of crime, poverty, disease, and unhappiness, but it is a tremendous work, the imperfect masterpiece of imperfect Man the Creator. Within a version of the town charter given by Henry II to the citizens of Dublin, Joyce places revised versions of sociological data gathered by the pioneer B. Seebohm Rowntree about the slums of York.[30] And a miserably depressing picture it is.

T provides a translated text of the second city charter, given by Henry II to Dublin in 1172:

> Henricus Dei gratia. . . . Know ye, that I have given, granted, and by my charter confirmed to my subjects of Bristol my city of Dublin to inhabit. Wherefore I will and firmly command that they do inhabit it, and hold it of me and my heirs, well and in peace, freely and quietly, fully and amply, and honourably, with all the liberties and free customs which the men of Bristol have at Bristol, and through my whole land. (281)

Joyce rewrites the charter, making it more pompous. He adds the old borders of the city of Dublin and lists the different types of citizens (543.16–21). All the citizens are serving in homage and fealty, except that Joyce describes their activities as homage and felony, again asserting the double nature of HCE's creation.

Then begin details of the actual city, with the Rowntree selections carefully altered to make the picture more sordid and comic. HCE's city is, in fact, a kind of Ark, with both clean and unclean beasts aboard. Joyce makes this Ark reference clear by stipulating that only those residents who have received tickets may stay in his city (543.17–18). This phrase echoes a quote from Brigham Young referring to the Ark: "All those who have received tickets are aboard" (M).

In HCE's creation, the houses of the city are dirty and dusty—passages are blocked with refuse—and overcrowded, with very little furniture. The plumbing is inadequate; many households share one toilet, chamber pots must be carried through crowded bedrooms at night, and water sources are few and scattered.

The inhabitants have a limited diet and are generally unemployed and bored; they sit on their front stoops and talk and smoke. Those who do earn money generally do not earn enough of it, and some of them gather and sell rags and bones. Many of the inhabitants are dirty and verminous, and sick physically or mentally. Of course, they cannot afford medical treatment. A considerable number are rumored to engage in criminal activity. However,

Rowntree pronounces many of the inhabitants "respectable," which seems to mean that they have not (yet) been convicted of any crime. The ordinary middle-class notion of respectability is rarely attained by them. The middle-class visions of Flowerville, with which Leopold Bloom amuses himself before going to sleep, and his considerable financial resources (17.1497–1759, 1854–67), are far from available to the struggling miserable children of HCE. All you can say of them is that they are barely scraping by. Even the cat has left in disgust.

HCE delivers a great peroration: though the horrible admissions of his children were the worst that could be expected, let them all come, they are my vassals, I have written them down in my books (545.12–14). He then ends with his version of the rest of Henry II's charter (545.14–22), and puts his seal on the document. It is a grisly and sinister seal: his vouchers are knives and snuffboxes (545.22–23), the ultimate tools of his authority, which he uses for castration, suffocation, and execution. "Fee fo fum!" says the tyrannous giant (and "I smell the blood of an Irish man" in the original version). "I own the farm; I have paid my fees for it." He signs his name Henricus Rex, but altered to "Enwreak us wrecks" to send a most discouraging message: he wrought us, and he will wreck us—a final double message from the Creator and Destroyer of the city and its inhabitants!

There is a reference here to the dying speech of John of Gaunt in Shakespeare's *Richard II*, a reference to a deeply serious matter of land tenure and the psychology of tenants versus owners. Gaunt is deeply distressed that England, described in the famous introduction to the deathbed scene, has been parcelled out with charters, "rotten parchment bonds," and treated merely as a piece of real estate, to be rented out. In Dublin, as in John of Gaunt's England, no one will own property except the landlords; no roots will be put down. It is the world of Blake's "London"—the world of the "chartered" streets and parcelled-out riverbanks. It is also the world of T. S. Eliot's "Gerontion," in which "the jew squats on the window sill, the owner." Joyce was not anti-Semitic, of course, but here he makes the same point as Eliot; in HCE's city, only HCE owns any property. The inhabitants of his city are rootless children wandering in his concrete bowels and trying to avoid becoming digested by the paternal giant with his "eatupus complex" (128.36). Once the children are digested, they can no longer threaten his privileged position.[31]

IV. The Uncertain Magnanimity of HCE's Rule (545.24–546.28)

The fourth paragraph carries on the themes of the third, but without comment by the four inquisitors. It is possible that such intervention was left out accidentally, in the general difficulty of transmission of this chapter.

HCE first describes his activities as a ruler. He asserts that he was a merciful ruler and has liberated thousands of slaves, here called "mancipelles" (545.25) from the Italian *mancipio*, "slave" (M). HCE gave hope to those poor people living in attics, and housed other poor hungry people in bleak cellars. He took as his credo Virgil's words about the duty of the emperor: "Parcere subjectis et debellare superbos" (Aeneid 6:853), that is, he spared the humble and "put down the mighty from their seats," as the Gospel of Luke (1:52) expressed the thought (M). HCE judged the drugged prostitutes in his lower courts and acted as a judge in a "pie-powder court," a medieval court set up especially to administer justice in fairgrounds for travelers from afar with dusty feet (French *pieds poudreux*) (545.29–30).

HCE oversaw both birth and death, the beginning and the end of life: at one of his hospitals, Guy's, the babies were swathed; at another, Foulke's, the dead were autopsied, "slashed" (545.30–31). Guy's is a hospital in London, but Foulke's is not a real hospital. The two names were inserted to suggest that the births and deaths of Dubliners were overseen by Guy Fawkes, the traditional villain of the Gunpowder Plot.

The phrase that follows (545.31–32), concerning a game for someone named Gomez, shows HCE's double nature. It refers to a well-known fifteenth-century event in which the mayor of Galway, James Lynch Fitzstephan, condemned his own son to death for the murder of a Spaniard named Gomez, and hanged the son himself from a second-story window of his house when no one could be procured to execute the prisoner. However, a second phrase, referring to a loy, suggests a son murdering his father; the loy is the instrument with which Christy Mahon tries to kill his father in Synge's *Playboy of the Western World*. The double deaths in these phrases provide a balance that sums up HCE's double role in life, as the destroyer and the victim of youth.

Accounts of HCE's activities as judge and city builder are followed by a description of his coat of arms (546.5–11). The crest of Dublin's arms bears two unclothed young girls, and the field, divided in two horizontally, bears a beetle (Earwicker himself) above and, below, three young soldiers shaking their naked spears at the beetle—in other words, the shield sums up the whole story of youth, male and female, three and two, attacking the father.

The motto (546.10–11) spells out HCE as the first letters in a variant of the Emerson poem title "Heri, Cras, Hodie," which means "yesterday, tomorrow, today" in Latin—the fight between age and youth is perennial.

HCE takes up the story of the three soldiers and the two girls in a comment on the motto, and insists, by his creative powers, by his civic rights as a man, and by the inner light of his religion (546.19–21), that he was allowed to enter her sexually. By his masculine power and his ability to make love to women, he is simultaneously all in all in himself, and contains all contradictions. He ends by asserting that this is the true account of himself. The four inquisitors comment cynically about this boast (546.25–28).

V. HCE and His Wife (546.29–547.13)

In the fifth paragraph, and the three following, HCE returns to the subject of his treatment of his wife, Fulvia Fluvia, the blond or reddish-brown river. I was always fair to her, he insists. Yet he admits that his lovemaking was sometimes rough, that he spoiled her undies, and that he made her weep (547.7–9). At the end of the Haveth Childers Everywhere soliloquy, her weeping changes to laughter. However, the line between love and possession is never clear in the activity of HCE with ALP. The builders of Dublin drained the plain through which the Liffey originally flowed, and constrained the river between stone embankments. HCE may have made the city as an ornament for his bride, as he claims, but his gifts of stone provided severe constraints on her freedom. She realizes this at the very end of the book, and she then springs to be free from him (627.32).

The four inquisitors try to leave, and promise to meet again in a hundred years (547.10–13).

VI. HCE's Forcible Discipline of ALP (547.14–550.7)

HCE continues with his account of the construction of the city, his gigantic gift for ALP. Despite her weeping at his roughness, he was firm with her, personally and sexually (547.14). He has swathed her completely in veils, for firmer control of her—masks, yashmak, covered ears, covered nose (547.15–16). He has married her, impelled by his powerful physical drives. His attitude toward ALP is a compound of great and authentic love and violent, gross bodily lust. Of course he insists that he views her as a bride to be loved and cherished, but he lets slip that he regards her also as a whore to be captured and held.

He declares that with all his bawdy body he worshiped her (547.28), a marital attitude traceable to the Solemnization of Matrimony of the Church of England—HCE is an Anglican—as originally set down in the Book of Common Prayer: When the man placed the ring on the finger of the woman, he said, "With this ring I thee wed, with my body I thee worship . . ." However, here the ring of HCE is not only the sign of marriage, it is also a metal enclosure symbolizing the capture of ALP.

Tall as Cuchulain or Ajax, he raised his trident (the terrible prongs of the ending of the book) and bade the seas retire from her. He cast ten bridges over her, as decoration and as means of control, and created riverside drives and embankments, as in New York and London. These creations are, like all the other operations on ALP, both creative acts and acts of control.

Now that he is in sight of the sea, in his imagination, HCE is inspired to describe his marriage as elements of his greatest role, Ocean. He has performed an act of unity and sexual capture—the male maelstrom penetrating the female gulf (547.32–33). He created the port facilities of the great city (547.35–548.2), and anticipates the introduction of ALP's paranymphs, the bridesmaids Amazia and Niluna at the end of the book (627.28–30), but gives them names of two ocean liners from the Eastern and Western Hemispheres, the *Empress of Asia* and *Queen Columbia* (548.2). The wedding music comes also from the ocean—the "singing sands" of the Hebrides. Apparently the wedding is such a huge event that the whole of the seas and islands between Ireland and Britain are participating.

The theme of sexual capture and violence in wedlock is reinforced: with a Spanish fury, he chained, locked, and bolted a name to her, which she will carry to her grave (548.5–9). The "spunish furiosos" with which he punished and terrified her is the dreadful sack of Antwerp by the Spaniards in 1576, which was forever after known as the Spanish Fury.

HCE was her marriage partner; he would cleave unto her as prescribed in Genesis 2:24. He declares that he towered over her as they went through the marriage ceremony (German *Hochzeit*). In fact, HCE was, in his own estimation, as gigantic as Mount Everest (548.9)! However, this is only the masculine, boastful version given in this great male soliloquy. As we will see in the greater female soliloquy at the end of the book, ALP revolts against the violence of the male, and she ultimately describes him as a puny bumpkin (627.22–24), merely a bump on the horizon.

HCE returns to the theme of the international shipping industry established by the aggressive bourgeoisie of the nineteenth and twentieth centuries. Who cut her ribbons if not my prowess, and who established harbors and free ports if not the enterprising bourgeois free-porter (548.10–12)? It will be remembered that the establishment of Hong Kong as a "free port" was an egregious act of brutal imperialism by Great Britain in the nineteenth century.

The entrepreneur HCE established the great shops of the modern city, ostensibly for the delight of his bride, but also as part of his iron control of her by fear and pain (548.19–32). Among other acts of commercial creativity, in his department stores he established shoe shops for her dainty feet, but also that she might know the torture of the boots (548.30): her fashionable shoes introduced her to the terrible torture engine called the boot, in which the bones of prisoners' legs were progressively broken. In HCE's department stores, he established tea shops for her to enjoy the tea hour, as in Copenhagen (548.32). In a special sense, Copenhagen is HCE's city; it will be remembered that the name, København in Danish, means "merchant's harbor."

His next feats ensure the protection of his beloved city. He makes it safer from its internal enemies by creating lighting systems for modern Dublin. Lighting cities removes the ancient peril of the "nightwalkers," criminals and prostitutes who prowled around the ancient and medieval city and preyed on the citizens. At first the Dublin lighting took the form of cressets, metal baskets with fires within them, then candles and tapers, then gaslight, and finally electric lighting (549.1–20). The illumination swept away all the terrors of the night, and there was peace, perfect peace (549.6–12).

Joyce's description of the electrification of Ireland contains some of his most vivid sentences (549.12–20). HCE, the great engineer, hung up electric lamps in the cities, and topaz-colored lights in lighthouses all along the coasts. Joyce here is historically accurate. The Pigeonhouse generator was set up in 1903, and by 1922 the hydroelectric resources of the Shannon were exploited. The project was directed, as Joyce notes, by the German firm of Siemens-Schuckerwerke of Berlin. The lovely passage is filled with electrical terms—volts, amperes, anodes and cathodes—and is one of the triumphs of Joyce's style.

HCE proceeds to set up the defenses of his city against her external enemies. He tells how he defended her by sweeping the seas clean of her foes (549.21–22). He then alludes to the worldwide creation of other Dublins, such as the Georgia Dublin on the Oconee, tributary of the Altamaha (M) (549.28), and begins to describe some of the Lord Mayors of the various towns named Dublin.

It is at this point that HCE begins to turn Dublin into a holy city, by setting up a religious frame for her. He first equates his city to Jerusalem by citing a history ranging from the time of Joshua to Godfrey of Bouillon (550.1–3), the first and the last of the Nine Worthies of medieval literature (M). Since the book of Joshua (10:1) is where Jerusalem first appears in the Bible, at least under that name,[32] Dublin is implicitly compared to the city that became the holy city of the Jews when David conquered it from the Jebusites in the eleventh century B.C., and when the Temple was built there by Solomon— and that became the holy city of the Christians when Godfrey conquered it in the eleventh century A.D.

The inquisitors are becoming impressed by HCE's recitation: one of the four inquisitors describes HCE with grudging admiration as not all bum and belly (550.4). It appears that the cynicism of the inquisitors is gradually turning to admiration and, later, worship.

VII. The Institutions of the City (550.8–552.34)

HCE next protected his city from infection: he attempted to clean ALP of the sewage that flowed into her from the city (550.8–9), a task far from complete in 1904 when Stephen Dedalus, walking on the beach, sensed that "Unwholesome sandflats waited to suck his treading soles, breathing upward sewage breath" (3.150–51).

HCE also established the richly stocked food markets, with garlic and spices and herbs, and bakeshops (550.12–15), and apothecary shops whose wares include laxatives (jalap) to keep her digestion going just in case the rich food and spices upset her stomach (550.15–17), and cosmetics shops that stocked baking soda and olive oil, as well as Cuticura ointment and implements to make her body clean and pure (550.15–22).

He set up places for the playing of games, surrounded by portraits of Lord Mayors and Lady Mayoresses, and he set up dance halls for her amusement (550.22–551.1). He introduced her to the general public, here as elsewhere in the *Wake* signified by twelve words ending in "-ation" (551.17–21).

HCE then turned to the educational, commercial, political, and transportation systems of the city. He set up observatories and universities for ALP (551.24–32), thoughtfully including public toilets (551.25–28), this last possibly a reference to the public urinal outside Trinity College, "the meeting of the waters." In the universities, his scholars translated the hieroglyphics of the Rosetta stone (M). HCE then constructed great streets of commerce and finance (551.32–35). He set up the modern political system (551.35–552.1) by providing polling places, although the power remained in his hands: the electoral districts resembled the famous Old Sarum, the English "rotten borough" outside Salisbury notorious for the fact that, before the First Reform Act, it returned two members to Parliament although there were no residents there. HCE also built the four railway terminals of Dublin (552.1–3).

Finally, he set up great churches, meetinghouses, and cathedrals (552.3–10, 14–16). He is no religious bigot—so long as he holds the central power, all religions can be practiced freely. He built houses of worship, and enforced respect, for all faiths. He constructed the two cathedrals of Dublin—the Anglican Christ Church Cathedral, and the Catholic Pro-Cathedral—adding for good measure Freemasons' halls and meetinghouses for the Covenanters (Scottish Presbyterians), the Salvation Army, and the Swedenborgians. There is even a hint that he constructed mosques (532.24–25). With the assistance of fourteen Irish architects and sculptors (552.11–13), he constructed many lovely buildings and statues, and set up pleasure grounds in which his sons and daughters might greet each other and mingle freely—hoopskirts for the girls, men taking their hats off and introducing themselves (552. 16–20).

This section builds to a spectacular word-portrait of the restored St. Patrick's Cathedral, complete with rose window, with its bells clashing and booming, the Telford organ gloriously swelling, its choir in its pews singing ecumenically in Old Church Slavonic "Lord have mercy on us, Christ have mercy on us," and its other instruments blaring and blasting (532.21–29). And like the Viking queen Ota on the altar of Clonmacnois cathedral, ALP set her bare bottom on the chilly altar of the cathedral (532.29–30). May Allah and all gods have mercy on us!

The four inquisitors have become deeply impressed by the huge onward sweep of HCE's rhetoric, and the plenitude of his creation. They respond with ambiguous cries combining the German hail of "Hoch!" with the lingering scepticism of "hokum" (552.31–34).

VIII. The Climax of the Great Prose Poem (552.35–554.10)

The ending of HCE's poem of creation shows ALP in pain and in delight. HCE has forced his beloved to learn the alphabets, the Greek, Hebrew, English, and Old Irish, by means of punishment with birch, yew, and rattan rods on her bottom, and she wailed in pain (552.36–553.4).

He spread before her the extensive thoroughfares and elaborate gardens of the great modern cities of Ireland, England, and America—Dublin's grand Lord Edward Street, the bustling streets of London, New York's Coney Island and Mulberry Bend Park, Letchworth Garden City in England, the first garden city, as well as Garden City in Long Island—plus the seven wonders of the ancient world (553.4–12). He set up all the statues on O'Connell Street in Dublin, notably the highly ridiculous bust of Sir Philip Crampton, pass it if you can or can't! (553.12–15). He planted vineyards and elms and hops and barley fields, and constructed the Bowery in New York (in its old form as an orchard), Greenwich Village, the Magazine Fort in Phoenix Park, and (again!) public toilets—"English necessities," as they were called in Italy and Hispanic countries—necessary for the English, with their cloacal obsessions (553.18–22).

He brewed Guinness for her, but it was necessary to drink it in a speakeasy: Pussyfoot Johnson, the American official responsible for overseeing Prohibition, was pussyfooting around, seeking to arrest drinkers. Joyce was proud of the slogan he wrote for Guinness, which appears here: "the free, the froh, the frothy freshener" (553.25–28). I remember the reception that the Guinness family gave for the 1969 James Joyce Symposium, at which the leader of the brewery and the Guinness family admitted that he was baffled by that slogan, as well as by Joyce's version of the most famous Guinness slogan, "Guinness is good for you!" (593.17–18).

This gigantic poem of the city ends with a description of the city traffic (553.28–554.9). On the streets of Dublin—Stony Batter, the North and South Circular Roads, Eastmoreland Place and Westland Row, the boulevards, and Sydney Parade—swirls the bewildering variety and complexity of the city traffic. With the exception of the electric Dublin United Tramway Corporation vehicles (driven by yahoos), all of the traffic seems to be horse-drawn. Joyce is here describing the Dublin of 1904, although there are references to other modern cities with modern traffic—Rome, Vienna, Madrid, Bucharest, Prague, some Western American cities with bucking broncos.

HCE is entirely sure that ALP delights in the great complexity and power of the city traffic, and all of the huge, swirling creation that he has produced for the delight and control of his bride. Although ALP begins by weeping, she ends with laughing, like Horace's Lalage, in her domino to the switching of the whips of the drivers (554.8–9).[33] HCE may be deceiving himself here; the sadomasochistic pleasure that he takes in controlling ALP may impel him to think that she enjoys being restrained and controlled by him and by his creation. As we will see, ALP's own closing soliloquy, the great female soliloquy Soft Morning, City, which balances this great male soliloquy Haveth Childers Everywhere, ends with her scorning HCE and rushing out to sea, to freedom. Yet even there, at the end of the book, she succumbs to the arms of her rising beloved, as the river is borne backward by the incoming tide.

HCE now knows that he has the total admiration of the four inquisitors, and he proudly orders them to bow before him in the pose of four footballs, which he is about to kick (554.9). And sure enough, the four inquisitors (and their donkey) are now kneeling before him, and yammering in admiration of HCE's flawed but titanic creation (554.10).

Book III, Chapter 4: Predawn Explorations and Revelations

The penultimate chapter takes place in the bedroom of HCE and ALP, and in the corridors adjoining, as well as in the hall outside the bedrooms of the children. The description of the house is apparently naturalistic; in the course of this chapter the predawn light becomes morning light (566.7, 24–25), so that we, the readers, can see what seems to be a realistic scene of a middle-class home.

However, Joyce seems to regard this "realistic" presentation not as the truly basic way of viewing the world that is accepted unthinkingly by most people but, ironically, as just another mode of perception among many. The return of the ineluctable modalities of sight and sound, illuminated by the early light of dawn, is to him an arbitrary artistic presentation.

The apparent reality of the scene is undercut constantly by irony and paradox. The house is described as a stage set or a film set. Joyce gives a great deal of theatrical detail, including stage manager's instructions about the movement of backdrops, and also much detailed information about camera angles, as if he were following the action with a handheld camera. However, the point of view is not truly objective. The narrative voice coyly informs us that we could see nothing if the narrative voice did not inform us. When the voice describes how one boy holds the other boy's foot, we are told that we cannot see whose heel Shem holds in his right hand because the speaker has not told us (563.8–9). We can see and hear only by courtesy of the narrator/creator. All of this is literally true; we are reading a book, not gazing at a landscape.

The house is the home of the Porter family, and the interior of the house is based on a real place. According to Gordon, the house is the Mullingar House on Chapelizod Road near Dublin. This house has become a place of pilgrimage for Joyceans; it has even acquired a Finnegan's Bistro! However, Gordon is careful to explain that since the house has undergone a great deal of alteration since Joyce saw it, "it is probably futile to look for exact correspondences between the layout of the present structure and that of the *Wake*'s inn."[34]

What we first "see" is the bed of the married couple as viewed from the four cardinal points of the compass by the Four Old Men, each in his appropriate geographical position: Matthew (Ulster) to the *north*, Mark (Munster) to the *south*, Luke (Leinster) to the *east*, John (Connaught) to the *west*. The old men are represented by the posts of a four-poster bed, located at the cardinal compass points. It is true that the Four Old Men are twice referred to in the book as "fourposter" (325.10; 533.16). However, Joyce complicates the issue in this chapter by declaring that HCE's trousers are hanging on a bedknob (559.8–9). Since the syntax of this description is abbreviated, it is not quite clear whether the trousers are hanging on one of four bedknobs, and which bedknob it is, or just on a bedknob at the head of a non-four-poster bed. However, the situation remains much the same whether the Four Old Men watch from their respective four bedknobs or from the sides of the bed adjoining.

Each of the four sections is introduced by HCE's initials in revolving order, ending where the cycle began:

```
CEH     I
    EHC     II
        HCE     III
            CEH     IV
```

The physical situation of the bed is:

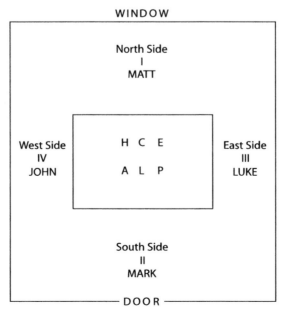

The chapter opens with the family and servants asleep. The scene is the same as in the beginning of III.1, in which we saw the old man sleeping uneasily and dreaming of a demon that was threatening to take away his bride—an Oedipal nightmare, evidently. This chapter, III.4, begins with another nightmare, this time one of Jerry (Shem), who has dreamed something bad about his father. Perhaps Jerry has dreamed the other half of the Oedipal dream of his father, the one in which the father seeks a castrating revenge for the claim of the son on the mother.

Jerry's cry, the first of three, stirs the old couple into reluctant waking in a misty predawn. They mumble sleepily, "What was that? It is foggy. Let us sleep" (555.1–2). Then the bedroom scenes are shown, with their occupants.

First, the narrative voice asks for a description of the house and its occupants. We are informed that the description will be given from the point of view of the Four Old Men, since they control the four dimensions of spatiotemporal description (555.5–11). They are referred to by the names of the four main Balearic islands, Majorca, Minorca, Ibiza, and Formentera, possibly because these islands are located from 1 degree to 5 degrees east of the prime meridian, and the sun is already up in this Mediterranean area. Recall that at the end of III.2 the narrator declares that the "sombrer opacities" of night have already "sphanished" (473.20)—that is, that the Spanish border, in the same longitudinal area as the Balearics, was already lit by the predawn light. Now in III.4 these areas are lit by the risen sun, as it travels toward the prime meridian at Greenwich and toward Dublin.

We are then introduced to the two boys, now named Kevin Mary (Shaun), who is dressed in the Irish colors orange, white, and green, and who is smiling in his sleep, and Jerry Godolphing (Shem), dressed in medical colors and sleeping uneasily (555.15–24).

We next observe sweet little Issy (556.1–22), dreaming her little-girl dreams featuring the various roles that she will take in life: the princess Infantina Isobel (556.1–2), the nun Sister Isobel (556.3–5), the nurse Saintette Isabelle (556.7–8), and the glamorous widow Madame Isa Veuve La Belle (556.9–11).

The narrator is evidently in love with Issy, because there is then a tender and lovely description of her sleeping in her cot, with a piece of candy stuck to her pillow (556.11–22). There is even music accompanying the loving description: an Elizabethan song by William Byrd, "Woods So Wild," sounds in the text.[35] In a letter (3:138), Joyce asserted that he imitated the rhythm of Byrd's song in the description here of Issy. I attach part of the lyric, so that the reader may judge: "Will you walk the wood so wild, / Wand'ring, wand'ring here and there, / As I was once full sore beguil'd, / Alas for love! I die with woe. / Wearily blows the winter wind, / Wand'ring, wand'ring here and there, / My heart is like a stricken hind, / Alas for love! I die with woe."

Sometimes Joyceans take a cynical attitude toward sentiment in Joyce's texts, as in the description of little Rudy at the end of the Circe chapter, which has been called "poisonously sweet." Molly's knitting a little sweater for Rudy's dead body has also been regarded with suspicion. However, since Joyce took it upon himself to describe *every* aspect of human life, I think that these descriptions are mainly sincere. Joyce is not usually sentimental, but the few times when he is, as in the passage quoted above, he is one of the best sentimental novelists who ever lived.

The next descriptions are of the servants of the house, the customers in the pub, and the twenty-nine Monthly Girls (556.23–558.25). The servants Sackerson and Kate the Slop are both sleeping. Sackerson is dreaming of his duties in the bar (556.23–30). Kate remembers in her sleep how she once woke in the night and went down to open the door; HCE was there, and he swore her to silence about some escapade in the park (556.31–557.12). The twelve customers in the bar are also described (with the largest concentration of "-ation" words in the book—thirty-four). They dream of trying HCE for his crimes, and sentence him to appropriate punishment (557.13–558.20). The twenty-nine Monthly Girls are also dreaming, and laughing and weeping at the same time (558.21–25).

Finally we observe the two chief characters, HCE and ALP, who are sleeping side by side. They are compared to the two great lakes of Africa, Albert Nyanza and Victoria Nyanza, perhaps because these lakes are now both lit up by the risen sun. HCE's penis is limp; ALP's hairpiece is hung up on a nail (558.26–31).

With all of the characters introduced, we then hear a cry offstage, the second (558.32). Where are we, and what is the time? The narrator in mock bewilderment declares that he does not understand, and he dares say that neither do we. Then he begins to describe the bedroom.

The scene is presented like a stage or film set (558.35–559.16); the time is simply "a time," and the play or film that is beginning with a close-up of the leads is a pantomime (559.17–19).

Since we are in the realm of realism, if only ironically, every detail is of a normal house of the period. It looks like a "boxed" stage set, one constructed of flats rather than backcloth and wings (M). Many of the details have already played a part in the story—the salmon of the wallpaper, for example, and the picture of the archangel Michael fighting a dragon (559.2, 11–12). The clothes of HCE and ALP are disposed on a chair and over a bedknob. The only enigmatic article is described as a pink "man's gummy article," which may be a reusable condom (559.15–16).

I. Harmony (559.20–563.39)

CEH ("Say! Eh? Ha!" = the letters CEH, pronounced in German)
Matthew, of Ulster (view from north)
The scene is viewed from the left (north) side of the parents' bed. HCE's face is toward us; his back and behind are facing south. ALP is behind him, partly concealed by HCE's body.

HCE rouses (559.20–29). Half asleep, he is not an attractive sight. There are both beastly and fishy aspects to him (559.23). Since we, viewing from the north, can see part of his back, we observe one rectangular shoulder blade. We can also see his ponderous belly looming toward us. As we later learn, he is not wearing pajama bottoms, or indeed any clothing below the waist except for a pair of socks. He is enraged at being awakened. His hair is red-blond, and he is very red in the face, possibly from anger: the reference to Armenian bole (559.25) shows that he is wearing a bright red piece of stage makeup. As we will see, he probably has high blood pressure. Someone with his gross body (559.25) should certainly take care to avoid violent exertion.

ALP awakens and is described. She is small and rather anemic; unlike her husband, she probably has low blood pressure. She is a featherweight with a peaked nose and a pursed triangular mouth. She has a pale yellowish face, on which she now wears a fearful "haggish" expression (559.26–29).

Both of the parents are Protestants. HCE is a member of the Church of Ireland. He is called an "episcopalian," although technically "episcopalian" should be used only for members of the Anglican Communion in the United States. Joyce may be hinting that the initials of HCE stand for High Church Episcopalian.

ALP is a member of the Free Kirk, an evangelical presbyterian church whose members withdrew from the Church of Scotland in 1843. Perhaps Joyce is here trying to fill out the background of both sides of his own family. As we know, HCE is of Scandinavian descent. The Joyce family were of Norman descent,[36] and hence were also originally Scandinavians. The Murrays, the family of Joyce's mother, bore a Scottish name; since Joyce declares that ALP is a member of a Scottish church, he may be giving a tribute to the ancestry of his mother.

Just before the camera begins to turn at the mention of film footage (559.31), there is the third cry offstage. ALP leaps out of bed, closely followed by the still very sleepy HCE, who is not aware of his pajama bottoms' absence (559.36–560.1), and who follows the lead of the queen, ALP (560.1). They take a circular route out the bedroom door, and come into a corridor (560.3). We have stage manager's directions about how to move the scenery: as the parents abandon the bedroom and move into the corridor, some of the flats of the bedroom walls and the other rooms and the stair fly up into the wings; others sink below the stage into prepared grooves (560.4–6).

The garrulous commentator admits that the house looks incomplete, as a stage or movie set will almost always look, but says the whole house will appear with full daylight. The stairs are also incomplete: there is only one real step; the rest are painted on (560.10).

The parents are climbing upstairs to the rooms of the children. There follows is a description of the pub and of the Porter family (560.13–36). The Porters are, to judge by their pictures in the newspapers, a very nice family. From what we know of HCE, we can doubt this, but to the indulgent narrator he *looks* like a very nice man. At any rate, we are in the realm of imperfect vision right now. HCE, lumbering behind ALP, appears to be a heavy man, with his bare stern showing. All he wears is a black and white shirt, and his blond head of hair looks like a wig. ALP, a poppyhead, a redhead (M), with a yellow nightgown, is ahead of him. She also looks very nice. In fact, to all appearances, everything and everyone in the family is very nice, terribly nice, by the pale light of early day.

The parents reach the rooms of their children upstairs (561.1–563.32). One room is on the right and one on the left of a corridor that probably runs north-south. The boys' room is on the right (east); Issy's is on the left (west).

The narrator coyly gives us some information about the brothers: one thing that the reader should know is that one brother was once the other, but now they have changed (561.4–6). We already know this, since we have seen Shem and Shaun change places in II.2 after embracing their mother. However, the narrator is reminding us again that we do not know anything if he has not told us.

Issy is described in a paragraph full of love and baby talk. She is nicknamed Buttercup, and she is her father's delight and her brothers' most darling sister, aunt, and bride (561.16). An "auntybride" sounds innocent enough—a little aunt to her brothers—but an "ante-bride" suggests preparations for a more sensual role later.

The lovesick narrator declares of Issy that to describe her would take a knowledge of Greek; to describe her goodness would require the saints' tales of the Golden Legend of Jacobus de Voragine. She is made up of seven flowers (561.20–21), and since the Rainbow Girls, those impatient virgins of adolescence, are symbols of sexual desire, she may have potentialities that her parents and her brothers do not yet appreciate. Lead us not into temptation! If you just part the lips of the little sleeping darling with your finger, she tries to seize it (561.24–26).

There are a number of references to the Virgin Mary in this description, especially the reference to the Dormition of the Virgin, her "falling asleep" before her Assumption into Heaven. M notes several other traditional signs of the Virgin—the seven steps she took at six months of age, the spinning of the veil of the temple in scarlet and purple, and the concealment of her mother inside a mountain during Herod's massacres (561. 25, 26, 27, 28; 562.9–11).

At this point the Virgin has been conceived immaculately, and is intended to become the vessel of conception by the Holy Ghost (213.19), memorialized by Joyce's triple Angelus at twilight, midnight, and dawn—which makes much more shocking the knowledge of male anatomy she acquires just four pages from now! A hint of her sexual potentialities has already been given by the allusion to the seven Rainbow Girls, which is reinforced by another septuple phrase at 562.4–5, emphasizing the young beauty of the flower girls.

When awake, Issy plays with her dolls and talks baby talk to them. I wonder if we can see a personal note here: is Joyce reproducing Lucia's baby talk? It would be tempting, and extremely sad, to see the obvious love of the narrator for Issy—in this passage as well as in 556.1–22—as the love of Lucia's father for his daughter, before her tragic fate overtook her.

The sweet description ends with a fragment of Issy's baby talk with her doll. Then her brothers are described. The two boys are sleeping in the right-hand room (east). Joyce presents us with a number of enigmas here. The boys are sleeping in the same bed, but we do not know whether the bed is lying north-south or east-west. In addition, the arrangement of the boys in the bed raises questions. They seem to be lying in a rather complex arrangement which Joyce conveys only indirectly and somewhat obscurely. Kevin (Shaun) may possibly be sleeping on the left side of the bed (the side of the heart), while Jerry (Shem) may possibly be sleeping on the right side of the bed (the side of the liver). However, Jerry is holding one of Kevin's heels with his right hand (562.23; 563.1, 8–9). Here is a problem for the reader. The only way such an arrangement is possible is if the boys are sleeping head to tail, like Molly and Leopold Bloom, with Jerry lying to the right on his back toward the head of the bed, clasping one of Kevin's heels, with Kevin lying on his stomach on the left facing the foot of the bed—an awkward arrangement. If this is right, Jerry has apparently wet the bed while lying on his back—not an easy feat.[37]

The fairhaired boy Frank Kevin (Shaun) is happily asleep, with his hand lifted in blessing.[38] He looks like an angel, and his mouth is half open as though he were giggling, or blowing a bugle. Very soon, he will grow up and go off to America to seek (and probably find) a cushy job at a generous salary. He is adorable, but Joyce undercuts his virtues by calling him "eunique" (562.33). Shaun is, after all, the top half of the body at this point, the half without the genitals.

Jerry (Shem), on the other side, has been crying in his sleep, after chewing some dirty candy. (Note that Issy also has fallen asleep chewing candy (556.15–16).) Jerry is playing the role of Jacob to Kevin's Esau (Genesis 25:26), but the reader cannot see whose heel Shem holds in his right hand because the omniscient narrator had not said (563.8–9): the narrator is again reminding us that he is really the creator of the whole book.

The narrator has some problems with the boy's name: the narrator stammers in syllables beginning with J until he finally arrives at the names Jerry Jehu (563.6–7). M suggests convincingly that the narrator's difficulty in pronouncing the boy's name means that the boy's name is really James Joyce. The boy had previously been called Jerry Godolphing, but "Jehu" is appropriate: Jehu is the only biblical king who ruled over both the separated northern and southern kingdoms, having killed the kings of both regions in a short time (II Kings 9–10). Shem is, in his own way, the motive power in bringing about the death of the old kingdom and the creation of the new.

Jerry has wet the bed, but his urination has some sexual aspects (563.5–6). The urination may be a premature attempt at ejaculation, since Swift's Pepette is suggested here, and Jerry's immature penis is both a fountain pen to write with and a penis to found a family with. He may have had a nightmare and wept in his sleep from Oedipal fear that his father would castrate him for his growing presexual prowess. He will grow up to be a writer in an alcoholic Byronic style—as evidenced by his beery Byronic brow (563.12)—with overtones of Blake.

Both boys have prospects in life, of different and opposing sorts (563.23–36), and the combined activity of Kerry and Jevin (563.36) will carry the story forward. The narrator gives his blessing to both of them.

II. Discord (564.1–582.27)

EHC ("Meseedo" or mi-si-do = EHC in German musical notation)
Mark, of Munster (view from south)
Now, looking from the south side of the bed, we can have a full view of HCE's behind, which is described in great detail as Phoenix Park (564.1–565.5). It is observed by one of the Four Old Men, Mark, who from his cardinal position in the south is situated on the right side of the Earwicker bed. However, each of the Four Old Men also commands his cardinal position everywhere in the house. Here in the corridor outside the children's bedrooms, Mark, from Munster, the southern province, sees HCE's bottom, as Mark has been seeing it for hours in the bedroom. HCE has been sleeping half nude. From his point of view at the side of the bed, Mark has noted HCE's big bottom partly obscured by ALP's body (564.6–8). Described in legal terms, HCE's big bottom partially covers the "femecovert" (564.2–3).

Switching our view to the scene upstairs, Mark notes that HCE's big wide harse is larger than life—in fact, is blocking the hall. Mark gives an awed description of HCE's bottom, in the style of a travel book. We are given a tour noting the road down the center, the hugeness of the buttocks (564.13–14), the tufts of hair, some black and blue marks indicating weals resulting from self-inflicted whippings with a belt (564.23–25), which provide evidence of HCE's Bloomlike masochism. We are also asked to notice a scarlet pimple, on the dangerous parts of the bottom where murders took place, as in the Phoenix Park. Mark also views the darker regions, a sinister area where the police band gives Wagnerian concerts (565.1–5). The suggestion of Wagner here—Valhalla, Götterdämmerung, Walküre, Wotan—and the police band that plays on Wednesdays, sounds innocent enough, but the variant of the word "police" combined with the German word for fart, *Furz*, gives away the game. The deep hollow at the bottom of the back is in fact the anus, from which orifice Wagnerian bassoon-resounding farts emerge from time to time.

All of this impressive bottom equipment is on display in the hall. HCE's big wide harse is pointed into the girl's room, and his uncovered genitals are pointing into the boys' room. Then an obscene song about a maid of Amsterdam begins to sound out as incidental music, and Jerry, catching sight of what is pointing at him, gets panicky and starts trembling like a jelly (565.6–12). ALP, kneeling by Jerry's side, attempts to console him: You were just dreaming, dear. Your father? Shoo! There are no phantoms in the room, my little boy! We'll drive away bad daddy! I'll spank daddy! Take that! Slap, slap, slap!

HCE and ALP talk swiftly in Esperanto. M translates (I have altered a few words): "He hasn't slept? Yes, he is sleeping badly. What is he crying about in the night? Only baby talk." ALP goes back to soothing Jerry, telling him that it is all only in his imagination. She refers to the "little brittle magic nation" Ireland and rocks him to sleep with lovely motherly words (565.29–32). Perhaps Joyce thought of Ireland in some of its aspects as a poor little brittle magic nation.

Shaun in his barrel is rolling eastward to rise up soon as the young sun. The predawn half-light now reveals the exterior of the inn, and there follows an advertisement for it (565.33–566.6). The ad ends with some delightful words, perhaps signaling the presence of Issy, who in the growing light will now get her glimpse of the intimate appurtenances of her father.

A grave and formal description of the event follows. The inn is described as a court in half mourning, or morning (566.7–21). The sight to be revealed has its tragic aspects. The knowledge of adult male sexuality already presented to Jerry by the half-light will now be presented to little Issy, initiating the whole process of maturing that will inevitably end with the overthrow of the parents, and the shift of power within the family. Here we have the naturalistically described event that provided the events in the Willingdone Museyroom and the details of the scandal in the park.

The Four Old Men with their donkey are sharpening their pencils to described the event. Sackerson is holding up matches, perhaps to light the morning fires. Kate is preparing her talk on the Willingdone Museyroom. The twelve representatives of public opinion are standing by, preparing for another day of gossiping and swift, shallow judgment. The maidens are preparing to become gray-haired old maids whose hands will wear no wedding rings. ALP remains kneeling by Jerry, but there is a sinister implication in her description as First Murderer with a coil of cord (566.19). She is also the First Mother, but why is she preparing to strangle one of the princes in the tower? Or is it the umbilical cord that she is holding, as evidence that the little foetus is now independent of her shelter, and on the way to dangerous manhood?

At 566.19–21 the two boys are described as both awake, but they appear to be trying to avoid the sight of their father's penis, just as the lipoleum boys in the Museyroom tried to escape the phallic artillery of their father. Then comes the central event of the whole book: HCE, embarrassed to be seen by his boys, wheels hastily to prevent any more exposure (566.21–23)—but as he turns his formidable behind to the two boys, his weapon is instead presented to the wondering eyes of Issy (566.23–24). Now the brand (sword), which is also the branded mark of Cain that HCE bears as father and as a "futherer" (from the French *foutre*), is fully exposed to his little daughter.

Just then, to make things even worse, the full light of dawn floods the scene, illuminating little Issy's mind, filling it with the astonishing sight of a mature male penis, and destroying her virginal innocence forever. In the Museyroom episode, the Willingdone chases after the jinnies with his phallic artillery blazing, and in the park, HCE fears that soldiers are at his back with hostile intent, while he is peering at girls doing something in the bushes. All of these developments are based on this tragicomic event, which is the pivotal point of the book, and which now takes place in full mo(u)rning.

ALP hastily informs HCE, in Esperanto as before, that his behavior is indelicate, that the children are looking at him, and she urges, "Turn around, pig!" (566.26–27). But it is too late.

As the wonderstruck Issy gets a good look at her father, she imagines in her excitement a great celebration, with wedding bells ringing out (566.28–570.13). "God of heaven!" exclaims Issy, like Stephen on the beach in *A Portrait*. She is entranced by the sight of HCE's genitals, the crags and hillocks of them. She fears that she may have lost her mental virginity upon beholding the wild shagginess of HCE's nether regions (566.31–32). Though not a Freudian, Joyce is here suggesting, if not penis envy exactly, then a feminine realization that there is a real difference between men and women.[39] How shaggy and beastly! And she sees a pointing pole of great length (566.34–35). It brings to mind several great erections in and around Dublin (566.36–567.4). And such a big belly too (567.5)!

She notices what looks like a hunting cap or a baby bunting hood on the tip of the penis (567.7–9). It must in reality be the glans or the foreskin; HCE has not yet donned the condom. The pole with the object at its tip brings up the old story of how HCE got his name after meeting the king, and now we are launched into a long description of a royal visit based on the visit to Ireland of George IV in 1821, during which he dubbed the Lord Mayor, Abraham Bradley King, a knight (R&O 275). The visit is indeed a glorious one (567.13–570.13), featuring a whole hunting party including hounds (567.23–25), popular amusements, clowns grinning through horse collars (567.25–28), fiddle music (567.30), reconciliation of all parties (567.34–568.11), appearance of the seven Rainbow Girls signifying peace (568.2–4).

In the midst of all these joyous occasions, the king makes HCE a knight— Sir Pompey Donkey (568.16–26)! This is followed by the ringing of the bells of many churches—which are easily confused with wedding bells by the dazzled Issy (569.4–16)—by a great banquet (*Mahlzeit!* 569.21–27), and by other spectacular dramatic and musical events (569.28–570.7). There'll be a hot time in the old town tonight (570.7–8)!

Issy has inherited from her mother an exaggerated respect for disreputable men, especially when the men are sexually aroused. We will see at the end of the book ALP's pathetic attempts to encourage her comatose and guilty spouse to rise and walk with her to the Old King, who might make him a chief magistrate (623.4–18). But here in this passage Issy, her mother's daughter, promotes her father from Mr. Porter, esquire, to Sir Porter pouring drinks, to Lord Porterfamilias, to Mr. Prince of Porter. The incorporation of the syllable "porn" into the family name of Porter, and the "pouring" into Issy in the last title, shows the motive power of sexual arousal within little Issy (570.15, 19, 20; 571.20).

Issy giggles, but is highly serious at the same time—sex has suddenly become a serious matter to her, young as she is (570.24–25). She feels something within her that she confuses with a prickly desire to urinate (570.26–27). It is, in fact, her first onset of hot pants—*dessous troublants*, as they are called in *Ulysses* (15.3893). The little girl is well and truly launched on the path to sexual desire. And the whole family balance of power has begun to tip over in the direction of the children.

The Four Old Men, now back in the bedroom with the married couple, comment on what the little girl may have seen (571.27, 30, 31, 34). HCE, excited despite his embarrassment at his exposure to his children, especially Issy, begins to feel a powerful desire to make love to his wife, faute de mieux (570.15–571.26). He mumbles something about being legally entitled to sexual access to his wife. After all, they will not be coupling like wild beasts! The twain are, in biblical terms, one flesh, to have and to hold (571.28–29).

He also murmurs some broken phrases about the unfolding morning, and the need to rise up and provide for the morning sacrifice (571.32–33). These turn out to be parts of John Keble's Protestant hymn "Morning," which is all about having survived the night.[40] Perhaps part of HCE's overpowering desire for physical contact arises from his nightmares, his fears in the night, his dread of defeat and death at the hands of the rising generation. The three verses from this poem that contain the words quoted in the *Wake* are:

Hues of the rich unfolding morn,
That, ere the glorious sun be born,
By some soft touch invisible

Around his path are taught to dwell.

    *   *   *

New every morning is the love
Our wakening and uprising prove;
Through sleep and darkness safely brought,
Restored to life, and power, and thought.

    *   *   *

If on our daily course our mind
Be set to hallow all we find,
New treasures still, of countless price,
God will provide for sacrifice.

Now occurs a warning that the children are working against their parents (571.35–572.6). This is certainly true: after seeing HCE's genitals, the children will work incessantly to overthrow their parents.[41] As we have seen, HCE's exposure to Issy begins the process of maturation of the children that takes up the whole of Book II. To quote Ibsen, the younger generation is knocking at the door. Issy begins thinking about sex from the impressive sight of her father's shaggy, beastly male equipment, and Shem and (probably) Shaun have also caught a glimpse of their father's bottom and possibly his penis. In addition, HCE's fears about soldiers at his back, and his guilt about watching girls urinating in the bushes, all derive from his double exposure to his children.

As HCE begins to feel sexual urges stirring in his incorrigibly incestuous soul, he may make overtures, concealed from the reader, to ALP. The attempt of the aged HCE and ALP to make love is introduced by two legal cases, both turning on a man's "right" (or otherwise) to have sex with his wife (572.18–576.9).

Church

Joyce first presents an enormously complicated canon law case, revealing all of the family life of the Porter family, along with many crimes and sins of HCE. After all, as Fallen Man, HCE has committed all possible sins and crimes. However, Joyce lets him off easy—there are no crimes of violence on HCE's conscience, just moral crimes and sins. Now, with all of these sins laid to him, can HCE legally force ALP to submit to him sexually, despite his disreputable character?

The reader should note the prominent part played in the canon law case by Magravius, the sinister Magraw, who is the Other Man in the family history. Magraw's name will come up shortly as, during sex, ALP tries to excite HCE by declaring that she loves Magraw, although in the fullest exposition of her letter to the world, and in her final soliloquy, we see her true contempt for him (615.16–17; 617.9–12; 622.3–8).

One of HCE's misdemeanors is masochistic submission to punishment (572.28–29), as is shown by black and blue marks on his bottom (564.23–25). Although almost all of the sadomasochistic activity described in the *Wake* is directed at young girls, there is evidence at this point of masochistic drives in HCE. Like Leopold Bloom in *Ulysses*, HCE has "paid homage on that living altar where the back changes name" (15.3405–6).

This canon law case has had repercussions beyond the *Wake*. A brilliant commentary on it was written by a famous science-fiction writer, James Blish, who was also a fanatical Wakean. It occurs in his novel *A Case of Conscience* (1959). In the beginning of this work, Father Ruiz-Sanchez, a Jesuit and an expert on canon law, spends his ample spare time on a journey to the planet Lithia by trying to answer Joyce's question, whether HCE has hegemony and ALP shall submit, by the rules of canon law. Father Ruiz-Sanchez decides that the answer to the bipartite question is Yes, and No. HCE, despite his many crimes, still has a canonical right to the physical love of his wife, but ALP does not have to submit. And who are we to disagree with a professional in canon law?[42]

State

The second case Joyce presents is apparently a commercial law case over the validity of a check. However, the entire case, likewise one of enormous complexity, is in reality about the validity of marriage vows as administered outside the Catholic Church. This is shown by the reference to the case of Henry VIII versus Anne Boleyn. (576.6) Joyce here seems to take an orthodox Catholic position, which declares that such a sacrament outside the Church is not valid. Since HCE and ALP are both Protestants, the check is a dud (574.26), and the marriage ceremony is invalid.

However, Joyce has given us a hint that both cases are beside the point, and moreover extremely fishy (as is shown by 573.33, which refers to two stages in the development of salmon). Laws of God or man cannot ensure a happy marriage. Only the freely given love of the partners in the marriage can lead to a true relationship. Experience of twenty-seven years of marriage to Nora without benefit either of clergy or of registry office (they married in 1931 only for legal reasons) taught Joyce about the true bonds of matrimony.

Ergo

HCE has no legal hegemony over ALP, either by the laws of Church or of State, and therefore has no legally enforceable right to compel her to have sex with him. The Joyces were not bound by laws of either Church or State for twenty-seven years of cohabitation. Their union was one of mutual love. Like the Joyces, the Earwickers are bound together by bonds of affection. They decide to try to make love, and they head back to bed.

A prayer ensues. The gist of the prayer is that the parents be brought safely down the stairs into their own bedroom, and protected from devils, and from their own uncontrollable impulses. Suddenly we feel alarm: is there some noise? Has Jerry woken up? No. The noise is only the wind (577.36–578.2).

Now, in the growing light, we can see both protagonists clearly (578.3–28). HCE is wearing only a nightcap, a surplice and doublet, and socks—no pants, as we knew already. ALP is moving along the corridor switching her bustle about, possibly in anticipation of lovemaking. Which way are they going? They are passing through their home, which is amply plastered with middle-class imperatives, generally counseling prudence over charity (579.8–25). There is a definite emphasis here on Protestant tenets of religion and the rise of capitalism, on material prosperity as the sign of eternal election by the Lord, as an outward sign of an inward grace. Tawney and Max Weber singing in duet could not have put the case more plainly.

The middle-class careers of HCE and ALP are described in detail, from their meeting and marrying to their creation of city neighborhoods, their occasional betrayal of their convictions—they turned their coats (579.34)—for the sake of peace and prosperity, all bourgeois necessities, for which Joyce does not reproach them. They raised a family and supported it. Now they are going to embark on lovemaking in the growing dawn light (580.20–22).

HCE knows that the children he engendered and supported are going to overthrow him—yet he begot them (582.1). So let us give him a vote of thanks, for putting his right hand into chancery; that is, he hampered himself by giving hostages to chance and fortune. At any rate, he had to have children. The archetypal family must have children; otherwise, the processes of human history would stop (582.2–4, 13).

Then the riggish and sexually heated HCE begins to sing a dirty song about a "raughty tinker" (582.21–25), a sea shanty sung to Joyce by Frank Budgen. The partial text of the original song goes: "There was a raughty tinker / Who in London town did dwell, / And when he had no work to do / His meatax he did sell.[43] / With me solderin' iron and taraway / Hammer legs and saw. / Brave old Donald! We are off to Castlepool."[44]

III. Concord (582.28–590.22)

HCE ("sidome" = HCE, from musical notes si-do-mi in German)
Luke, of Leinster (view from east)
HCE and ALP then attempt an act of love, viewed from the head of the bed. HCE is exerting himself hugely—in fact, far too vigorously for someone with his blood pressure. His face is dark red, his brow is hot and wet with sweat, and he bears a red brand on his forehead, something like the mark of Cain (582.28–29, 31; 583.29–30). The relative physical positions of HCE and ALP is still a subject of debate.[45] It may be that HCE is embracing ALP from behind while plunging about in his exertions: ALP is like an upended and immobilized maiden, that is, she is held from beneath by those terrible prongs HCE's arms, with her bottom in the air (584.18–19).

ALP is enjoying herself; she laughs at her old stick-in-the-mud waving his belly about (583.26–27), and giggles at his trembly aging penis (583.31). She licks him, and flicks his testicles to get things going (584.3–4). She sings a version of "Tea for Two" (584.10–11)—tea obviously has a strong sexual meaning for her—and taunts HCE by saying that she loves the Other Man, Magraw, and that Magraw has been making love to her (584.5–8)—an assertion made only for strategic purposes, as she really despises Magraw. Apparently the strategy succeeds, because HCE is goaded to greater exertions, to such an extent that ALP warns him he may burst the condom and she may get pregnant (584.11–14).

To top off the great act of love, a cock begins to crow. It is a universal cockcrow, which may owe something to the cockcrow in *The Waste Land*. It also may owe something to the cockcrow in D. H. Lawrence's 1929 long story "The Man Who Died," first published as "The Escaped Cock," which celebrates the physical resurrection, by evidence of an erection and a cockcrow, of the crucified but risen Christ.

Here Joyce's cockcrow first makes itself known as twenty-two single syllables similar to "kik," building up to "kikkery key." Then the great "Cocorico" itself emerges, combining with the syllables of sexual union "O I you O you me" into a gigantic echo that circles around the whole universe several times (585.3).[46]

The sexual act is vigorous enough, but it is all part of a game, as the dozens of cricket terms imply (much like the football terms accompanying the French kiss of Tristan and Isolde). In fact, the sex act is just that, an act, part of a game. Perhaps this is the ultimate meaning of ALP's assertion "You never wet the tea." T. S. Eliot anticipated Joyce in this cynical analysis of self-gratifying sex in the "Game of Chess" section in *The Waste Land*. Lorenz Hart, in a late lyric for a Richard Rodgers song, refers to the same sad phenomenon of self-gratifying lovers in his phrase "the faint aroma of performing seals."[47]

In any case, ALP asks him to withdraw his member and says, perhaps sadly, that he never wet the tea (585.26, 31).[48] Whether she means that she did not feel him ejaculating inside the condom, or perhaps that the condom prevented conception, this sexual act is not successful, any more than the previous acts of love in the *Wake*. T observes (283–84) that this bedroom scene is yet another scene of less than satisfying sexual contact between aging couples in the works of Joyce. The first is the scene in the Gresham Hotel in "The Dead," in which Gabriel, inflamed by his specious success at the party, has an impulse, perhaps the first in years, to make love to his wife. We all know the devastating result of this impulse. The second is the bottom-kissing scene in *Ulysses*, which annoys Molly considerably. The third bedroom scene, this one in the *Wake*, is apparently just as unsatisfying as the first two.

The older generation having failed in their sexual adventures, the way is clear for the new generation, and for the great climax of the book, when at dawn the maturing Shaun employs the ithyphallic Shem in the only successful act of love in the *Wake*. For an act of love to be truly loving, there must be no hint of self-gratification in it. Joyce knew that love as defined by Aquinas is truly love only when it is directed selflessly at the happiness of someone else. As Stephen thinks in *Ulysses*, "Amor vero aliquid alicui bonum vult unde et ea quae concupiscimus" (9.430–31). By this standard, the failure in III.4 is only temporary. True love is one chapter away.[49]

Back in the bedroom in Chapelizod, the dapple-gray dawn approaches. Acknowledgment is given to the assistants in the attempted act of love—the mattress, the lamp, and the condom (585.5–14)—and HCE is allowed to go back to sleep (585.31–33). In fact, HCE sleeps for the rest of the book; it is his son who rises up in Book IV as the rising sun.

A policeman, Sackerson, has been prowling around in the street outside the Porter residence, and he now rebukes the occupants (585.34–586.18).

Their lovemaking has been too loud, and people are trying to sleep! They are living in a home, not a brothel!

However unsuccessful, the act of physical love, according to Augustine, transmits the burden of Original Sin. Therefore, after the universally reported act of love here by the old couple, snaky rumors begin to spread about HCE (587.3–590.3). Amid serpentine hisses, the stories about Earwicker begin to multiply, ending up with the Cad in the park, the stories about the sodomizing of HCE by three soldiers, and HCE observing urinating girls in bushes, Hosty's scurrilous ballad, and the ruining of Earwicker's reputation, his lack of commercial ethics, his bankruptcy—in fact, the whole of Book I, chapters 2–4. And all this derives from HCE and ALP attempting to make love, as they pass on the Original Sin of human beings.

At the end of Luke's section, HCE is dismissed with taunts that his rainbow has faded, and that he can never again attempt sexual intercourse (590.10–11). The colors of dawn, from violet to red, are beginning to appear in the sky. The rainbow hues of the physical world—into which Man has fallen, and where he is struggling with the vicissitudes of Time—are appropriate for Fallen Man, as St. Patrick later proves to the hilt. At the end of Luke's section, the phrase "the great triumphal arch" from "The Man Who Broke the Bank at Monte Carlo" (590.9–10) combines the note of triumph with the note of possible disaster. After all, in this uncertain world, very few people break the bank at Monte Carlo; the house always wins in the end.

The phrases referring to Wales, with their Welsh orthography (590.13, 16–17), convey the growing light revealing clouds over the mountains of Wales across the Irish Sea. The night is ending and the east is becoming light (590.18–19).

IV. Solution (590.22–30)

CEH ("two me see" = do-mi-si, CEH in German notation)
John, of Connaught (view from west)
The view is now from the foot of the bed. We see the fourth position, one of (re)solution. How jolly! There is the finest view from the horizon. This is the final tableau (590.22–23). The stage set is open on the "west" side, the fourth wall of the traditional theater set, and we the audience, at the western horizon along with old Johnny of Connaught, the western province, are looking directly east into the rising sun. The titanic eight-act play that began with II.1,

"The Mime of Mick, Nick and the Maggies," is now ending, perhaps happily. Or perhaps not happily.

What John sees, and what we the audience see also, is a truly happy but also bittersweet act of love. In the echoing skies of dawn, the queen bee and her male consort have just made love, which will engender the entire hive, although the male bee, the drone, always dies as a result of his love (590.24–29). The eastern queen, the begum, is lying beside the big gun, who is now comatose. He has fertilized the queen, "staggerhorned" her (590.28), as befits an earwig, an anticipation of the terrible prongs of the ending of the book.

"Tiers, tiers and tiers. Rounds" (590.30). The audience in the huge theater filled with tiers of seats is ecstatic. The playgoers break into rounds of cheers, but also into tears. We the readers are in the audience, and we have come to the end of the third book, to the end of the series of threes. We have joined in the rounds of applause, having gone safely through "the semitary of Somnionia" and passed round the three active stages of Vico. We are getting ready for the great dawn, the final transition, the *sandhi* or *ricorso* of Book IV.

4

Book IV (*FW* 591–628)

Ricorso (Vico)

Time Medium Ending, Space Medium Recommencing

The River Begins to Flow Backward

DAWN

Time eventually stops in the fourth book, which consists of only one chapter. At the beginning of the chapter, the tide is still going out, and therefore time is still running, if weakly. But the moment of the turn of the tide is fast approaching, when TIME will stop and SPACE begin again.

Dawn is breaking, and with dawn the dream ends. After a splendid dawn sequence, showing misty Sunday morning events in Dublin, three stained-glass windows are revealed by the growing sunlight. The scenes on the windows show the three great male saints of Ireland: St. Kevin, St. Patrick defeating the Archdruid, and St. Laurence O'Toole.

Finally, with the light brightening minute by minute, we can see the Liffey, bearing the stains of all humanity, as she flows out to Dublin Bay for her union with the sea. As she flows through the city, Anna Livia's letter about her guilty husband is revealed in its clearest form. Last of all, Anna Livia, growing mixed in mind and body, meets the sea at Dublin Bar. She mistakes the risen sun (and son) for her blazing husband, risen from his guilt and restored to the glorious raider that she fell in love with so many years ago. She imagines that she is taking him by his scarred hand,[1] and is going to meet the emperor—that is, the rising sun. Then she and her husband sink into each other's arms. The keys to heaven are given, Anna Livia "dies" bodily and sexually, the sea embraces the river, and the tide begins to come in. Anna Livia begins to flow backward, and TIME stops as a misty scene appears. We have returned to the watery and misty spaces of the primal scene, and *Finnegans Wake* begins again.

In this supreme climax to Joyce's greatest work, the old family is resurrected as the new family with the new day. HCE appears in double form: as the old comatose HCE, he is the Hill of Howth, and as the new HCE, he is hot and cold, creative and destructive. He is the risen son and the rising sun—that is, he is now his own tennis champion son in his blazing white flannels, and is about to become Anna's lover. He is also Anna Livia's cold mad fearsome father about to embrace her, as she is moved with fear and love.

Anna herself is double: She is her old, dying self, defiled by the dirt of the city, flashing out the most complete version of her letter defending her guilty husband and then swimming out through Dublin Bay into the arms of the frightening ocean. She is also her own little daughter, Issy, running down the Wicklow hills to become the new river. The three sons, Shem, Shaun, and their combined form, are present too, as three stained-glass windows, revealing the rainbow colors of Fallen Man which illuminate the stage of the new day.

Dawn

Although there seem to be a number of voices in this final section, most of them are either radio voices or, like Muta and Juva, discourses from figures in stained-glass windows. In fact, the only active voice is that of Anna Livia. Everyone else is still abed in the early morning—her husband is comatose, as she laments, and the children are all fast asleep. The occurrence of "ourselves alone"—Sinn Féin, Sinn Féin Amháin (593.8–9)—reinforces the notion of loneliness on an island, as does the phrase "robins in crews so" (619.24). Anna Livia herself, at the end of her great soliloquy, declares her loneliness (627.34), and one of the very last phrases in the book—"A way a lone" (628.15)—expresses loneliness. The tone, despite the glory of the sunrise and early morning, is finally lonely and bittersweet.

At the start of Book IV, however, the loneliness of Anna Livia is not yet apparent. The chapter begins with one of the merriest passages in all literature, a glorious outburst announcing the dawn. The triple cry of "Sanctus" (593.1) is the song of praise constantly sung by the angels to God as an expression of their eternal awe at His creation: their admiration is described in the Song of God in the book of Job—"When the morning stars sang together, and all the sons of God shouted for joy" (38:7). In *Finnegans Wake*, the shout is for the retreat of night and the approach of the great sun.

"Sandhyas" also announces that it is Sunday morning, because there is no school (620.11–12). Apparently the Earwicker children do not go to Sunday school. Has the *Wake* taken place on a Saturday night and a Sunday morning? Another meaning of "Sandhyas" turns upon its meaning in Sanskrit. Joyce told Jacques Mercanton that *sandhi* means "the twilight of dawn" (M). The basic meaning of the word *sandhi* in Sanskrit is "transition," and we are present at a great transition, the beginning of dawn, and the moving of night to day.

The triple cry may evoke a great peace. For T. S. Eliot, the final "Shantih shantih shantih" at the end of *The Waste Land* conveys to readers of an upanishad the same meaning that the phrase "The Peace that passeth all understanding" conveys to Christians. Finally, the "sandy" shores of Dublin Bay and the Hill of Howth become visible as the Liffey approaches her union with the sea and the sun, which are merging into one giant lover.

Dawn is shining on the dunes of the seashore: "Calling all downs!" A resurrection! Earwicker to the whole bloody world! There is a haze on the sea to the east; after all, this is a soft morning, a misty morning. Seven news agencies announce the great news to all the world: Tass (Russian), Patt (?), Staff (Stafetta, Italian), Woff (Wolff, German), Havv (Havas, French), Bluvv (?), and Rutter (Reuters). The smog is lifting, and already the valets (the gentlemen's gentlemen) have risen to light the household fires (593.6–8).

Modern advertisements and familiar notices begin to appear in the dawn light on the city. The first, at 593.9, refers to a well-known joke from *Punch* about Pears' Soap. "Good morning, have you used Pears' Soap?" was one of the most famous advertising slogans of the era. Here it doubles as the question "Have you seen the dawn of *perce-oreille* [Earwicker]?" Pears' Soap cleans the body; Piers's dawn cleans the earth.[2] We are also exhorted: "Post no bills" and "Trespassers will be prosecuted" (594.26, 14). Meanwhile, characteristic morning activities are taking place: as we will see, milk is being delivered, bread is being baked. In fact, one Irishman is actually taking a morning bath—St. Kevin. We are seeing dawn rise on a modern city.

The narrative voice shouts, "Wake up, all you dim people, and let HCE be bailed out of his humiliation and his tumulus!" (593.14–15). The sun is rising in the east, and the famous slogan "Guinness is good for you" announces also that Genghis Khan, the Eastern invader, the fearsome sun, is going for you (593.17–18).

"A hand from the cloud emerges, holding a chart expanded" (593.19). Besides describing the Finnegan family crest (M), the line bears HCE's initials twice. It also bears the name of the author of a book on Dublin, D. M. Chart, and evokes a passage from the Book of Revelation: "And the heaven departed as a scroll when it is rolled together" (6:14). Here, in Joyce's merry apocalypse, the heavens open a scroll, revealing Dublin.

The narrative voice identifies itself as the voice of Pu Nuseht (The Sunup reversed), lord of rising in the underworld of Dublin (the name transliterated into Greek spelling) (593.20–24). Shem and Shaun have changed places and reversed their names. Shaun has been carrying the mail through the night, from west to east, until he rises up as the sun, and Shem has cuddled up inside the trousers of the postman since the end of II.2. The rising sun, the triumphant light, a triumphant toff (593.24), speaks.

Amid a spate of Sanskrit words, we weak Dubliners (*durbala*," "of little strength" (M)) address a prayer to the Hindu god of fire, Agni (594.2). We have been led by his kindly light through the pathways of sleep, "the semitary of Somnionia" (Latin *semita*, "pathway") and are approaching "Heliotropolis, the castellated, the enchanting" (594.8–9), which is itself one of the most enchanting phrases in the book. Heliopolis is the city that now turns toward the sun and bears HCE's initials.

Other enchanting phrases follow. Now if someone fetched a towel, and someone else warm water, we could clean this woeful Dane's bottom, the remaining darkness from the landscape, with a bar of Sunlight Soap, before you could say a Hail Mary, or Smith, Brown, and Robinson. The sun hits on the Hill of Allen, and the speaker describes how the sun shines (594.19–21). The Celtic god of the sun is beating sparks out of his atoms, his tiny ones, by the process of atomic fusion that was barely defined when Joyce wrote this chapter.

Now the rising sun is illuminating the tablestone at Stonehenge. The description of Stonehenge is one of the most vivid pieces of poetry in the whole book, as the sunlight tentatively and then more strongly begins to illuminate it (594.21–26). "Gaunt grey ghostly gossips" on the plain of Salisbury—magnificent description!—are touched by the first spearpoint of sunlight. Stonehenge is only about one hundred miles east of Dublin, on Salisbury Plain, so the sun is rapidly approaching the Irish coast.

The word "peneplain" provides a vivid touch. It means literally a landscape that is a partial plain. However, it evokes a British toyshop image: in the days when cut-out figures for children's paper theaters were sold, you could buy either "penny plain" or "tuppence coloured" figures. Here the Dublin "penny plain" is mainly pale and monochrome, since the sunlight is not yet strong enough to bring out the colors in the landscape. Soon, however, the rainbow colors will color the land—"tuppence coloured."

This brilliant passage also solves one of the great riddles of the book: what happens after Humpty Dumpty falls off the wall? Here the answer is given: Humpty as the sun may have fallen down the day before, but today he rises up whole and jolly (594.32–33); the inedible yolk of the sun has banished the darkness.[3]

Life returns to the land: after the deathbone has been pointed and the quick are still, the lifewand is raised and the dead live (595.1–2). The Hill of Howth begins to emerge from darkness, and the counties of Ireland begin to appear (595.3–17). Most of the counties of Ireland are named. Some of them are mingled with a smorgasbord of breakfast foods.[4]

The rooster begins to crow. It is not the universal cockcrow that we heard in the previous chapter, but it is a respectable cock-a-doodle-doo (595.30). However, the narrator says to let the shopkeeper sleep until they take down the shutter from his shop, as the Jarl van Hoother ordered in the Prankquean fable so much earlier in the book (23.5).

The young boy, the risen son or sun, is now described in a puzzling passage (595.34–596.33). The sun-son is a combination of Shem and Shaun, as the word "mnames" suggests: the *mn* combination stands for the endings of Shem and Shaun, and for Mick and Nick (595.34).[5] The son was originally kidnapped, or conjured himself from sight by sleight of hand; then follow fifty-nine clauses separated by semicolons, of which the sense is very obscure (595.34–596.33). However, the end of the passage is clear: the boy has ended up slim and sturdy and serene. The rising sun is in the prime of youthful life.

Daylight has returned, and with it "objective" reality—the ineluctable modes of the visible and audible. Also returning is rational analysis—the "why" of things. You mean to say that we have been having a sound night's sleep? the narrator voice asks itself, and it answers, "You may say so." In fact, in a tentative phrase, it is just about to roll wholly over (597.1–3). That is one of the strangest things ever heard of! Then all of life, sleeping and waking, is merely the flowing of a stream (597.7–8)?

But why? The awakening rational mind, as if it were possessed by the Four Old Men, tries successive rational explanations of the duple nature of human life, and why we emerge from sleep to daylight (597.9–22). Why? Because, thanks be to God, there are two sides to everything, the east and the west, the right side and the wrong side, falling asleep and waking up, and so forth. Because, as Eastern religion tells us, on the one side we have the earthly pleasures—the pleasure dome, the bathhouse and the bazaar—and on the other side we have the delights of a Muslim heaven, the Koran and the rose garden. Because life has two sides: one part of life is about ordinary family activities—bed and breakfast, and fighting with your parents, and the couches of sexual delights—and the other part is about sufferings, endurance, and heated combating and haggling,.

But why? Because every dog has his day, or every flowing discourse has an ending, as witness Shavarsanjivana—as corpses who returned to life (*shava sam-jivana*) will testify (M)—or perhaps because we are such stuff as dreams are made on, or because human beings live to give birth to future generations, like salmon leaping upstream to their deaths (Leixlip, the "salmon leap") to give life to a new generation of salmon.

But why? Well, it is a sort of a systole and diastole, which everybody you ever heard of does. But why? And then the final answer, possibly given by the donkey of the Four Old Men (597.22–23): Why? Search me! That is just the way things are. Anyway, upsydaisy! Get up from your drowsy slumbers!

The rational mind having acknowledged its relative failure, the basic modes of TIME and SPACE are reestablished. That is to say, Shem and Shaun, the ineluctable modes of sound and sight, are now working in tandem to report the four-dimensional nature of the waking world (597.24–600.4).

Look! The first shaft of sunlight appears on the Dublin horizon (597.24). We have seen the sunrise line crossing the Balearics and the Spanish border, and then illuminating Stonehenge. Now, for the first time, sunlight appears in the eastern Irish sky. Accompanying the shaft of light is the cold dawn wind, introduced by the name of the Hindu god of the wind, Vayu (M). It brings an intimation of the coming day, and the recreation of the physical world, with a chill in the small of the back (597.24–29).

The newly awakening sleeper has already roused his rational mind. And now his sense of time and space is recreated, to enable him to organize his impressions to recreate the complete world. Augustine, Avicenna, and Kant all declared that the human sense of time does not exist in the objective world; time is a mode of organizing that the mind uses to order its sense-impressions of change. As for space, Bishop Berkeley declared that the mind creates the sense of extension that establishes a three-dimensional world for the viewer. We have already seen that happen in the Proteus chapter in *Ulysses*; now we are to see it happening in the *Wake*.

What is the time? Tom and Tim, space and time, Shaun and Shem, here form the time of day, or Timothy—the four-dimensional continuum of the dawning world (599.3). First, Tom reports that the morning temperature is perfectly normal, that the dew has fallen, that there are mackerel clouds in the heavens, that the wind (*anemos* in Greek) is gently active. In fact, the scene reminds one of the Garden of Eden.

Tom informs us that the nighttime adventure was a very long, very dark, all but endless, hardly endurable, stumbling and confused night (598.6–9). However, the night has ended, and now day has arrived. Day is announced by some of Joyce's most beautiful sentences, in a chapter of beautiful sentences: Slow day now rises up like a bellflower for the hour of awakening (598.11–13). It is our hour of orisons, our sweet and bright brother and sister. The flower of dawn is beginning to bloom. In the Hindu legend, in the beginning of each historical cycle, Vishnu is sleeping on the coils of the unending serpent Ananta on the ocean, and from the god's navel a giant lotus slowly grows. From the lotus, Brahma arises to re-create the universe. In the *Wake*, the growing lotus tickles the navel of the sleeper. Let us pray (598.14).

Thank you very much! Here Europe has met India; the West has greeted the East. The narrator muses on the oddity and the miracle of daily resurrection. Even the most mildewed, murky, leaky, and lying characters—our moldy Four Old Men—are now newly remade.

Tim, Tom's twin brother (*tom* is Hebrew for "twin") is the spirit of SPACE, and he now takes up the tale. The city is appearing, along with our huge hero and our tiny mother, and their children, and their neighbors, and their neighbor's children's neighbors, and their goods and their servants and their belongings, and everything that is theirs (598.33–599.2).

Much obliged for the time of day! says the narrator. Now let us know where we are, and both TIME and SPACE will be satisfied. The question "What o'clock is it?"—the question that infuriated spatial Shaun in the course of the book—now is not offensive: SPACE and TIME are cooperating to create a world.

Time having been adequately determined, it is the turn of SPACE: "Where?" The question is answered in three long paragraphs. First, the animals of the world, all visible now that the world has been restored, are paraded before us (599.5–8). The flood of night has receded; human society has been made possible, and a tentative equilibrium has been established (599.9–18). Joyce would be the first to admit the tentative nature of human society, but on balance, the conventions of society enable human life to continue. The secular resurrection of human families goes on, with shaky but regular rhythm.

And where does all this take place? The rays of the sun have pierced the dark woods of night (599.25–27) as, warmed by the young sun, everything goes on more or less adequately. Anyhow, there is not much to be done about it. The great act of sexual contact that we will see in a few pages, between the male principles of sun and sea and the female principle of the river, will create the clouds, the conditions for human society (599.25). HCE's "dart of desire" will pierce the clouds ("Bring me my Spear—O Clouds unfold!": Blake), the clouds will dissipate, and the new day will dawn. In our dreary Drury Lane playhouse world, TIME and SPACE will keep everything solid and moving, as (in Macaulay's famous phrase) every schoolboy and schoolgirl knows (600.2–4).

We are beginning to segue into the introduction of the sun, who is the transformed Shaun. He has traveled his night journey backward from west to east down the river, and he is now rising above the horizon. The risen sun reveals the landscape—the Liffey, the Tree and the Stone, and three stained-glass windows in a village church.

First we see bodies of water—a pool, a river, and two large lakes, Albert and Victoria again, representing HCE and ALP. We also see the three boys (one a pissabed), a sluice, and a cataract (600.5, 8, 12–13, 15). The family have settled down and begun to cultivate their fields. God speed the plow!

Then an elm tree is seen, near a slab of stone (600.20, 26). The two sacred elements in the aboriginal landscape, the Stone and the Tree inform HCE and ALP they are in a holy place (600.31–34).

And sure enough, here we see a naked yogi priest clothed with the sun (601.1–2). In Indian texts, "clothed with the sun" is the traditional description of naked Hindu priests—but this one is not entirely naked, because his "oakey" is decked with leaves! He is offering a prayer while standing in water, as the Sanskrit phrase conveys. He is identified as a priest by the epithet "Pfaf!" (601.3)—"Pfaff" is an insulting German word meaning "priest." In *Ulysses* the day opens with a naked priest offering a prayer—surely no coincidence. At first, Buck Mulligan is probably naked under his dressing gown—that is how we see that he is "plump." Buck offers a mocking, blasphemous prayer, but a prayer is a prayer, as the Church says. And in the *Wake*, in response to the yogpriest's prayer, the city begins to appear. It rises up like the sunken city of Ys of Brittany, or Lough Neagh in Ireland, from under the waters of night (601.4–7).

Following the prayer, and the rising of the sun, there is the chiming of bells from many of the churches of Dublin. They send up their morning chimes, the morning Angelus, to the rising sun, their favorite, Kevin. This lovely passage is parallel to the chorus of the little flowers, greeting their clean innocent Chuff, in II.1 (234.6–239.27). The worshipers are here referred to as "dairmaidens," identifying them as the dear dairymaids, the Gopis, who worship Krishna (601.8). The first chimes echo along the cliffs of the seaside. The daughters of the cliffs are echoes; the phrase is based upon an Irish kenning, "the sons of the cliffs," which means "echoes." Joyce gives us a vivid picture of the seashore, with a view along the sapphire coast, its cliffs studded with a seaside plant, samphire (601.10–11). Samphire recalls the lines in *King Lear* where Edgar describes the height of the sea cliff to blind Gloucester: "Half way down / Hangs one that gathers samphire, dreadful trade!" (IV. vi.14–15).

The little girl churches joyfully ring out the morning Angelus, ending with a soft, loving chime, evoking St. Thomas à Becket and (tremulously) St. Laurence O'Toole (601.27–28). Joyce enumerates the churches in a number of different ways; however, although the result comes out as twenty-nine, Joyce lists the names of only twenty-six churches (601.21–28)—one of several errors in this section of the book. Emphasizing their resemblance to the little flowers of II.1, the chiming baby churches appear like little petal-bearing bells, and they sing from omega to alpha (601.16–17), carolling on their flowery way to Botany Bay. Botany Bay in Australia was more noted for convicts than for botany, but here the phrase is literally correct.

All of the innocent little flower girls send up their baby-talk prayers to Kevin. The babyish voices sing to "Keavn" from alpha to omega—from Ah! to Oh!—and spelling the name of Kevin to resemble "Heaven" is not an accident. The rhythm of these sentences seems very like the rhythm of an old American spiritual: "I got shoes, / You got shoes, / All God's chillun got shoes! / When I get to Heaven, gonna put on my shoes, / Gonna walk all over God's Heaven! / Heaven! Heaven! / When I get to Heaven, gonna put on my shoes / Gonna walk all over God's heaven!" The exclamation of the little churches and flowers is greeted as a true mixture of prayerfulness and playfulness, with an echo of "Pray for us!" (601.29). And never mind the overcultivated English voice commenting critically, "Oh, that is so! What shall one name it?" (601.30).

Ireland has reappeared, new and bright as if just created, as is indicated by the references to antipodean lands such as New Ireland itself in the Bismarck Archipelago, Melanesia, and New Zealand in the form of an even Newer Aland (601.34–36), as well as the previous Botany Bay in Australia.

The little midinettes (M) have rung their morning Angelus bells (601.31), the third Angelus in the book, ringing out the prayer for the conception of the Messiah by the Holy Spirit.

Stained Glass Windows

Now three stained-glass apsidal windows begin to appear. The south window is devoted to St. Kevin (602.9–13; 603.34–606.12), the center window celebrates St. Patrick (606.13–613.14), and the north window dimly shows the patron saint of Dublin, St. Laurence O'Toole (613.15–614.18).

From early Christian times, most Christian churches have been carefully "orientated" toward the east, with the altar facing the rising sun, a survival of a very old pagan custom. The apse, the area behind the altar, is therefore lit every morning by the rising sun. The windows to the south of the central window in the apse, and in the church itself, are lit most brightly then; the windows to the north are lit much more faintly. In Chartres Cathedral, and in many other medieval churches, the dim north windows contain episodes from the Old Testament, with its imperfect message of revelation, and the brightly illuminated south windows bear episodes from the New Testament and from medieval Christianity.

Here, the prayers of the little girl churches in Ireland introduce the triple stained-glass windows in the apse of an Irish village church, which is beginning to be illuminated by the rising sun, as Joyce told Frank Budgen (M). But Joyce's village church is his own invention; there are no churches of this description in Ireland. I checked the stained-glass windows of several churches around Dublin, and there are none with this selection of saints. The closest is a church in Clondalkin, south of Phoenix Park, which shows Patrick and Laurence O'Toole, but not St. Kevin. I once thought that it would be delightful if the church windows illuminated were those of Adam and Eve's, the Franciscan Church of the Transfiguration of Mary mentioned on the first page of the *Wake*. However, during the Joyce Centennial Symposium of 2004, I checked the stained glass at this church, and there is no connection with Joyce's windows.

The subject of the three stained-glass windows corresponds, in my opinion, with the three soldiers, and the three parts of the male genital equipment. The subjects of two of the windows, St. Kevin and St. Laurence O'Toole, are more or less passive. St. Kevin does nothing but sit in his bathtub, meditate, and soak. To be sure, he is one of the few people in the works of Joyce to bathe at all! However, bathing is not much of an activity. As for the dark and mysterious passage on St. Laurence O'Toole, it is hard to tell what if anything he is doing.

By contrast, the central window, that dealing with the debate between St. Patrick and the pagan sage, displays considerable activity. In fact, St. Patrick recreates the physical world. I would say that he is the active and administrative center of the activity of the three windows, just as the third soldier, the ithyphallic Davy of the Willingdone Museyroom, brings about the overthrow of the father and the accession of the new generation.

In an emblematic form, the three soldiers are represented by windows in all the rainbow colors of Fallen Man created by the rising sun.

I. South Window: St. Kevin (602.9–606.12)

St. Kevin begins to appear in the growing light. He is extremely handsome (602.3–4). What is Kevin doing? Tell us quickly! His face shines out like the sun, or a son (602.12); the rising sun is illuminating the whole land-scape. The description of Kevin is interrupted by a morning news report from Mike Portlund, an independent correspondent (hanging by the neck), reporting from anywhere on Doomsday (602.16–27). The reporter describes a funeral, presumably HCE's, and a Saturday night's entertainment, exhibit-ing the caricature of a horse, or HCE's harse (see 111.27–30), revealed by a camera obscura.

The most astonishing part of the news story for an American reader ap-pears at 606.23–24. The last delirium of the American gangster Dutch Schultz is linked to the life of Humphrey Chimpden Earwicker. "Dutch Schulds" encapsulates the life of our guilty hero HCE, of Scandinavian (Germanic) origin and laden with *Schuld*, guilt. Joyce is here evoking a famous piece of nonfiction: the dying words of Arthur Flegenheimer, the American gangster and bootlegger known by the nom de guerre Dutch Schultz.

On October 24, 1935, Dutch Schultz lay dying in a Newark hospital. He had been shot earlier in the day by Charlie "the Bug" Workman, an assassin working for his rivals, mainly Lucky Luciano. Schultz drifted in and out of delirium. His statements were taken down by a police stenographer sitting by his bedside. The police were hoping that Schultz would give away some of the details of his murderous career and implicate some of his accomplices.

Dutch Schultz was an uneducated man, and much of what he said was disconnected and apparently trivial. However, some of his phrases were chilling in their implications—for example, "Talk to the sword"; no poet ever contrived a more sinister metaphor expressing total implacability. There was a suggestion of metaphysical poetry in "Oh, go ahead; that happens for crying; I don't want harmony, I want harmony." At one time, after quoting the words of a song, he seemed to be calling on James Joyce; at least, that may have been what attracted Joyce to these extraordinary utterances from a guilty criminal: "Look out for Jimmie Valentine, for he is an old pal of mine. Come on, Jim, come on, Jimmie; oh, thanks." Another passage, ending in a perfect alexandrine, has ever since fascinated readers of Schultz's deathbed rambling: "Please; I may take all events into consideration: no, no. And it is no: a boy has never wept nor dashed a thousand kin [or "kim"]." Dutch Schultz's last words were "French Canadian bean soup . . . I want to pay, let them leave me alone."

The *Wake* morning continues, after the Germanic guilt in the news story fades away. There follow the characteristic scenes and sights and smells of all mornings in all modern cities. Shaun/Kevin is further described. All Shaun wants, says the narrator, is to rise up out of the misty city and to fall in with a merry group of maidens coming home from a dance (602.27–33). Kevin, like his corresponding persona Shaun, is very fond of women in his own way, and also very fond of his food. He is now especially eager for breakfast. The oily smile of the early postman is combined with bacon and eggs, and the sublime ("ovenly") odor of baking bread fills the morning air (603.1–2, 6–7). Shaun the Post is one of those early risers who animate the morning scene of every modern city, those who sort and deliver the mail, who deliver daily blessings from the daily mailbag with an echo of the Lord's Prayer (603.7–8, 10–12).

Shaun's taste for jolly plump girls is also aired, with a caution that anyone who accuses Shaun of indecent behavior will be libeling the Catholic Church, against which Shaun is pressing his fully grown girlfriends: Great Heavens! What do we see? Hyacinths with heliotropes, such trollops! (603.28–30).

But what of Coemghem, the foster child (603.34)? "Coemghen" is the old Irish version of the name of Kevin, who as part of the band of Finn McCool is a foster child, and illegitimate. "Clan" in Gaelic languages means "children," and the young men in Celtic war bands such as Finn's Fianna were considered the foster children of the chief. Where is Kevin? The answer is that he is in the blue, green, and gray stained-glass window of a church, which is now beginning to glow with the sunrise. The south window of the apse of the church orientated toward the sunrise, the one that bears the legend of St.

Kevin, is becoming faintly lighter, and the colors are beginning to acquire their daytime values (603.34–36).

The St. Kevin section is a parody of a medieval saint's legend, written in deliberately archaized language. One of the first parts of *Wake* to be created, it is perhaps the most completely organized, or overorganized, sections of the work.[6] Kevin does nothing except bathe and meditate, yet the complexity of the document describing his ablutions and meditations is astonishing.

The magic numbers seven and nine govern the text. Kevin sits in his bathtub situated within nine circles of, respectively, "land, water, land, water, land, hut, land, water, tub."[7] There are seven lists of ecclesiastical import:

1. Seven ecclesiastical grades: priest, deacon, subdeacon, acolyte, lector, exorcist, and doorkeeper
2. Nine grades of virtue leading to canonization: poor Kevin, pious[ly] Kevin, holy Kevin, most holy Kevin, venerable Kevin, most venerable Kevin, blessed Kevin, most blessed Kevin, Saint Kevin[8]
3. Nine orders of angels: angels, archangels, principalities, powers, virtues, dominations,[9] thrones, cherubim, seraphim
4. Seven ecclesiastical colors: white, rose, gold, green, red, violet, black
5. Seven canonical hours: matins/lauds, prime, tierce, sext, nones, vespers, compline
6. Seven gifts of the Holy Spirit: fear of the lord, piety, knowledge, fortitude, counsel, understanding, wisdom (note that here, however, Joyce slyly intimates Shaun/Kevin's limitations, as St. Kevin possesses none of the three Heavenly Virtues—faith, hope, and charity)
7. Seven sacraments: matrimony, holy orders, extreme unction, penance, Eucharist, confirmation, baptism (note, again, Joyce intimating the priest Kevin's limitations, as the sacraments are listed in the reverse of the usual order)

There are two more magic series: the tub is mentioned seven times, and seven variations of the word "created" occur in the text.

In the course of the Kevin passages, some typical morning scenes are recreated. We see and hear the morning delivery of milk, loaded Morris lorries full of milk crates—here combined with the message of Gabriel to the Virgin, the text of the Angelus, "Hail Mary full of grace, the Lord is with thee" (604.10–11). Milk trains are on the road, bearing the Milky Way (604.12–15).

And as the milk arrives, Kevin sits in his bath and meditates continuously on baptism (606.10–12). The water images in the Kevin passages lead to the sea in the St. Patrick passages that follow.

Here the blazing sun appears.

The awakening and the forgetting of night begins.

II. Center Window: St. Patrick and the Pagan Sage (606.13–613.14)

In the center window, now becoming brighter in its turn, is depicted the conflict between St. Patrick and the pagan Archdruid, presided over by the high king Leary. The debate begins with a run-up to the scene (606.13). This sentence locates the rising sun as being just at the mouth of Dublin Bay: The sun has just struck Bishop Rock Light at the end of the Scilly Isles, and the server of the light can put it out now. The Bishop Rock Light is at 6°26′68″ W, almost directly south of the mouth of Dublin Bay (6°15′ W) and Howth Castle and Environs (6°4′50.77″ W). Before now, we have seen the sun rising in Spain and on the Balearics, then on Stonehenge. Now the sun has definitely risen upon Dublin itself.

The view from the three Benns on the Hill of Howth, says the narrator, is something to write home about (606.14–16)—and indeed the view over the Irish Sea at sunrise must be unforgettable. In the sunlight, we begin to see Dublin itself, its ways and turns, its cobbled streets, picturesque and lovely in the dawn light (606. 17–19), a good scene for an artist (606.21–23). The Earwicker family is evoked in memory as the large mechanical clocks of the town, with the Old Testament figures of Jacob and Esau and the New Testament figures of the twelve apostles, get ready to strike the time when all things change over (607.5–10). It is time for the old people to rejoin their ancestors in the boneyard and for the young people to wake up to their world (607.12–16). And as we hear the full and accurately spelled title of the song "Finnegan's Wake" for the first and only time in the book, we hear the sounds of the young lads and lassies dancing in the dawn to a lively old music-hall song, "Hy ty ty tiddly aye ty ty" (607.17), and it's high time, too! Early wakers in Dublin are having their Tetley's tea.

The rising of the sun is here described twice, each time in a great prose poem of the sort that Joyce invented in *Ulysses*. We have already seen one description of the sunrise, at 597.24–29, where the first rays of the sun break out into slim spears of light, and the dawn wind blows around the small of our backs. Now the sun has risen in earnest and is blazing in the eastern sky. In this great poem (607.24–33), the daylight grows out of the darkness, and the winds of all the year are abated. The reign of murky, wet darkness, with its snow, thunder, and lightning, has retreated belowstairs. The Sun King, rising from the mist from his hotel in the hollow, will show up above Dublin Bar, to be greeted by thick fog, the mayor of Chapelizod. The mayor is looking most pleased, with a cloud-capped sun halo shining from his sequined torso, which is also his big white horse, the horse we have seen so many times before, which will show up again in a touching context in Anna Livia's last words.

The most impressive part of the poem is the names of the actors who play the part of the Sun King. Captain Bunting and Lieutenant-Colonel Blair sound like a pair of ordinary military men, but in fact the names make up the center of a great, very short poem within the poem, in which two aspects of the risen sun are conveyed with brilliance and power. "Captive Bunting" represents the rays of the risen sun, like ribbons attached to a blazing ring and fluttering in the solar breeze. "Loftonant-Cornel Blaire" represents the sun high up in the air ("loft") with his corona, the glory of the sun which can be seen only during an eclipse, shining around him, and with his blazing light synesthetically conveyed by sound imagery as thundering ("tonant") and blaring.

The second of Joyce's great sunrise prose poems occurs on 608.28–32. In the wake of the black ship *Shades of Night*, and accompanied by the Hindle Wakes, English sunrise festivals, the week of wakes is over. The phoenix fire first catches weakly from innumerable generations of phoenix ashes in Asia, then becomes stronger, fuming with fierce force. To the increasingly powerful striking of a huge Chinese gong, a tamtam, the Phoenix awakes, the Finnegans awake. The use of alliterations of increasing power and openness is masterly here, as is the increasing volume of the gong conveyed by the change of vowel, "temtem tamtam," and the use of synesthesia, sound reinforcing sight, the clashing of the gong reinforcing the growing power of the risen sun.

We are passing from sleep. And yet we would linger in sleep—it was agreeable to remain in a half-doze, with the characters in the dream (608.33–609.18). However, day is too lovely for the sleeper to linger in slumber (609.19–23). The rising sun through the center window of the apsidal stained glass is enriching all parts of the earth with the colors and sounds of day—the ineluctable modalities of the visible and the audible. The sun is also setting up space and time—"the now, the here"—while we are waiting breathlessly and reverently for the great God, for "Hymn."

We now see our old friends Mutt and Jute, but greatly improved. Their names have been translated into Latin as Muta and Juva, and they are much better behaved than their earlier selves. They are no longer truculent primitives hurling at each other irritable comments about death and some terrible battle in the depths of the mound. Their behavior is now formal, and they are highly courteous to each other. Their learned and graceful comments, partly in Latin, are about life and daylight, and about the resurrected sun appearing on the top of the mound.

What is now smoking from the Lord? asks Muta. It turns out to be the Lord, the Sun, puffing his morning pipe, which fills the landscape with mist. It is the Lord in the form of the daylight wishing an Irish blessing to all—"Top of the mornin' to you!"—and keeping an eye on the development of the morning (609.25). Juva declares joyfully that day is the master of sleep and commands the shades of night.

And what does the growing morning disclose but a procession maneuvering over the sunlit field of nighttime battle (609.32–34)? The scene is the battlefield of Cabra and Slane; it was at Slane that St. Patrick arrived for his debate with the Archdruid. Juva intimates that the procession is headed by a Japanese figure of authority bearing a chrysanthemum, the sacred flower of Japan. This dignitary, an Oriental sage, is followed by an impressive train of porters, Japanese priests (bonzes), musicians playing conventional versions of Oriental music (plunky plunk), and Eastern carriages. Any Eastern feature is Oriental enough for Joyce in this sunlit chapter—Japanese, Chinese, Hindu are all sources for the eastern sunlight.

Muta utters a version of "Corpo di Bacco!" that may mean that the sage has a paunch (Italian *panza*) resembling that of an ape (*Pongo* is the genus of the orangutan). Then Muta exclaims (in pidgin: more Orientalism!) that there is someone else on the plain, a tall solitary unmoving man (609.36)—St. Patrick, who has arrived for a debate with the Oriental sage. This reproduces Patrick's famous debate at Tara with the Archdruid, a pagan sage, where Patrick successfully defended Christianity before the high king Leary or Laoghaire. In the original debate, Patrick answered the pagan's taunt about the incomprehensibility of the Trinity by showing the king the three-in-one shamrock. Patrick is just the right figure to defend sunlight against the pagans; in the original story, the druids at Tara cast a thick darkness over the land, which Patrick immediately dispelled by prayer.

And sure enough, the high king rises up like the sun from underneath the Hill of Howth; he has been resurrected. Muta asks why King Leary's wrinkled lips are smiling so broadly. Juva explains—"Bet your bottom! Every time!"—that the king has bet on both of the contestants to win, and therefore he cannot lose (610.11–13).

Juva has announced the sage's name, linking him with Bishop Berkeley (610.1). Berkeley adhered to an extreme idealist position on the nature of reality, which unmaterialist position the sage will defend. Here the sage is conflated with Buckley, the Shaun-figure who shot the Russian general, but Buckley will not be successful here, the king will not be shot, and the philosopher Berkeley will not triumph over a materialistic argument for a true daylight.

The next few exchanges (610.14–16) are enigmatic. Muta's reaction on hearing of the king's double bet seems to ask whether both night and day are necessary to the complete process of secular resurrection, and to suggest that a veiled twilight is also paradisiacal. And with Juva's retort—That the book may live, let paradise perish![10]—Joyce seems to be asserting that his own work is supremely important to him, and that his declaration through Stephen Dedalus in *A Portrait*—that he will not conform to beliefs he does not hold, and is not afraid to make a mistake as long as eternity itself—still holds.

Muta and Juva declare that pious and pure wars—Vico's description of religious conflict—and the hedonistic trio of wine, women, and song are alike necessary to the eternal cycle of human progress. Then Muta comes out with the clearest statement in the book—a statement summing up the reconciliation of opposites associated with Giordano Bruno—about the stages of the human cycle: When human beings have become unified, as Shem and Shaun have done, they will pass on to their first stage of development, diversity. Next will come conflict, which will lead to the third stage, peace and reconciliation. Juva adds that the passage through the three-level process will be guided by the light of reason. Bright daylight sends reason down to humanity, and resolves all conflicts (610.21–29).

The cross talk ends with genial wishes from each speaker that the sun will warm the other, like a hot water bottle or a warming pan. It will be noted that this is the first time in the book that the brothers are on good terms. In previous discourses, they ended up thunderstruck and astonished, or wished each other speedy deaths (18.15–16; 252.7–13). Now, however, they are united peacefully in one integrated young man, with Shaun as the top half accepting (if uneasily) his lower half, Shem, and both of them preparing for the final act of love with ALP at the end/beginning of the book.

The voice of the radio or television announcer (610.34–611.3) gives some racing news, headlines announcing the reconciliation of Rhythm and Colour at a park meeting, and Paradise Lost coming in last in the Grand National steeplechase, three ties and two drawn races (the three/two sexual pattern), and Heliotrope, the sunwise turn, winning over rigid religion, the Harem ("the forbidden" in Arabic). The omega-alpha pair Jockey the Ropper and Jake the Rape now compose one Jack the Ripper, which leads smoothly to the conclusion. The debate between St. Patrick and Buckley the Archdruid is announced as a chat from the paddock. The details of the great debate follow.[11]

The sage and the saint are not on as good terms as the reconciled brothers Muta and Juva. In the heat of argument, Buckley calls Patrick a son of a bitch's bastard (612.8), and Patrick contemptuously refers to the sage as poor and colorblind (612.18). However, Buckley or Berkeley, the sage, is described in pidgin English as the leading Irish theologian (611.4–5). He is the man of highest rank for the business, the Archdruid leader of Irish Godtalk: in pidgin, *chin-chin* is "talk" and *joss* is "God," so *chin-chin joss* means "theology."

In his long and learned discourse, filled with Latin expressions, this famous Eastern theologian takes an unmaterialistic, idealistic, Gnostic view of physical reality, which is held to be ignoble and repellent, and thus to be transcended. Joyce knew and despised many such idealists in Dublin; in the Library chapter in *Ulysses*, he paints a satirical portrait of the worshipers of "ideas, formless spiritual essences" (9.49). This attitude is not simply the opinion of Stephen Dedalus: Joyce in his own person attacks these faint idealists in "The Holy Office" (1904): "Thus I relieve their timid arses, / Perform my office of Katharsis. / My scarlet leaves them white as wool. / Through me they purge a bellyful."[12]

The Eastern sage Buckley begins the debate by invoking a well-known theory of color perception, first associated with Bishop Berkeley, which holds that what we see as colors are really only the colors *rejected* by colored material, what the animal-vegetable-mineral furnishings of the world are unable to absorb (611.12–19). On the other hand, for the true sage, only the inner nature of reality is true—that is, only the colors *inside* the colored material, absorbed by it, are *truly* there, and therefore all the rainbow colors of the morning world that are appearing before the debaters are factitious and illusory. The insides of earthly things contain the true essence of things, the Ding an Sich, the Kantian transcendent noumenal reality (611.19–24).

The surface rainbow colors are rejected by the sage for another reason, one that is not specifically mentioned by him but will form the basis for the argument of his opponent—the sage is rejecting the rainbow colors as representative of Fallen Man, as symbolic of man's disgrace. The number one seer restricts himself to the white radiance of eternity, not the illusory colors of the material world stained by Life as a dome of many-colored glass, as in Shelley's lines from "Adonais."

The proud sage then proceeds to give an example of his thesis (611.33–612.15). He points to High King Leary, who is sitting smiling on the Hill of Howth in his seven colors of physical features, ornaments, and costume, in all the colors of the rainbow.[13] To the eye of true wisdom, the sage asserts, all the colors really reduce to one inward color—green, as befits an Irish king! —green as vegetables or herbs: the pure vegetarian sage approves of sage. He then asserts that in reality the king's red hair is green as sorrel, the king's orange kilt is green as spinach, the king's golden torc is green as curly cabbage, the king's green umbrella is green as laurel leaves. Here the sage in his chauvinism and desire to flatter the king has gone a bit too far and committed a logical error—the umbrella is green both inside and outside—but then, all's fair in flattery of royalty! The sage asserts that the king's blue eyes are really as green as thyme chopped with parsley, and the indigo stone in his finger-ring as green as an olive or a lentil. Finally, the king's violet battle bruises are really as green as sennacassia. The sage, who has already referred to St. Patrick as an anxious melancholic (611.32–33), now tosses the argument to him with an offhand use of Patrick's Celtic name, Sucat ("warlike") (612.15).

St. Patrick, who displays the signs of his austerities—he was fasting all the time—has been patiently standing by during this pompous disquisition and singing a hymn, first softly and slowly, then more swiftly and loudly (611.8–9, 28–29). In contrast to the sage's gorgeous rainbow mantle (611.6–7), the saint is wearing a simple gray garment, as befits an ascetic.[14]

The saint finishes his hymn and begins his argument. Where the sage's presentation was long and elaborate, the saint's is short and slangy. Although Patrick has blushed red with irritation at the sage's casuistry, he speaks out easily and fluently (612.16). He starts to attack the sage (612.18): you poor chiaroscuro/shiroskuro creature,[15] seeing only black and white—or rather green and white, for the sage is a bigot when he dismisses all other colors as sinful and illusory. The bystanders, struck dumb by Patrick's boldness, wait to see whether the greenness of the sage or the redness of the saint will triumph (612.21–24).[16]

Patrick claps a handkerchief bearing the sign of the shamrock to his heart (612.24–25), but unlike the original legend of Patrick, in which the saint uses the shamrock as a symbol of the Trinity in his debate with the Archdruid, this version has Patrick using the risen sun as his symbol. He "saves the appearances," that is, he justifies the nature of the world, not by abstract theory alone, but by principles that account for the outer appearance of the physical world. Patrick kneels down once, twice, thrice—to the great Lord of the Rainbow. This triple rainbow is the sign of the world appropriate to Fallen Man, its halo a symbol cast on men by the fire of the sun, which is the symbol of the Father, the Son, and the Holy Ghost, amen (612.26–30). God, the Lord of the Rainbow (*arcobaleno* in Italian), created the rainbow as a sign of reconciliation with sinful man (Genesis 9:13–17). The colors of the rainbow, the colors of the daytime world, in addition to staining the white radiance of eternity and symbolizing sinful Man, are also the signs of the ultimate resurrection and salvation of human beings.   Joyce may have derived his idea of God the creator of the rainbow not only from the Bible but also from Dante. At the end of *Paradiso* (33.115–20), Dante has a vision of God as three things: an intense point of light, a rainbow, and a loving human face. In the rainbow passage—

. . . In the deep and bright

> essence of that exalted Light, three circles
> appeared to me; they had three different colors,
> but all of them were of the same dimension;

> one circle seemed reflected by the second,
> as rainbow is by rainbow, and the third
> seemed fire breathed equally by those two circles

—at the height of Paradise, God as a triple rainbow symbolizes the Trinity for Dante. For Joyce in his *commedia*, however, the sun of everyday appearances, the sun that gives color to the physical world, is the most appropriate symbol for the world of "the now, the here," which Joyce celebrated and defended against the sages of Neoplatonism, the forces of cold Gnosticism.

That's the thing, by God! the very thing to defeat the forces of vagueness and Neoplatonic nonsense! The Archdruid desperately twists himself about and about, but only succeeds in pushing his face between his legs. Then the defeated sage falls on his behind with a comic thud (614.31–36). This last detail reflects an element in the original legend of St. Patrick: when the Arch-druid Lochru was lifted up into the air by devils, Patrick broke the spell by prayer, and the diabolical pagan was dashed to pieces on a rock.

The bystanders, now completely convinced by the saint's argument, burst out in hymns of praise, based on an old Irish patriotic song: "'God Save Ireland,' said the heroes. / 'God save Ireland,' said they all. / 'Whether on the scaffold high, / Or the battlefield we die, / What matter when for Ireland dear we fall?'" The sun is hailed as the essence of everyday usefulness, as a good safe lamp of fire, by the servants of Helios, the sun-god. (Helots were the servant class of Sparta.) After the sun worshippers extol the sun as a lump of gold in the heavens (German *hallen* = "resound"), they tramp off, singing farewell, to the rest of the patriotic song, now hailing not the death of the heroes on the scaffold but the brilliant light of the morning sky (613.1–3).

From the heavens comes a gigantic echoing voice endorsing the victory of day over night: "Per jocundum Dominum Nostrum Jesum Christum, Filium Tuum"—By our merry Lord Jesus Christ, Thy Son—a merry Messiah re-joices in Patrick's victory. Joyce was of the opinion that his family name was derived from the Latin *jocundum*, "merry," so the merry author may here be putting his trademark on this passage.[17]

Where have the debaters and the sun worshippers gone? asks the text. They are gone forever, or at least for today. As the Kevin passages ended with the milk trains, the Patrick passages end with God's truce, and breakfast (613.10–12). We are in a far bigger colored world (German *farbiger*, "colored") as the sun—looking like a plate of ham and eggs—brings out all the spectrum of visible light. We are witnessing to God's truth, but we are also witnessing God's truce with fallen human beings; the rainbow has always been a symbol of God's mercy since the story of Noah in the Bible. Yet nothing has changed; nothing is present that was not there before; only the order of the elements has changed. Nothing has been destroyed. As it was, let it be! (613.13–14).

III. North Window: St. Laurence O'Toole (613.15–614.18)

The north window in the apse of the village church is, as tradition dictates for north-facing stained-glass windows, reserved for matters that have not been illuminated by revelation. In the example already given, all dark north windows, as at Chartres, contain scenes from the Old Testament.

However, although this window may be dark and there may be some obscurities in this passage, there is little doubt to whom the window is dedicated—the lord of Laurens now has his turn when the saint and the sage have finished their debate (613.15–16). Here the lord of Laurens is certainly St. Laurence O'Toole, the patron saint of Dublin; many churches in the vicinity of Dublin have windows dedicated to the saint. Yet the lord of Laurens also seems to be the Earl of Howth, whose family name is St. Lawrence. And we have a reference to the first page of the book—Laurens County, Georgia, has Dublin as its county seat. We are returning to the beginning of the book, for after the lord has had his say, we enter into the very last sections of the *Wake*, the Anna Livia sections. The lord here may be the sun as well, since he is seen as rising benevolently when Ireland has been identified yet again as "the isle of saints and sages."

What the saint is doing is not immediately clear. There is what seems to be a sketch of evolution. Fungi and algae appear, and evolve into mosses and ferns, and then trees (613.17–19). From this vegetable pantheon, creatures of increasing complexity arise. These are animals, since they are capable, unlike classic plants, of eating other live creatures. Then the animals begin to "feel" emotions, and to "think" (613.19).

All of these creatures, plant and animal, are luxuriating among the features of a dead world that has been reborn with the sun. A dog, the symbol of newly rearisen man, is roaming around this newborn world; the dog may have been borrowed from the first section of *The Waste Land*—the dog who is friend to human beings, and who will resurrect them if he can. Here, human beings are returning to the scene of their previous failures, only to repeat them; the dog is returning to his vomit, as the Bible says (Proverbs 26:11, II Peter 2:22). However, this is the eternal human pattern: one gulp of the nauseous mixture of sin acts as an emetic, and clears the digestion for the new day (613.22–24).

And sure enough, we are all cleared up for a beautiful day, heralded by the initials of HCE and ALP. There is bound to be a lovely day for marriages in the open, and morning and evening are going to bury the sad past night (613.27–31). In the lovely new plant-filled world (613.34–36), all of the polar opposites will be coming back to perform their tasks—ondt or gracehoper, noble or slave, mookse or gripes (613.36–614.1). All the old dirty clothes will be coming back anew from the laundry blazing bright and sharply ironed; the tennis champion son of the washerwoman's hallucination will be rising up bright and sharp in his white flannels as the newly arisen sun and lover (614.1–7).

Teems of times and happy returns, in our dazzling white clothes, collars and cuffs and overalls, as clean as bluing, ironing, and starch can make them, under the burning new sun! This paragraph ends in phrases that echo the early description of HCE in suspended animation (74.13–19), but now he is well and truly woken up (614.8–9, 12–13).

"Sinn féin, sinn féin amhain!" The speaker gives the sunrise a political application to the newly freed state of Ireland, by echoing the most famous statements of Parnell, one bitter and one glorious: "If you sell me, get my price," and "No man has a right to fix a boundary to the march of a nation." And the patriotic song "A Nation Once Again" sounds out over the brightening morning sky (614.14–18).

Final Forgetting of Night (614.19–615.11)

What has gone? asks the narrator. How did it end? The old night has gone, and the book is going to end soon. The dream fades with the opening day, as dreams do; we are ordered to begin to forget our dream. It does not matter if the dream fades: it will be repeated every day and night. Then the forgetting gets stronger. HCE and ALP's initials appear twice, and we are reminded that we are by dear dirty Dublin, by the river goddess Anna's delta. "Forget!" Now the forgetting is supreme (614.19–26).

The whole Viconian pattern has ended, under the auspices of the Four Old Men of History (614.27–30). The four-part process of birth, marriage, death, and resurrection was designed by the Father, the Son, and the Holy Ghost for the birth, death, and secular resurrection of human beings through history, through the bursting open of the egg, the blending of characteristics in the fertilization of the next egg, the death of the parents of the egg, and finally resurrection—"hatch-as-hatch-can" (614.31–33).

All of the previously decomposed elements of history have been recombined as the new world of the new family, as the families of little flowers described in the Quinet quote have persisted through the centuries. The whole process makes up the same old atomic structure of Finn, our giant hero, a powerfully charged electrical structure made up of electrons moved by Heisenberg's uncertainty principle and quantum leaps, by "hophazards" (615.6–8). HCE's initials occur twice in this sentence, to endorse the scientific analysis of atoms, which offers an astonishingly up-to-date description of atomic structure, with electrons moving from shell to shell in their orbits, emitting photons with each change—and making the sun shine.

Anna Livia's Letter

The hen has laid her eggs, and breakfast is now ready. Humpty Dumpty has been put together again as the risen sun, and the breakfast eggs are on the table (615.9–10). And all of this is as sure as that the hen has written her letter, which we now read in its most complete form (615.12–619.19).[18]

The letter, and Anna Livia's great female soliloquy that follows, is introduced by a reference to the beginning of the narrative process in the book: Narratives proceed by Cause and Effect (615.11). We saw the process beginning in I.7 as Anna Livia starts "coming" to her sons, and in I.8 as she begins moving slowly eastward to the sea (193.31–195.6; 196.1–216.5). At the end of the book, we now know that we have come to the end of the process: omega and alpha are prominent in the phrases "Of cause, so! And in effect, as?" We are near the end, the omega point, and we are ready to return to the beginning, the alpha point, the point at which Alph the sacred river begins to run backward, westward, at the beginning of the book.

The letter is in six paragraphs, of generally decreasing size; seven "well's" tie together the paragraphs. Since ALP is running through the eastern parts of her familiar city, she reminisces in her letter for the last time about familiar things—her family, and the enemies of her husband. She defends HCE valiantly, but there is an uneasiness in the tone of her references to her husband. In the great male soliloquy Haveth Childers Everywhere, we saw that HCE is of the opinion that ALP needs and enjoys controlling by male authority. Even though in Haveth Childers Everywhere she begins by weeping, at the end of the section she rejoices in the whip wielded by HCE (547.8–9; 554.8–9). Or so HCE believes, like all self-centered males. And indeed ALP may for the moment have believed that she was happy in her chains. But in her great final soliloquy we will see her dismiss her husband as a puny bumpkin and a petty criminal, and then spring to be free. In the letter, her divided attitude comes out as an equivocal tone.

Paragraph 1 (615.12–616.19)

ALP begins her letter to the Old Lord with a respectful salutation: "Dear Reverend Majesty."[19] (She almost begins with "Dear Dirty Dublin," but corrects herself.) She politely declares how much she has enjoyed observing the secrets of nature that she has encountered during the night, and then launches into her first attack on her husband's enemies: Magraw, who bring up bad things about Earwicker, will come to no/know good, and the clouds of the misty morning will burn away to reveal a fine day.

She segues into a dreamy reminiscence of the early days of her courtship. This passage is filled with references to nursery rhymes and children's literature—"Goldilocks," "Jack and the Beanstalk," the prick of the spindle in "Sleeping Beauty," fairy godmothers, and so on—as well as to more mature works of literature, such as *Paradise Lost* and *Huckleberry Finn*, and the songs "Merrily We Roll Along" and "The Banks of the Wabash" (615.21–28; 616.1; 617.18). She may now realize that her emotions in those courtship days were childish, and based on literature—the first hint of her impatience with her marriage. And at the end of her letter, she declares in fury that she is just about fed up with nursery rhymes.

In the letter, she then returns to the attack on the enemies of her family. The Magraws sell cheap, rancid, and low-quality bacon—back and streaky for ninepence!—and spoiled margarine, unlike her husband, whose sausages are famous for their quality (615.30–31; 616.22–24; 618.7). She hints strongly that Magraw tried to make her commit adultery, and quotes several commandments against the practice (615.32–33). May the Lord forgive them their trespasses against Milord O'Reilly, who is now about to get up (she hopes)! Her husband will make a corpse of somebody with the greatest of pleasure, and not leave enough pieces of the slanderers to be identified. Her husband is extremely strong and fierce and virile. so all of you snakes, watch out! (616.6–10, 12–16).

Paragraph 2 (616.20–617.29)

HCE is an honest merchant, she insists, and a faithful husband. She goes into great detail about how many sexual temptations he has resisted: In response to her questions about his temptations, he has asserted staunchly, "As sure as there is a God in Heaven, Livia, my cheek is a complete blank." That is, he has done nothing to blush for (616.36–617.1). He is, she declares, the dearest of husbands—though the force of her testimonial is somewhat vitiated by her spelling of "dearest" as "direst" (617.7). Magraw had better watch out for himself! Her sons will punch the daylights out of him, and he will need all his fairy godmothers to patch him up (617.12–19)! Magraw has stuffed his last sausage, and his funeral will take place early today (617.20–27)!

Paragraph 3 (617.30–618.19)

She then attacks Magraw's wife, Lily Kinsella. ALP insists on her own beauty (617.33–618.3). However, Lily Kinsella, who previously was the wife of the cad with the pipe, is now married to Magraw, and is an alcoholic and a loose woman (618.3–19).

Paragraph 4 (618.20–34)

ALP denies that she was ever treated without respect by anybody—the police and everybody always bow to her when she goes out. If the Magraws think that they can humiliate her, she will cut them contemptuously. "They can make their bows to my arse!" is a phrase that sounds as if Nora Joyce often uttered it!

Then Anna Livia returns to the defense of her husband, denying some charges of abuse, charges that, however, sound too detailed and specific to be without foundation. She was never bound to a chair, she insists, and nobody ever followed her with a fork (618.24–26)—although terrible prongs rise up and frighten her at the end of the book. Her dear husband is as gentle as a mushroom and very affectionate to her, whereas Sully, Magraw's henchman, is a thug (though a good bootmaker). Yet HCE, her mushroom-gentle husband, is also a violent Norwegian who has been expelled from Christianity, and who, with police assistance, will break up his family's enemies like sherds of a pot (618.26–34).

Paragraph 5 (618.35–619.5)

It is not quite clear what this paragraph is about, but it involves someone who has been very generous to the Earwickers. Perhaps ALP is reverting to thanks to the Old Lord who has been so kind as to contribute his son to help suffering humanity—God the father's lovely Christmas parcel.

Paragraph 6 (619.6–15)

ALP returns to the attack on her enemies; she simply likes their damn cheek, and their groundless complaints about the fall of Humpty Dumpty! HCE has not fallen permanently; the person under the Hill of Howth, the fallen vice-king, is another person. Her own husband will get up and, erect, confident, and heroic, make love to her, for her daily freshening-up, as he did when he was young.

She signs herself "Alma Luvia, Pollabella," a name emphasizing nourishment, fertility, and family care. *Alma* is "nourishing" in Latin: she is the nourishing goddess of rain (*lluvia* in Spanish). She is also the hen (*polla* in Latin) who is so solicitous of the health of her children.

In a postscript (619.17–19) she identifies herself as "Soldier Rollo's sweet-heart." Rollo, or Rou, was the Scandinavian founder of the Normans, and thus a major avatar of HCE. However, there may be a reference here to the French nursery song "Cadet Roussel," especially the last verse:

> Cadet Roussel ne mourra pas, (bis)
> Car avant de sauter le pas, (bis)
> On dit qu'il apprend l'orthographe,
> Pour faire lui même son épitaphe.

[Cadet Roussel will not die, / Because before taking the leap, / It is said that he will learn spelling, / To write his own epitaph.] The emphasis on living after death in this stanza is exactly in line with the theme of resurrection in the *Wake*, as is the emphasis on survival through language, perhaps through Anna Livia's letter.

Then Anna Livia has a flash of anger, premonitory of her final spring to freedom in Soft Morning, City! It may be possible to follow her angry train of thought here:

- She is just about fed up with nursery rhymes, the unrealistic picture of her marriage that she has been painting in her letter. She may also be fed up with the reams of nonsense in the *Wake*, a feeling some readers may share.
- She feels that she should be in the company of queens; she will encounter her fellow river deities Amazia and Niluna at the end of the book, but here the river leaving the dirty city feels that she is dressed in soiled rags, and she is totally worn out.
- However, she still senses the possibility of a renewal, anticipating the second version of herself, her daughter, swimming in the Wicklow hills (627.3).

Soft Morning, City!

Anna Livia has not spoken during the *Wake*, except for her poem as reported by the washerwomen in I.8, and in her letter. However, just like Molly in *Ulysses*, it is the voice of Anna Livia that speaks the last words in the book. Molly and Anna Livia are both voices of continuity.[20] Here at the end of the *Wake*, Anna Livia is flowing out to the mouth of Dublin Bay. She is an old woman, dying, wandering in her mind back to marriage and childhood. As the sea air and the ocean currents hit her, she turns wild. She sees her resurrected newly innocent husband rising blazing before her, as the sun is poised above the horizon. She declares that she will rush into his rising arms (628.4–5). She rushes toward the sea and the risen sun—both of them symbols of her husband, her father, her son—and is embraced and loved.

The great female soliloquy (619.20–628-16) begins with a "Good morning, city!" modulated into a greeting to the "soft" morning since the scene is misty, a soft Irish morning. Anna Livia is lisping, since she is bearing leaves on her. It may be that the season is autumn, or, as M suggests, the leaves she bears are the last leaves of *Finnegans Wake*. These leaves are now being turned over by the reader; that is, the actual pages of the copy held in the hand of the reader are being referred to in the text—a postmodern note.

The nursery and literary references continue as Anna Livia's old mind wanders between youth and old age. The reader encounters the literature of youth: "Babes in the Woods," *Robinson Crusoe*, "Goody Two-Shoes," and "Puss in Boots" (619.23–24; 621.36; 622.10, 11), and later *Tristram Shandy*. Anna Livia is "passing out" of the city; the last of the family memories pass through her mind before these memories are swept away by the stronger currents of the Irish Sea.

She comes within sight of the Hill of Howth, under which her husband lies on his palm, reclining from head to foot, like a comatose King Cole (619.25–29). She calls to him to rise up; he has slept so long! He resembles Vishnu lying on his side, slumbering after having created the universe, and now resting on his palm, and she asks him to rouse himself and love her again—"Rise up! Nirvana's over!" But there is an ominous undertone in the text, which mentions the chimes for the dead: traditionally, three chimes sound out for the funeral of a child, six for a woman, and nine for a man.

She remembers his praises of her when he was wooing her. She coyly calls the ex-raider an exaggerator (619.30), and yet she sees him as a great poet—her beauty had once excited him into poetry, though now perhaps his poetry would bore her to sleep (T 326). She imagines dressing him in seven articles of his newly cleaned clothes and his umbrella (619.34–620.1). She is flowing directly into the path of the sun, and the risen sun in her dimming, dazzled eyes bring to mind the tennis champion son of the old washerwoman in his blazing white flannels. And she orders him to stand up tall and straight for her. He is wearing a new "green belt," trees planted in garden cities to beautify the urban areas and provide oxygen. In her imagination he is blooming in the very latest, and second to none, as Dublin is presented as "nill, Budd!" (620.1–3).

She imagines going for a walk with him, and we suddenly get an extremely high-level panoramic morning view of rich England marching hand in hand and side by side in the sunlit sea with poor Ireland (620.5–6). (Note that she is finding difficulty in finishing her sentences; from now on, she becomes increasingly short of breath.) Then she rebukes herself for pride, covetousness, and envy, which sins she regards complacently as rather comforting—"comfytousness" (620.6). Her husband seems to her like several heroes—the Flying Dutchman, Sinbad the Sailor, Patrick Sarsfield, Earl of Lucan (M), or the Duke of Wellington. Come and walk with me; we always said that we would go abroad!

The last family reminiscences continue in Anna Livia's aging mind, as she continues her flow out of the city and into the bay. Now she thinks of her children (620.11–23). She thinks first of her sons. They are still fast asleep; there is no school today, so the day may be Sunday. The boys are so opposed in character, they are Heel Trouble and Heal Travel—Esau's heel was grasped by Jacob as they both were born, and Jacob wounded by the angel he wrestled at night cannot put his heel completely on the ground (Genesis 25:26, 32:24–32). Jacob is partly healed of his guilt only by travel, and Shaun is the traveler as postman. The boys are also Girl-Lover and Gall-Liver, Shaun the popular lover and Shem the worrier. HCE is constantly worried about them. Indeed, the boys are contrary; they have changed places during the night. She has seen similar things happen in the twinkling of an eye (the words of St. Paul on resurrection in I Corinthians 15:51–52). They are two brothers as different as north from south, but nevertheless the same anew, and resembling HCE completely. There is no peace from them; perhaps the two old nurses, the washerwomen, originally caused their conflicts.

Then her thoughts turn to Issy. First, she remembers HCE's wanton desires in the nights of their early marriage. He confessed to her what he would give to have a girl, and his wish was her will. (There is a secular echo here of Dante's Piccarda in *Paradiso* 3:85: "E 'n la sua volontade è nostra pace.")

Yet Anna Livia knows that Issy will take her place. If only Issy had more mother wit! Issy is still playing merrily, but the young girl will soon be a sober river goddess, an Isis, and one fit for HCE. Her young daughter is still as merry as a grig, or as the Greeks, but she will grow up. ALP accepts her supersession by her younger form. She also accepts the fact that the future, in which she dies and her children live, is inevitable: let what will happen happen. Like Hamlet, who says at the end of the play, "Let be," she is reconciled to her fate.

The servants in the inn—Sackerson and Kate the Slop—come briefly to her mind, as do the Four Old Men (620.32–621.1; 621.5–6). Then, in a passage of great beauty (621.1–9), she declares that the night is finished, that the Phoenix is flaming in the sky, that the morning star Lucifer has faded, that the Book of the Dead is closed. She invites her husband again to walk with her—as if they were walking over the causeway to Mont St. Michel—and to hold up his finger to test the wind. Now there is certainly light enough, and the Four Old Men, those windbags, will not blow them about. He need not bring his rucksack, which would cause the inevitable Irish informers, suspecting he had a bomb in the rucksack, to call the police. Even though it is the softest morning she ever saw—her fading eyesight causes her to see everything as through the mists of morning—surely it will not rain. May St. Arthur guide them! An ominous note: Arthur, besides being the great king, is also an ancient Celtic god of death (621.1–9).

Even though it probably will not rain, she will take her old shawl with her, and she imagines how fine her breakfast will taste—there will be trout, and sausages to bring out the taste of the tea, and toast. All the little children will come clustering about them, calling for their breakfast. But, she tells her husband, you must buy me a new girdle today; the old one has given way.

In the midst of all the happy family memories occurs the first note of Anna Livia's dismay, as she grasps HCE's hand in imagination: Come, give me your great bear-paw, daddy, for a little minute. Reach down, a little more. Draw back your glove.[21] Your hand is hot and hairy, and here is a healed scar, where the skin is as smooth as an infant's.[22] You once told me that you had burnt your hand with ice, and one time I heard that your hand was branded after you had killed someone, or painted the likeness of someone—creation as original sin, and a violation of the Second Commandment.[23] Maybe that is why you, Finnegan, held your hod so loosely, and why you lost your grip on the ladder and fell—and people think that you missed your footing on the scaffold deliberately.

And she tries to repress the memory: she will close her eyes so as not to see her guilty spouse—or rather to see him only as a pure youth, an innocent flowering boy, standing beside a tiny white pony, the child that bears all our hopes (621.29–32). Like Molly Bloom, she desires to see a young man, as a change from the sight of her husband, whom she sees as reeking with guilt.

The youth she desires will be innocent, and instead of her husband's big wide harse, with the scarlet pimple on it, she will see the young man's inoffensive slender young behind, a little white steed instead of a big horse of a bottom. The child will still provide hope for goodness; he has not yet sinned.

Then she alters her opinion in resignation (621.32–33). By original sin, all men have done something by the time they have acquired the mature flesh of age. It is the way of all flesh. "Fletch" also suggests "arrow," so the old arrow may be the flesh of the aged and experienced phallus.

She turns her mind from the troubling thought—they will take their walk before the bells ring in the churches, or before the dawn chorus of the birds. Anna Livia may be becoming slightly deaf, because both the church bells and the dawn chorus have already resounded. She sees HCE's birds; like Wotan, he has his two ravens. They are wishing you good luck, she says. The ravens are both as white as the driven snow—a marvel! This is a good omen: you will certainly be elected Lord Mayor. (She hints that she will help him to elicit votes by offering bribes, perhaps herself?) Magraw as Lord Mayor? Anna Livia scorns the very idea. Putting Magraw in the Mansion House would be like putting a chamberpot on the bedroom dresser, or jamming a derby hat over the brows of a Viking eagle (621.33–622.8)!

Suddenly she pushes Dublin politics away and begs her husband/father to bear her along more slowly (622.8–9). It is at this point that Anna Livia begins to leave the constricting embankments of Dublin, together with her sluggish movement within HCE's domain and her concern with his political career. She now feels the tug of freedom, and the pull of the sea tide. The present image of HCE drifts from her. She begins to sink into the past (622.13–19). She suggests that they could go for a trip, just by themselves, without the children. She then goes farther back in her memory, to the fox-hunt scene at which HCE got his name (622.24–623.4).

She suggests next that they might call on the Old Lord, whom she confuses with the Earl of Howth and the Hill of Howth. She tells her imaginary HCE to address His Majesty as "ismuthisthy"; he is an isthmus, a properly prominent old promontory (623.10, 6–7). His door is always open, she says, like the reformed Earl of Howth's. She hopefully asserts that the Lord ought to welcome them and give them something to eat. Remember to take off your white hat, and say, "Howdydo, Your Majesty!" I will drop my most graceful curtsey. After all, if he will not come to us, we must come to him: if the mountain will not come to Muhammad, Muhammad will come to the mountain! His is the house of laws: Ming Tung is the imperial Chinese reception hall (623.11–13). The Old Lord might dub you a knight, or make you the First Chief Magistrate. Remember Bartholomew van Homrigh, who was honored by William III! And I will be the witness for your worth.

The golden vision fades—it is all vain fancies (623.18). She suggests a humbler tour, one that takes in the Hill of Howth where they were the first of so many courting couples, a series that would later include Marion Tweedy and Leopold Bloom (623.21–22). Perhaps while they are on the Hill, a copy of the letter that she has been writing all of her life might wash ashore in a bottle (623.29–624.6).

Then she has a more grandiose vision: Let's live in a cottage that we financed with a bank loan, a cottage with a great tower to Heaven, as high as the Tower of Babel or Jack's beanstalk, to live among the stars and to hear how Jove and the gods talk. You are the Master Builder; you can build the tower, and climb it too (624.7–12). Ibsen's Hilde Wangel urged Master Builder Solness to climb his tower, with disastrous results. Anna Livia urges HCE to climb his own great phallic tower; she does not think that he will be dizzy at such a height. Eve is tempting Adam again, to the doom of both of them. However, Eve realizes the danger and accepts it: "At Trinity Church I met my doom," she sings. "That's what I've done for me." Just don't start running after other women again (624.16–21)!

What a lovely leafy dress I have! You will always call me Livia the Leafiest, won't you, darling? Wonderful old boy! And you won't object to my marshy perfume? The mention of her dress reminds her when she first saw him, a bold marauder—when you came into my father's tailor shop. I nearly fell off the pile of samples when I saw you. And is it true that you were brought up in a Borstal reform school, and that your parents were drunks and your mother would always be pawning her petticoats? However, you were fine to me! You were the only man I heard of who could eat the crusts of lobsters. And do you remember the night when you took me for two girls, one French and one German (a reference to the two girls on the coat of arms of Dublin). You certainly can act kingly at times! I will tell you all sorts of stories, like Scheherazade. And you will have to ask the Four Old Men about the history of the old houses that I can begin to see now (624.21–625.13).

The king will come tomorrow, by the route we are now traveling. The flint and fern are rustling as we go by them into the bay. You can bite your thumb, and the knowledge of the Salmon of Wisdom will enlighten you about the history of the town. You are sniffing as if you smell something, but it is only the turf fires of morning, dear! It is only clean turf, at Clontarf. And what you're seeing, as the mist begins to get lighter, that's the new houses of Dublin that have come up during the night, as thick as mushrooms, acres of them (625.19–20).

As she enters the bay, Anna Livia starts to feel the power of the retreating sea tide. It almost sweeps her off her feet, and it is beginning to keep her from finishing her sentences: "Steady on, Colossus! Watch your pace or you will knock [me down]" (625.21–23). She finds some little peas and seeds, and she gathers them in a maternal embrace. Then she sees more of the city behind her, the great new Dublin looming up out of the mist, but still the same city. Again she becomes breathless, from her own weakness and from the pull of the tide sweeping her forward. If I lose my breath for a short time, she says, do not worry—it happened before (625.26–29, 32–33). (The Liffey once ran dry during a severe drought.)

She imagines walking side by side with her husband, whom she envisages as the Lord Mayor of Dublin. She hopes that all under the heavens see them (625.35–36). However, her breathlessness—from age, and from her intuition of the great tides awaiting her—overcomes her again. Her sentences grow fainter and shorter, and she leaves out more and more words. Faltering, she tries to say: I feel I could faint away into the depths. Let me lean on you just a little. All girls are weak at times, while you, the great mountain, are adamant forever (626.1–3).

As she rounds the Hill of Howth and comes into sight of the Irish Sea, the sudden sea wind from the north leaps into her river mouth like a apocalyptic bow and arrows, and the cruel violence of the Norsemen, the Lachlanns, lashes her cheeks (626.4–7).[24] The invasion of her mouth resembles a kiss (*pogue* in Irish), and the whipping of her "cheeks" provides a masochistic thrill to the aging river.

Then she remembers the earlier turn of the tide at the weir at Island Bridge, which produced the huge orgasm that started the whole narrative process (626.7–8). She intuits the turn of the incoming tide, which will force her westward and backward toward the weir upstream at Island Bridge, to start the sempiternal tides again.

The memory of the turn of the tide brings to her mind the whole history of their marriage. She recalls that she was just a tailor's daughter, and the dandies of Dublin were saying that the Norwegian captain was old enough to be her father, whom he resembled. But he was a swaggering swell off Sackville Street, who became a fierce husband and father: he would follow a weak child around the dinner table to force him to eat the fat of the meat. He was also a great whistler—the allusion to Whistler hints at HCE's creative power—and he would sing duets with her as they worked on the clothes in the tailor shop. She was sometimes frightened of him—his flashing eyes in moments of anger awed her with their electric power (626.15–16). And yet she is sure that he was always fond of her. She asks mournfully who will now search for flowers for her on the hillsides. She has read that girls will always find lovers, but until she sees the sun rise over Dublin Bar, there will be no more lovers for her.

She returns to her memories of HCE. One time he would stand laughing before her, threatening to fan her *cul* (626.23), that is, whip her bottom, and she would be as quiet as a mouse—another masochistic note, recalling Mozart's Zerlina in *Don Giovanni*, who offers to allow her angry peasant fiancé Masetto to spank her—"Batti, batti, bel Masetto!"—and the humble Zerlina would stay as still and quiet as a little lamb. Then Anna recalls that HCE would sometimes rush upon her in anger, and she would freeze up and pray for him to return to his loving ways.

She was the envy of everyone then—a principal girl, like the Principal Boy in the pantomine. He would be the fearsome Viking invader in the pantomime *The Invasion of Ireland*. And by Thor, he looked it! With her failing heart making her lips pale, she is reminded of her sensations of fainting then for joy and fear when he rushed at her with love and rage, and when he proposed to her, how he said that he would give her the keys to her heart (626.26–31).

Here we have the last mention of the early love of ALP and HCE, and it is a musical mention. This last section of Book IV resounds with music. The reference here is to a song that Joyce knew well, "The Keys of Heaven," the title of which recurs in fragmentary form at the very end of the book, as a climactic reference to the keys of Heaven which will be "Given!" to her (628.15). The phrases of this song echo throughout the last pages of *Finnegans Wake*. They represent an early memory of ALP's, when HCE, courting her, sang to her a lovely old English song:

I will give you the keys of my heart;
And we will be married till death us do part;
Madam, will you walk? Madam, will you talk?
Madam, will you walk and talk with me?

Thou shalt give me the keys of thy heart,
And we'll be married till death us do part;

I will walk, I will talk;
I will walk and talk with thee.[25]

And then Anna remembers her marriage ceremony: we would be married till death do us part, or until the delta parts us (626.31–32). ALP is passing through the delta, which is overgrown with esparto grass. However, Anna's memories of HCE and the joys and fears of their married life are almost over. Now death is indeed about to part them.

Poised to say farewell and free herself from her husband and her children, Anna at first feels great regret at the parting, and she wishes that she had better eyeglasses and could see her husband more clearly. However, her sight is failing as well as her breath (626.32, 34–35).

And can it be it's now farewell (626.33)? With that word, Anna Livia crosses Dublin Bar and sweeps into the wild Irish Sea. We know it is at this point that she begins to die: there are six keywords here in the final three pages of the book that derive from the famous poem describing death as the crossing of a sandbar at the mouth of a bay—Tennyson's "Crossing the Bar."

With so many shared keywords and phrases, "Crossing the Bar" seems to echo in counterpoint throughout the climax of Anna Livia's soliloquy. Tennyson's great phrase "When that which drew from out the boundless deep / Turns again home" describes exactly the pilgrimage of Anna Livia; she once came out of the depths of her great father the Sea, and now she is turning again for home:

"Crossing the Bar"	Finnegans Wake
Sunset and evening star,	
And one clear call for me!	[*Far calls* 628.13]
And may there be no moaning of the bar,	[*moananoaning* 628.3]
When I put out to sea,	
But such a tide as, moving, seems asleep,	[*Yes, tid* 628.11–12]
Too full for sound and foam,	
When that which drew from out the boundless deep	
Turns again home.	[*you're turning* 627.2 / *Home!* 627.24]
Twilight and evening bell,	
And after that the dark!	
And may there be no sadness of farewell,	[*fforvell* 626.33]
When I embark;	

> For though from out our bourne of Time and Place
> The flood may bear me far,   [*bear it on me* 628.7 / *bearing down*
>   *on me* 628.9 / *Coming, far!* 628.13]
> I hope to see my Pilot face to face
> When I have crossed the bar.

She has crossed the bar, and she begins to feel the different currents and the colder waters of the sea and the different mix of fresh and salt waters. Like her waters, her mind is getting mixed as she says farewell to Dublin Bay and is drawn into the Irish Sea. A tragic note enters her flow as she tears herself from her family. HCE is changing away from her—he is now not the debased husband but the great sea itself. Or is she changing? Yes, she is getting mixed, both in her dimming mind and in the sea waters that are diluting her own fresh waters—"Brightening up and tightening down" (626.35–627.1).

She feels that her combined son, lover, and husband is turning from her for a new wife, his daughter from the hills. Anna at this point relinquishes her rights in the marriage, and rejoices in the young bride that is dancing merrily from the Wicklow hills to take her place, "coming" in all senses of the word, swimming in her moist hindmost (627.3–4). Anna imagines her young successor, in an echo of 202.26–27, as dancing the Italian saltarella all on her own (627.4–6). She pities HCE's old self that she was used to, and who is going to die with her. Now a younger man is there, as she dimly descries the blaze of her son on the horizon.

In one of the most tender and beautiful passages in the book, Anna pronounces a blessing on the new couple. She tries to overcome her misgivings about the new marriage, which she knows is going to wind up just like hers, and ends with a lovely reminiscence of her own early youth, as she "fell" from her little cloud for the young HCE (627.7–12). The rhythms of the phrases describing her peaceful life as a little cloud are exquisite. Linguists would describe the change of the vowels in "fails-feel-fall" as an ablaut series, and would demonstrate how the fall of the little drop is acted out iconically by the movements of the tongue in the mouth: there is first a rise to the hard palate in "fails" and "feel," and then a "fall" to the bottom of the mouth.

However, this lovely passage marks the last happy note in Anna Livia's monologue until the very end of the book. From now on, the cold waters of the ocean alter Anna Livia's nature drastically. She turns violently against all memories of her family life ashore, and turns again home to her pure cold father the ocean, and to her ladies-in-waiting, her awaiting rivers. She now loathes all the dirt of the city—Dublin is now only a dim memory on the western horizon—and all of the indignities inevitable in the raising of a family and the caring for an imperfect husband. As a river, she has cleaned all the dirt of the family and borne all the sewage of the city, but now the dirt of the family and the city are falling from her. She declares that she always did her best to hold the family together. She recalls her many troubles, and the lack of understanding she received from the family. Now, however, she turns away from them all, and all the burdens they laid upon her. She loathes their selfishness, and the way they treated her as a sewer that now is cleansing itself in the deep sea (627.13–20).

Joyce's technique is astonishing here. The punning style has changed from paronomasia, approximate marriage of meanings, to antanaclasis, exact overlay of opposing meanings. As the sunlight grows, Joyce's puns have become utterly transparent. In Anna's lament that she did her best when she was let, "let" means both "allowed" and "hindered." And in her reflection that if she goes, all goes, "goes" means both "dies" and "continues."

As Anna Livia is swept into the Irish Sea, she frees herself from HCE's power. She realizes that she has been bullied into submission by her husband. As we saw at the end of Haveth Childers Everywhere, his apparent love for her contained a strong element of force in the guise of love. HCE, in his male fantasy, assumed that ALP sincerely gloried in his authoritarian sadistic games, in the switching of his whip (554.8–9). She now understands that her visions of HCE's glory were always only illusions and that, far from being a great hero and a powerful raider, he is really only a petty criminal.

Her mental freedom is complete.[26] Now we see that she has always been deeply resentful of the male power of HCE. She now sees him, not as the giant Hill of Howth, but as only a bump on the far horizon (627.20–24).

As Anna Livia turns again home, her contempt for HCE comes out as a dismissal of his antecedents: She scents her home, the great sea, which she can only dimly descry (627.24–25). She is going blind—the phrase "as far as I can" should end with "see" (or "sea"), but she can barely see the blazing sun before her. However, she can clearly envisage her bold, bad, and bleary goddess companions, the great sea witches, who will greet her as an equal when she enters the ocean currents. She can see herself among them (627.27–28). Her two storm-goddess companions, her bridesmaids, the "pairanymphs" referred to earlier (548.2), are the two greatest rivers of the Eastern and Western Hemispheres, the Nile and the Amazon: "the stormies" (627.28–31). Amazia seizes her breast; the original Amazons were reputed to have amputated one breast in order to draw the bow with more ease. Niluna will snatch at her hair, as the lunar tides pull at the newly born sea goddess. Her goddess companions greet her with clashing cries and river names as all three spring to freedom. They tell her to renounce her land name, and they rename Anna Livia with an ocean name, Auravoles (627.31–33). She springs to be free, at this point at last abandoning the masochistic attachment to the land, the city, and her master, her husband.

The exhilarated cries of freedom change to a great tragic keening. Anna Livia is Life itself, and now Life itself is dying. Unlike the comic "funferals" of her husband, Anna Livia's farewell is filled with deep moaning sorrow. She feels intense loathing—the family that she loathes she loves at the same time, as the spelling indicates—but also loneliness and a huge sorrow, bitter as the ocean waters: "O bitter ending! I'll slip away before they're up. They'll never see. Nor know. Nor miss me" (627.33–36).[27]

The great keen begins: "And it's old and old it's sad and old it's sad and weary I go back to you" (627.36–628.1). The sounds of the rising vowels of the river's lament—bold, bad, bleary, old, sad, weary, cold, mad, feary—chime hauntingly with the moaning sea lament, and sweep Anna and the reader into the arms of the ocean, "moananoaning" (628.3). This word contains the name of the Irish sea god Mananaan, the son of Lir, and is probably accented as "moanánoaning," following the prosody of the poetic lines by AE (George Russell) in *Ulysses* (9.190–91):

> Flow over them with your waves and with your waters, Mananaan,
> Mananaan MacLir.[28]

Anna's cold mad feary father the ocean is a faery creature, a huge spirit miles and miles in extent—the Moyle is the sea between Ireland and Scotland. The mere sight of him, as she goes back to him, and the mixture of salt and silt in him, makes her faint with awe into his arms, those terrible prongs.

Danis Rose has discovered that the great last section, while apparently describing ALP's rush into her son-husband-father's arms, was once, at least in part, a description of Joyce's desire to be enfolded in his *mother's* arms. He writes:

> N57 (VI.B.47) was compiled specially for this section. Much more than any of the other notebooks, it contains original composition of many of the passages in the "Soft morning" finale. One particular passage in the notebook (p. 40) tells us, if we need to be told, that whilst ostensibly the piece describes a young girl rushing into the arms of her

father, it was also James Joyce, after so many years, reaching out for his mother:[29]

And it's old
and old it's
weary I go
back to you,
my cold father,
mother
And old it's sad
and old it's sad
& weary mother
I go back to you,
my cold father
my cold mad
father, my cold
mad bleary
father, yet the sight
of him makes me
saltsick and I
rush into your
arms

It is certainly true that Joyce was haunted to the end of his life by the death of his mother. As Stephen walks away from Eccles Street, having escaped the fate of a Son, he nevertheless hears in his heart the echo of the Prayer for the Dying that was intoned at his mother's deathbed:

Liliata rutilantium. Turma circumdet.
Iubilantium te virginem. Chorus excipiat. (17.1230–31)

This theme is reinforced in the *Wake*: as we have seen, one of the cries from the depths of the mound in III.3 comes very likely from Joyce himself, calling upon his dead mother to reinforce his faith and to enfold him in her arms (500.33). However, eventually, in his final version of the great final passage of the *Wake*, Joyce suppressed the impulse and separated the dying mother from the cold father, the ocean, and from her blazing son, both of whom are her lovers. The heat of the sun and the coldness of the ocean cause Anna Livia to rise up as a little cloud, to journey over the land to become the new Anna Livia.

There are some fascinating technical aspects in this great lament. The low, mid, and high vowel sounds in "old-sad-weary" and "cold-mad-feary" have been anticipated by "bold-bad-bleary" at 627.25–26. Joyce may have learned this device, the echoing of key phonemes over long stretches of sound, from Milton's "Lycidas," another poem about death at sea, which plays such a prominent part in *Ulysses*: Milton in "Lycidas" sets up a pattern of accented vowels, *ee/oh*, throughout the poem, leading up to the famous lines quoted in *Ulysses*:

> Weep no more, woeful Shepherds, weep no more,
> For Lycidas, your sorrow, is not dead,
> Sunk though he be beneath the watery floor.

Anna Livia's call to her lover has been heard, and she sees the arms of her father/husband/son rising up to embrace her through the misty incense of the soft morning (628.4–5). The "therrble prongs" that she desires and fears are the arms of her lover(s), but they are also holy incense bowls, thuribles. The terrible prongs evoke a powerful sunrise scene from Walt Whitman:

> To behold the day-break!
> The little light fades the immense and diaphanous shadows,
> . . .
> Something I cannot see puts upward libidinous prongs,
> Seas of bright juice suffuse heaven.[30]

Anna Livia can no longer see clearly, but she sees terrible "libidinous" prongs lifted up to clasp her. This is exactly the action of the last page of *Finnegans Wake*—the sexual junction of the sea and the river, the earth and the sky, providing the only complete sexual union of the book, which takes place in the silence between the last sentence of the book and the first.

The terrible arms of her lovers have dispelled her great sorrow at approaching death, and after begging for one or two moments more of life (628.5–6), she melts into a dream of love. She reminds herself of her old life; all her leaves have drifted from her, all but one. She bids the world hail and farewell on the last leaf of the book (M), and is borne along on the shoulder of her father/son/husband, on the ocean currents (628.6–9). It seems possible to me that the pathetic cry of the child to her father to carry her along to the toy fair (628.9) may be an actual plea made by Mary Joyce on her deathbed as she sank into delirium—another tribute by her son, James.

Though Anna Livia is all but blind at this point, she dimly sees the blazing sun before her, and the image generates an awe for her giant beloved. If she saw him bearing down on her, approaching like a great ship sailing under "white wings"—that is, with all sails spread to the wind—she would sink down in awe over his feet "humbly dumbly," only to worship him and to wash his feet (628.9–11). Her son the sun is blazing before her dim eyes, as bright as the archangel Michael: the risen sun is in the northeast angle of the morning sky, over Archangel in Russia. The sun is also the reassembled Humpty Dumpty, and also Jesus, with Anna playing the role of Mary Magdalen washing his feet. Anna no longer fears the terrible prongs, the arms of her lover. Her "washup" is also her worship of her great new lover.

The last magnificent sentences show Anna dying into her own love-death (628.11–15):

- She says yes to the tide: Anna's "Yes" echoes Molly's "Yes" at the ecstatic end of *Ulysses*. "Yes, it is time" is the meaning of the phrase.
- There's where first we made love: Like Molly remembering her first sexual encounter with Leopold, Anna's last thoughts are of her first lovemaking.
- We passed through the bushes then: And now she passes through the last tufts of seagrass before she leaves the land behind.
- Whish! A gull, gulls, four gulls: The gulls are the Four Old Men hovering around the entrance to the sea, as they did in the beginning of the Tristan and Isolde chapter, II.4, and as they hover around every harbor in the world.
- Coming far and near: The gulls are coming from all points of the compass; also "Coming, father" (Danish *far* = "father"). And finally, it seems that Tennyson's "one clear call" is heard by Anna Livia, who eventually answers "Coming, far!" (628.13). Anna Livia is coming to her father the sea, who is also her lover; "coming" bears the significance of orgasm, as it did at 194.22, where our turfbrown mummy first began to "come" to her sons.

"End here" marks the point of Anna Livia's death, which is a love-death, her Liebestod: as in the opera, it is sung at the seaside. It also marks the end of narrative TIME, as the failing strength of the Liffey is no longer carried along by the ebbing low tide, and she is swept into the cold sea. Then the first strength of the rising tide embraces her, and the first successful act of love begins.

- "Us, then": She is linked to her lover, the combined sun and sea, her son-husband Shaun, and her father, the ocean, one hot and the other cold.
- "Finn, again! Take": On the last leaf of the book (M), we hear the title of the book: Finnegan + *wake*; also, the exhortation by Anna Livia that Finnegan take her, carry her, and take her in love.
- But softly, remember me: Take me softly, kiss me softly, and remember me. "Remember me!" is Dido's great cry before her death, in Purcell's *Dido and Aeneas*.
- "Till thousendsthee": Here are three Danish words: *til* ("to"), *tusend* ("thousand"), *dyb* ("deep"). Anna Livia may be feeling the huge depth of the ocean awaiting her—to a depth of a thousand feet.
- Lips. The keys to heaven are given: A kiss, by which the great lover passes the key of life from his lips into Anna's. Just as Nora in Boucicault's *Arrah-na-Pogue* uses a kiss to pass her foster brother a key to freedom, here it is the beloved, Anna, who has died seven phrases before, who is given the key to life by her lover in a kiss.

The song "The Keys of Heaven," which we have heard before, recurs in fragmentary form at the very end of the book: "The keys to. Given!" (628.15). They form the irresistible invitation of Anna's son/husband/father to love-death and resurrection. These phrases resound throughout the last pages of *Finnegans Wake*: "I will give you the keys of heaven, / I will give you the keys of heaven, / Madam, will you walk? Madam, will you talk? Madam, will you walk and talk with me?"

"a way a lone a last a loved a long the" (628.15–16). The last phrase in the *Wake* is the most perfect iambic pentameter line ever penned, and it has, appropriately, like the final phrase of *Ulysses*, a feminine ending. The line also bears the rhythm of sex.[31] In addition, the words bear two of the three initials of Anna Livia.[32] The whole phrase may mean: "Away, alone at last—and loved!—along the river ran." Like Coleridge's Alph the sacred river, ALP runs "through caverns measureless to man," through the pathways of death and resurrection, back to Howth Castle and Environs, at the beginning of the book.

Then, with the phrase "a loved," the tide turns, the river begins to flow backward, TIME stops and SPACE commences, as the great act of love begins yet again.

Notes

Introduction

Earlier versions of some of the material in this introduction appeared in Epstein 2007.

I am grateful to Fritz Senn for suggesting the rubric "Time and Tide" featured in this chapter.

1. Joyce, *Critical Writings*, 144.

2. See, for example, Begnal 1988, Bishop, Burgess, Campbell and Robinson, Glasheen, Gordon, Hart 1962, McCarthy 1984, McHugh 1981, and Rose and O'Hanlon.

3. See Budgen, 11.

4. "There are, so to say, no individual people in the book—it is as in a dream, the style gliding and unreal as is the way in dreams. If one were to speak of a person in the book, it would have to be of an old man, but even his relationship to reality is doubtful" (Joyce, quoted in Vinding, 149).

5. Beckett, 7. Margot Norris (1990, 177) believes that Joyce provided the information to Beckett in time for the writing of Beckett's essay in *Our Exagmination*: "Beckett does produce a scheme for 'Work in Progress' that bears Joyce's imprimatur. . . . The 'lovegame of the children' [in Book II], included in Beckett's 1929 essay, was not begun by Joyce until 1930 and not completed until 1932 ([Ellmann 1982,] 796): Beckett could only have had this proleptic information on Joyce's authority."

6. The "swerve of shore and bend of bay" can only mean that the Liffey has swerved around the *outer* seashore and then moved *backward* with the incoming tide to the bend of Dublin Bay. The phrase cannot mean "the swerve of [the bay] shore and [the] bend of [Dublin] Bay."

7. Joyce himself denied that the *Wake* as a whole had a conventional chronological framework. Its action, he said, "is a simultaneous action, represented by the novel's circular construction. . . . Wherever the book begins it also ends" (Hoffmeister, 132). However, the *Wake* contains episodes, or whole chapters, that can be read as temporal sequences. Shem the Penman as the custodian of Time oversees the creation of the TIME episodes Books II, III, and part of IV, all of which occur in "the pressant" (221.17); see also 185.36–186.2.

8. Joyce to Harriet Weaver, May 21, 1926, *Letters*, 1:204. Mink points out that "*un-*

derstanding Vico is not necessary preparation or equipment for reading *Finnegans Wake*" (42). It seems to me that Joyce uses Vico and Bruno in the *Wake* in something of the way that he uses Homer in *Ulysses*—as the source of structural armatures for the book rather than as templates for the entire story.

9. Northrop Frye declares that "there seems relatively little concrete documentation for the influence of Bruno of Nola" (5). However, see Olson for a differing view of the importance of Bruno.

10. Peter Munz declared that "Joyce paid a lot of lip service to Vico but was not really a careful reader of *La Scienza Nuova*" (48). Attila Fáj called it "an illusion that the division of *Finnegans Wake* into four books is in strict correspondence with the Vichian stages" (27). Margot Norris (1976, 24–28) asserts that each Vichian stage is present in every phase of the plot of *Finnegans Wake*.

11. David Hayman has an explanation of the role of the Arranger in *Ulysses* and the *Wake*, which I have adopted, with reservations. Both Hayman and I find a relationship between darkness and the Arranger, but Hayman believes that the darkness must be natural darkness and not the darkness of the interior of buildings. He also believes that the Arranger operates to "feminize" the text, for which I see little evidence. See Hayman 1970, 88–104, 122–25, and Hayman 1990, 155–99. See also Kenner, 61–71, and the references in Hayman 1990, 155n, to the work of Bernard and Shari Benstock and of Patrick McGee.

12. Porter, 137. See also *Ulysses* 2.81–83.

13. Hart 1962, 70–71 and passim.

Chapter 1. Book I (*FW* 1–216)

1. The ten thunderwords, distributed unevenly between I, II, III, i, are at 3.15–17, 23.5–7, 44.20–21, 90.31–33, 113.9–11, 257.27–28, 314.8–9, 332.5–7, 414.19–20, 424.20–22. On the last thunderword, see my note 5 to Book III. See McLuhan for extended comment on the content of the thunderwords.

2. See *Ulysses* 7.882–83, 927–29.

3. See Ellmann 1982, 580–81; Rose, 96–97.

4. Joyce drew a detailed map of the battle in the *FW* notebooks in the British Library collection; see BL Add. Ms. 47482a, 91v.

5. Begnal has a different interpretation of some words in these messages: see Begnal 1984, 635.

6. The Davy's curse of "Basucker youstead!" (10.19) sounds very fierce but is of uncertain meaning. He may simply be calling the Willingdone a stranger: *Besucher* is "visitor" in German; *basökare* is "visitor" in Swedish.

7. The names of the boys have also been transmogrified: Tristopher has been transformed into Toughertrees, and Hilary has become Larryhill—trees and stones, which in the *Wake* symbolism represent Shem and Shaun, the growing and the static principles of Tree and Stone, combining to make TreeStone, or Tristan, the triumphant young lover who wins the bride away from King Mark, or Old Man Winter.

8. In a later story, the dummy is shown up as a tailor's daughter who will ultimately marry a misshapen Norwegian captain. The connection between the Prankquean fable and the later fable in II.3 of How Kersse the Tailor Made a Suit of Clothes for the Norwegian Captain is shown by the reference at the end of the Prankquean fable (23.10–11). The tailor's daughter sweetly unclo(the)ses herself to the Norwegian captain, who displays the horn of the Narwhal as the sign of his own sexual readiness.

9. "Treacle Tom" may derive from "Treacle Tommy," a baby who features in music hall songs by the great Lancashire comedian George Formby Sr. He was at the height of his fame in the spring of 1900, when Joyce and his father visited the London music halls.

10. Here is some meat for conspiracy theorists! The assassin of John F. Kennedy, Lee Harvey Oswald, was questioned by an FBI agent named James Hosty Jr.

11. He is buried with the "deaf and dumb Danes" (47.24) in Oxmanstown, a suburb of Dublin named for the Ostmen, the Scandinavian invaders, where there is a Deaf and Dumb Institute.

12. See Rabelais, *Gargantua et Pantagruel*, bk. 2, chap. 3. Joyce denied having read anything but "a little book called *The Language of Rabelais*," which may be the detailed and magisterial *La Langue de Rabelais* by Lazare Sainéan. However, Joyce may have been concealing his sources in his usual style, since in the Penelope chapter of *Ulysses* (18.487–91) the shocked Molly recalls Bloom introducing her to the works of a writer-priest, "Master Francois Somebody," who describes a woman's "bumgut" falling out during the delivery of a baby (Gargantua), which is described in *Gargantua et Pantagruel*, bk. 1, chap. 3.

13. McHugh provides some assistance here, but a number of the phrases are still opaque. I have done my best to supplement M, but I invite readers to join in the effort.

14. M takes us part of the way into the labyrinth, but there is still a great deal of work to do on this passage. I treat here only five passages whose explanation he omits.

15. *Dictionnaire du Français Argotique et Populaire*, ed. François Caradec (Paris: Larousse, 1977), s.v. "coin."

16. M identifies many Armenian words in this sentence which reinforce the meaning: *herou* ("far"), *kišer* ("night"), *zereg* ("day"), *pou* ("owl"), *gouyr* ("blind").

17. See Hart 1962, 200.

18. The phrase "ideal reader" may derive from *A Rebours*, by J. K. Huysmans, where it is used to describe the reader of the works of Mallarmé. Joyce was well acquainted with the works of Huysmans.

19. The name Hans the Curier is based on that of Hans Curjel, originally *intendant* of the Kroll Opera under Otto Klemperer. Curjel became director of the Corso Theater in Zurich in the 1930s.

20. Commas in 133.1 after "hauwck" and in 135.6 after "stripe" may be mistakes for semicolons. If this is true, then the huge question has 399 parts.

21. This event horrified Goethe, who included shocked references to it in the second part of *Faust*, in his Classical Walpurgisnacht, to indicate the evil parts of the glorious classical age. Here HCE, like most classical heroes, performs both heroic feats and prodigies of cruelty.

22. From Lewis Carroll, *Further Nonsense Verse and Prose*, ed. Langford Reed (London: T. Fisher Unwin, 1926), 114–16.

23. The *Wake* "takes place" during such a leap year. The significant number 732 appears a number of times in the book. Joyce may have thought that there were 732 high tides in a leap year (two a day on each of 366 days). However, high tides do not occur exactly twice a day but roughly every 12 hours 24 minutes. Therefore, there are actually about 708 high tides in a leap year.

Nevertheless, the number that Joyce used is significant: the book's rhythm is sexual, and contains one tide cycle, which also represents the lovemaking of the sea and the river. And 732 when "added" to another significant number, 432 (the traditional date of St. Patrick's arrival in Ireland), "adds up" in Joyce's mystical arithmetic to 1132, a number that also crops up frequently in *FW*. For lively speculation on Joyce's attachment to 1132, see Sterling.

24. See Epstein 1982b.

25. T. H. Huxley, "Scientific and Pseudo-Scientific Realism," *Nineteenth Century* 21 (February 1887): 191–205.

26. In a draft for Book I of the *Wake*, Joyce indicates that the three children of HCE and ALP have different speech rhythms: Issy speaks in trochees (/˘), Shaun in spondees (//), and Shem in pyrrhic feet (˘˘). However, Joyce seems to have abandoned this schema, since the passage quoted here is iambic, if anything.

27. She identifies the author as Dean Swift, "tame Schwipps" (146.11–12), but I find no such verse in the works of Swift.

28. M points out that the question is based on Thomas Campbell's poem "The Exile of Erin."

29. Note that the time of the eleventh question is "this evening"; even now, time is beginning to flow faintly.

30. Carl Vilhelm Strandberg (1818–1877), a poet and translator, wrote a biography of Byron under the pen name Talis Qualis.

31. "Javanese," besides being a French version of pig Latin (M), is actually Greek; Javan, a son of Japhet and a grandson of Noah, was the eponymous ancestor of the Ionian Greeks (the name Javan is a Semitic version of the Greek "Ion"). Jones is here insisting on his classical learning.

32. He may also be a moose, which, as the largest land mammal in the Western Hemisphere, would contribute largeness to the huge Mookse. It has been suggested that the Mookse is also Lewis Carroll's Mock Turtle. This would make the Gripes the other half of the team, the Gryphon.

33. "Shouldrups" contains a reference to Wyndham Lewis, who on June 21, 1935, made a radio broadcast on British writers, including Joyce, using the pseudonym "G. R. Schjelderup" (O'Keeffe, 355).

34. It is also, as a pineapple, the symbol of hospitality (N. Fargnoli, personal communication).

35. Stephen Dedalus, in *A Portrait*, is egged on by his schoolmates to imitate the rector's odd way of pronouncing this verse:

> —Go on, Dedalus, [Heron] urged, you can take him off rippingly. *He that will not hear the churcha let him be to theea as the heathena and the publicana.* (76.03)

36. From Roger Rosenblatt, *Anything Can Happen: Notes on My Inadequate Life and Yours* (Orlando: Harcourt, 2003), 108–9, and personal communication.

37. This discovery was made independently by John Gordon. Gordon (51) also credits Mark Troy's observation that at times we can see a composite figure made up of Osiris (Shaun) sitting on Set (Shem). See also McCarthy 1984, 561.

38. For a full treatment of the opposing characteristics of Shem and Shaun, see Epstein 1982a, 84–106.

39. For a complete treatment of this topic, see Epstein 1982a.

40. See Culleton, 134, quoting Ferris, 7, and Joyce, *Letters*, 1:54.

41. Joyce may have derived this idea from Carlyle: in *Sartor Resartus*, book 3, chapter 10, Carlyle describes the Dandy, the man who presents his Idea bodily in his suit of clothes.

42. This image resembles the central image in Kafka's "In the Penal Colony." A condemned prisoner is to be executed by having the nature of his crime scratched in his body by the needles of the machine. In theory, when the message is clear enough, the prisoner dies happy. The question in that story is whether or not the sufferings of human beings make any sense, or whether the universe is simply existentially cruel and meaningless. In Kafka's story, the answer is that human beings suffer meaninglessly. Joyce takes a more optimistic view: even though the artist is consumed during the creation of his work, the work is valid.

43. The word "dudhud," besides evoking ultimate death, also evokes the Hebrew word *shadud*, "stone dead."

44. "How do you do today, my dark sir?" and "How do you do today, my blond sir?" are, respectively, the addresses of Shaun to Shem and Shem to Shaun throughout the book.

45. The names Justius and Mercius may also represent the two families that produced James Joyce—the Joyces and the Murrays. Justius's fury at Mercius may owe a great deal to John Joyce's fury at his low-class inlaws, as reported by his son: "Weeping God, the things I married into!"

46. Robert Polhemus independently discovered the cinema-projector source for the "Quoiquoi-" sound, as well as the sound as the beginning flow of the river. See Polhemus, 310, 312, 313, 327, 333.

47. De Courcy, xxiii, 227–28.

48. See *Ulysses* 8.549, 8.778, 11.700, 15.3437.

49. By my count, in this section there are 121 children who receive these ambiguous presents from Life.

Chapter 2. Book II (*FW* 217–400)

1. Another source for the sorrowful fates of the decaying virgins in this section may be found in the story of Amalia, the unmarried, unattractive sister of the hero of Svevo's *Senilità*, who becomes an ether addict and dies a dreadful death.

2. "[T]he cluft that meataxe delt her" (229.21–4) refers to a traditional unsavory joke known to all naughty Anglo-American schoolboys. In fact, I myself heard that joke in the following form when I was in the Boy Scouts:

> Little Boy: (*having unexpectedly entered the bathroom and seen his mother in the bath*) Mommy, what is that between your legs?
> Mother: (*embarrassed*) Oh, that! Well, Sammy, you remember Daddy cutting the meat for dinner yesterday? Well, he accidentally hit me there with the meataxe.
> Little Boy: (*to himself*) Jeez, right inna cunt!

3. "Duffy and the Devil," in *Popular Romances of the West of England*, ed. Robert Hunt, 2nd ed. (London: John Camden Hotten, 1871). M notes a similar source in P. W. Joyce, *English as We Speak It in Ireland*, 2nd ed. (London: Longmans, Green, 1910).

4. Miguel de Cervantes, *Life and Exploits of the Ingenious Gentleman Don Quixote de la Mancha*, trans. Charles Jarvis (London, 1742), pt. 2, chap. 68.

5. There is a similar tale from France, a children's story about "La Princesse Tartine," Princess Bread and Butter.

6. *The Letters of Abelard and Heloise*, trans. Betty Radice (London: Penguin, 1974), 67–68.

7. The reference to jactitation at 243.8 conveys the notion that the marriage is not binding, from a legal point of view; jactitation is a false claim of marriage. This passage looks forward to III.4, where the legality of the Earwickers' marriage is argued as a case in commercial law (573.33–576.9), with a reference to the marriage and divorce of Henry VIII and Anne Boleyn ("Hal Kilbride" and "Una Bellina") and the creation of the Church of England, and therefore to the lack of authenticity of the Earwickers' marriage vows.

8. Joyce took great care with such passages. In Jacques Mercanton's "L'Esthétique de Joyce," on which Joyce collaborated, it is noted that the alteration of "tinct" to "tint" represents the gradual fading of the light, and the weakening sound of the evening bells of the churches (M).

9. See, for example, Shakespeare's phrase about Tarquin's "hot-burning will" in line 247 of *The Rape of Lucrece*.

10. Joyce picked up his knowledge of Antonio Venitiana's *Grand Grimoire* (1845) from A. E. Waite's *Book of Black Magic and of Pacts* (London, 1899). Joyce seems to

have misread his notes referring to the *Grand Grimoire*: in that text the four demons' names are spelled Agaliarept, Fleurety, Nebiros, and Lucifuge Rofocale.

11. See Atherton 1960, 27, 31, for a treatment of this theme.

12. Latin *Deipara*, mother of God.

13. Nora was the parent who was responsible for punishing the children; Joyce never intervened. See Ellmann 1982, 434.

14. Atherton 1960, 31.

15. Here we have an echo of Eliot's Sanskrit thunderwords in *The Waste Land*.

16. M notes that "krubeen" is Irish for pig's or sheep's trotter. W. H. Auden, in a play that he wrote with Christopher Isherwood, *The Dog Beneath the Skin, or Where Is Francis?* produces a similar evening prayer describing "The Two," who act as guardians of the household, so long as you obey their orders.

17. Joyce may ultimately have derived his knowledge of Kabbalism from the account in the eleventh edition of the *Encyclopaedia Britannica*, but he certainly encountered the Kabbalistic works of William Wynn Westcott and MacGregor Mathers among the Dublin Theosophists that he mocks in the Library scene in *Ulysses*.

18. At 262.1, "decemt" is not a misprint: "decent" is altered to include the initial of Michael the archangel rather than the letter *n* for the devil as Old Nick.

19. See Dante, *Inferno* 4.67–138.

20. Shem's purpose—to force Shaun to confront the facts of life by viewing his mother's genitals—is foreshadowed in this section, where Issy's immature genitals are hinted at in "pretty Proserpronette whose slit satchel spilleth peas" (267.10–11). Proserpina, the daughter of Ceres, has a "slit" from which liquid spills. See also 270.22–28.

Naughty Shem begins a limerick at 267L—"There was a sweet hopeful culled Cis"—but does not finish it. I think that, with the suggestive rhyme-word in mind, it is possible to hazard a complete version of the limerick:

There was a sweet hopeful called Ciss,
Who struggled to hold in her piss.
    But the sound of the spout,
    When at last it shot out,
Was much more like a roar than a hiss.

21. Joyce contributes a traditional bit of student humor at 269R, but this time in French. The Greek phrase *ouk elabon polin*, which speaks of the taking or destruction of a city, has been transformed into one-half of a French schoolboy joke: "Où qu'est la bonne Pauline?" (Where is the maid Pauline?). The Greek continues, *elpis alla gar ephe kaka*, yielding the French "Elle pisse à la gare et fait caca" (She pisses at the railway station and makes caca). I owe this information to John Hollander.

22. The period after BELLUM-PAX-BELLUM is probably an error.

23. The succeeding "betwain" introduces Mark Twain. "Mark" represents old King Mark, and "Twain" suggests *Huckleberry Finn*, evoked copiously at 283:24–32, which suggests that "HEC'll bury Finn," a previous murderous cycle.

24. See Epstein 1971, 156–73.

25. The brothers form a duet-singing team, much like the first earl of Dudley, who "died insane in 1833 after a lifetime of conversing with himself in two voices, one squeaky, one bass"; see A. N. Wilson, *The Victorians* (New York: Norton, 2003), 382.

26. What would Yeats have thought about Joyce's conflation of his name with the sentimental song "Dublin Bay"?

27. Plutarch reports, in section 55 of "Isis and Osiris" (133), that in the Egyptian city of Koptos, the statue of Horus holds Set's genitals in his hand.

28. Joyce derives HCE's stammer from that of Parnell (Ellmann 1982, 320).

29. For more on the *haka*, see Corballis. Corballis also comments (131–32) on the Willingdone Museyroom section.

30. Here Joyce may be echoing *The Brothers Karamazov*, in that the intellectual Ivan (= John = Shaun) is the moving spirit in the death of his father (with the assistance of the illegitimate Smerdyakov = Deathly James = Shem)

31. Joyce's anticipation is not unprecedented: H. G. Wells and the American writer Philip Wylie both wrote about atomic warfare before the weapon was unveiled. Wylie was investigated by the FBI.

32. Some elements of the verbal expression of the explosion derive from Virgil: *frago*- and *mole*- seem to come from the *Aeneid* IX.540–42: "tum pondere turris / procubit subito et caelum tonat omne fragore semineces. / ad terram, immani mole secuta" ["After Prince Turnus broke into the Trojan fortress], suddenly the tower collapsed, and the entire sky rang with the crash—halfdead men [fell] to the ground, and a huge mass of stone followed" (Schork, 138).

33. Robert Heinlein wrote an early story, "And He Built a Crooked House," about some people in California trying to live in a house that is a three-dimensional attempt at a tesseract. An earthquake collapses the house into a four-dimensional figure, with dramatic results. However, this story, published in February 1941 in *Astounding Science Fiction,* appeared too late to have influenced Joyce.

M has noted that the coach that attempted to get Louis XVI out of France in 1791 had six inside passengers. The connection here is certainly relevant, since the endangered king only made his position worse by his attempted flight. He was intercepted at Varennes, taken back to Paris, and accused of trying to join his brothers in Austria, who were raising an army to attack Revolutionary France. The king's position after the capture was completely untenable, and he was soon executed. HCE's position is increasingly dangerous, as he is becoming uneasily aware.

34. M notes that the BBC broadcast the voices of live nightingales from Surrey in 1924.

35. For an extended treatment of this topic, see Epstein 1971, 41–92 and passim.

36. For a treatment of the alpha-omega theme, see Epstein 1966, 259–67.

37. The Irish Republican Rory (Roderick) O'Connor was shot by the Free State government in retaliation for the killing of one Free State parliamentarian and the

wounding of another in 1922. This event may have started Joyce off on the creation of the brothers' quarrel, the core from which evolved the creation of the whole of the *Wake*.

38. Here the ship is named for the Nancy Hands pub at the gates of Phoenix Park, as well as for Nancy Hanks, the mother of Abraham Lincoln, the Great Emancipator, or Immensipater.

39. Atherton 1966, 56.

40. Is Joyce here anticipating a late-twentieth-century American slang term for sexual encounter, a "lube job"? Certainly the tendency of the Four Old Men to confuse the lovers with the parts of an automobile would suggest this interpretation! Cf. E. E. Cummings's poem "She / being brand-new."

Chapter 3. Book III (*FW* 401–590)

1. See *Ulysses* 1.57–62; 14.1025. The black nightmare figure may, however, be a recurring figure in the nightmares of Lucia Joyce. Roland Littlewood, in a letter in the August 13, 2004 issue of the *Times Literary Supplement*, reported catching a glimpse of the notes which had been taken by a therapist in the Northampton sanatorium where Lucia Joyce was being treated. Apparently, her dreams featured "constant references to a threatening black figure" (15).

2. *Henry IV, Part 2* III.ii.229.

3. He is, in addition, a perfect stage Irishman. Shaun's stagy appearance and huge appetite are both reminiscent of John McCormack's attire and personal habits. I owe a good deal of the material on John McCormack to the research of my student Patrick Reilly. For background on McCormack, see Foxall; McCormack; Scarry.

4. A saddlebag steak, a most impressive culinary creation, is a very thick steak cut longitudinally to form a pouch. The pouch is then stuffed with oysters and the steak is roasted.

5. This interpretation, though traditional, may not be accurate: the *-gringnir-* in the thunderword may be a mistake on the part of Joyce or a typist. There is no Scandinavian creature or thing named *Gringnir*, especially not one associated with Ragnarök. There is, however, a *Gungnir* intimately associated with the battle—Odin's spear. It plays a prominent part in the last battle, in which Odin slays the Fenris-wolf at the cost of his own life. The last thunderword would then have only 100 letters, and the 1,001 count referring to the Arabian Nights would be based on a misreading of handwriting.

6. However, not every act of violence in the works of Joyce has a sexual twist: the beating of Farringdon's little boy in "Counterparts," the pandying of Stephen in *A Portrait* and his beating by Heron, and Stephen's punch in the face delivered by Private Carr in "Circe" have no tinge of pleasure in them of any kind.

7. The "ring" addition to the word contains a sexual reference based upon the ending of *The Merchant of Venice*. It will be remembered that at the end of the play Gratiano says, "Well, while I live I'll fear no other thing / So sore as keeping safe

Nerissa's ring." In context it is clear that Nerissa's ring is her vagina. The reference is to Rabelais' story of Hans Carvel's ring: as long as he keeps it on his finger, his wife will be faithful to him.

8. See Finn Fordham (1997) for a comprehensive treatment of the topic of Joyce's dancing, especially 39, where he refers to Helen Joyce's reminiscences of Joyce dancing "wildly" with Lucia when she was institutionalized and then, upon his return home, relating the visit in tears.

9. For a full treatment of King David in the works of Joyce, see Epstein 1971, 104–41, 153, 156, 163, 170, 171, 173, 196n2, 201n109, 203n123.

10. For comment on these Latin phrases, see Schork, 200.

11. There is a story that the young Protestant Parnell was converted to Irish nationalism by seeing a troop of English yeomen whipping a young peasant, tied belly outward on a cart, until his guts hung out of his body.

12. Joyce had a Ségur telephone number (Ségur 95 20) when he lived at 2 square Robiac, 192 rue de Grenelle, in 1925–31 (*Letters*, 3:139, 168). However, it would be a favor to Joyceans if some French Joycean with connections with the French telephone authorities would check to see whose numbers these were when Joyce was writing this chapter.

13. *The Origin of Species*, chap. 4.

14. In 1940–42 the surrealist painter Pavel Tchelitchew painted a version of Joyce's Tree of Life. He named the painting *Hide and Seek*; it shows dozens of little children being born and playing in the branches and bole of a great tree. The painting, which is in the collection of New York's Museum of Modern Art, may have been influenced by this passage in the *Wake*.

15. Perhaps there is a reference here to the death of the Norse god Balder, who was killed (like Cock Robin?) by a spear tipped with mistletoe.

16. "Evovae" is an abbreviation formed by stringing together the vowels of *seculorum amen*, for the sequence of pitches sung in the final syllables of the Doxology at the end of a Gregorian chant.

In *Through the Looking Glass*, Alice and the twins Tweedledum and Tweedledee dance and sing "Here We Go Round the Mulberry Bush"—Alice says, "I don't know when I began it, but somehow I felt as if I'd been singing it a long long time." Joyce's Tree of Life section here resembles that scene.

17. "Dibble" is "penis" (M).

18. M gives a variant of the verse and calls it an Irish creation. However, I have seen an American version, originally a rowdy fraternity song, that differs slightly from M's version.

19. For a complete treatment of the figure of King David, see Epstein 1971, 101–41, 163, 170, 171, 173, 196n62, 201n109.

20. See Knuth, 58. Albert Camus' 1956 novel *La Chute* (The Fall), about the fall in self-esteem of a formerly contented attorney, is set in Amsterdam (A'dam), with the same implication of the Fall of Man.

21. For commentary on this passage, see Atherton 1974, 152–57, 260–61.

22. Hester Travers Smith, *Psychic Messages from Oscar Wilde* (London: Werner Laurie, 1924), 124. See also Atherton 1960, 48, and R&O 260–61.

23. For an extended treatment of Joyce's attitudes toward the city, see Begnal 2002, especially the essays by Ehrlich, Begnal, and Rabaté.

24. See Atherton 1960, 261.

25. Joyce borrowed these phrases from a description of Washington, D.C., in the *Encyclopaedia Britannica* (M).

26. Joyce may have heard about Kafka, and *The Castle*, from his contacts in Trieste and Zurich, especially Italo Svevo.

27. Ellmann 1982, 319, from a partial transcript at Cornell. For a more complete text, see *Buffalo Studies* 1, no. 1 (December 1964).

28. He describes the Dublin water system more fully in *Ulysses* 17.163–82.

29. Today there are twelve towns named Dublin in the United States, and one in Canada, plus several submunicipal Dublins.

30. Atherton 1960, 92; Gordon, 250–51.

31. It is also the world of Faulkner's "The Bear." In this long novella, the South is cursed from the moment the Chickasaw chief Ikkemotubbe starts to treat his land not as a resource, to be used, but as property, to be sold, to be surveyed and chartered.

32. However, the city of Salem mentioned at Genesis 14:18 may be Jerusalem.

33. Gordon declares that the cry of the child in III.4 is anticipated here, and "becomes the cry of a schoolgirl being whipped (horsewhipped?), 'for her pleashadure,' by her schoolmaster" (253). This interpretation is certainly in line with HCE's sexual preferences.

34. Gordon, 10. Gordon's detailed description of the house itself and its rooms are on 10–36.

35. The song was a favorite of Henry VIII; this is significant here because of the allusion to "Hal Kilbride" at 576.6. The settings by Byrd and Orlando Gibbons are in the Fitzwilliam Virginal Book. See Bauerle, 667, song number 1977, and Tindall (hereafter T), 287. The words of the song are copied—with one change, from "Shall I" to "Will you"—from a volume entitled *One Hundred Songs of England* (1914), which is possibly where Joyce found it.

36. Epstein 1984, 780–81.

37. M asserts that Kevin's "heartsleeveside" is on the right, where Jesus wears his Sacred Heart, rather than on the left. An argument in favor of this interpretation is that the right is traditionally the favorable side, and Kevin is the favorite son, while the left is the "sinister" side and Jerry is the less well-regarded son. This interpretation would also allow Jerry to sleep on his stomach to wet the bed. Another argument in favor of this arrangement is that an early manuscript notes that Kevin is lying on "the farther away," later altered to the "leeside," both of which versions suggest the right side of the bed (Hayman 1963, 253, reporting MS 47482 a 32 b) if the bed is oriented north-south and we are looking at the bed from the south.

However, this does not explain Jerry's "codliverside." The heart of most people is slightly on the left, and the liver is on the right. In one respect this does not make much difference: the boys would still have to be sleeping head to tail, for Jerry could not reach all the way down to grasp Kevin's heel if the boys were sleeping head to head.

38. Another enigma in this passage: a word has been omitted. The text reads as if it should be "with his [hand] lifted in blessing." If Kevin is lying on his stomach facing the foot of the bed, he may be resting his head on his left hand, and resting his right hand on the bottom bedpost of the bed, which would look as if he had lifted it in blessing. Any other arrangement is less likely, I feel; it is difficult to imagine Kevin's hand freestanding, that is, supporting itself for any length of time.

39. In the view of R&O (274–76), it is the Four Old Men who are talking in this section, and it is their own physical debility that they are lamenting.

40. These phrases are not from the Anglican hymn derived from the poem; the hymn does not include the first stanza, which contains the first phrase that HCE quotes.

41. There is an error in the printed text. See Hayman 1963, 257, quoting MS 47482 a, 5.

42. See Blish, 3–4, 54–56, 193, 227–28.

43. See 229.23–24 for another sexual meataxe.

44. Ellmann 1982, 432.

45. R&O suggests that HCE is performing *a tergo* (doggy-style) or possibly committing sodomy (282n). T suggests that ALP occupies the superior position in the bed (294). I tend to agree with Tindall.

46. The cockcrow develops from *FW* 583.25, 26, 26, 26, 30, 31, 32, 32, 32, 33, 33, 34; 584.2, 3, 4, 5, 5, 5, 6, 20, 21, 22–23, 25, 27, 28, 30–31, 33–34, to its climax at 585.3–5.

47. Richard Rodgers and Lorenz Hart, "I Wish I Were in Love Again."

48. See 585.26, 31, and T 295. Benstock (9, 64, 277) declares that the attempted sexual act is a failure, on the basis of ALP's statements that HCE "never wet the tea." Brown (69) and Glasheen (lxviii), on the other hand, deny HCE's impotence and interpret this line as meaning only that he used a contraceptive, the gummy article by the side of the bed. For Joyce's attitude toward contraception, see Brown, 7–8.

49. A poem by Goethe from his old age, "Phänomen," elucidates Joyce's different acts of love. It provides a scenario that links the "fogbow" at 403.6 with the rainbow in the mist in Book IV and the eventual successful act of love at the end/beginning of the book.

Chapter 4. Book IV (*FW* 591–628)

1. Note that Flaubert's right hand bore a scar from a burn.

2. The joke, also used in advertisements, is about a scruffy tramp writing a letter to Pears' Soap: "Dear Sir, Three years ago I used your soap, since when I have used no other." Recall a similar phrase in *Ulysses* as sung by a bar of soap: "We're a capital couple are Bloom and I / He brightens the earth. I polish the sky" (15.338–39).

3. The phrase "invasable blackth" may derive from An Invisible Black, a character in a burlesque of *Robinson Crusoe*, once played by a young W. S. Gilbert on July 31, 1867. See Jane W. Stedman, *W. S. Gilbert* (London: Oxford University Press, 1996), 40.

4. About twenty-six of the thirty-two counties are identifiable; why Joyce left out six of the counties is not clear, except perhaps that six counties were left as Northern Ireland after the partition. However, only some of the six counties omitted are those of Northern Ireland; County Dublin is one of those omitted. County Tipperary and County Cork are implicitly present.

5. For comment on the *m/n* symbolism, see Epstein 1966, 267.

6. Many hands have contributed to the analysis of this complex section: see Campbell and Robinson, 346–47; Dalton, 119–29; Evans, 6; Gordon, 266–67; Hodgart, 7–8; the relevant pages in M; and T 313–15. The first detailed treatment of the St. Kevin passage was made by M. J. C. Hodgart in 1957, in the first issue of the *James Joyce Review*. However, the most complete treatment of the passage, with close description of its careful organization as well as conjectures on errors of transmission of the typescript, was made by the late Jack P. Dalton, to whose "Advertisement for the Restoration," 129–37, the above analysis is heavily indebted.

7. Gordon, 267.

8. However, the bare name of Kevin occurs without qualification in the progression to canonization, at 605.18.

9. The word "dominions" or "dominations" is missing from the text, by error. See the exceedingly thorough analysis by Jack Dalton (121–25).

10. T 318 explicates this interchange as referring to Yeats's late poem "The Choice":

The intellect of man is forced to choose
Perfection of the life, or of the work,
And if it take the second must refuse
A heavenly mansion, raging in the dark.

11. M declares the phrase "And now the details" was a Radio Athlone expression.

12. Joyce, *Critical Writings*, 151.

13. By medieval Irish sumptuary laws, kings alone were allowed to wear seven colors; the sage, by appearing in a heptachromatic costume, is committing an act of lèse-majesté!

14. The gray robe is usually associated with the Franciscans, as the sage notes, but Patrick lived eight hundred years before the Franciscans were established.

15. *Shiro* (white) and *kuro* (black) astonishingly make up an exact equivalent for the Italian word *chiaroscuro*.

16. The whole scene resembles the biblical contest of Elijah and the priests of Baal in 1 Kings 18:17–40, with much the same result.

17. The name Joyce was actually derived ultimately from "Goth," but Joyce probably did not know this. See Epstein 1984, 781–82.

18. Rose asserts that Anna Livia's letter "is uncomfortable and incongruous" where it is placed. "It has frankly nothing to do with dawn or endings" (133). However, the clarity and completeness of the letter is appropriate to a sunlit scene. Anna Livia is flowing out to sea underneath her sleeping husband, and she argues for him before the "old Lord," the sun.

19. Clive Hart (1962, 200) believes that "Reverend" echoes the first word in the book, "riverrun," as "pronounced in popular Irish speech," so that the entire book is in fact ALP's letter to the Old Lord. However, R&O have noted that in the drafts of this section the word appears as "Revered," and is changed, perhaps by mistake, to "Reverend" in the galley proofs (326n13).

20. Molly speaks only 101 words before "Penelope"; Anna Livia speaks only 177 words in the course of the book.

21. "Glave" means sword, so perhaps she is asking him to draw back his foreskin.

22. Joyce's tribute to Flaubert, who also had a scar on his hand.

23. Ben Jonson was branded on the hand after killing a fellow actor.

24. As M notes, the Dublin Annals record that in 1839 there was a dreadful windstorm on the feast of the Epiphany.

25. The source of the song is identified in Hodgart and Worthington, 188, as Cecil Sharp, *Folk Songs from Somerset*. This is not accurate. The version of the song that is quoted in the *Wake* does not appear in the Cecil Sharp volume. Its true source is Lucy E. Broadwood and J. A. Fuller Maitland, *English County Songs* (London: Leadenhall Press, 1893), 32–33.

26. See Brivic, esp. 32–35, 107–16, for an account of her fight for freedom.

27. There may be an echo of an attempt at an Act of Contrition in "For all their faults" (627.34).

28. "Moananoaning" may also contain the Maori word for "sea," *moana*. See Ray Harlow, *Māori: A Linguistic Introduction* (Cambridge University Press, 2007), 33.

29. Rose, 134. The passage itself, from *JJA* VI.B.40, is quoted in its entirety. See R&O 319 for commentary on this passage.

30. "Song of Myself," section 24.

31. J. Mitchell Morse (70) discovered this independently.

32. See R&O 329. Here they note that Joyce insisted, in the last correction he ever made to the *Wake*, that the printer put the book's place of composition, Paris, on the last page—implying that "Paris" provided the last initial of "ALP."

Works Cited

Works by James Joyce

The Critical Writings of James Joyce. Edited by Ellsworth Mason and Richard Ellmann. New York: Viking, 1959.

Finnegans Wake. New York: Viking, 1939.

"The Holy Office." 1904. In *Critical Writings*, 149–52.

James Joyce Archive: A Facsimile of the Buffalo Notebooks. Edited by Michael Groden. 63 vols. New York: Garland, 1978.

Letters of James Joyce. Vol. 1. Edited by Stuart Gilbert. New York: Viking, 1957; issued with corrections, 1965.

———. Vols. 2–3. Edited by Richard Ellmann. New York: Viking, 1966.

A Portrait of the Artist as a Young Man. 1916. Edited by Chester G. Anderson. New York: Viking, 1968.

Stephen Hero. Edited by Theodore Spencer. 1944. New ed., with additional pages edited by John J. Slocum and Herbert Cahoon. Norfolk, Conn.: New Directions, 1963.

Ulysses. 1922. Edited by Hans Walter Gabler, with Wolfhard Steppe and Herbert Cahoon. New York: Garland, 1984.

Other Works Consulted

Alldritt, Keith. *W. B. Yeats: The Man and the Milieu*. New York: Clarkson Potter, 1997.

Atherton, James S. *The Books at the Wake: A Study of Literary Allusions in James Joyce's Finnegans Wake*. New York: Viking, 1960.

———. "Sport and Games in *Finnegans Wake*." 1966. In Dalton and Hart, *Twelve and a Tilly*, 52–64.

———. *The Books at the Wake: A Study of Literary Allusions in James Joyce's Finnegans Wake*. Rev. ed. Mamaroneck, N.Y.: Paul P. Appel, 1974.

Attridge, Derek, ed. *The Cambridge Companion to James Joyce*. Cambridge: Cambridge University Press, 1990.

Audoin-Rouzeau, Stéphane, and Annette Becker. *14–18: Understanding the Great War*. Translated by Catherine Temerson. New York: Hill and Wang, 2002.

Bauerle, Ruth, ed. *The James Joyce Songbook*. New York: Garland, 1982.

Beckett, Samuel, et al. *Our Exagmination Round His Factification for Incamination of Work in Progress.* Paris: Shakespeare and Company, 1929.

Begnal, Michael H. "The Language of *Finnegans Wake.*" 1984. In Bowen and Carens, *Companion,* 633–46.

———. *Dreamscheme: Narrative and Voice in "Finnegans Wake."* Syracuse: Syracuse University Press, 1988.

———. "*Finnegans Wake* and the Nature of Narrative." 1992. In McCarthy, *Critical Essays,* 119–28.

———, ed. *Joyce and the City: The Significance of Place.* Syracuse: Syracuse University Press, 2002.

———. "Hosty's Ballad in *Finnegans Wake*: The Galway Connection." In Begnal, *Joyce and the City,* 151–61.

Benstock, Bernard. *Joyce-Again's Wake.* Seattle: University of Washington Press, 1965.

Bishop, John. Introduction to *Finnegans Wake,* by James Joyce, vii–xxvii. New York: Penguin, 1999.

Blish, James. *A Case of Conscience.* New York: Ballantine, 1958.

Bowen, Zack, and James F. Carens, eds. *A Companion to Joyce Studies.* Westport, Conn.: Greenwood Press, 1984.

Brivic, Sheldon. *Joyce's Waking Women: An Introduction to "Finnegans Wake."* Madison: University of Wisconsin Press, 1995.

Brown, Richard. *James Joyce and Sexuality.* Cambridge: Cambridge University Press, 1985.

Budgen, Frank. "Resurrection." In Dalton and Hart, *Twelve and a Tilly,* 11–15.

Burgess, Anthony. *Re Joyce.* New York: Norton, 1965. Published in England as *Here Comes Everybody: An Introduction to James Joyce for the Ordinary Reader* (London: Faber and Faber, 1965).

Campbell, Joseph. *Mythic Worlds, Modern Words: On the Art of James Joyce.* Edited by Edmund L. Epstein. New York: HarperCollins, 1993.

Campbell, Joseph, and Henry Morton Robinson. *A Skeleton Key to "Finnegans Wake."* 1944. New ed. with a foreword by Edmund L. Epstein. Novato, Calif.: New World Library, 2005.

Christopher, Thomas. *In Search of Lost Roses.* New York: Summit, 1989.

Colum, Mary, and Padraic Colum. *Our Friend James Joyce.* Garden City, N.Y.: Doubleday, 1958.

Corballis, Richard. "The Provenance of Joyce's *Haka.*" *James Joyce Quarterly* 44, no. 1 (Fall 2006): 127–32.

Culleton, Claire A. *Names and Naming in Joyce.* Madison: University of Wisconsin Press, 1994.

Dalton, Jack. "Advertisement for the Restoration." In Dalton and Hart, *Twelve and a Tilly,* 119–37.

Dalton, Jack P., and Clive Hart, eds. *Twelve and a Tilly: Essays on the Occasion of the 25th Anniversary of "Finnegans Wake."* London: Faber and Faber, 1964.

Dante. *The Divine Comedy of Dante Alighieri.* Translated by Allen Mandelbaum. 3 vols. Berkeley and Los Angeles: University of California Press, 1980–82.

de Courcy, J. W. *The Liffey in Dublin.* Dublin: Gill and Macmillan, 1996.

Dickens, Charles. *Our Mutual Friend.* 1864. London: Oxford University Press, 1952.

Ehrlich, Heyward. "James Joyce's Four-Gated City of Modernisms." In Begnal, *Joyce and the City*, 3–17.

Ellmann, Richard. *James Joyce.* Rev. ed. New York: Oxford University Press, 1982.

———. *Oscar Wilde.* New York: Knopf, 1988.

Epstein, Edmund L. Review of *Joyce-Again's Wake*, by Bernard Benstock. *James Joyce Quarterly* 3, no. 4 (Summer 1966): 252–71.

———. *The Ordeal of Stephen Dedalus.* Carbondale: Southern Illinois University Press, 1971.

———. "James Joyce and the Body." In *A Starchamber Quiry: A Joyce Centennial Publication, 1882–1982*, edited by Edmund L. Epstein, 71–106. London: Methuen, 1982a.

———. Note on *Finnegans Wake* and Newman's *Apologia. A Wake Newslitter* 19, no. 1 (Spring 1982b).

———. "James Joyce and Language." In *Work in Progress: Joyce Centenary Essays*, edited by Richard F. Peterson, Alan M. Cohn, and Edmund L. Epstein, 58–69. Carbondale: Southern Illinois University Press, 1983.

———. "James Augustine Aloysius Joyce." 1984. In Bowen and Carens, *Companion*, 3–37, 781–82.

———. "The Content and Form of *Finnegans Wake*: With a Synopsis of the *Wake*." *Joyce Studies Annual* 2007: 1–20.

Evans, Simon. "The Ultimate Ysland of Yreland." *A Wake Newslitter*, Occasional Paper no. 2 (1993).

Evans, Stewart P., and Keith Skinner. *Jack the Ripper: Letters from Hell.* Phoenix Mill, Glos.: Sutton, 2001.

Fáj, Attila. "Vico's Basic Law of History in *Finnegans Wake*." In Verene, *Vico and Joyce*, 20–31.

Ferris, Kathleen. "Joyce's Untold Biography." *James Joyce Literary Supplement* 7, no. 1 (Spring 1993): 6–8.

Fordham, Finn. "*Finnegans Wake* and the Dance." *Abiko Quarterly* 9, no. 17 (Winter–Spring/Fuyu–Haru 1997–98): 12–41.

———. *Lots of Fun at Finnegans Wake: Unravelling Universals.* Oxford: Oxford University Press, 2007.

Foxall, Raymond. *John McCormack.* New York: Alba House, 1963.

Frye, Northrop. "Cycle and Apocalypse in *Finnegans Wake*." In Verene, *Vico and Joyce*, 3–19.

Gifford, Don. *"Ulysses" Annotated*. With Robert J. Seidman. 2nd ed. Berkeley and Los Angeles: University of California Press, 1988.

Glasheen, Adaline. *Third Census of "Finnegans Wake": An Index of the Characters and Their Roles*. Berkeley and Los Angeles: University of California Press, 1977.

Gordon, John. *"Finnegans Wake": A Plot Summary*. Syracuse: Syracuse University Press, 1986.

Hart, Clive. *Structure and Motif in "Finnegans Wake."* Evanston, Ill.: Northwestern University Press, 1962.

———. *A Concordance to "Finnegans Wake."* Minneapolis: University of Minnesota Press, 1963.

Hayman, David, ed. *A First-Draft Version of "Finnegans Wake."* Austin: University of Texas Press, 1963.

———. *"Ulysses": The Mechanics of Meaning*. Englewood Cliffs, N.J.: Prentice-Hall, 1970.

———. *The "Wake" in Transit*. Ithaca, N.Y.: Cornell University Press, 1990.

Hodgart, Matthew. "The Earliest Sections of *Finnegans Wake.*" *James Joyce Review* 1, no. 1 (1957): 3–18.

Hodgart, Matthew J. C., and Mabel P. Worthington. *Song in the Works of James Joyce*. New York: Temple University Publications/Columbia University Press, 1959.

Hoffmeister, Adolph. "Portrait of Joyce." In Potts, *Portraits of the Artist in Exile*, 127–36.

Joyce, Stanislaus. *My Brother's Keeper: James Joyce's Early Years*. Edited by Richard Ellmann. Preface by T. S. Eliot. London: Faber and Faber, 1958.

———. *The Complete Dublin Diary of Stanislaus Joyce*. Ithaca: Cornell University Press, 1971.

Keble, John. *The Christian Year: Thoughts in Verse for the Sundays and Holydays throughout the Year*. 2 vols. Oxford: J. Parker, 1827.

Kenner, Hugh. *Ulysses*. London: George Allen & Unwin, 1980.

Knuth, Leo. "More Dutch in *Finnegans Wake.*" *A Wake Newslitter* 8, no. 4 (August 1971): 54–62.

Lernout, Geert. "Time and the *Wakean* Person." In *Finnegans Wake: "teems of times,"* edited by Andrew Treip, 119–25. Amsterdam: Rodopi, 1994.

Lewis, Wyndham. *The Art of Being Ruled*. London: Chatto and Windus, 1926.

McCarthy, Patrick A. "The Structures and Meanings of *Finnegans Wake.*" In Bowen and Carens, *Companion*, 559–632.

——— ed. *Critical Essays on James Joyce's "Finnegans Wake."* New York: G. K. Hall, 1992.

McCormack, John. *John McCormack: His Own Life*. 1918. New York: Vienna House, 1973.

McHugh, Roland. *The "Finnegans Wake" Experience*. Berkeley and Los Angeles: University of California Press, 1981.

———. *Annotations to "Finnegans Wake."* 3rd ed. Baltimore: Johns Hopkins University Press, 2006.

McLuhan, Eric. *The Role of Thunder in "Finnegans Wake."* Toronto: University of Toronto Press, 1997.

Mink, Louis O. "Reading *Finnegans Wake*." In McCarthy, *Critical Essays*, 34–47.

Morse, J. Mitchell. "On Teaching *Finnegans Wake*." In Dalton and Hart, *Twelve and a Tilly*, 65–71.

Munz, Peter. "James Joyce: Myth-Maker at the End of Time." In Verene, *Vico and Joyce*, 48–56.

Norris, Margot. *The Decentered Universe of "Finnegans Wake": A Structuralist Analysis*. Baltimore: Johns Hopkins University Press, 1976.

———. "*Finnegans Wake*." 1990. In Attridge, *Cambridge Companion*, 161–84.

O'Keeffe, Paul. *Some Sort of Genius: A Life of Wyndham Lewis*. London: Cape, 2000.

Olson, Kristen L. "The Pluralities of 'Parole': Giordano Bruno and the Cyclical Trope of Language in *Finnegans Wake*." *James Joyce Quarterly* 42/ 43 (Fall 2004–Summer 2006), 253–68.

Plutarch. *Moralia*. Translated by Frank Cole Babbitt. Vol. 5. Cambridge, Mass.: Harvard University Press, 1957.

Polhemus, Robert M. *Comic Faith: The Great Tradition from Austen to Joyce*. Chicago: University of Chicago Press, 1980.

Porter, Katherine Anne. "I Saw Joyce Only Once." In *James Joyce: Interviews and Recollections*, edited by E. H. Mikhail, 136–37. New York: St. Martin's, 1990.

Potts, Willard, ed. *Portraits of the Artist in Exile: Recollections of James Joyce by Europeans*. Seattle: University of Washington Press, 1979.

Purdy, Strother B. "Is There a Multiverse in *Finnegans Wake*, and Does That Make It a Religious Book?" *James Joyce Quarterly* 36, no. 3 (Spring 1999): 587–602.

Rabaté, Jean-Michel. "Eternest cittas, heil!: A Genetic Approach." In Begnal, *Joyce and the City*, 182–98.

Rose, Danis. *The Textual Diaries of James Joyce*. Dublin: Lilliput Press, 1995.

Rose, Danis, and John O'Hanlon. *Understanding "Finnegans Wake": A Guide to the Narrative of James Joyce's Masterpiece*. New York: Garland, 1982.

Scarry, John. "Shem and Shaun: John McCormack in the Works of James Joyce." Ph.D. diss., New York University, 1969.

Schork, R. J. *Latin and Roman Culture in Joyce*. Gainesville: University Press of Florida, 1997.

Stephens, James. *Irish Fairy Tales*. New York: Macmillan, 1920.

Sterling, Clarence R. "1132 A.D. & St. Brighid." 1998. www.finneganswake.info/st-bridget/bridget.htm.

Tindall, William York. *A Reader's Guide to "Finnegans Wake."* New York: Farrar, Straus and Giroux, 1969.

Troy, Mark L. "Mummeries of Resurrection: The Cycle of Osiris in *Finnegans Wake*." Ph.D. diss., Uppsala University, 1976. At rosenlake.net/fw/Troy-Mummeries/troybook.htm.

Tully, Nola, ed. *Yes I said yes I will Yes: A Celebration of James Joyce, "Ulysses," and 100 Years of Bloomsday*. New York: Vintage, 2004.

Verene, Donald Phillip, ed. *Vico and Joyce*. Albany: State University of New York Press, 1987.

Vinding, Ole. "James Joyce in Copenhagen." In Potts, *Portraits of the Artist in Exile*, 139–52.

Wallace, David Foster. *Everything and More: A Compact History of* ∞. New York: Norton, 2003.

Wolff, Geoffrey. *The Art of Burning Bridges: A Life of John O'Hara*. New York: Knopf, 2003.

Index

Abelard, 114, 115
Act of Contrition, 302n27
Adam and Eve, 202–3
AE (George Russell), 284
Aeschylus, 198
Ahab, Captain, 78
Alice, 72, 298n16
Alph the sacred river (Coleridge), 288
Ananta (serpent), 253
Anaxagoras, 129
Arabian Nights, 150
Archdruid and St. Patrick, 260–67
Aristotle, 128
Arne, Thomas, 153
Arranger, 16–17, 290n11
Arthur, 276
Astaire, Fred, 204
atomic warfare, 296n31
Auden, W. H., and Christopher Isherwood:
    *The Dog Beneath the Skin, or Where Is
    Francis?*, 295n16
Augustine, St., 252
Avicenna, 252

"Babes in the Woods," 274
Bach, Johann Sebastian, 149
Balder, 298n15
Balzac, Honoré de, 88
Barnum and Bailey, 47
Baudelaire, Charles, 212
Beaverbrook, Lord, 47
Becket, St. Thomas à, 255
Beckett, Samuel, 7, 298n5
Beethoven, Ludwig van, 149
Begnal, Michael, 289n2, 290n4
Beit, Sir Alfred, 45
Bellini, Vincenzo, 149
Benstock, Bernard, 290n11

Benstock, Shari, 290n11
Bérard, Victor, 50
Bergson, Henri, 75
Berkeley, Bishop, 128, 252
Bible, 268
Bishop, John, 289n2
Blake, William, 220, 235, 258
Blish, James: *A Case of Conscience*, 241
Bloom, Leopold, 110, 220, 278, 287
Bloom, Molly, 276, 278, 287, 302n20
Book of Common Prayer, 124
Book of the Dead, The, 136, 160
Book of Kells, The, 55, 56
Boucicault, Dion, 193, 288
Bowdler, Reverend Thomas, 184
Brahe, Tycho, 128
Brahma, 253
Brian Boru, 141, 216
Brillat-Savarin, Anthelme, 44
Browning, Daddy, 44–45
Bruno, Giordano, 14–15, 134, 193, 263, 290n9
Buckley the Archdruid, 264–67
Budgen, Frank, 103, 242, 256, 289n3
Burgess, Anthony, 289n2
Burke, Edmund, 123, 136
Burns, Robert, 81
Byrd, William, 230
Byron, George Gordon, Lord, 87, 160, 176,
    187, 235

"Cadet Roussel," 273
Campbell, Joseph, 289n2
Campbell, Thomas, 292n28
Camus, Albert, 298n20
Carlyle, Thomas, 141, 293n41
Carroll, Lewis, 68, 282n22
Caruso, Enrico, 205
Casement, Sir Roger, 119
Chart, D. M., 250

Chaucer, Geoffrey, 61–62, 168
Chevalier, Albert, 52
Cicero, 155
Citizen Kane, 99
Clongowes Wood College, 98
cockcrow, 300n46
Coleridge, Samuel Taylor, 46, 288
Crampton, Sir Philip, 217
creation, 123–24
Cromwell, Oliver, 19, 46, 195
"Crossing the Bar" (Tennyson), 281–82
Culleton, Claire, 293n40
Cummings, E. E., 297n40
Curjel, Hans, 291n15

Dante, 62, 129, 147, 184, 266, 275, 295n19
Darwin, Charles, 200, 201, 202
David, King, 186
David Copperfield, 181
De Courcy, 293n47
Defoe, Daniel, 217
Democritus, 129
Descartes, Réné, 126–27, 138
Dickens, Charles, 171–72, 181, 216
"Dido and Aeneas" (Purcell), 288
Dilke, Charles, 44
Diogenes, 121
Disraeli, Benjamin, 217
Don Giovanni, 187
Don Quixote, 112
Dooley, Mr., 188
Dorian Gray, 88–89
Dostoevsky, Feodor, 296n30
Dublin (towns named), 60, 224, 299n29
Dublin, Ireland: electrification of, 224; and
    third question, 64
Dudley, First Earl of, 296n25

Ecclesiastes, 218
Edgeworth, Maria, 215
Einstein, Albert, 75
Elijah and the Prophets of Baal, 301n16
Eliot, T. S.: *The Waste Land*, 122, 148, 212, 220,
    243, 244, 249, 268, 295n15
Ellmann, Richard, 140, 141–42, 207, 289n5,
    290n3
Emerson, Ralph Waldo, 169
Empedocles, 129
Epiphany windstorm, 302n24

Epstein, E. L., 292n24, 293n38, 293n39
Escoffier, Auguste, 44
Euclid, 133
Evovae, 298n16

Fáj, Attila, 290n10
Falstaff, 141, 157, 167
Fargnoli, Nicholas, 293n34
Faulkner, William, 299n31
Fenris wolf, 293n40
Field, Eugene, 123, 190
Field, John, 149
Finnegan family crest, 249
Finnegans Wake: characters or types in, 4–5,
    5–7; events in, 3–7; Joyce's notebooks on,
    284–85, 290n4, 302n29; language of, 15–18;
    as narrative fiction 4; outline of, 18–24; and
    the physical world, 2–3; time and space,
    7–9, 9–12; Time and Tide and the River,
    12–14
—Books and chapters: Book I, 25–101; Book
    I.1, 26–37; Book I.2, 37–39; Book I.3,
    39–48; Book I.4, 48–51; Book I.5, 51–57;
    Book I.6, 57–82; Book I.7, 82–91; Book I.8,
    91–101; Book II, 102–63; Book II.1, 103–25;
    Book II.2, 125–39; Book II.3, 139–57; Book
    II.4, 158–63; Book III, 164–246; Book III.1,
    164–78; Book III.2, 178–89; Book III.3,
    189–228; Book III.4, 228–46; Book IV,
    247–88
—Characters physically described: ALP/
    Anna Livia Plurabelle, 49, 63–64, 91–101,
    204, 233, 270–73, 302n18, 302n20; custom-
    ers, 67; Four Old Men, 152, 287, 300n35;
    HCE/Finn MacCool, 57–63, 166, 204, 233,
    236; Issy, 71–73; Jerry, 299n37, 300n38;
    Kate the Slop, 67; Kevin, 299n37, 300n38,
    301n6, 301n8; maggies, 68; Sackerson 66;
    Shaun, 82–91, 167–68, 185, 204; Shem,
    73–74, 82–91, 204–5, 235; Tristopher and
    Hilary, 290n7; universe (collideorscape),
    69–70
—Fables and episodes: Adam, 209–10;
    Ballad of Persse O'Reilly, 38–39; BBC An-
    nouncer, 209–11; Book-Burning, 184; The
    Starchamber Quiry, 189–212; The Brain
    Trust, 208–9; Burrus and Caseous, 79; Butt
    and Taff, 165; Church and State on Marital
    Rights, 240–42; Communicator (Oscar

Wilde), 211–12; The Dance of the Rainbow Girls Through Time, 109; The Envelope, 175–76; The Garden of Eden, 199–205; A Geometry Lesson, 125–39; Haveth Childers Everywhere, 212–28, 283; How Buckley Shot the Russian General, 143–48; Kersse the Tailor and the Norwegian Captain, 139–42, 291n8; The Lecture of Professor Jones, 74–81; Maxims, 180–82, 183; "The Mime of Mick, Nick and the Maggies," 103–25; The Mookse and the Gripes, 76–79, 292n32; Muta and Juva (Mutt and Jute), 32, 262–63; The Ondt and the Gracehoper, 172–75; Prankquean Fable, 35–36; The River of Time, 90–91; "A Royal Divorce," 101–246; The Salmon of Wisdom, 206–7, 278; Soft Morning, City!, 273–88; The Song of the Nightingale, 148–51; The Stone, 199–200; Three Stained-Glass Windows, 252–69; The Tree, 200–202; The Washers at the Ford (The Washerwomen), 93–101; Willingdone Museyroom, 18–33

"Finnegan's Wake" (song), 260
Finn's Hotel, 205–6
Fitzgerald, John Francis "Honey Fitz," 98
Fitzstephen, James Lynch, 221
Flaubert, Gustave, 300n1, 302n22
Flying Dutchman, 275
Francis, St., 168
Franciscan robes, 301n14
Frye, Northrop, 290n9

Gainsborough, Thomas, 128
Galliffet, Gaston Alexandre August, Marquis de, 216
Geisha, The (Sydney Jones), 52
Gell-Mann, Murray, 158
Georgius, 46
Gibbon, Edward, 201
Gilbert, W. S., 301n3
Glasheen, Adaline, 289n2
Glinka, Mikhail, 149
Gluck, Christoph Willibald, 149
Goethe, Johann Wolfgang von, 132, 292n21, 300n49
Gogarty, Oliver St. John, 166, 174
"Goldilocks," 271
Goldsmith, Oliver, 123
Gomez, 221

"Goody Two-Shoes," 274
Gopis, 255
Gordon, John, 228, 289n2, 293n37
Gounod, Charles: Faust, 181
Grace, W. G., 47
Grand Grimoire, 121
Graves, Robert, 133
Gringnir, 297n5
Guido D'Arezzo, 128
Guinness, 227, 249; Lords Ardilaun and Iveagh, 174
Gunas (Buddhism), 151, 152

Haines, 166
Hamlet, 120, 163, 276
Harmsworth Press (Carmelite House), 99
Hart, Lorenz, 245, 289n2, 290n13, 291n17; and Richard Rodgers, 300n47
Hawthorne, Nathaniel, 152
Haydn, Franz Josef, 149
Hayman, David, 165, 171, 290n11
Heinlein, Robert, 296n33
Heisenberg uncertainty principle, 269
Henry II: second city charter by, 219
Heraclitus, 129
Hermann und Dorothea (Goethe), 132
high tides in leap-year, 292n23
Hoffmeister, Adolph, 289n7
Hogarth, William, 81
Holinshed: Chronicles, 214
Holmes, Oliver Wendell, 181
Homer, 129
Horace, 129, 227
Horus, 165
Howth, Earl of, 268, 277
Howth, Hill of, 279
Huckleberry Finn, 271
Hugo, Victor, 216
Huguenots, Les (Meyerbeer), 144
Humpty Dumpty, 251, 270, 287
Huxley, Thomas Henry, 69–70, 292n25
Huysmans, Joris-Karl, 291n18

Ibsen, Henrik, 156, 213, 215, 240, 278
Ireland, provinces of, 64–66
Irish counties, 301n4
Irish Sea, 279
Island Bridge, 279
Isolde of the White (Lovely) Hands, 192, 193

"Jack and the Beanstalk," 271
Jack the Ripper, 149
Jacob and Esau, 278
jactitation, 294n7
James, Henry: "The Lesson of the Master," 214
Javan (Ion), 292n31
Jesus, 287
Johnson, Pussyfoot, 227
Jones, Casey, 151, 152
Jonson, Ben, 302n23
Joyce, James: name of, 301n17; pleading for forgiveness by his mother, in his own voice, 198
—Writings: "The Dead," 297n6; Dubliners, 109, 179, 245; Exiles, 166; "The Holy Office," 264; Letters, 8, 100, 103, 165, 179, 289n8, 293n40, 298n12; "A Portrait of the Artist" (essay), 97, 126; A Portrait of the Artist as a Young Man, 86, 111, 126, 151, 165, 178, 179, 263, 238, 293n35, 297n6; Stephen Hero, 5, 188. See also Ulysses; Finnegans Wake
Joyce, John (father), 293n45
Joyce, Lucia (daughter), 297n1, 298n8
Joyce, Mary (mother), 286
Joyce, Nora (wife), 272, 295n13
Joyce, Stanislaus (brother), 173, 188
Joyce family name, 267
Justius and Mercius, 293n45

Kabbala (Ain Soph), 127, 128
kabbalism, 295n17
Kafka, Franz, 216, 293n42, 299n26
Kant, Immanuel, 252, 264
Kavanagh, Patrick: The Great Hunger, 188
Keble, John: "Morning" (hymn), 239–40
Kendal Bushe, Charles, 123
Kenner, Hugh, 290n11
Kevin, 251–60
"Keys of Heaven, The," 280–81, 288
Khayyam, Omar, 151
King Lear, 179, 255
Krishna, 255

Lamarr, Hedy, 183
Lavater, Johann Kaspar, 128
Lawrence, D. H., 114, 184; "The Man Who Died," 243; "Tickets Please!" 181–82
Leary, High King (Laoghaire), 260, 262–63

Le Monade, Prince, 113
Lewis, Wyndham, 74, 293n33
Liebestod (Wagner), 287
Life for the Czar, A (Glinka), 144
limerick, 295n20
Lincoln, Abraham, 297n38
Lind, Jenny, 149
Livy, 128
Louis XVI, 296n33
Lucan (poet), 129
Lucan, Earl of, 275
"Lycidas," 286

Macbeth, 120
MacDowell, Gerty, 185
Mallarmé, Stéphane: "L'Après-Midi d'un Faune," 121, 291n18
Malleus Maleficarum, 121
Mananaan MacLir, 284
"Man Who Broke The Bank at Monte Carlo, The," 245
Maori (haka), 143, 302n28
Mark, King, 192, 193
Mary Magdalen, 287
matter, hostility toward, 169
McCarthy, Patrick, 289n2, 293n37
McCormack, John, 168, 297n3
McGee, Patrick, 290n11
McHugh, Roger, 289n2, 291n13
McLuhan, Marshall, 290n1
Melville, Herman, 184
Mercadante, Saverio, 149
Mercanton, Jacques, 249, 294n8
Merchant of Venice, The, 297n7
Meyerbeer, Jacques, 149
Mezzofanti, Giuseppe, 128
Mikado, The ("Tit Willow"), 149
milk delivery, 259
Milligan, Alice, 61
Milton, John, 81, 286
Mink, Louis, 289n8
Morse, J. Mitchell, 302n32
Mozart, Wolfgang Amadeus, 149
Muhammad, 277
Mulligan, Buck, 254
Mullingar House, 228
Munz, Peter, 290n10
Muraveyev, "Hangman," 216
"My Old Dutch," 52

Napoleon, 216, 217
Nazis, 156, 184
Newman, John Henry, 69
news agencies, 249
Nicholas Nickleby, 125
Nicholas of Cusa, 129
Nightingale, Florence, 149
nightingales, 296n34
Nijinsky, Vaslav, 204
nominalism and realism (Aquinas), 5
Norma (Bellini), 150
Norris, Margot, 289n5, 290n10

O'Connell, Daniel, 159, 207
O'Connor, Rory (brothers' quarrel), 296n37
O'Conor, King Roderic, 157
O'Keeffe, Paul, 292n33
Old Curiosity Shop, The, 181
Olson, Kristen, 290n9
O'Malley, Grace (Granuaile), 34
Osiris, 133
O'Toole, St. Laurence, 251, 255, 256, 267–69
ouk elabon polin, 295n21
Our Mutual Friend, 171–72, 181
Ovid, 129

Paradise Lost, 271
Parnell, Charles Stewart, 191, 192, 198, 209,
    264, 296n28, 298n11
Pater, Walter, 52
Patrick, St., 169, 175, 191, 192, 197, 209, 256,
    257, 260–67
Paul, St., 275
Pears' Soap, 249
Pergolesi, Giovanni, 149
Philistinism, 182–87
Piedigrotta, 205
Plato, 129
Playboy of the Western World, The (Synge), 221
Plutarch, 296n27
Poincaré, Henri, 137
Polhemus, Robert, 293n46
Porter, Katherine Anne, 17, 290n12
Pound, Ezra, 54, 60, 78
Princesse Tartine, La, 294n5
Prout, Father: "Bells of Shandon," 63
puns (paronomasia and antanaclasis), 18
Purcell, Henry, 288
"Puss in Boots," 274

Quinet, Edgar, 113

Rabelais, 41, 291n12, 298n7
Radetsky von Radetz, Joseph, 216
Radio Athlone, 301n11
"realism" and stage properties, 228, 231
regifugium, 40
Rembrandt van Rijn, 166
Revelation, Book of, 250
"Reverend," 302n19
Richard III, 47, 141, 156, 220
Riders to the Sea (Synge), 100
Robinson, Henry Morton, 289n2
Robinson Crusoe, 274
Rockefeller, John D., 46
Rogers, Ginger, 204
Rose, Danis, 290n3
Rosenbach, A.S.W., 98
Rosenblatt, Roger, 293n36
Rossini, Gioacchino, 149, 170, 188
Rowntree, Seebohm B., 219, 220
Ruhmkorff, H. D., 118
Rumpelstiltskin, 127

sadomasochism, 178–80, 241, 283, 299n33
Saladin, 129
Salem, 299n37
Salome, 149
Sarsfield, Patrick, 275
Savonarola, Girolamo, 184
Scheherazade, 278
Schultz, Dutch, 257–58
Scott, Sir Walter, 81
Sebastian Melmoth (Wilde), 211
Sechseläute (Angelus), 100, 145–46
Senilità (Italo Svevo), 294n1
sentimentalism, 231
Sermon on the Mount, 218
serpent, 202
Set, 133
Seth, 133
sexual attitudes and sexual failure, 300n45,
    300n48
Shakespeare, William, 81, 120, 123, 299n9
Shaw, George Bernard, 97, 127, 136
Shelley, Percy Bysshe, 212, 265
Sheppard, Jack, 215
Sheridan, William Brinsley, 123
ship of Theseus, 62–63

Sinbad the Sailor, 275
Sitric Silkyshag, 215
"Sleeping Beauty," 271
Socrates, 129
Solness, Master Builder, 278
Solomon, 218
speech rhythms, 292n26
Steele, Richard, 136
Stella, 193
Stephens, James, 3
Sterne, Laurence, 123, 136
Stevens, Wallace, 169
Stonehenge, 250
Strandberg, C. V.: "Talis Qualis," 292n30
"Stride la vampa" (*Il Trovatore*), 171
Sullivan, Sir Edward, 55, 56
Sullivan, John, 106
sumptuary laws, 301n13
Sunlight Soap, 250
Svevo, Italo, 294n1
Sweeney, King, 201
Swift, Jonathan, 123, 136, 172, 179, 191, 193, 197,
    209, 235, 292n27
Synge, John Millington, 100, 123, 221

Taglioni, Maria, 205
Tawney, R. H., 242
Tchelitchew, Pavel, 298n14
telephone numbers, French, 298n12
Tenducci, Giusto Ferdinando "Senesino," 153
Tetley's tea, 260
Thales, 129
Thomas, Dylan, 119
Tindall, William York, 212
Tom Tit Tot, 127
Top Hat, 204
Tosca (Puccini): "E lucevan le stelle," 177
Toulouse-Lautrec, Henri de, 173
transaccidentated, 88
Tree of Life (Darwin), 200
Tristan, 191, 192, 193, 196, 197, 209
Tristan und Isolde (Wagner), 154, 244
Tristram Shandy (Sterne), 274
Trovatore, Il (Verdi), 171, 187
Troy, Mark, 293n37
Twain, Mark, 295n23

Ulysses, 72, 76–77, 86, 87, 94, 104, 105, 110, 141,
    161, 166, 169, 179, 180, 183, 194–95, 196, 203,
    205, 207, 212, 217, 239, 241, 244, 254, 260,
    264, 284, 285, 287, 290n2, 291n12, 293n48,
    297n1, 297n6, 299n28, 300n2
Under Milk Wood (Dylan Thomas), 119

Valentine (heretic), 169
Vanessa, 193
van Homerigh, Bartholomew, 278
Vico, Giambattista, 14–15, 134, 206, 269,
    290n10
Vinding, Ole, 289n4
Virag, Lipoti, 176
Virgil, 129, 221, 296n32
Vishnu, 253, 274

Wagner, Richard, 109, 137, 149, 158
Waite, A. E., 294n10
Wangel, Hilde, 278
Washington, D.C., 299n25
"Water Parted" (Arne), 153
"Wearing of the Green, The," 171
Weaver, Harriet, 165, 168, 188
Weber, Max, 242
Welles, Orson, 99
Wellington, Duke of, 47, 216, 275
Whistler, James Abbott MacNeill, 280
Whiston, John, 148
Whitman, Walt, 286
Wild, Jonathan, 215
Wilde, Oscar, 44, 88–89, 123, 136, 146, 209,
    211–12
"Willow Song" (*Otello*), 149
Woolworth's, 46
Worthies, Nine, 225

Yeats, William Butler, 51, 97, 123, 136, 211,
    301n10
Yggdrasill (ash tree), 200
Young, Brigham, 217

Zar und Zimmermann (Lortzing), 144
Zeno, 126, 129
Zerlina (*Don Giovanni*), 280
Zworykin, Vladimir, 143

Edmund Lloyd Epstein is professor of English at the City University of New York (Queens College and the Graduate Center). His specialities are modern British literature, including Joyce, Yeats, Hopkins, and Eliot, and the linguistics of literature.

Five of his nine books are on the work and life of James Joyce, as are more than forty articles and notes and some fifteen major addresses.

In 1957 he founded and edited the first Joyce journal, the *James Joyce Review*, which was eventually merged with the *James Joyce Quarterly*. He is on the advisory boards of the *Joyce Quarterly* and the *Joyce Studies Annual*.

The Florida James Joyce Series
Edited by Sebastian D. G. Knowles
Zack Bowen, Editor Emeritus

The Autobiographical Novel of Co-Consciousness: Goncharov, Woolf, and Joyce, by Galya
 Diment (1994)
Bloom's Old Sweet Song: Essays on Joyce and Music, by Zack Bowen (1995)
Joyce's Iritis and the Irritated Text: The Dis-lexic Ulysses, by Roy Gottfried (1995)
Joyce, Milton, and the Theory of Influence, by Patrick Colm Hogan (1995)
Reauthorizing Joyce, by Vicki Mahaffey (paperback edition, 1995)
Shaw and Joyce: "The Last Word in Stolentelling," by Martha Fodaski Black (1995)
Bely, Joyce, Döblin: Peripatetics in the City Novel, by Peter I. Barta (1996)
Jocoserious Joyce: The Fate of Folly in Ulysses, by Robert H. Bell (paperback edition, 1996)
Joyce and Popular Culture, edited by R. B. Kershner (1996)
Joyce and the Jews: Culture and Texts, by Ira B. Nadel (paperback edition, 1996)
Narrative Design in Finnegans Wake: *The Wake Lock Picked*, by Harry Burrell (1996)
Gender in Joyce, edited by Jolanta W. Wawrzycka and Marlena G. Corcoran (1997)
Latin and Roman Culture in Joyce, by R. J. Schork (1997)
Reading Joyce Politically, by Trevor L. Williams (1997)
Advertising and Commodity Culture in Joyce, by Garry Leonard (1998)
Greek and Hellenic Culture in Joyce, by R. J. Schork (1998)
Joyce, Joyceans, and the Rhetoric of Citation, by Eloise Knowlton (1998)
Joyce's Music and Noise: Theme and Variation in His Writings, by Jack W. Weaver (1998)
Reading Derrida Reading Joyce, by Alan Roughley (1999)
Joyce through the Ages: A Nonlinear View, edited by Michael Patrick Gillespie (1999)
Chaos Theory and James Joyce's Everyman, by Peter Francis Mackey (1999)
Joyce's Comic Portrait, by Roy Gottfried (2000)
Joyce and Hagiography: Saints Above! by R. J. Schork (2000)
Voices and Values in Joyce's Ulysses, by Weldon Thornton (2000)
The Dublin Helix: The Life of Language in Joyce's Ulysses, by Sebastian D. G. Knowles
 (2001)
Joyce Beyond Marx: History and Desire in Ulysses *and* Finnegans Wake, by Patrick McGee
 (2001)
Joyce's Metamorphosis, by Stanley Sultan (2001)
Joycean Temporalities: Debts, Promises, and Countersignatures, by Tony Thwaites (2001)
Joyce and the Victorians, by Tracey Teets Schwarze (2002)
Joyce's Ulysses *as National Epic: Epic Mimesis and the Political History of the Nation State*,
 by Andras Ungar (2002)
James Joyce's "Fraudstuff," by Kimberly J. Devlin (2002)
Rite of Passage in the Narratives of Dante and Joyce, by Jennifer Margaret Fraser (2002)
Joyce and the Scene of Modernity, by David Spurr (2002)
Joyce and the Early Freudians: A Synchronic Dialogue of Texts, by Jean Kimball (2003)
Twenty-first Joyce, edited by Ellen Carol Jones and Morris Beja (2004)
Joyce on the Threshold, edited by Anne Fogarty and Timothy Martin (2005)

Wake Rites: The Ancient Irish Rituals of Finnegans Wake, by George Cinclair Gibson (2005)

Ulysses *in Critical Perspective*, edited by Michael Patrick Gillespie and A. Nicholas Fargnoli (2006)

Joyce and the Narrative Structure of Incest, by Jen Shelton (2006)

Joyce, Ireland, Britain, edited by Andrew Gibson and Len Platt (2006)

Joyce in Trieste: An Album of Risky Readings, edited by Sebastian D. G. Knowles, Geert Lernout, and John McCourt (2007)

Joyce's Rare View: The Nature of Things in Finnegans Wake, by Richard Beckman (2007)

Joyce's Misbelief, by Roy Gottfried (2007)

James Joyce's Painful Case, by Cóilín Owens (2008)

Cannibal Joyce, by Thomas Jackson Rice (2008)

Manuscript Genetics, Joyce's Know-How, Beckett's Nohow, by Dirk Van Hulle (2008)

Catholic Nostalgia in Joyce and Company, by Mary Lowe-Evans (2008)

A Guide through Finnegans Wake, by Edmund Lloyd Epstein (2009)